REFORMATION EUROPE:
A Guide to Research

REFORMATION EUROPE:
A Guide to Research

edited by
Steven Ozment

Center for Reformation Research
St. Louis

Center for Reformation Research,
6477 San Bonita Avenue,
St. Louis, Missouri 63105

ISBN 0–910345–01–5

Contents

Introduction

There is no field of historical study today that is more alive with change and fresh ideas than that of Reformation Europe. This may come as a surprise to those who have considered the Reformation the stodgiest of subjects. Indeed, the variety and rapidity of change has even shocked Reformation scholars themselves. Yet, as recently as 1965, Bernd Moeller pleaded with historians of the Reformation to broaden their interests. "It seems high time," he wrote in an influential article,

> that the *Reformation movement as a whole* once again become an object of research in church history. Let us hope that many historians, who at present may be scared off by the theological monologue, will now resume studies in this area. Through careful observation and analysis of political, socioeconomic, intellectual, and spiritual forces, we should try to see more clearly the broad outlines and the interplay of events and their profound effects . . . . We must attempt to understand the end-lessly varied framework of phenomena as they clash and catch fire, and as totally different assumptions and experiences, motives and goals are exchanged and unified.[1]

Moeller here protested against the predominance of dogmatic theology, especially scholarly obsession with the theology of Martin Luther, within German Reformation research. While appreciating the achievements of four decades of theological studies of the Reformation, Moeller believed that the price of such progress had been very high: the loss of the Reformation "as history."

To a very large extent this problem is peculiar to German scholarship with its long tradition of internal confessional strife, and Moeller's famous protest needs to be kept within its proper historical

[1]"Probleme der Reformationsgeschichtsforschung," *Zeitschrift für Kirchengeschichte* 14 (1965): 246–57. I cite from the English translation by H. C. Erik Midelfort and Mark U. Edwards, Jr. in: Bernd Moeller, *Imperial Cities and the Reformation: Three Essays* (Philadelphia, 1972), p. 15.

context. In no other land have the reflections of Martin Luther proven so divisive of religious, cultural, and even political life. This is not to say that the polemical contrast: "theology" versus "history" has not also been heard in the Anglo-American world, for certainly it has, and especially of late. But it remains more an imported problem than an expression of true native conflict, more indicative of Anglo-American fascination with German scholarhip than of a serious scholarly ill. Indeed, one may even suspect that it is invoked today in the Anglo-American world as much out of mischief as in true criticism, as if to suggest that a scholarly work that keeps the theologies of elites at arm's length has, by such abstinence alone, more firmly grasped the Age of Reformation.

English and American scholars of Reformation Europe have never been so one-sidedly theological and confessional as to require rebuke, nor have they ever been mesmerized by the life and thought of Martin Luther—facts no doubt related to the plurality of their religious traditions, their different social and political experience, and perhaps also to what one may risk calling their greater secularity. If anything, American Reformation scholarship, with its deep pragmatic and moralizing bent, has tended for centuries to slight the abstractly theological for the concretely historical, favoring the broad political narrative, social history, biography, and psychohistory; and those Anglo-American scholars who have tried to compete with their German counterparts in the maze of theological Luther scholarship have usually seemed to be more borrowers and imitators than true pioneers. Other fields, in particular urban history, humanism and education, witchcraft and the occult, and popular culture, have been far more authoritatively explored by Anglo-American scholars.

Over the last two decades an international community of scholars has given the most detailed attention to the "historical" side of the Reformation, making possible an unprecedented broadening of Reformation Studies. The seeds of this flowering had long been planted, but several factors worked together to bring it about. The marvels of modern technology have provided scholars with ever expanding textual resources. In addition to a flood of source editions and related scholarly aids, microfilm and microfiche collections now place thousands of pamphlets and tracts at the fingertips of every Reformation historian, and computers enable a single scholar to sift through a mountain of data that previously would have exhausted the best efforts of a team of scholars over a lifetime. Historical anthropologists and sociologists, the imperial *Annales* school, and Marxist studies have stimulated scholars with imaginative new theories and methods as well as with fresh data. Another contributing factor is upheaval in the modern world, especially the counter-culture movements of the 1960s, which has forced a new generation of Reformation scholars to raise different historical questions and develop new historical sympathies. So prominent, indeed, has the "historical" side of the Reformation become that Moeller himself recently raised the specter of a reductionist social history ("sociologism") tyrannizing the field of Reformation scholarship as German Lutheran theology once threatened to do.[2]

The chances of the latter happening are surely very slim; the study of Reformation Europe has become too broad and too vital to tolerate the leash of any one or even a few special interests. The present popularity of social history, even in its most dogmatic form, is simply another of the field's many growing pains, particularly its willingness to exploit new data and to test the theories of modern philosophers and social scientists.

The contributors to the present volume are scholars whose work in the particular field reported is both fresh and on-going. Although they are American and English, each has spent extended periods of time in the land in which he or she specializes and each would doubtlessly consider himself or herself a scholarly "citizen of the world." And despite occasional expressions of fervent devotion to a particular field and method of study, I suspect each would be quick to acknowledge that history is a house of many mansions, each as spacious and beautiful in its way as the others.

Each contributor was asked to answer succinctly three questions. First, what is the present state of research in the field in question, especially the trend-setting new studies that are challenging traditional points of view? Secondly, what are the key issues scholars in the field will be trying to resolve in the immediate future? Finally, where are the strategic research collections and/or centers for research in the particular field? In sum: where are we; where do we seem to be going; and how do we get there? Owing to the individu-

[2]"Stadt und Buch. Bermerkungen zur Struktur der reformatorischen Bewegung in Deutschland" in *Stadtbürgertum und Adel Reformation*, ed. by Wolfgang J. Mommsen, Peter Alter, and Robert W. Scribner (Stuttgart, 1979), pp. 25–40.

ality of the contributors and the different stages of research in the various fields, not every essay has followed this sequence of questions literally. However, each essay has in its own way provided an assessment that speaks to each of these concerns. As a group, the essays range from the eve of the Reformation to the confessional struggles of the late Reformation. They document the present transformation of Reformation Studies and set an agenda for future research.

S.O.
June, 1981

Religious and Ecclesiastical Life on the Eve of the Reformation

Francis Oakley

Of the later Middle Ages late-medieval men and women knew nothing. Unlike modern Reformation historians, properly concerned to probe the conditions governing their religious and ecclesiastical life, they themselves neither knew that they were "late medieval" nor realized that they were living on "the eve of the Reformation." Those interested, then, in beginning their exploration of Reformation history with a scrutiny of the late-medieval "background" would do well to be particularly self-conscious about the perspective from which they choose to view the evidence.

Though some truly major disagreements persist among historians of the period,[1] few would want to challenge the traditional perception that the later Middle Ages did indeed constitute a time of troubles. Incipient over-population at the beginning of the fourteenth century, abnormally wet weather and Europe-wide famine shortly thereafter (1315–17), recurrent and catastrophic visitations of plague from mid-century onwards, economic strain and social unrest in both town and country, a papal schism of unprecedented intractability and length (1378–1417), the outbreak of protracted warfare between France and England, the concomitant breakdown in some regions of the basic structures of public order, the contraction in Eastern Europe of the very boundaries of Christendom—all of these developments (and others, too) hardly conduce to the framing of any positive appraisal of the period. Long ago, indeed, they helped establish the sense that this was an era of civilizational decline, a gloomy hiatus between two great periods of drama and high achievement—the economic, political, religious, and intellectual

---

[1]E.g. disagreements concerning the relative health or sickness of the late-medieval European economy—see Lopez and Miskimin and Cipolla (1976).

flowering of Europe in the twelfth and thirteenth centuries and the great age of exploration, High Renaissance, and Reformation in the late-fifteenth and sixteenth centuries.

In few areas of historical endeavor was that view more clearly manifest than in the writing of church history. At the beginning of the present century it was commonplace to assume that by the later Middle Ages the medieval Church "had reached the term of its natural development," and that the fourteenth and fifteenth centuries were of interest mainly because "they were the age that nursed the Reformation."[2] Medieval historians were apt, accordingly, to perceive the religious and ecclesiastical life of those centuries as no more than an epilogue to the history of medieval Christianity, something to be treated more superficially and imprecisely than the history of earlier centuries, a piece of undesirable territory readily conceded to the Reformation historians. The latter, in their turn, were understandably preoccupied before all else with tracing the roots of the great upheaval to come and with identifying those "Reformers before the Reformation"[3] whose abortive or quasi-abortive endeavors providentially anticipated the secure achievements of their great Protestant successors.

As a result, the picture emerged of a late-medieval Church characterized by a degree of ecclesiastical decadence, theological bankruptcy, and religious decline so grievous as to be destined, finally, to alienate from the traditional patterns of churchly life the most truly committed and most deeply devout. Central to that picture was the assumption that in certain critical respects the period was in sharp discontinuity with the great age of medieval religion that preceded it. The French degradation of Boniface VIII at Anagni in 1303 and the subsequent removal of the papacy from Rome to Avignon was seen to mark a critical turning-point in its history, laying the foundations for the Great Schism of the West and signalling the incipient collapse of the whole structure of ecclesiastical governance within which medieval Catholicism had contrived to flourish. Reflected also in that picture was the countervailing tendency to recognize in the seemingly disparate late-medieval phenomena that we identify as heresy, mysticism, conciliarism, increasing temporal control of ecclesiastical affairs, the *Devotio moderna*, and humanism, the re-

[2]Sohm, pp. 135–39.
[3]K. Ullmann.

demptive stirrings of inter-related movements of reform. These movements were seen to draw their impulse in part from common well-springs of religious vitality and to converge upon the great up-heaval of the Protestant Reformation.

Old perspectives, like old habits, die hard. In one or another of its several dimensions that traditional picture continues to be reflected in at least some of the more recent literature.[4] Nonetheless, the scholarly research of the past several decades has served to shatter its unity and to blunt the force of its impact. Sensitive to the danger of relying too exclusively on the frequently propagandistic accounts of contemporary chroniclers and publicists, mindful of the intrusion of non-historical canons of judgment (confessional, nationalistic, theological), alert to the refractions and distortions that occur when the late-medieval Church is seen too obsessively through the lens of the Reformation, and conscious of the dilemma posed by the comparative abundance of evidence concerning late-medieval as opposed to earlier medieval religious life, scholars have heaped qualification upon cautious qualification and have generated a multiplicity of interpretations distinguished above all by their rich and frequently daunting complexity. But the cumulative impact of their work has been to suggest very forcefully that (no less in its weaknesses than in its strengths) the continuities binding the late-medieval church with that of the earlier period were a good deal more insistent than historians once thought them to be. Second, that the alleged links binding the disparate stirrings of late-medieval "reform" both with one another and with phenomena characteristic later on of the Reformation era were a good deal more problematic than the traditional picture suggests. Further, that the doomed sense of accelerating decline evident in so many writings of the period, however revelatory of the *mood* of ecclesiastics and intellectuals, is a less than adequate index to the varied, fluctuating, but frequently vital realities of late-medieval religious life. These shifts in interpretation cannot be traced in their fullness here, but they have been conveniently signalled in several recent interpretative surveys and collective volumes.[5] And they can at least be illustrated by glancing in what follows at some of the most important contributions made to the field over the past several decades and in the following areas: ecclesiasti-

---

[4]E.g., Spinka (1958); Léonard; Lortz (1964, 1968); Gilson; Iserloh (1956); Bouyer.
[5]Ozment (1971); Trinkaus and Oberman; Thompson; Hendrix; Duggan.

cal institutions and governance; currents of reform, both orthodox
and heretical; theological developments; modes of spirituality, both
clerical and lay.

Ecclesiastical institutions and governance

As long ago as 1903 Haller sounded the warning that although the
publicistic writings of the period are of great value in so far as they
give us "a picture of the prevailing mood," they simply cannot be
relied upon to give us an accurate picture of the ecclesiastical and
religious conditions of the day.[6] To few topics has that warning
proved more pertinent than to the history of the late-medieval
papacy in general and the Avignonese papacy in particular. Referring to the Avignonese period as the "Babylonian Captivity" implied
that it involved the tragic exile of the papacy from its proper home
as well as a scandalous subordination to the exigencies of French
royal policy. As long as historians had to rely on the literary sources
of the day—especially the English, German and Italian chronicles—
they continued to portray the Avignonese papacy as morally corrupt, financially extravagant, administratively tyrannical, the principal source of the numerous evils besetting the Church at large and
of the disastrous schism that began in 1378. With the opening of the
Vatican archives a hundred years ago and the publication of the
papal registers, a more nuanced appraisal became possible. Over the
years it has been the achievement especially of Mollat, Guillemain,
and Rénouard to modify the traditionally negative representation of
the Avignonese papacy's relationship with the French monarchy,
which was much less subservient than was once assumed, and to re-
habilitate the moral character of the pontiffs themselves (of the
seven, four were men of reforming instincts; only under Clement VI
are there truly convincing signs of the dissipation and luxury once
associated with Avignon *tout court*). They have also taken a more
positive view of the growing centralization and absolutism of papal
government, which they see as the continuation of an institutional
logic established long ago by the reforming popes of the late-
eleventh, twelfth, and early-thirteenth centuries.[7]

On the last point, it has been the concern of Barraclough, Lunt,
Pantin, and others to emphasize the degree to which the much-

[6]Haller. Cf. Hay; Duggan.
[7]Samaran et Mollat; Mollat (1921, 1963); Guillemain (1952, 1953, 1962); Renouard
(1941, 1970).

maligned Avignonese "fiscalism," and especially its intensification of the traffic in ecclesiastical benefices, was a response to the characteristic failure of late-medieval peoples to accord their rulers, royal no less than papal, the general taxing powers they needed if they were effectively to discharge their increasingly onerous range of governmental responsibilities. They have also recognized the degree to which it presupposed the twelfth-century enshrinement in law of early-medieval conception of the benefice as a material thing, an object of proprietary right rather than a focus of spiritual duty.[8] Only during the later years of the fourteenth century in the midst of economic depression and of the marked financial strain and administrative dislocation occasioned by the schism does one find clear evidence for the type of uncontrolled "fiscalism" once attributed to the Avignonese papacy throughout its career.[9]

In the wake of this revised estimate of the "Babylonian Captivity," historians have scrutinized with renewed interest the rich collection of manuscript materials in the Vatican archives pertaining to the dramatic events of 1378.[10] They are no longer as disposed as once they were to blame the outbreak of the schism on the policies of the Avignonese cardinals or of their French sympathizers. Recent studies of the disputed election and its background have converged on the conclusion that the doubts later expressed by the cardinals concerning the validity of Urban VI's title must be taken more seriously than was once the case.[11] As a result historians have come to challenge the theologically (or canonistically) conditioned tendency to treat Urban and his successors in the Roman line as the only legitimate claimants to the papal title and to write the history of the Councils of Pisa (1409) and Constance (1414–18) accordingly, a tendency particularly prominent in the aftermath of the First Vatican Council.[12] In the distinguished contribution which Delaruelle, Labande, and Ourliac made in 1964 to the Fliche and Martin *Histoire de l'Église*, we now have at our disposal an informed and thorough account of the Conciliar era as a whole.[13] Though a

[8]Barraclough; Lunt (1934, 1939–62); Pantin. Cf. Labande, in Delaruelle (1962–64), I, 295–313; Southern (1970), 151–69.

[9]Favier; Jacob; Labande, in Delaruelle (1962–64), I, 295–313.

[10]For a description of this collection, see Seidlmayer (1940a).

[11]Seidlmayer (1940b); Přerovský; Fink (1962); Trexler (1967). W. Ullmann marks something of an exception to this trend.

[12]On which, see the discussion in Franzen and Oakley (1969a), pp. 105–31.

[13]Delaruelle (1962–64)—though see the criticism of Ourliac's treatment of the Council of Basel in Stieber, p. 396. Cf. the fine chapters on the conciliar era contributed by K. A. Fink to Jedin and Dolan.

controversy as yet unresolved has erupted concerning the meaning, dogmatic status, and historical significance of *Haec sancta synodus* (1415) (the Constance decree concerning the superiority of council to pope),[14] studies subsequent to Delaruelle's have served to illuminate the histories of the Councils of Constance and Pavia-Siena (1423–24) more effectively than that of Basel-Ferrara-Florence (1431–48).[15] Nonetheless, the work especially of Jedin, Bäumer, and Stieber[16] has made it clear how widespread was support for the conciliarist position throughout Europe during the Basel years and the decades immediately thereafter. Similarly, the continuing credibility of the conciliarist threat until well into the sixteenth century helps to account for the fateful delay of the popes in assembling the general council for which, in the early years of the Reformation era, even the most papalist of reformers repeatedly called. That work has also underlined the degree to which the triumph of the fifteenth-century popes over the constitutionalist challenge represented by the Conciliar movement had been bought at the price of a constitutional revolution of a different type. It was nothing less, in fact, than the parcelling out among the secular rulers of Europe of the pope's sovereign authority over the Church universal and, along with it, the revenues that had once flowed to Rome from provincial churches all over Europe. If by the eve of the Reformation the popes had in no small degree been transformed into typical Renaissance princes intent upon protecting and building up the resources of their Italian principality, Partner's studies have indicated that behind that transformation lay, at least in part, a very urgent financial impetus.[17]

Currents of reform

If late-medieval reformers and publicists were prone to represent the religious and ecclesiastical life of their day as a pitiable story of decline and to universalize its defects accordingly, it has been the tendency of the more recent scholarly literature to recognize that such strictures cannot be taken at face value.[18] They may well reflect

[14]For analyses of the pertinent literature, see Oakley (1969a), pp. 104–41; Oakley (1971); Vooght (1970); Schneider; Morrissey.

[15]See esp., Franzen and Müller; Vooght (1965); Brandmüller. Though see also Gill on Florence.

[16]Jedin; Bäumer (1971) and (1972); Stieber. See also Klotzner; La Brosse; Oakley (1965, 1969b, 1972, 1977 and 1981); Black (1970, 1979).

[17]Partner (1958) and (1960).

[18]Thus, Hay; Duggan; O'Malley (1968); Heath; Binz.

rising standards of expectation as much as declining levels of performance. Their constant repetition may also reflect the thoughtless repetition of propagandistic stereotypes as much as the stubborn persistence of abuses,[19] and the sense that things were going from bad to worse may itself have been something of a convention fostered by the myth of a golden age of apostolic poverty.[20]

Nonetheless, from the late-thirteenth century onwards the papacy ceased to provide the effective leadership of the reforming and crusading movements by virtue of which it had risen to a position of jurisdictional supremacy in the universal Church. As a result, the call for reform now began to come from other quarters, some of them heretical, to assume even in orthodox circles an increasingly hostile tone, and to take the form of an imperative cry for "reform in head and members." That call, emanating from the provincial churches, was heard already in 1245 and 1274 at the first and second Councils of Lyons, and again in 1311 at the Council of Vienne. From the outbreak of the schism in 1378 until the Reformation era it became a central theme of Church history. While Haller's old work on this matter continues to maintain its value, scholars are now fortunate enough to have at their disposal important works of synthesis by Jedin, by Delaruelle, Labande and Ourliac, and by Fink, all of which serve to highlight the continuity of struggle for church-wide reform during the Conciliar epoch and its aftermath.[21] Of the more specialized studies on this topic, attention should be drawn to the contributions of Brandmüller on the abortive Council of Pavia-Siena (1423–24), Zwölfer on the reform work of Basel, and Fink and Bäumer on the reform programs of the Conciliar era as a whole and of its aftermath.[22] Ozment, Pascoe, Bernstein and O'Malley have made valuable contributions to our understanding of the reform ideology of such leaders as Jean Gerson, Pierre D'Ailly, and Giles of Viterbo.[23] In connection with more localized attempts at reform, Weinstein's careful study of Savonarola's ascendancy at Florence and Sullivan's rather negative reappraisal of Nicholas of Cusa's reforming mission to Germany and the Netherlands in 1451–52 both serve to illustrate further, though in differing fashion, the growing dominance of the political factor in the arena of religious and eccle-

---

[19]See Delaruelle (1962–64), I, 320 and n. 3.
[20]O'Malley (1968), 2, 184.
[21]Haller; Jedin; Delaruelle (1962–64); Fink in Jedin and Dolan.
[22]Brandmüller; Zwölfer; Fink (1946, 1965); Bäumer (1971, 1972).
[23]Ozment (1970); Pascoe; Bernstein; O'Malley (1968); cf. Oakley (1967).

siastical reform to which Renaudet called attention over fifty years ago.[24] Delaruelle, Knowles, and Origo together convey at the Europe-wide, national and individual levels respectively, a good sense of the general condition of monastic life and of the specifically late-medieval movement of monastic reform that focused on the ideal of a return to strict observance of the original rule,[25] while in his magisterial study of the Brethren of the Common Life and their monastic cousins, R. R. Post illustrates with a wealth of detail the marked degree to which the highly conservative "back to roots" impulse of the Observantine reform movement informed the spirit of the Windesheim congregation and sustained its leadership in the work of spreading the *Devotio moderna*.[26]

Those interested in the type of late-medieval reform that transgressed the boundaries of orthodoxy now have at their disposal two excellent bibliographical aids[27] as well as two up-to-date works of synthesis in English—one by Lambert covering the greater part of the Middle Ages and one by Leff devoted specifically to the late-medieval centuries.[28] Works by Gonnet and Molnár on the Waldensians, Bloomfield and Reeves on Joachim of Fiore and the Joachites (including their legacy to the era of Renaissance and Reformation), and Lerner on the Brethren of the Free Spirit provide reliable access to the intricacies of recent scholarship on those particular groups.[29] Responding as carefully as it does to Grundmann's warnings about the danger of taking the Inquisition records at face value[30] and painting a sober picture of the Free Spirit far removed from the older sensational evocations of a movement of antinomian libertines, advocates of mystic eroticism,[31] Lerner's book is especially valuable. This is particularly the case since Leff's treatment of the Free Spirit is much less carefully nuanced and has accordingly met with severe criticism.[32]

On the structure and direction of Wycliffe's theology, however,

---

[24]Weinstein; Sullivan; Renaudet.
[25]Delaruelle (1962–64), II; Knowles (1950–59); Origo.
[26]Post.
[27]Grundmann (1967); Leff (1967), II, 739–77.
[28]Lambert; Leff (1967).
[29]Gonnet and Molnár; Bloomfield; Reeves; Lerner.
[30]Grundmann (1965).
[31]Evident in as recent a book as Cohn's.
[32]See the reviews by H. Grundmann in *Deutsches Archiv für Erforschung des Mittelalters*, XXIV (1968), 284–86, and by H. S. Offler in *English Historical Review*, LXXXIV (1969), 572–76.

Leff is particularly effective, and, along with McFarlane's fine little biography and the contributions of Aston and Thomson,[33] he helps to provide us with a clear picture of the lineaments of Wycliffe's heterodoxy, the dimensions of his legacy to fifteenth-century religious life in England, and the precise manner in which he may have helped promote the spread of Protestant ideas in the century that followed.

Not all of those concerned with the continuity of medieval heterodoxies into the Age of Reformation have been as cautious or precise in their conclusions, and it is proper to evince a certain reserve towards claims that some Anabaptist groups in Switzerland and Germany reveal the survival in those areas of the heresy of the Free Spirit, or that the view of the Eucharist ultimately adopted by Zwingli was in direct continuity with a tradition of "sacramentarianism . . . endemic for centuries" in the Netherlands.[34] In the case of the Czech reformer, John Hus, however, the big *quaestio disputata* has not been the continuity of Hussite doctrines on into the sixteenth century, but rather the precise relationship of Hus's own views to the unquestionably heterdox commitments of Wycliffe. It was the conclusion of those other reformers, the Conciliarists of the Council of Constance who in 1415 tried him and condemned him to death, that Hus was a more thorough-going Wycliffite than he would have had them believe, and such scholars as Loserth and Kalivoda have been inclined to agree.[35] But the trend (at least of recent Western scholarship) has been to distance Hus from Wycliffe and to see him as the product of an indigenous Czech reform focused overwhelmingly on moral and practical issues, the victim of his own failure to bring his theology under any single controlling principle and of a temperament that betrayed him into such "gratuitous acts of bravado" as that of employing provocatively Wycliffite terminology when formulating perfectly orthodox postions.[36] If, as Kaminsky has said in his excellent account of the Hussite movement in Bohemia, the Hus who served the Hussites as symbol and inspiration was "Hus as the Council of Constance judged him to be: turbulent, seditious, subversive,"[37] the Hus who emerges from the pages especially

[33]Leff (1967), II, 494–605; McFarlane; Aston; Thomson, J. A. F.
[34]Clasen; Williams (1962), pp. 26–37.
[35]Loserth; Kalivoda (on whom, see Kaminsky).
[36]Vooght (1960a), esp. pp. 64–71; Vooght (1960b); Thomson, S. H.; Spinka (1966), 1968).
[37]Kaminsky, 6.

of De Vooght is much closer to what he himself claimed to be: doctrinally ambivalent, perhaps, but at least in intention fundamentally orthodox.

Theological developments

The years since the Second World War have witnessed some very significant shifts in interpretation of developments in three distinct areas of theological discourse, all of them directly pertinent to an understanding of the positions staked out during the ideological turbulence of the Reformation era.

Noting in 1954 the lack of scholarly attention paid to the views of fourteenth-century theologians concerning the sources of Christian doctrine, De Vooght helped stimulate a surge of interest in the subject.[38] His own work, along with contributions by Tavard, Xiberta, Hurley, Oberman, Tierney, Preus, and Steinmetz (though they are by no means in accord one with another), has conspired to undermine the older tendency to understand the controversies of the era in terms of an alleged clash between proto-Protestant appeals to "Scripture alone" and traditionally Catholic appeals to "Scripture and Tradition."[39] Rather than precocious proclaimers of *scriptura sola*, Wycliffe and Hus emerge instead as defenders of the older patristic view that made no sharp distinction between Scripture, Tradition, and the magisterial authority of the Church in relation to both.[40] The late-medieval theologians, rather than their patristic or scholastic predecessors—or, indeed, than their canonist colleagues—have been identified as the developers of the "two-sources" (Scripture and Tradition) theory of revelation that was destined to become so prominent in the theology of the Counter-Reformation era.[41] And in thinkers of such different stamp as Jean Gerson, the conciliarist, and John Pupper of Goch (traditionally portrayed as a "Reformer before the Reformation") there has been detected a commitment to the notion of the Church as itself a "living tradition"—a notion often linked in the modern era with the doctrine of papal infallibility.[42]

Comparable perplexities, it seems, attend any attempt to chart the subsequent career of the two-sources theory, which, if it did feed

[38]Vooght (1954).

[39]Tavard; Xiberta; Hurley, Oberman (1963); Tierney (1972); Preus; Steinmetz.

[40]Vooght (1954), esp. 233, 259–60. Hurley, esp. 276–79, 337–52, dissents from his view of Wycliffe's position, but see the reply in Oberman (1963), 375, n. 41.

[41]Tierney (1967). Cf. the conflicting views in Oberman (1963), 369, and Tavard, 37–40, 47–48.

[42]Preus, 79–81; Steinmetz.

into the mainstream of Counter-Reformation theology, numbered among its late-medieval adherents not only papalists but also such critics of high-papalist claims as Ockham, Pierre D'Ailly, and Johannes Breviscoxe.[43] And the older patristic position (taught later on by Bonuccio at Trent and clearly not to be identified with the Protestant appeal to *scriptura sola*) was actually embraced during the fourteenth and fifteenth centuries by men of such different sympathies as Pope John XXII, Wycliffe and Hus, and Guido Terreni, an early proponent of papal infallibility. The truly important ecclesiological disagreements of the era centered less, it seems, on the specifically magisterial power of the Church than upon its jurisdictional power in general.

This view has been powerfully suggested by Tierney's recent and provocative claim that the doctrine of papal infallibility, far from being one of the bulwarks of the high-papalist position, was instead a late-medieval invention, first explicitly proposed by Franciscan propagandists eager to defend as a matter of revealed truth the inviolability of Nicholas III's endorsement (1279) of the doctrine of apostolic poverty. In 1324 John XXII dismissed the doctrine as a "pestiferous novelty."[44] Though Tierney's claim has predictably given rise to a storm of controversy,[45] it has weathered that storm and remained more or less intact.[46] It now seems proper to conclude that the doctrine of papal infallibility was not prominent in Catholic theology until the sixteenth and seventeenth centuries.

That conclusion is itself pertinent to the shift in our understanding of Conciliar theory that has taken place over the course of the past twenty-five years. The unexamined assumption that the doctrine of papal infallibility was widely held in the fourteenth and fifteenth centuries may well explain the ease with which in the past the Conciliarist position was misrepresented as an unorthodox ecclesiology of revolutionary vintage foisted upon the Church by those dangerous radicals, Marsilius of Padua and William of Ockham. It is now commonplace to admit that Ockham was not a conciliarist at all and that Marsilius was something much more radical.[47] Furthermore, the Conciliar theory itself is seen as an essentially moderate doctrine

[43]For the last, see Oakley (1978).
[44]Tierney (1972).
[45]Bäumer (1973) and (1974) is the most unrestrained attack on the claim. See Tierney (1974) for a reply. For the most instructive exchange in English see Stickler (1974, 1975); Tierney (1975).
[46]With the further nuances suggested by Turley.
[47]Oakley (1969a), 56–71.

of ecclesiastical constitutionalism with unimpeachably orthodox foundations in the cozy respectabilities of the pre-Marsilian era. These insights are a witness to the current flowering of studies in the history of medieval canon law,[48] particularly to the decisive contribution of Tierney. In pursuing suggestions made over the years by Otto von Gierke, H. X. Arquillièrre, Walter Ullmann, and others, he established that the conciliarist assertion of the jurisdictional superiority under certain conditions of council to pope, far from being a reaction against canonistic views or a profane importation onto ecclesial soil of secular constitutionalist ideas, was in fact a logical outgrowth of certain strands of canonist thought.[49] If, as a result, it has become clear that the Conciliar theory was neither as recent nor as revolutionary in its origins as was once commonly assumed, it has likewise been the achievement of Jedin, De la Brosse, Bäumer, and others to have made the case that the demise of that theory after the closing of the Council of Basel (1449) was neither as sudden nor as final as we were formerly led to suppose.[50] It was rather the pressure of an essentially ultramontane historiography that led to the placing of so anachronistic an emphasis on Pius II's bull *Execrabilis* (1460).[51] The persistence of conciliarist ideas from the early-fourteenth century down to the mid-sixteenth must now be taken as a simple matter of fact, and scholarly attention has come to focus, accordingly, on the more intricate problem of determining the precise nature of that persisting conciliarism.[52] It is clear, however, that without the persistence of such ecclesiological hesitancies into the Age of the Reformation, it would be hard to explain the failure of the Council of Trent, despite the challenge laid down by the Protestant ecclesiologies of the day, to promulgate any dogmatic decree on the nature of the Christian Church.

If such shifts in the interpretation of late-medieval theological developments help explain one of the silences of Trent, they also throw light on some of its utterances, notably its decree on justification which is no longer regarded as being merely a "*via media* between the extremes of a Pelagian nominalism and a Lutheran Au-

---

[48]See Tierney (1953).

[49]Tierney (1955, 1957). Cf. Seidlmayer (1957); Moynihan.

[50]Jedin; La Brosse; Bäumer (1971, 1972); Klotzner; Oakley (1965, 1969b, 1972, 1981); Stieber.

[51]Thus Denzinger prints *Execrabilis* while excluding the decree *Haec sancta synodus* of the Council of Constance and *all* the decrees of the Council of Basil.

[52]Bäumer (1971), 14–15, 265; Bubenheimer; Oberman (1975).

gustinianism."[53] That this should be so reflects the impact of a recent
and impressive surge of scholarly studies devoted to late-medieval
philosophy and theology—to William of Ockham, subsequent Ock-
hamists, and nominalism in general, to the theologians of the Augustinian order whose influence on the humanists is now coming to be
appreciated, and to the religious thinking of the humanists themselves.[54] Junghans, Courtenay, Oberman and Ozment having fur-
nished us with good, up-to-date bibliographical essays and interpretative surveys of the scholarly literature,[55] it will suffice to note that
the traditional interpretation of the history of late-medieval philosophy and theology as a sad declension from former greatness[56] has
come under severe attack especially at the hands of Vignaux, Trapp,
Boehner, and Oberman.[57] The orthodoxy and sobriety of Ockhamist
treatments of justification have been increasingly vindicated,[58] and
the sheer intricacy of the ties that bound late-medieval and Reformation theologies of grace and the gaps that divided them have been
dauntingly underlined.[59]

Modes of spirituality

Something similar may be said with reference to the great flowering of mysticism that occurred during the course of the fourteenth
century, in Italy, in England, but above all in the Netherlands and
Germany, where Grundmann has portrayed this "complicated phenomenon" as the product of a particular confluence of "Dominican
theology and care of souls, vernacular preaching, feminine piety,
and the special place that Germany occupied in the religious movements of the thirteenth and fourteenth centuries."[60] While of late
scholars have shown a renewed willingness to stress "the revolutionary possibilities of mystical theology" and to explore the links between late-medieval mystical writings and the spirituality of the
Reformation era, especially that cultivated by the Anabaptist and
radical reformers, they have also reminded us that the exploitation

[53]Oberman (1964, 1966).
[54]Notably Boehner; Oberman (1963); Leff (1975); Trapp; Zumkeller; Trinkaus
(1970) and Trinkaus and Oberman (1974).
[55]Junghans; Courtenay (1972, 1974); Oberman (1974); Ozment (1980), 1–21.
[56]Set forth with such authority by Gilson.
[57]Vignaux; Trapp; Boehner; Oberman (1963).
[58]Dettloff; Vignaux (1935); Leff (1975). Iserloh (1956) is a dissenting voice.
[59]See especially the volumes in the series edited by Oberman, *Studies in Medieval
and Reformation Thought* as well as Hägglund.
[60]Grundmann (1961), 527.

of those possibilities involved "a decision extrinsic to mystical theology itself."[61] As with other aspects of late-medieval spirituality, they have also taken pains to stress how very much the mysticism and mystical theology of the day were the beneficiaries of the great awakening of spiritual life in the late-eleventh and twelfth centuries cultivated by the Victorines and the Augustinian canons and diffused abroad by the efforts especially of the Cistercians and Franciscans.[62]

Of the general works on late-medieval mysticism published in recent years, perhaps the most helpful is a characteristically insightful little book by David Knowles which has a broader pertinence than its title would suggest.[63] Of the various areas of more specialized concern two have witnessed developments of particular interest: first, the relationship between nominalism and mysticism and second, the appropriate classification of different forms of mysticism. In relation to the former, Dress and Oberman have challenged the traditional assumption that nominalism and mysticism were mutually exclusive.[64] In relation to the latter, Ozment has stressed the inadequacy of the traditional tendency to classify the differing forms in "speculative" as opposed to "affective" categories (or "intellectualist" as opposed to "volitional"), and has suggested instead that late-medieval mystics be placed within a common conceptual framework based on the scholastic distinction between the *potentia dei absoluta* and *potentia dei ordinata*.[65] In relation to both, and in striking vindication of Delaruelle's insistence on his centrality to the period,[66] Jean Gerson has emerged in scholarly literature as a principal focus of attention. And any attempt to come to terms with the nature of his philosophical position and its relation to his mystical theology must also come to terms with the fundamental contribution of André Combes.[67]

Of course, as the wide-ranging work of synthesis by Leclercq, Vandenbroucke, and Bouyer makes very clear,[68] mysticism, however important, was not the only strand even in the monastic spiritu-

[61]Williams (1967); Ozment (1974). Cf. the older work of Hegler.
[62]Grundmann (1961); Constable (1971a, 1971b).
[63]Knowles (1961).
[64]Dress; Oberman (1963).
[65]Ozment (1973, 1974).
[66]Delaruelle (1962–64), II, ch. 5 bears the title: "Le siècle de Gerson."
[67]Combes.
[68]Leclercq *et al.*

ality of the era. Knowles's distinguished work conveys, in an in-depth study of one country, a superbly informed, sympathetic, and finely-balanced insight into the enduring strengths as well as the accumulating weaknesses of that spirituality.[69] We now have a useful and ambitious study by McDonnell on the Beghard and Beguine communities of religious men and women who belonged to no monastic order, lived in accord with no official rule, and took no formal vows, but who, while continuing to pursue ordinary occupations, committed themselves to a community life of simplicity and celibacy.[70] On the Brothers and Sisters of the Common Life (the proponents along with the Windesheim monastic congregation of the *Devotio moderna*), who attempted to carve out new middle ground between the positions of the traditional monastic orders and those of the Beghards and Beguines, we now have two competing accounts. One, by Hyma, stresses the links between the *Devotio moderna* and the reforming movements of the sixteenth century. The other, by Post, stresses the width of the gap that divided the Brethren (and their monastic cousins) from the later piety at least of the Protestant reformers, as well as the links that bound them to the traditions of the monastic past and the degree to which they moved across time to embrace a fully monastic vocation.[71]

As Post himself says, however, "one must not take it for granted that everyone who showed any signs of piety at the end of the Middle Ages, or who was assumed to be devout, belonged to the Modern Devotion."[72] In recent years a broad array of studies—Delaruelle's fine essay in synthesis[73] as well as more specialized works, either thematic in their concern[74] or regional in their focus[75]—have deepened our knowledge of the modes of piety prevalent not only among the elites but also among the less articulate strata of society. Delaruelle's remark that "we are better informed about the abuses of the fifteenth century than we are about the virtues of the thirteenth"[76] relates with particular force to our knowledge of the religious sensi-

[69]Knowles (1950–59).
[70]McDonnell.
[71]Hyma; Post. For a recent qualification of Post's claims, see Oberman (1977), 56–71.
[72]Post, xi, 676.
[73]Delaruelle (1962–64), II, occupying nearly three hundred pages of the collective volumes and reflecting his own extensive researches as well as those of others; cf. Rapp.
[74]E.g., Tentler (1974) and (1977); Wood-Legh; Sumption; Cohen; Trexler.
[75]E.g., Pantin, Hay; Toussaert; Binz; Moeller (1965); Privat.
[76]Delaruelle (1962–64), I, xi; cf. Hay, pp. 72–73.

bilities of the broader masses of city and country dwellers. And
although we are increasingly better informed in this respect for the
later Middle Ages than for the earlier period, that fact generates its
own problems. As the evidence continues to accumulate—evidence
concerning the quality of popular preaching, the survival in the
villages of magical and quasi-pagan practices, the activities of confraternities, the nature of legacies left for religious purposes, the
means of religious instruction (liturgical, theatrical, catechetical,
penitential), the range of liturgical and paraliturgical rites, and the
dissemination of popular devotional literature—it is hard to know
what to make of it, what to compare it with, from what perspective
to view it.

This being so, the outstanding problem confronting scholars is as
much one of conceptualization as of information. Despite a widely-
shared tendency to credit late-medieval people with "un immense
appétit du divin"[77] and even to concede to one or another of its dimensions the genuine vitality of their religious life, scholars continue
to differ about the degree to which the prevailing modes of piety were
capable of satisfying the religious aspirations of the day.[78] And a me-
dievalist may perhaps be forgiven for suggesting that on this, as on
many another matter pertaining to late-medieval ecclesiastical and
religious life, an acquaintance with the spirituality of the earlier medieval centuries (and in its weaknesses as well as its strengths) is
more likely to conduce to a realistically balanced appraisal of the
quality of late-medieval piety than is a preoccupation with the programmatic aspirations of sixteenth-century reformers, whether
Catholic or Protestant.[79]

Of course, in assimilating the importance of the history of the
liturgy, medievalists cannot claim to have done much better than
the Reformation historians. Despite the availability in English of
three excellent liturgical histories,[80] treatments of late-medieval
spirituality rarely betray much sense of the degree to which late-

[77]Febvre, 41.

[78]See, e.g., the contrasting views of Ozment (1975) and Tentler (1974) and (1977)
concerning the oppressive or consolatory impact of the discipline of sacramental
penance.

[79]In this respect one is tempted, for example, to fault as simply anachronistic the
judgmental criteria invoked in their respective studies by Lortz (1964, 1968) and
Toussaert. It is one of Delaruelle's strengths that he has worked on the spirituality of
the eleventh and twelfth centuries as well as on that of the later Middle Ages—see
Delaruelle (1975).

[80]Jungmann; Klauser; Dix.

medieval liturgical and paraliturgical developments, however frequently deplored, reflect little more than the pursuit to its conclusion of the logic established by critical changes dating back to the late-antique and early-medieval periods.[81] Nor, for the proper understanding of popular piety in the later Middle Ages, does the future necessarily lie with either medievalists or Reformation historians *as such.* Rather, it seems likely to lie with those who, in pursuing the detailed local investigations we still need, are self-conscious about the dangers of anachronism, hesitant about distinguishing too confidently between "religion" and "superstition," and open in their interpretations to the insights of the sociologists, cultural anthropologists, and students of comparative religion.[82]

In such other areas as the history of late-medieval theology in general and ecclesiology in particular, of the Council of Basel, its aftermath, and the subsequent fate of conciliarism, the great need is for the continued proliferation of studies on a host of minor figures so that the territory can be mapped out properly and the judgments we make (freed now, by and large, from the receding shadows of neo-Thomism, ultramontane theology, and a too-anxious preoccupation with the debates of the Reformation era) will not continue to be distorted by too heavy a reliance on the views of major figures whose positions may well turn out to have been highly exceptional.

Finally, on the matter of ecclesiastical institutions, a considerable urgency attaches to our need to comprehend far better still than we do the early-medieval proprietary church system (*Eigenkirchenwesen*), the material conception of the benefice which it spawned, and its legacy to the later-medieval and subsequent centuries of such affiliated practices as lay patronage and papal provisions. Elsewhere, I have urged that the institution of the benefice was the rock upon which late-medieval attempts at church-wide reform were shipwrecked.[83] One is led to wonder in what measure it may have served also as a hindrance to the efforts of Lutheran reformers in Germany and Scandinavia. In France, after all, it was among other things Louis XIV's attempt to extend his regalian rights (a classically medieval gambit) that led in 1682 to the famous Declaration of the Gallican Clergy. When Southern wanted to illuminate the draw-

---

[81] Changes that had conspired to make the consecration of the mass the focus, the action the priest's rather than the people's, the sacrifice a repetition, the benefit a quantity, the number a consideration. Cf. Iserloh (1961).

[82] Cf. the remarks of Davis and of A. Vauchez in Privat, esp. 434ff.

[83] Oakley (1979), 219.

backs of the early-medieval proprietary church he was able to do so by referring to the continuing prevalence of the lay patronage system in early-nineteenth century England and to illustrate his point by quoting a most apposite passage from Jane Austen's *Mansfield Park*.[84] And in relation to the same issue, appropriately enough, Barraclough ventured the provocative claim: "[N]o one who knows the history . . . of the English Church from the sixteenth to the nineteenth century, will deny that the real reformers of the Church were, not Henry VIII or Elizabeth, but the Ecclesiastical Commissioners appointed by Peel in 1835."[85]

Bibliography

I. General Accounts
Standard lengthier accounts are: Mollat (1963); Delaruelle (1962–64); Aubenas and Ricard; Jedin, and Dolan. Shorter accounts: Rapp; Moeller (1966); Oakley (1979).

II. Bibliographical Aids
In addition to the extensive bibliographies contained in the general accounts listed above, the following bibliographies, bibliographic essays, interpretative surveys and collective volumes are very useful. On late-medieval church history in general: O'Malley (1969–70); Duggan. On heresy: Grundmann (1967); Leff (1967), II, 739–77. On nominalism and related topics: Junghans; Courtenay (1972, 1974); Ozment (1980), 1–21. On conciliarism: Alberigo. On late-medieval spirituality and the Reformation in medieval perspective: Ozment (1971); Trinkaus and Oberman; Thompson. Current contributions are listed in the very comprehensive classified bibliographies of new works published on a continuing basis in *Revue d'histoire ecclésiastique*.

[84]Southern (1961), 124–25.
[85]Barraclough, 64–65.

III. Works Cited

Alberigo, Giuseppe, "Il movimento conciliare (xiv-xv sec.) nella ricerca storica recente," *Studi Medievali*, 3rd series, XIX (No. 2, 1978): 913-50.

Aston, M. E., "Lollards and the Reformation: Survival or Revival," *History*, XLIX (No. 2, 1964): 149-70.

Aubenas, R. and Ricard, R., *L'Eglise et la Renaissance (1449-1517)* (Paris, 1951).

Barraclough, Geoffrey, *Papal Provisions* (Oxford, 1935).

Bäumer, Remigius, *Nachwirkungen des konziliaren Gedankens in der Theologie und Kanonistik des frühen 16. Jahrhunderts* (Münster, 1971).

_____, ed., *Von Constanz nach Trient: Beiträge zur Geschichte der Kirche von der Reformkonzilien bis zum Tridentinum Kirche von der Reformkonzilien bis zum Tridentinum* (Munich-Paderborn-Vienna, 1972).

_____, "Um die Anfänge der päpstlichen Unfehlbarkeitslehre." *Theologische Revue*, LXIX (1973): 441-50.

_____, "Antwort an Tierney," *Theologische Revue*, LXX (1974): 193-94.

Bernstein, Alan E. *Pierre d'Ailly and the Blanchard Affair* (Leiden, 1978).

Binz, L., *Vie religieuse et réforme ecclésiastique dans le diocèse de Genève pendant le Grand Schisme* (Geneva, 1973).

Black, A. J., *Monarchy and Community: Political Ideas in the Later Conciliar Controversy: 1430-1450* (Cambridge, 1970).

_____, *Council and Commune: The Conciliar Movement and the Council of Basel* (London-Shepherdstown, 1979).

Bloomfield, Morton W., "Joachim of Flora: A Critical Survey of his Canon, Teachings, Sources, Biography and Influence" *Traditio*, XIII (1957): 248-311.

Boehner, Philotheus, *Collected Articles on Ockham* (New York, 1958).

Bouyer, Louis, *The Spirit and Forms of Protestantism*, trans. A. V. Littledale. (Cleveland-New York, 1964).

Brandmüller, Walter, *Das Konzil von Pavia-Siena: 1423-1424*, 2 vols. (Münster, 1968-73).

Bubenheimer, Ulrich, Review in *Zeitschrift der Savigny-Stiftung für Rechtsgeschichte*, XC (1973), Kanonistische Abteilung, LIX, 445-65.

Cipolla, Carlo M., *Before the Industrial Revolution: European Society and Economy, 1000-1700* (New York, 1976).

Clasen, Claus-Peter, "Medieval Heresies in the Reformation," *Church History,* XXXII (No. 4, 1963): 392-414.

Cohen, Kathleen, *Metamorphosis of a Death Symbol: The Transi Tomb in the Late Middle Ages and the Renaissance* (Berkeley-Los Angeles-London, 1973).

Cohn, Norman, *The Pursuit of the Millennium,* rev. ed. (London, 1970).

Combes, André, *Essai sur la critique de Ruysbroeck par Gerson,* 3 vols. (Paris, 1945-59).

Constable, Giles, "Twelfth-Century Spirituality and the Late Middle Ages," ed. O. B. Hardison, Jr. in *Proceedings of the Southeastern Institute of Medieval and Renaissance Studies,* 5th Session, V (Charlotte, N.C., 1971), pp. 27-60. (a)

———, "Popularity of Twelfth-Century Spiritual Writers," eds. Anthony Molho and John A. Tedeschi, in *Renaissance Studies in Honor of Hans Baron,* (Florence and DeKalb, 1971), pp. 5-28. (b)

Courtenay, William J., "Nominalism and Late Medieval Thought: A Bibliographical Essay," *Theological Studies,* XXXIII (No. 4, 1972): 716-34.

———, "Nominalism and Late Medieval Religion," in Trinkhaus and Oberman, pp. 26-59.

Davis, Natalie Zemon, "Some Tasks and Themes in the Study of Popular Religion," in Trinkaus and Oberman, pp. 307-36.

Delaruelle, Etienne; Labande, E.-R.; and Ourliac, Paul, *L'Eglise au temps du Grand Schisme et de la crise conciliaire,* 2 vols. (Paris, 1962-64).

———, *La Piété Populaire au Moyen Age* (Turin, 1975).

Dettloff, Werner, *Die Entwicklung der Akzeptations-und Verdienstlehre von Duns Scotus bis Luther* (Münster, 1963).

Dix, Dom Gregory, *The Shape of the Liturgy,* 2d ed. (London, 1960).

Dress, Walter, *Die Theologie Gersons — Eine Untersuchung zur Verbindung von Nominalismus und Mystik im Spätmittelalter.* (Gütersloh, 1931).

Duggan, Lawrence G., "The Unresponsiveness of the Late Medieval Church: A Reconsideration," *The Sixteenth-Century Journal* IX (No. 1, 1978): 3-26.

Favier, Jean, *Les Finances pontificales à l'époque du Grand Schisme d'Occident* (Paris, 1966).

Febvre, Lucien, "Une question mal posée: Les origines de la réforme française et le problème de causes de la réforme," *Revue historique* CLXI (1929): 1–73.

Fink, K. A., "Papsttum und Kirchenreform nach dem Grossen Schisma," *Theologische Quartalschrift* CXXVI (1946): 110–22.

_____, "Zur Beurteilung des grossen abendländischen Schismas," *Zeitschrift für Kirchengeschichte* LXXIII (1962): 335–43.

_____, "Die konziliare Idee im späten Mittelalter," ed. Theodor Mayer in *Die Welt zur Zeit des Konstanzer Konzils*, (Konstanz, 1965), pp. 119–34.

Franzen, A., "The Council of Constance: Present State of the Problem," *Concilium* V (1965): 29–68.

Franzen, A. and Müller, W., *Das Konzil von Konstanz: Beiträge zu seiner Geschichte und Theologie* (Freiburg, 1964).

Gill, Joseph, *The Council of Florence* (Cambridge, 1959).

Gilson, Etienne, *History of Christian Philosophy in the Middle Ages* (New York, 1955).

Gonnet, Jean, and Molnár, Amadeo, *Les Vaudois au Moyen Age* (Turin, 1974).

Grundmann, Herbert, *Religiöse Bewegungen im Mittelalter*, 2d ed. (Hildesheim, 1961).

_____, "Ketzerverhöre des Spätmittelalters als quellenkritisches Problem," *Deutsches Archiv für Erforschung des Mittelalters* XXI (1965): 519–71.

_____, *Bibliographie zur Ketzergeschichte des Mittelalters (1900–1966)* (Rome, 1967).

Guillemain, B., *La politique bénéficiale du pape Benoît XII* (Paris, 1952).

_____, "Punti di vista sul Papato avignonese," *Archivio storico italiano* CXI (1953): 181–206.

_____, *La Cour pontificale d'Avignon: 1309–1376* (Paris, 1962).

Hägglund, Bengt, *The Background of Luther's Doctrine of Justification in Late Medieval Theology* (Philadelphia, 1971).

Haller, J., *Papsttum und Kirchenreform* (Berlin, 1903).

Hay, Denys, *The Church in Italy in the Fifteenth Century* (Cambridge, 1977).

Heath, Peter, *English Parish Clergy on the Eve of the Reformation* (London, 1969).

Hegler, Alfred, *Geist und Schrift bei Sebastien Franck: Eine Studie zur Geschichte des Spiritualismus in der Reformationszeit* (Freiburg, 1892).

Hendrix, Scott H., "In Quest of the *Vera Ecclesia*. The Crises of Late Medieval Ecclesiology," *Viator* VII (1976): 347–78.

Hurley, Michael, " 'Scriptura Sola': Wyclif and His Critics." *Traditio* XVI (1960): 275–352.

Hyma, Albert, *The Brethren of the Common Life* (Grand Rapids, 1950).

Iserloh, Erwin, *Gnade und Eucharistie in der philosophischen Theologie des Wilhelm von Ockham* (Wiesbaden, 1956).

————, "Der Wert der Messe in der Diskussion der Theologen vom Mittelalter bis zum 16. Jahrhundert," *Zeitschrift für katholische Theologie* LXXXIII (1961): 44–79.

Jacob, E. F., *Essays in the Conciliar Epoch*, 3d ed. (Manchester, 1963).

Jedin, Hubert, *A History of the Council of Trent.* trans. Ernest Graf, 2 vols. (London, 1957–61), Vol. I.

Jedin, Hubert, and Dolan, John, eds., *Handbook of Church History*, 7 vols. (Freiburg-Montreal, 1965), Vol. I.

Junghans, Helmar, *Ockham im Lichte der neueren Forschung* (Berlin, 1968).

Jungmann, Joseph A., *The Mass of the Roman Rite: Its Origin and Development*, trans. F. A. Brunner, 2 vols. (New York, 1950).

Kalivoda, Robert, *Husitská ideologie* (Prague, 1961).

Kaminsky, Howard, *A History of the Hussite Revolution* (Berkeley-Los Angeles, 1967).

Klauser, Theodor, *A Short History of the Western Liturgy*, trans. John Haliburton (London, 1969).

Klotzner, Josef, *Kardinal Domenikus Jacobazzi und sein Konzilswerk* (Rome, 1948).

Knowles, David, *The Religious Orders in England*, 3 vols. (Cambridge, 1950–59).

————, *The English Mystical Tradition* (New York, 1961).

La Brosse, Olivier de, *Le Pape et le Concile: La comparaison de leur pouvoirs à la veille de la Réforme* (Paris, 1965).

Lambert, Malcolm, *Medieval Heresy: Popular Movements from Bogomil to Hus* (New York, 1976).

Leclercq, Jean; Vandenbroucke, François; and Bouyer, Louis, *La Spiritualité du Moyen Age* (Paris, 1961).

Leff, Gordon, *Heresy in the Later Middle Ages: The Relation of Heterodoxy to Dissent c. 1250-c. 1450*, 2 vols. (Manchester, 1967).

_____, *William of Ockham: The Metamorphosis of Scholastic Discourse* (Manchester, 1975).

Léonard, Emile G., *Histoire générale des Protestantisme*, 3 vols. (Paris, 1961).

Lerner, Robert E., *The Heresy of the Free Spirit in the Later Middle Ages* (Berkeley-Los Angeles-London, 1972).

Lopez, R., and Miskimin, H. A., "The Economic Depression of the Renaissance," *Economic History Review* XIV (1962): 408-26.

Lortz, Josef, *How the Reformation Came*, trans. Otto M. Knab (New York, 1964).

_____, *The Reformation in Germany*, trans. Ronald Walls, 2 vols. (London-New York, 1968).

Loserth, Johann, *Wiclif and Hus*, trans. M. J. Evans (London, 1884).

Lunt, William E., *Papal Revenues in the Middle Ages*, 2 vols. (New York, 1934).

_____, *Financial Relations of the Papacy with England*, 2 vols. (Cambridge, Mass., 1939-62).

McDonnell, E. W., *The Beguines and Beghards in Medieval Culture* (New Brunswick, 1954).

McFarlane, K. B., *John Wycliffe and the Beginnings of English Nonconformity* (London, 1952).

Moeller, Bernd, "Frömmigkeit in Deutschland um 1500," *Archiv für Reformationsgeschichte* LVI (1965): 3-31.

_____, *Spätmittelalter*. Vol. 2, installment H (pt. 1), of *Die Kirche in ihrer Geschichte: Ein Handbuch*, ed. Kurt Schmidt and Ernst Wolf (Göttingen, 1966).

Mollat, G., *La collation des bénéfices à l'époque des papes d'Avignon* (Paris, 1921).

_____, *The Popes at Avignon (1305-1378)*, trans. Janet Love (New York, 1963), from the 9th French edition: *Les Papes d'Avignon*, (Paris, 1949).

Morrissey, Thomas E., "The Decree 'Haec Sancta' and Cardinal Zabarella," *Annuarium Historiae Conciliorum* X (No. 1, 1978): 145-76.

Moynihan, James M., *Papal Immunity and Liability in the Writings of the Medieval Canonists* (Rome, 1961).

Oakley, Francis, "Almain and Major Conciliar Theory on the Eve of the Reformation," *American Historical Review* LXX (No. 3, 1965): 673-90.

————, "Pierre d'Ailly," ed. B. A. Gerrish in *Reformers in Profile*, (Philadelphia, 1967), pp. 40–57.

————, *Council over Pope? Towards a Provisional Ecclesiology* (New York-London, 1969). (a)

————, "Figgis, Constance, and the Divines of Paris," *American Historical Review* LXXV (No. 2, 1969): 368–86. (b)

————, "The 'New Conciliarism' and its Implications: A Problem in History and Hermeneutics," *Journal of Ecumenical Studies* VIII (No. 4, 1971): 815–40.

————, "Conciliarism at the Fifth Lateran Council?" *Church History* XLI (1972): 452–63.

————, "Conciliarism in the Sixteenth Century: Jacques Almain Again," *Archiv für Reformationsgeschichte* LXVIII (1977): 111–32.

————, "The 'Tractatus de Fide et Ecclesia, Romano Pontifice et Concilio Generali' of Johannes Breviscoxe," *Annuarium Historiae Conciliorum* X (No. 1, 1978): 99–130.

————, *The Western Church in the Later Middle Ages* (Ithaca-London, 1979).

————, "Natural Law, the Corpus Mysticum and Consent in Conciliar Thought from John of Paris to Matthias Ugonius," *Speculum* LVI (No. 4, 1981): 786–810.

Oberman, Heiko, *The Harvest of Medieval Theology: Gabriel Biel Late Medieval Nominalism* (Cambridge, Mass. 1963).

————, "Das tridentinische Rechtfertigungsdekret im Licht spätmittelalterlicher Theologie," *Zeitschrift für Theologie und Kirche* LXI (No. 3, 1964): 251–82.

————, ed., *Forerunners of the Reformation: The Shape of Late Medieval Thought* (New York, 1966).

————, "The Shape of Late Medieval Thought: The Birthpangs of the Modern Era," in Trinkaus and Oberman, pp. 3–25.

————, "Et tibi dabo claves regni coelorum," *Nederlands Theologisch Tijdschrift* XXXIX (No. 2, 1975): 97–118.

————, *Werden und Wertung der Reformation. Vom Wegenstreit zum Glaubenskampf* (Tübingen, 1977).

O'Malley, John W., *Giles of Viterbo on Church and Reform: A Study in Renaissance Thought* (Leiden, 1968).

————, "Recent Studies in Church History," *Catholic Historical Review* LV (1969–70): 394–437.

Origo, Iris, *The World of San Bernardino* (New York, 1962).

Ozment, Steven E., "The University and the Church: Patterns of Reform in Jean Gerson," *Medievalia et Humanistica*, New Series I (1970): 111–26.

———, ed., *The Reformation in Medieval Perspective*, (Chicago, 1971).

———, *Mysticism and Dissent: Religious Ideology and Social Protest in the Sixteenth Century* (New Haven-London, 1973).

———, "Mysticism, Nominalism and Dissent," in Trinkaus and Oberman, pp. 67–92.

———, *The Reformation in the Cities* (New Haven-London, 1975).

———, *The Age of Reform: 1250–1550* (New Haven-London, 1980).

Pantin, W. A., *The English Church in the Fourteenth Century* (Cambridge, 1955).

Partner, Peter, *The Papal State under Martin V* (London, 1958).

———, "The 'Budget' of the Roman Church," ed. E. F. Jacob, in *Italian Renaissance Studies* (London, 1960), kpp. 256–278.

Pascoe, Louis B., *Jean Gerson: Principles of Church Reform* (Leiden, 1973).

Post, R. R., *The Modern Devotion: Confrontation with Reforma- and Humanism* (Leiden, 1968).

Přerovský, O., *L'elezione di Urbano VI e l'insorgere dello scisma d'Occidente* (Rome, 1960).

Preus, James S., *From Shadow to Promise: Old Testament Interpretation from Augustine to the Young Luther* (Cambridge, Mass., 1969).

Privat, Edouard, ed., *La religion populaire en Languedoc du XIIIe siècle à la moitié du XIVe siècle* (Toulouse, 1976).

Rapp, Francis, *L'Eglise et la vie religieuse en Occident à la fin du Moyen Age* (Paris, 1971).

Reeves, Marjorie, *The Influence of Prophecy in the Later Middle Ages: A Study in Joachimism* (Oxford, 1969).

Renaudet, Augustin, *Préréforme et Humanisme à Paris pendant les premières guerres d'Italie: 1494–1517*, 2d ed. (Paris, 1953).

Renouard, Yves, *Les relations des papes d'Avignon et des compagnies commerciales et bancaires* (Paris, 1941).

———, *The Avignon Papacy: 1305–1403*, trans. Denis Bethell (Hamden, Conn., 1970).

Samaran, Ch. and Mollat, G., *La fiscalité pontificale en France au XIVe siècle* (Paris, 1905).

Schneider, Hans, *Der Konziliarismus als Problem der neuren katholischen Theologie* (Berlin-New York, 1976).

Seidlmayer, M. "Die Spanischen 'Libri de Schismate' des Vatikanischen Archivs," *Gesammelte Aufsätze zur Kulturgeschichte Spaniens* VIII (1940): 199–262. (a)

————, *Die Anfänge des grossen abendländischen Schismas* (Münster, 1940).

————, Review in *Zeitschrift der Savigny-Stiftung für Rechtsgeschichte, Kanonistische Abteilung* XLIII (1957): 374–87.

Sohm, Rudolf, *Outlines of Church History*, trans. May Sinclair (Boston, 1958), from the 3d. German edition: *Kirchengeschichte im Grundriss* (Leipzig, 1889).

Southern, R. W., *The Making of the Middle Ages* (New Haven, 1961).

————, *Western Society and the Church in the Middle Ages* (Harmondsworth, 1970).

Spinka, Matthew, ed., *Advocates of Reform: From Wyclif to Erasmus* (London, 1958).

————, *John Hus' Concept of the Church* (Princeton, 1966).

————, *John Hus. A Biography* (Princeton, 1968).

Steinmetz, David C., "Libertas Christiana: Studies in the Theology of John Pupper of Goch (d. 1475)," *Harvard Theological Review* LXV (No. 2, 1972): 191–230.

Stickler, Alfons M., "Papal Infallibility—A Thirteenth-Century Invention," *Catholic Historical Review* LX (No. 3, 1974): 427–41.

————, "Rejoinder to Professor Tierney," *Catholic Historical Review* LXI (No. 2, 1975): 274–77.

Stieber, Joachim, *Pope Eugenius IV, The Council of Basel, and the Secular and Ecclesiastical Authorities in the Empire* (Leiden, 1978).

Sullivan, Donald, "Nicholas of Cusa as Reformer: The Papal Legation to the Germanies, 1451–1452," *Mediaeval Studies* XXXVI (1974): 382–428.

Sumption, Jonathan, *Pilgrimage: An Image of Medieval Religion* (London, 1975).

Tavard, George H. *Holy Writ or Holy Church: The Crisis of the Protestant Reformation* (New York, 1959).

Tentler, Thomas N., "The Summa for Confessors as an Instrument of Social Control," in Trinkaus and Oberman, pp. 103–26.

———, *Sin and Confession on the Eve of the Reformation* (Princeton, 1977).

Thompson, W. D. J. Cargill, "Seeing the Reformation in Medieval Perspective," *Journal of Ecclesiastical History* XXV (No. 3, 1974): 297–308.

Thomson, J. A. F., *The Later Lollards: 1414–1520* (Oxford, 1965).

Thomson, S. Harrison, ed., *Magistri Joannis Hus: Tractatus de ecclesia*. (Boulder, Colo., 1956).

Tierney, Brian, "The Canonists and the mediaeval state," *Review of Politics* XV (1953): 378–88.

———, *Foundations of the Conciliar Theory* (Cambridge, 1955).

———, "Pope and Council: Some New Decretist Texts," *Mediaeval Studies* XIX (1957): 197–218.

———, " 'Sola Scriptura' and the Canonists," *Studia Gratiana* XI (1967): 347–66.

———, *Origins of Papal Infallibility: 1150–1350* (Leiden, 1972).

———, "On the History of Papal Infallibility: A Discussion with Remigius Bäumer," *Theologische Revue* LXX (1974): 185–94.

———, "Infallibility and the Medieval Canonists: A Discussion with Alfons Stickler," *Catholic Historical Review, LXI (No. 2, 1975): 265–73.*

Toussaert, Jacques, *Le Sentiment religieux en Flandre à la fin du Moyen Age* (Paris, 1963).

Trapp, Damasus, "Augustinian Theology of the Fourteenth Century: Notes on Editions, Marginalia, Opinions and Booklore," *Augustiniana* VI (1956): 146–274.

Trexler, Richard C., "Ritual in Florence: Adolescence and Salvation in the Renaissance," in Trinkaus and Oberman, pp. 200–64.

———, "Rome on the Eve of the Great Schism," *Speculum* XLII (No. 3, 1967): 489–509.

Trinkaus, Charles, *In Our Image and Likeness: Humanity and Divinity in Italian Humanist Thought*, 2 vols. (Chicago, 1970).

———and Oberman, Heiko, eds., *The Pursuit of Holiness in Late Medieval and Renaissance Religion* (Leiden, 1974).

Turley, Thomas, "Infallibilists in the Curia of Pope John XXII," *Journal of Medieval History*, I (No. 1, 1975): 71–101.

Ullmann, Karl H., *Reformatoren vor der Reformation vornehmlich in Deutschland und den Niederlanden*, 2 vols. (Hamburg, 1841–42).

Ullmann, Walter, *Origins of the Great Schism* (London, 1949).

Vauchez, André, "Conclusion," in Privat, pp. 429–44.

Vignaux, Paul, *Justification et prédestination au xive siècle: Duns Scot, Pierre d'Auriole, Guillaume d'Occam, Grégoire de Rimini* (Paris, 1934).

_____, *Luther: Commentateur des sentences* (Paris, 1935).

Vooght, Paul de, *Les sources de la doctrine chrétienne d'après les théologiens du xive siècle et du début du xve* (Paris, 1954).

_____, *L'Hérésie de Jean Hus* (Louvain, 1960). (a)

_____, *Hussiana* (Louvain, 1960). (b)

_____, (1965), *Les Pouvoirs du concile et l'autorité du Pape au Concile de Constance* (Paris, 1965).

_____, "Les Controverses sur des pouvoirs du concile et l'autorité du pape au Concile de Constance," *Revue Théologique de Louvain*, I (1970): 45–75.

Weinstein, Donald, *Savonarola and Florence: Prophecy and Patriotism in the Renaissance* (Princeton, 1970).

Williams, George H., *The Radical Reformation* (Philadelphia, 1962).

_____, "Popularized German Mysticism as a Factor in the Rise of Anabaptist Communism," ed. G. Müller and W. Zeller in *Glaube, Geist, Geschichte: Festschirift für Ernst Benz*, (Leiden, 1967), pp. 290–312.

Wood-Legh, K. L., *Perpetual Chantries in Britain* (Cambridge, 1965).

Xiberta, B. M., "Scriptura, Traditio et magisterium juxta antiquos auctores ordinis Carmelitarum," ed. C. Balić *De Scriptura et traditione*, (Rome, 1963).

Zumkeller, Adolar, "Die Augustinerschule des Mittelalters: Vertreter und philosophish-theologische Lehre," *Analecta Augustiniana* XXVII (1964): 167–262.

Zwölfer, Richard, "Die Reform der Kirchenverfassung auf dem Konzil zu Basel," *Basler Zeitschrift für Geschichte und Altertumskunde* XXVIII (1929): 141–247, and XXIX (1930): 1–58.

Humanism and the Reformation

James D. Tracy

Moeller (1961) has stated the conundrum which still confronts students of the relationship between Renaissance humanism and the nascent Protestant movement. Although humanists "stood on the foundations of medieval Catholicism," a unity symbolized by Erasmus' dedication of his Greek New Testament to Pope Leo X, humanists in Germany and Switzerland rallied to Luther's banner from the very beginning, indeed they were "the one united group of men" who stood behind him in the crucial early years (Moeller notes that there was a generation gap between Luther's antagonists among the older humanists and his eager young supporters); only amid the turmoil of the 1520s did many humanists realize "that their religious assumptions were ultimately Catholic." Hence, Moeller speaks of a "constructive misunderstanding" in which the humanists, not sensing at first the conflict between Luther's doctrine of justification and their own faith in the powers of man, hailed him as one of their own because of his attack on scholastic theology and his exaltation of Scripture.

Clearly, it was no accident that Erasmus chose free will as the issue on which to attack Luther (*De Libero Arbitrio* has never been thoroughly treated, but the quality of previous works by *Boyle* and *Chantraine* give reason to hope that their forthcoming studies will answer this need). Studies of his educational thought from *Woodward* to *Margolin* (1966) highlight the "ethical optimism" Erasmus found in the classics and the Greek Fathers; as he wrote in *De Libero Arbitrio*, Scripture itself was full of exhortations for man to better himself—which was clearly impossible if, as Luther insisted, everything done by free will was a sin. True, recent research has swept aside the old tendency to think of humanism as a set of philosophical assumptions in which freedom of the will took pride of place. Yet in a long view of history the humanist and the Augustinian views of man stand on opposite sides of some great intellectual divide. The debate between Erasmus and Luther began a warfare between free will and predestination which reverberated for two hundred years in European religious thought, and free will invariably found its defenders among men with strong ties to the Renaissance humanist tradition: Philippists vs. Genesio-Lutherans in Germany, Remonstrants vs. Counter-Remonstrants in The Netherlands, Jesuits vs. Jansenists in France.

But the fact remains that most younger humanists—at least in Germany and Switzerland—did become Lutherans or reformed Protestants. *Spitz* (1967) finds an impressive number of men of humanist background among the Reformers, but very few older men. My own survey of those listed as "humanists" in the standard biographical dictionaries,[1] and born in Germany, Switzerland, and the Low Countries between 1450 and 1510, yields a total of 278, of whom 145 became and remained Protestants; the proportions are reversed for the generation born by 1480 (25 Catholics out of 35) and afterwards (135 Protestants out of 243, or 55.5 percent). Since it is a consensus of scholarship both old and new that Renaissance humanism was primarily an educational movement focused on reform of the liberal arts, one may usefully segregate out from other younger humanists the professional educators in liberal arts fields—for present purposes, those who taught for a total of five years or more in university arts faculties or gymnasia. Professional educators thus defined were significantly more likely to become Protestants (99–55, or 62.0 percent, as opposed to 45–53, or 45.9 percent, among the remaining younger humanists). Barring individual biographies of all 278 men, many of whom have never been studied, what such numbers may mean is open to question, but it does seem that Moeller's paradox may be stated even more emphatically: those closest to the educational core of the humanist movement were most likely to embrace a religious doctrine directly in conflict with certain assumptions about human nature without which humanist pedagogy would be unintelligible.

That university humanists mistakenly hailed the Saxon Reformer as an ally in their partisan struggle against scholasticism and clerical obscurantism is undoubtedly correct. Both in *Ijsewijn*'s lucid survey of Low Countries humanism, and *Herding*'s exemplary edition of

---

[1]P. S. Allen, *Allgemeine Deutsche Biographie, Biographie Nationale de Belgioue, Cioranescu, Gerloi Neve Deutsche Biographie, Nieuwe Nederlandsche Biographische Woordenboer, De Vocht.*

Wimpheling's *Adolescentia*, one can already see grounds for conflict between the pious timidity of the first generation of native-born humanists and their sophisticated successors, steeped in "pagan" eloquence. Particularly in Germany the Reuchlin affair and other controversies described by *Overfield* and *Nauert* had fused the humanists into a self-conscious party of "good letters." But Moeller's further argument that "as an independent movement humanism fell apart" after about 1523 is more dubious. Apart from those who changed careers and became Protestant preachers during the critical early years there were many others for whom the humanist reform of the liberal arts continued to provide a livelihood and possibly some common attitudes towards the religious issues of the day. Moreover, among those who embraced the new doctrines in the early years (1518–1523), the number of men who returned to the old faith was fairly small. The majority of these early converts as well as those who adhered to the new faith after about 1525 must have found in the Protestant cause something of more value than an alliance against scholasticism that was both misconceived and short-lived.

At this point the discussion may usefully turn to what has been accomplished in the study of Renaissance humanism in the twenty-two years since Moeller's article. Two major themes of current research will be noted and examined for their relevance to the question at hand: (1) the religion of the humanists, and (2) humanism as a phase in the rhetorical tradition of Western culture.

The Religion of the Humanists

According to a conception of the Renaissance that dates from the *philosophes* of the Enlightenment era the humanists, as Renaissance men, were thought to have emancipated themselves from medieval religion along with everything else pertaining to the "Dark Ages." If, in recognition of the piety of men like John Colet and Thomas More, it became conventional to place "Christian humanists" north of the Alps in a separate category, it also remained fashionable to regard Italian humanists as pagan in spirit if not always in outward profession. Early twentieth-century Italian scholars proposed that the humanists had anticipated the modern doctrine of philosophical idealism, according to which man is the creator of his own values and beliefs. This view is still noticeable in a major post-war scholar like *Garin*, and indeed may find partial confirmation in studies of humanist logic and in the connections that *Cantimori* and others have found between humanism and Italian anti-Trinitarians of the later sixteenth century.

Meanwhile, others have reaffirmed the humanists' place in the Catholic tradition. *Dulles* and *Monnerjahn* established that Pico della Mirandola (d. 1495), despite clear syncretist tendencies, was more orthodox than had been thought and much closer to scholasticism. Particularly interesting is the shift of opinion with regard to Lorenzo Valla (d. 1455), arguably the most original thinker among Italian humanists and sometimes thought to have no religious beliefs at all. During the last few decades an impressive consensus concerning his fundamental orthodoxy has emerged in Italian scholarship: Valla's distinctive sythesis of Christianity and Epicureanism (*De Voluptate*) represents not a rejection of transcendence, as the idealists thought, but a passionate affirmation, as against the Stoics, of the unity of soul and body (*Gaeta*). When Valla declares against his enemy Poggio that his life's work has been "to offer in the Lord's temple pig skins, as they say, if I am not capable of anything else," there is no reason not to take him seriously (*Camporeale*). *Fois* can even speak of Valla's "spirituality," and his fundamental concerns situate him according to *Di Napoli* in a line of development running from the Conciliar Movement to the Protestant Reformation. In this regard, *Bouwsma* (1968) draws an interesting parallel between the humanists with their skepticism in regard to philosophical systems and their love of the particulars of language and history, and Protestant rejection of the universal claims of the Church. But he strains credibility by employing as a foil for his argument a metaphysical caricature of the Catholic tradition. *Trinkaus* (1971), in pointing to the emphasis on man's passionate or emotional nature which Valla shared with earlier figures like Petrarch and Salutati, connects the humanists with the medieval Augustinian tradition, which can be shown to have exerted an influence on humanism and scholastic voluntarism as well as on the Reformers. This line of investigation promises to be fruitful.

Similarly, over the last several decades, northern humanists like Erasmus and Melanchthon—formerly claimed by free-thinkers, in the case of Erasmus, or scorned as traitors by many of their co-religionists—have come to be taken seriously as religious thinkers. For Erasmus studies the most important breakthrough was probably *Auer*'s book on the *Enchiridion Militis Christiani*, which shows Erasmus's heavy emphasis on the ethical dimension of religion, as distinct from formal dogma, must be understood in terms of his readings in the Greek Fathers, and therefore should not be considered a displacement of religious values by purely ethical norms derived from the classics. *Kohls*'s effort to demonstrate detailed correspondences between the thought structure of the *Enchiridion* and traditional theological *schemata* made it possible to speak of Erasmus's "theology" without raising eyebrows, but many of his arguments were tendentious. Far more valuable are *Payne*'s careful survey of Erasmus's sacramental views, and *Chantraine*'s subtle analysis of one of his mature works, the *Ratio Verae Theologiae*, which shows a humanist's understanding of language merging with Erasmus's patristic sources to shape a new biblical exegesis, once again colored by a strong ethical concern. *Oelrich* and *Augustijn*, addressing the question posed by Erasmus's apparently shifting attitudes toward the Reformation, each found an underlying consistency in his rejection of the new movement, partly for doctrinal reasons, but more because the Reformation—especially in its Swiss or south German variety—failed dismally, in his opinion, to live up to its promise of bettering the morals of Christian people.

For Melanchthon studies, too, a turning point was evident by about 1960 in the session on the "Praeceptor Germaniae" at the Second Luther Congress in Münster, and also in *Stupperich*'s brief biography, a clear vindication of Melanchthon's integrity, based on a fresh look at the sources. *Fraenkel*'s careful analysis of Melanchthon's use of patristic sources showed that he did not, as had sometimes been thought, set the Fathers on an equal footing with Scripture. Where theological issues are at stake *Maurer*'s important account of Melanchthon's intellectual development (to 1529) argues for his fundamental agreement with Luther, albeit from an independent standpoint. Finally, *Greschat* shows that Luther himself incorporated some of Melanchthon's views into his own understanding of the doctrine of justification as expounded in the 1532 *Commentary on Galatians*. There are important issues which remain in dispute—whether or to what extent Melanchthon in his later writings adopted a synergistic view of justification—but after the work of various German scholars during the 1960s it would seem difficult indeed to deny Melanchthon the place to which he aspired, at Luther's side.

French humanism was arguably more creative in the sixteenth century and less understood today than any other national segment of the humanist movement. The confusion lies partly in the bewildering diversity among sixteenth-century French thinkers, all of whom were steeped in classical culture, even if it may not always be strictly correct to think of them as humanists; and partly in the profound interpenetration of Latin humanism and vernacular literature in a country more deeply influenced than any other by the culture of Renaissance Italy. Nonetheless, there are superb surveys for the early period (1495–1535) by *Renaudet* and *La Garanderie.*

The question of religious identity is usually clear enough in the latter part of the century when many humanists produced polemical tracts during the religious wars. To be sure, there was Bodin, whose *Heptaplomeres* still leaves readers guessing whether he was a Catholic, a Protestant, a Jew, or none of the above (*Kuntz*), and there were others (like Montaigne, if one who wrote only in French may be accounted a humanist) who found solace in the skeptical philosophy of antiquity. Although this revival of skepticism has been linked in recent studies (*Popkin, Brown*) to the fideist tradition among French Catholic apologists, it does point up certain ambiguities about the religious aspect of French humanism which trace back to the earlier part of the century.

Men like Rabelais or Lefèvre d'Etaples have at various times been claimed as their own by Catholics, Protestants, and anti-clericals; in this context, *Febvre's* discussion (1947) of the "limits of unbelief," with special reference to Rabelais, was a classic demonstration of the necessity of entering into the mental categories of the age in question. *Imbart de la Tour* contended that men like Lefèvre and Rabelais should be considered partisans of what he called "evangelisme," a more personal form of religion based on the Scriptures and severely critical of Catholic practices, yet not Protestant. *Lovy* countered by arguing that the "Meaux circle" was evolving in a clearly Protestant direction. A more plausible connection between humanism and the Reformation is suggested by *Bohatec*, whose intriguing study of Budé displays a powerful and original mind gradually coming to the conclusion that, contrary to what the philosophers said, man's reason was unable to hold in check his turbulent emotions, and that a resurgent pagan belief in the power of "fortune" could only be countered by a firm belief in divine predestination. Meanwhile, Imbart's conception of "evangelisme" continues to seem useful. If an attempt to apply it to certain Italian thinkers of the same period has come to grief,[2] it is still an important considera-

---

[2]*Sixteenth Century Journal* 9 (1978): 118–119.

tion in *Screech*'s studies of Rabelais and *Bedouelle*'s account of Lefèvre.

Religious syncretism represents still another dimension of humanist religious thought, in which beginning with the mysterious figure of Gemisthus Plethos (*Masai*),[3] many humanists probed the esoteric lore of various non-Christian traditions. In studies of Renaissance magic by *Yates* and *Walker*, and of Christian cabalism by *Bouwsma* (1957) and *Secret*, scholarship since the 1950s has uncovered a major component of the humanist movement which was probably considered slightly indecent so long as it was customary to think of the humanists as enlightened men. In fact, new awareness of the depth and breadth of Renaissance esoterism has done (or at least ought to have done) much to discredit the notion that humanists in general were spiritually akin to the sober rationalism of eighteenth-century *philosophes*. If the new humanist science of philology (see the following section) did indeed nurture among some of its devotees a critical spirit of which the eighteenth century might have been proud (*Holmes*), the religious yearnings of the Italian Neo-Platonists and their mystical exaltation of man's passionate nature have much more in common with the Romantic period (*Burger*). That there was a connection between this interest in the dark realm of magic and some more pervasive crisis of confidence in the powers of human reason is suggested by Goethe's re-working of the Faust legend as well as by *Nauert* (1960).

Possibly related to the influence of Italian thinkers like Ficino and Pico, whose importance for Germany is shown by *Spitz* (1964), is the latitudinarian view of doctrinal disputes to be found among so many humanists, both Catholic and Protestant. Alternatively, one may see, for instance, in Erasmus's complaints about those, including Luther, who seek to make dogmas of their private opinions, an echo of the rhetorical tradition—e.g., Cicero's slightly supercilious references to the wrangling among the philosophical "sects" of antiquity. However it be explained, humanists did have a tendency to view theological disagreements with a certain equanimity. To claim that they originated modern ideas of religious toleration would be wrong, as is made clear by *Lecler* and *Kamen*. True, More's Utopians permit anyone who believes in God to expound his views, pro-

---

[3]There is a more recent book in Russian by Igor Pavlovich Medvedev.

vided he observes moderation in censuring others, while Erasmus generally disapproved of the death penalty for heresy. Moreover, the impetus for Lutheran-Catholic dialogue in the 1530s and 1540s came from men of humanist sympathies (starting with Melanchthon's *Augsburg Confession*), including, on the Catholic side, several disciples of Erasmus (see *Stupperich* [1936], *Lipgens, Augustijn* [1967], *Pfnur, Matheson, Nugent*). But nowhere in humanist writings during the first half of the century does one find a statement of the crucial principle that a state can or should tolerate within its boundaries more than one organized religious establishment. As is well known, More initiated numerous prosecutions for heresy during his tenure as Lord Chancellor, and even the irenicists were hopeful of restoring the shattered religious unity of the *corpus Christianum*. Instead, something resembling the modern idea of toleration is first defended by Protestant radicals like Castellio, and first put into effect by practical men (e.g., the French *politiques*) who saw a co-existence of rival churches as the only alternative to something even worse, namely, religious war. Yet, in the forms of actual toleration which came into being in the later sixteenth century, whether by official sanction (France) or informally (The Netherlands), there is still a visible connection with humanism, since the foremost defenders of the novel idea of toleration were often of a humanist background, like L'Hôpital or Coornheert (*Kaegi, Di Caprariis, Güldner*). Theologians could also find a rationale for toleration, as *Lecler* shows, yet it seems at least appropriate that the later, eighteenth-century discussion of toleration was begun by a group of Protestant refugees in Holland, one of whose accomplishments was the first complete edition of Erasmus's works (on Jean Leclerc, see *Flittner*).

To speak of L'Hôpital, or even Montaigne, raises an important question concerning the boundaries of humanism as an historical movement. The further one moves into the sixteenth century, the less sense it makes to speak of "humanists," since, subject to national or local variations, the humanist curriculum and its influence eventually became all-pervasive. At some point, perhaps with the generation of Lipsius and Scaliger, one should speak rather of "classical scholars." But even as the humanist movement disappeared amidst its success, men who began their careers as humanist teachers or scholars were occupying important positions in government, directing the affairs of state in a manner that may sometimes betray the influence of their earlier training. In principle one must be skeptical of efforts to explain political actions in terms of political ideas, much less ideas about literature or education; but the studies of English statesmen and churchmen by *L. Smith* and *McConica*, showing their role in shaping the latitudinarian character of the Anglican religious settlement, make a convincing case that the careers of "humanist" statesmen in other countries are well worth studying.

Humanism and the Rhetorical Tradition

The single most important development in studies of Renaissance humanism over the last twenty-five years has been the broad acceptance of *Kristeller's* thesis[4] that humanism should be understood as a phase in the rhetorical tradition of Western culture. As a result, scholars no longer assume that anyone identified as a humanist will share in a set of philosophical assumptions. Rather, they assume he will share a set of intellectual interests starting with a love of classical Latin, as distinct from the language of the Church and the universities, and branching out into new conceptions of the traditional arts of language, grammar, rhetoric, and logic.

Even before Kristeller, *McKeon* pointed to the difference in method by which a scholastic logician like Abelard and a humanist grammarian like Erasmus would approach a given text, one in search of the author's opinions on philosophical questions of general interest, the other dwelling on the details of vocabulary and syntax by which one author differs from another. The way in which humanist eagerness to recapture the fine points of classical Latin led to the emergence of a new science of philology is clear in the career of Lorenzo Valla: first the laborious compilation of classical usages leading towards his *Elegantiae*, then his exposure of the *Donation of Constantine* as a forgery, and finally his *Annotations* to the Greek New Testament. If Scripture was the most important text to which humanists applied their new techniques, the results of their work are nonetheless very often much closer to traditional exegesis than might be expected, as is evident in the studies of Lefèvre d'Etaples and his disciple, Clichetove, by *Bedouelle* and *Massaut*. Erasmus, with his remarkable independence of mind and the extraordinary acuity of his critical method, was very different; *Bentley* shows that he was the founder of modern biblical scholarship, and also that those who came after him were too preoccupied by the theological concerns of

---

[4]See especially "The Humanist Movement" in *Kristeller* (1961), plus comments by *Gray* and *Nauert* (1980).

the Reformation and the Counter-Reformation to view textual problems quite so dispassionately as he did. His like was not to be seen in
Europe again until Richard Simon (d. 1712), a priest of the Oratory,
who had almost as much difficulty with Sorbonne theologians as
Erasmus (*Mirri, Steinman*). In other areas, humanist philology
opened a new, historical approach to Roman law, soon found competing in law faculties with adherents of the traditional *glossatores*,
and it was applied also to a critical study of textual sources for
various national and regional histories. But in the kind of history
which prevailed in the end, as is clear from *Huppert's* account of
French historiography, there was less attention to source criticism
than to fictive speeches by great actors on the stage of history; exciting though philology may be as an intellectual breakthrough which
does indeed separate the Renaissance from the Middle Ages, the fact
is that most humanists were more interested in rhetoric.

Studies of humanist rhetoric and its implications may conveniently be divided into a *Quellenforschung* approach on the one hand,
relating humanist thought to psychological or epistemological insights to be found in the ancient rhetoricians, including the Greek
sophists, and a *Sitz-im-Leben* approach on the other, which recog-
nizes that many humanists were in their professional lives attempting to restructure a curriculum traditionally dominated by the art of
logic, or dialectic. The former approach is more valuable for major
thinkers like Valla or Budé, for whom it can plausibly be argued
that they had a penetrating grasp of their sources, while the latter is
more suited to the generality of schoolmasters and liberal arts professors who, especially north of the Alps, fought humanism's daily
battles.

Among the classical rhetorical sources whose influence on humanist thought has most often been commented on are Aristotle's *Posterior Analytics* (along with similar works, like Cicero's *Topica*), and
the conception of *kairos*, the opportune moment, adapted from
Greek rhetorical *theory* by certain historians, notably Thucydides.
(Quintilian's educational theory was just as important, but a discussion of its influence would involve re-stating points made earlier in
this essay about the optimistic assumptions which underlay humanist pedagogy.) In the *Posterior Analytics* Aristotle proposes a list of
"topics" (literally, "places") into which all matters for discussion
may be grouped. Unlike the "ten categories" of the *Prior Analytics*,
this list makes no claim to reflect the structure of being outside the

mind, and it was for that reason particularly useful to practitioners of rhetoric, whose art consists in talking about things in a plausible and persuasive manner, eschewing the claim to certitude which, according to Plato and Aristotle, philosophical knowledge in the strict sense requires. Among the many humanists who sought to develop a topical logic congenial to the needs of rhetoric, and likewise intended to prune back the intellectual thickets which in the medieval schools had grown up out of Aristotle's demonstrative logic, the most interesting philosophically was Lorenzo Valla, who fully accepted the implication that mental categories are arbitrary products of the human mind. For Aristotle's "ten categories" he substituted a list of three, equivalent to the major parts of speech: nouns, verbs, and modifiers.

The connection between certain technical notions of classical rhetoric (*kairos*) and a new form of historical explanation developed by humanist writers that stresses the importance of particular circumstances rather than more general moral or religious categories is made by *Struever* for Bruni and Poggio (an intriguing argument, if at times it seems to strain the texts) and by *Kelley* (1970) for Budé and other French scholars. Both suggest a plausible comparison between the humanist historians they have studied and the beginnings of modern historicism, starting with Vico, himself a classical scholar. Thus, there was at least one strain in the broad humanist critique of Aristotle which involved a philosophical defense of the irreducible particularity of human reality, more amenable to historical description than to logical analysis. In regard to human nature, the complement to this rejection of abstract logic would be to insist that man's life is propelled by passions and desires too powerful for reason to control, a point of view which may be called Augustinian at least in its emphasis on the insufficiency of a rational moral philosophy. As *Trinkaus* (1948, 1949) suggested some time ago, Lorenzo Valla represents precisely this combination of a radical attack on Aristotle's logic and a definition of the soul's grandeur in terms of passion rather than reason. Among northern humanists of the Reformation era, Budé is the one who resembles Valla most closely in his stature as a philologist and historical scholar, in his conviction that reason cannot tame human emotions, and, finally, in his belief that man's will is in the hands of God. Though neither Valla nor Budé seems to have rejected free will altogether, both are close enough to the classical Protestant doctrine of predestination to cast serious doubt on the proposition that a humanist *qua* humanist must inevitably reject

Luther's or Calvin's teaching on this point. In light of the parallels between these two great humanists—they are among the very few who may be acclaimed as peers of Erasmus—it might be interesting for some young scholar with a fair bit of courage to undertake a comparative study.

For the large number of humanists who (unlike Budé or Valla) made their living in a classroom, the rhetorical traditional was less a source of epistemological questions, and more a practical means of organizing their teaching matter. The method of making a list of "common places" in which arguments could be "found" for a given subject had application also to theological debates, as is witnessed both by Melanchthon's famous textbook of Lutheran theology, the *Loci Communes*, and in the notion of an age-long *consensus Ecclesiae* invoked by Erasmus and More, albeit in different ways, in their defenses of Catholic doctrine. (The common consent of mankind was, according to the rhetoricians, a standard "place" in which arguments could be "found" for almost any subject.) There is considerable disagreement as to the intellectual value of the *loci* method, particularly as it was developed into a new form of rhetorical logic which in many schools displaced the traditional Aristotelian logic. *Ong*, in a masterful study of humanist logic north of the Alps as it evolved from Rudolph Agricola through Peter Ramus, argues that the natural desire of teachers to make things clearer and simpler for their pupils resulted in a "pedagogical juggernaut," in which the complicated nuances of Aristotelian predication gave way to Ramist "dichotomies" (whatever was to be taught was divided in two parts, each of which in turn was divided in two, etc.), which had the great advantage of being able to be presented in diagrams. But *Vasoli* gives more attention to the substantive critique of Aristotle's logic by Italian humanists not subject to the same professional constraints as northerners of a later generation, and *Gilbert* suggests that even Ramist logic may have played some part in displacing Aristotle by a new conception of scientific method. To some extent the same disagreement may be found in assessments of Melanchthon's humanist logic. *Breen*, who cites a good number of texts to support his contention that, for Melanchthon, "clarity was the text of truth," is nonetheless in a minority. More typical especially among German scholars is Maurer's view that there was nothing in Melanchthon's *loci* method that was not also to be found in the (perfectly respectable) *Posterior Analytics* of Aristotle.

No one would contend that classical or humanist rhetoric underlies Luther's vivid sense of God's Word as a power in the lives of men, nor his conviction that the whole of Scripture proclaims a coherent promise of forgiveness. Evocations by some humanists of the transrational power of human speech (*Tracy*, 1980) are at best dimly analagous to Luther's understanding of *fides ex auditu*. More congenial to the common assumptions of humanist rhetoric are the rhetorical or pedagogical corollaries which Melanchthon drew from Luther's message: that God's Word is a "teaching" (*doctrina*), and that the Church is a "school" (*coetus scholasticus*) in which this saving *doctrina* bears fruit in the lives of the pupils (*Haendler*). Understood in this way, the Lutheran Reformation could be seen as a fulfillment of the long-standing promises of humanist pedagogy. From the very beginning, humanist educators had contended that the study of "good letters" would cultivate gentle qualities useful to the commonwealth, as opposed to the combative spirit nurtured by the dialectical disputations of medieval schoolrooms. From here it was a short step to the belief that Scripture itself, purged of allegory and scholastic accretions, could form men in the image of God (one need only recall Erasmus' exclamation, from the 1515 *Paraclesis*, that if the Gospel were truly preached, "the Christian people would be spared many wars"). Since many humanists, and certainly Erasmus, already had a tendency to minimize elements of religious practice which had no clear instructional content, it might have seemed only another short step to embrace, as Melanchthon did in *Loci Communes*, the principle that theology might usefully and clearly be organized around a single, saving *doctrina* which provided a key to the whole of Scripture. Conversely, Johann Sturm, Melanchthon's friend, spoke very much as a humanist when he contended that the obvious lack of formal religious instruction in the medieval Church (after all, the catechism as a literary form was invented by Luther) was the cause of the deplorable state of Christian morals:

> For if we wol haue the world amended, we must haue the people good, well-instructed and taught, they must be as a felde well tilled. . . . Many men are sorie, that in this your deuise (the *De Ecclesia Emendanda* of the papal reform commission of 1538) no mencion is made, *De doctrina religionis*, which most specially ought to haue been intreated of. For to speak somewhat of this, what people, what citie, what multitude of men, in especiall through your dominions, can you finde, that is well instructed in poyntes of religion.[5]

[5] *The Epistole That Iohan Sturmius . . . sent to the Carcynalles*, tr. Richard Morysine (London: 1538), sig. Bi^v.

If, starting with Erasmus if not earlier, humanists fervently believed that a correct teaching of Christian doctrine would greatly improve public morals, there was perhaps a strong case to be made for choosing that form of Christianity which, both in its proclamation of a single saving truth and in its severe pruning back of the ritual elements of religious practice, gave promise of focusing the entire authority of religion upon the related functions of preaching and teaching. Hence, there may have been a second, broader approach along which a humanist *qua* humanist might, with all consistency, enter what *Strauss* (1978) has called Luther's house of learning.

From the foregoing discussion three conclusions may briefly be indicated. First, the concept of humanism must either be abandoned altogether, or treated as poly-valent in its capacity for combinations with other currents of thought. Not only are there clear connections between the humanist movement and Catholicism, both before and after the Council of Trent (e.g., the Jesuit schools), and likewise with the Protestant Reformation, as has been suggested here, but humanism can also be linked to the radical theology of the Italian anti-Trinitarians, or to Vico's historicism, or perhaps even to Hegel's philosophical idealism. If the eighteenth-century *philosophes* regarded themselves as successors of the humanists they were not entirely wrong, but in certain other respects the Romantic thinkers of the following generation might have claimed the humanists as their predecessors. So long as scholars were searching for some underlying philosophical unity in the humanist movement, such multi-sided affinities would not have been admissible. But Kristeller's re-definition of the humanist movement as a network of intellectual interests permits precisely the sort of distinctions that may help to explain humanism's varying ramifications. Thus, in the foregoing sections, major humanist scholars (Budé and Valla) were seen to approach an Augustinian conception of man by way of a profound critique of Aristotelian rationalism, while other and lesser figures may have been attracted to the Reformation because it promised to make religion more teachable.

Secondly, as was just suggested, one must distinguish between original thinkers like Erasmus or Valla, and the more pedestrian concerns of the many who but follow along in their footsteps. No one can read much of Erasmus, Budé, or Valla without recognizing in these pages the presence of a powerful mind; at the other extreme, whoever occupies himself with the writings of lesser known humanists cannot escape the conclusion that in some cases their obscurity is only too well deserved. One's view of the intellectual significance of humanist logic, for instance, may vary a great deal depending on whether one concentrates on thinkers like Valla (*Vasoli*), or on textbooks written to meet the needs of struggling schoolmasters (*Ong*). Scholars usually prefer to concentrate on the great lights of a movement, but a rounded historical picture would give more scope to the fact that humanism was at the same time highly original and supremely pedantic. Were there only Fausts and no Wagners, humanism would have remained an affair of the *cognoscenti*, with at most an ephemeral influence on the broad reading public.

Finally, one may ask what impact humanism actually did have upon the population at large. *Bolgar* contends that the classical authors themselves recede from view once humanism moves into the confessional age, while *Bot* finds that, despite the grand theories of Erasmus, such things as corporal punishment continued more or less undiminished in the crowded classrooms of humanist schools in The Netherlands. Rather similar is Strauss's conclusion that Lutheran schoolmasters and preachers in the end failed to impose upon a refractory populace their vision of a renewed moral discipline. Other studies may possibly yield a different verdict (e.g., *Monter*'s assessment of Geneva's post-Reformation patricians), but Strauss's work is a major landmark of the dawning realization among scholars that humanism, Reformation, Counter-Reformation, and certain late medieval reform movements were all in different ways efforts by religious and learned elites to elevate the behavior of ordinary folk to a new moral standard. Thus in the next twenty-five years students of humanism and the Reformation may very well find Strauss's questions of more interest than traditional problems concerning the initial relationship of the two movements.*

Bibliography

1. Bibliographies and Libraries

For works published after 1963, the most thorough bibliography, though always published a few years behind time, will be found in the annual *Bibliographie Internationale de l'Humanisme et de la Renaissance*. Useful guides to works by or about individual humanists include the printed catalogues of the British Museum and the

Bibliothèque Nationale in Paris, and in A. Cioranescu, *Bibliographie de la littérature Française du XVIe Siècle* (Paris, 1959), and A. Gerlo, *Bibliographie des Humanistes des Anciens Pays-Bas* (Brussels, 1972). For German humanists, secondary works prior to 1960 are listed in Karl Schottenloher, *Bibliographie der deutschen Geschichte im Zeitalter der Glaubensspaltung* (7 vols.; Wiesbaden, 1937–1960); the best listing of printed works by German humanists is in the handwritten, nineteenth-century Bandkatalog (access to which is by permission) at the Bayerische Staatsbibliothek in Munich. For Italian humanists, see M. E. Cosenza, *Biographical and Bibliographical Dictionary of the Italian Humanists* 2d ed. (6 vols.; Boston, 1962–1967). European centers for research on humanism include the "Centre des Etudes de la Renaissance" (Jean Claude Margolin) at the University of Tours and the "Seminarium Humanisticae Philologiae" (Jozef Ijsewijn) at the University of Leuven. Apart from Paris and London and Munich, other important collections for the study of humanism are in the national libraries in Brussels and The Hague, Wolfenbüttel, and the University libraries of Basel, Cologne, and Göttingen. As for northern humanist works still in manuscript, there is, unfortunately, nothing comparable to P. O. Kristeller's *Iter Italicum*.

2. Modern Editions and Translations

Fundamental is P. S. Allen, *Opus Epistolarum Erasmi* (2 vols.; Oxford, 1906–1958), now supplemented by the well-launched Amsterdam *Opera Omnia* under the general direction of Cornelis Reedijk, who earlier edited *The Poems of Erasmus* (Leiden, 1956). Meanwhile the Yale edition (with translations) of *The Complete Works of Sir Thomas More, Saint*, under Clarence H. Miller, is nearing completion. *Melanchthon's Werke im Auswahl* was begun some years ago by Robert Stupperich, while Heinze Scheible's critical edition of Melanchthon's correspondence has only recently started to appear. There are no modern editions of Budé's works, but there are useful translations by La Garanderie and Pelham, and, for Bodin, by Kuntz (see following section). The Toronto *Collected Works of Erasmus* is by far the most ambitious translation project, and its auxiliary material will be particularly useful to scholars.

3. Secondary Literature

Angeleri, Carlo, *Il Problema Religiosa del Rinascimento* (Florence, 1952).

_____, *Interpreti dell'Umanesimo e del Rinascimento* (Milan, 1965).

Ankwitz van Kleehoven, H., *Johannes Cuspinian* (Graz, 1969).

Arnold, K., *Johannes Trithemius* (Würzburg, 1971).

Auer, Alfons, *Die vollkommene Frömmigkeit eines Christen* (Düsseldorf, 1954).

Augustijn, Cornelis, *Erasmus en de Reformatie* (Amsterdam, 1962).

_____, *De Godsdienstgesprekken tussen Rooms-Katholieken en Protestanten van 1538 tot 1541* (Haarlem, 1967).

Bady, René, *L'Homme et son Institution de Montaigne à Berulle, 1580-1625* (Paris, 1965).

Bainton, Roland, *Erasmus of Christendom* (New York, 1969).

Bangs, Jeremy, *Cornelis Engelbrechtsz's Leiden* (Assen, 1979).

Battenhouse, Roy W., "The Doctrine of Man in Calvin and in Renaissance Platonism," *Journal of the History of Ideas* 9 (1948): 447-471.

Bedouelle, G., *Lefèvre d'Étaples et l'Intelligence des Écritures* (Geneva, 1975).

Béné, Charles, *Érasme et Saint Augustin* (Geneva, 1969).

Bentley, Jerry H., "Humanists and Holy Writ: The Pauline Scholarship of Lorenzo Valla and Erasmus," Ph.D. dissertation (University of Minnesota, 1976).

_____, "New Testament Scholarship at Louvain in the Early Sixteenth Century," *Studies in Medieval and Renaissance History*, n.s. 2 (1979): 51-79.

Bertin, G. M., *La Pedagogia Umanistica nei Secoli XV e XVI* (Milan, 1961).

El Cardinale Bessarione nel V Centenario del Morte. Rome, 1974.

Bohatec, Josef, *Budé and Calvin: Studien zur Gedankenwelt des französischen Frühhumanismus* (Graz, 1950).

Bolgar, R. R., *The Classical Heritage and Its Beneficiaries* (New York, 1964).

Bonorad, C., *Vadians Weg vom Humanismus zur Reformation* (St. Gallen, 1962).

Bot, P. J. M., *Humanisme en Onderwijs in Nederland* (Utrecht, 1955).

Bouwsma, William, *Concordia Mundi: Guillaume Postel* (Cambridge, Mass., 1957).

_____, *Venice and the Defense of Republican Liberty* (Berkeley, 1968).

_____, "The Two Faces of Humanism: Stoicism and Augustinianism in Renaissance Thought" in *Itinerarium Italicum*: 3–60.

Boyle, Marjorie O'Rourke, *Erasmus on Language and Method in Theology* (Toronto, 1977).

———, *Christening Pagan Mysteries: Erasmus in Pursuit of Wisdom* (Toronto, 1981).

Breen, Quirinius, *Christianity and Humanism: Studies in the History of Ideas* (Grand Rapids, 1968).

Brown, Frieda, *Religious and Political Conservatism in the Essays of Montaigne* (Geneva, 1963).

Burger, Heinz Otto, *Renaissance, Reformation, Humanismus* (Bad Homburg, 1969).

Caccamo, D., *Eretici Italiani in Moravia e Polonia, 1558–1611* (Florence, 1971).

Camporeale, Salvatore I., *Lorenzo Valla, Umanesimo e Teologia* (Florence, 1972).

Cantimori, D., *Eretici Italiani del Cinquecento* (Florence, 1939).

———, *Prospettive di Storia Ereticale Italiana del Cinquecento* (Bari, 1960).

Cassirer, E., *The Individual and the Cosmos in Renaissance Philosophy* (New York, 1964).

Chantraine, S. J., Georges, *Mysterium et Sacramentum dans le 'Ratio Verae Theologiae' d'Erasme* (Namur, 1972).

Church, F. C., *The Italian Reformers* (New York, 1932).

Cochrane, E., ed., *The Late Italian Renaissance* (New York, 1970).

———, *Florence in the Forgotten Centuries* (Chicago, 1973).

D'Amico, J. F., "Beatus Rhenanus, Tertullian, and the Reformation," *Archiv für Reformationsgeschichte* 71 (1980): 37–63.

Daxhelet, E., *Adrien Barlandus, Humaniste et Historien* (Leuven, 1937).

Di Caprariis, V., *Propaganda e Pensiera Politico in Francia durante le Guerre di Religione, 1559–1572* (Naples, 1959).

Di Napoli, G., *Giovanni Pico della Mirandola et la Problematica Dottrinale del suo Tempo* (Rome, 1965).

———, *Lorenzo Valla: Filosofia e Religione nell'Umanesimo Italiano* (Rome, 1976).

Dolan, John P., *The Influence of Erasmus, Witzel and Cassander on the Church Ordinances . . . of Cleves* (Münster, 1957).

Douglas, Mary Tew, *Natural Symbols* (New York, 1970).

Duhamel, P. Albert, "The Oxford Lectures of John Colet," *Journal of the History of Ideas* 14 (1953): 493–510.

Dulles, Avery, *Princeps Concordiae: Pico della Mirandola and the Scholastic Tradition* (Cambridge, Mass., 1941).

Etienne, Jacques, *Spiritualisme Erasmienne et Théologiens Lovanistes* (Leuven, 1956).

Febvre, Lucien, *Origène et Des Periers: l'Engime du "Cymbalum Mundi"* (Paris, 1942).

————, *Le Probleme de l'Incroyance au XVI$_e$ Siècle: la Religion de Rabelais* (Paris, 1947).

Fleischer, H. H., *Dietrich Gresemund der jüngere* (Mainz, 1967).

Fleisher, Martin, *Radical Reform and Political Persuasion in the Life and Writings of Thomas More* (Geneva, 1973).

Flittner, Andreas, *Erasmus im Urteil seiner Nachwelt* (Tübingen, 1952).

Fois, S. J., Mario, *Il Pensiero Cristiano di Lorenzo Valla* (Rome, 1969).

Fraenkel, Peter, *Testimonia Patrum: The Function of Patristic Argument in the Theology of Melanchthon* (Geneva, 1960).

————, and Greschat, Martin, *Zwanzig Jahre Melanchthonstudium* (Geneva, 1967).

Franzen, A., "Das Schicksal des Erasmianismus am Niederrhein," *Historisches Jahrbuch* 88 (1968): 300–324.

Gaeta, Franco, *Lorenzo Valla: Filologia e Storia nell'Umanesimo Italiano* (Naples, 1955).

Garin, Eugenio, *Italian Humanism*, trans. Peter Munz (Oxford, 1965).

Gebhardt, Georg, *Die Stellung des Erasmus zur römischen Kirche* (Marburg, 1966).

Gilbert, N., *Renaissance Concepts of Method* (New York, 1970).

Gleason, Elisabeth G., "On the Nature of 16th Century Italian Evangelism: Scholarship, 1953–1978," *Sixteenth Century Century* Journal, 9 (1978): 3–26.

Gray, Hannah, "Renaissance Humanism: The Pursuit of Eloquence," in *Renaissance Essays*, ed. P. O. Kristeller and P. Wiener (New York, 1968), pp. 199–216.

Greschat, Martin, *Melanchthon neben Luther: Studien zur Gestalt der Rechtfertigungslehre zwischen 1528 und 1537* (Witten, 1965).

Güldner, Gerhard, *Das Toleranzproblem in den Niederlanden am Ausgang des 16en Jahrhunderts* (Lübeck, 1968).

Gundersheimer, Werner, ed., *French Humanism* (London, 1969).

Haendler, Klaus, *Wort und Glaube bei Melanchthon* (Gütersloh, 1968).

Hatzfeld, Helmut, "Christian, Pagan, and Devout Humanism in Sixteenth-Century France," *Modern Language Quarterly* 12 (1951): 337–352.

Hay, Denys, *Polydore Vergil, Renaissance Historian and Man of Letters* (London, 1952).

Heath, Terence, "Logical Grammar, Grammatical Logic, and Humanism in Three German Universities," *Studies in the Renaissance* 18 (1971): 9–64.

Herding, Otto, "Erasmus und Isokrates und die *Institutio Principis Christiani*," in *Dauer und Wandel der Geschichte: Festschrift für Kurt von Raumer* (Münster, 1966), pp. 101–143.

———, *Jacobi Wimfelingi Opera Selecta*, Vol. 1: *Adolescentia* (Munich, 1965).

Hitchcock, James F., "More and Tyndale's Controversy Over Revelation: A Test of the McLuhan Hypothesis," *Journal of the American Academy of Religion* 39 (1971): 448–466.

Hofer, J. M., *Die Stellung des Erasmus und des J. L. Vives zur Pädagogik des Quintilian* (Erlangen, 1910).

Hoffmann, Manfred, *Erkenntnis und Verwirklichung der wahren Theologie bei Erasmus* (Tübingen, 1972).

Holmes, George, *The Florentine Enlightenment* (London, 1960).

Holoczek, Heinz, *Humanistische Bibelphilologie als Reformproblem bei Erasmus von Rotterdam, Thomas More, und William Tyndale* (Leiden, 1975).

Howell, W. S., *Logic and Rhetoric in England, 1500–1700* (Princeton, 1956).

Huber, Paul, *Traditionsfestigkeit und Traditionskritik bei Thomas Morus* (Basel, 1953).

Huppert, George, *The Idea of Perfect History* (Urbana, 1970).

Huschke, R. B., *Melanchthons Lehre vom Ordo Politicus* (Gütersloh, 1968).

Ijsewijn, Jozef, "The Coming of Humanism to the Low Countries," in *Itinerarium Italicum*, 193–304.

Imbart de la Tour, Pierre, *Les origines de la Reforme*, 4 vols. (Paris, 1919–1935).

Iternerarium Italicum, edited by H. A. Oberman and Thomas A. Brady, Jr. (Leiden, 1978).

Jayne, S. R., *John Colet and Marsilio Ficino* (Oxford, 1963).

Joachimsen, Paul, *Geschichtsauffassung und -Schriebung in Deutschland unter dem Einfluss des Humanismus* (Leipzig, 1910).

————, "Loci Communes: eine geistesgeschichtliche Untersuchung," *Luther Jahrbuch* 8 (1929): 7–97.

Kaegi, Werner, *Castellio und die Anfänge der Toleranz* (Basel, 1953).

Kamen, Henry, *The Rise of Toleration* (New York, 1967).

Kelley, Donald, *The Foundations of Modern Historical Scholarship* (New York, 1970).

————, *Francois Hotman* (Princeton, 1973).

Kisch, Guido, *Humanismus und Jurisprudenz. Mos Italicus und Mos Gallicus an der Universität Basel* (Basel, 1955).

————, *Zasius und Reuchlin. Eine rechtsgeschichtlich-vergleichende Studi zum Toleranzproblem im 16en Jahrhundert* (Konstanz, 1961).

————, *Studien zur humanistischen Jurisprudenz* (Berlin, 1972).

Kittelson, James M., *Wolfgang Capito: From Humanist to Reformer* (Leiden, 1975).

Koelker, A. J., *Alardus Amstelredamus en Cornelius Crocus. Twee Amsterdamsche Priester-Humanisten*, (Nijmegen, 1963).

Kohls, Ernst Wilhelm, *Die Theologie des Erasmus* (Basel, 1966).

Kristeller, Paul Oskar, *The Philosophy of Marsiglio Ficino* (New York, 1943).

————, *Renaissance Thought* (New York, 1961).

————, *Renaissance Thought II* (New York, 1965).

————, *Eight Philosophers of the Italian Renaissance* (Stanford, 1965).

————, *Studies in Renaissance Thought and Letters* (Rome, 1969).

————, *Renaissance Concepts of Man* (New York, 1972).

Kraus, Michael, "Patronage and Reform in France of the Préréforme: Clichetove," *Canadian Journal of History* 6 (1971): 45–68.

Kuhlow, H. F. W., *Die Imitatio Christi und ihre kosmologische Überfremdung: die theologischen Grundlagen des Agrippa von Nettesheim* (Hamburg, 1969).

Kuntz, Marian Leathers Daniels, *Colloquy of the Seven About Secrets of the Sublime: Jean Bodin's "Colloquium Heptaplomeres"* (Princeton, 1975).

Lachmann, E., *Johannes Rhaegius Aesticampianus* (Heidelberg, 1961).

La Garanderie, Marie Madeleine de, *Christianisme et Lettres Pro-*

fanes, 1515–1535: Essai sur les Mentalités des Milieux Intellectuels Parisiens et sur la Pensée de Guillaume Budé (Lille/ Paris, 1976).

———, *La Correspondence d'Erasme et de Guillaume Budé* (Paris, 1967).

Lecler, Joseph, *Toleration and the Reformation*, 2 vols. (New York, 1960).

Levi, A. H., *Humanism in France at the End of the Middle Ages* (New York, 1970).

Lipgens, Walter, *Kardinal Johannes Gropper* (Munster, 1951).

Lovy, R. J., *Les Origines de la Réforme Francaise: Meaux 1518–1546* (Paris, 1948).

Lutz, Heinrich, *Conrad Peutinger: Beiträge zur einer politischen Biographie* (Augsburg, 1958).

MacNeil, D. O., *Guillaume Budé and Humanism in the Reign of Francis I* (Geneva, 1975).

Maeder, K., *Die Via Media der schweizerischen Reformation* (Zurich, 1971).

Margolin, Jean-Claude, *Douze Années de Bibliographie Erasmienne* (Paris, 1963).

———, ed., *Erasmus, Declamatio de Pueris Instituendis* (Geneva, 1966).

Masai, Francois, *Plethon et la Platonisme de Mistra* (Paris, 1956).

Massaut, J. P., *Josse Clichtove*, 2 vols. (Paris, 1968).

———, *Critique et Tradition à la vieille de la Réforme en France* (Paris, 1974).

Matheson, P., *Cardinal Contarini at Regensburg* (Oxford, 1971).

Maurer, Wilhelm, *Der junge Melanchthon*, 2 vols. (Göttingen, 1967–1969).

McConica, James K., *English Humanists and Reformation Politics Under Henry and Elizabeth* (Oxford, 1965).

McKeon, R., "Renaissance and Method in Philosophy," *Studies in the History of Ideas*, (Columbia University), 3 (1935): 36–114.

Mirri, F., *Richard Simon e il metodo storico-critico di B. Spinoza* (Florence, 1972).

Moeller, Bernd, "The German Humanists and the Reformation," in *Imperial Cities and the Reformation*. Philadelphia, 1972; German original 1959.

Monnerjahn, E., *Giovanni Pico della Mirandola: Ein Beitrag zur philosophischen Theologie des Humanismus* (Wiesbaden, 1960).

Monter, E. W., *Calvin's Geneva* (New York, 1965).

Nauert, Charles, *Henry Cornelius Agrippa of Nettesheim* (Columbia, Mo., 1960).

_____, "The Clash of Humanists and Scholastics: An Approach to Pre-Reformation Controversies," *Sixteenth Century Journal* 4 (1973): 1–18.

_____, "Renaissance Humanism: An Emergent Consensus and its Critics" *Indiana Social Studies Quarterly* 33 (1980): 5–20.

Norena, Carlos G., *Juan Luis Vives* (The Hague, 1970).

Nugent, Donald, *Ecumenism in the Age of the Reformation: The Colloquy of Poissy* (Cambridge, Mass., 1974).

Oelrich, Karl Heinz, *Der späte Erasmus und die Reformation* (Münster, 1961).

O'Malley, John W., *Praise and Blame in Renaissance Rome* (Durham, NC, 1979).

Ong, S. J., Walter J., *Ramus, Method, and the Decay of Dialogue* (Cambridge, Mass., 1958).

Overfield, James, "A New Look at the Reuchlin Affair," *Studies in Medieval and Renaissance History* 8 (1971): 165–207.

_____, "Scholastic Opposition to Humanism in Pre-Reformation Germany," *Viator* 7 (1976): 391–420.

Ozment, Steven, "Humanism, Scholasticism, and the Intellectual Origins of the Reformation," in *Continuity and Discontinuity in Church History Essays Presented to G.H. Williams*, eds. F.F. Church and T. George (Leiden, 1979), pp. 133–49.

Payne, John B., *Erasmus: His Theology of the Sacraments* (Richmond, 1970).

Paulsen, Ludwig, *Geschichte des gelehrten Unterrichts*, 2 vols. (Leipzig, 1919–1921).

Pelham, D. F., *Guillaume Budé's De Transitu Hellenismi ad Christianismum* (Ann Arbor, 1955).

Pfnur, Vinzenz, *Einig in der Rechtfertigungslehre? Die Rechtfertigungslehre der Confessio Augustana* (Wiesbaden, 1970).

Phillips, Margaret Mann, *The Adages of Erasmus* (Cambridge, 1964).

L'Opera et il Pensiero di Giovanni Pico della Mirandola nella Storia dell'Umanesimo, Convegno Internationale, 2 vols (Florence, 1965).

Popkin, Richard, *The History of Scepticism from Erasmus to Descartes* (New York, 1968).

Prévost, Andre, *Thomas More et la Crise de la Pensée Européenne* (Lille, 1969).

Renaudet, Augustin, *Préréforme et Humanisme à Paris pendant les*

Premières Guerres de l'Italie, d 1495–1515, 2d ed. (Paris, 1953).

Rice, Eugene, *The Prefatory Epistles of Jacques Lefèvre d'Etaples and Related Texts* (New York, 1971).

Rotondo, A., *Studi e ricerche di storia ereticale del Cinquecento* (Turin, 1974).

Schmitt, C. B., *Gianfrancesco Pico and His Critique of Aristotle* (The Hague, 1971).

Schöffler, H., *Die Reformation* (Bochum, 1936).

Screech, Michael, *L'Evangelisme de Rabelais* (Geneva, 1959).

_____, *Rabelais* (Ithaca, 1979).

Secret, F., *Le Zohar chez les Kabbalistes Chrétiens de la Renaissance* (Paris, 1957).

_____, *Les Kabbalistes Chrétiens de la Renaissance* (Paris, 1964).

Simone, Franco, *The French Renaissance* (London, 1969).

_____, *Culture et Politique en France a l'epoque de l'humanisme* (Turin, 1974).

Smith, Lacey Baldwin, *Tudor Prelates and Politics, 1536–1558* (Princeton, 1953).

Smith, Preserved, *Erasmus* (New York, 1923).

Spitz, Lewis W., *Conrad Celtis, The German Arch-Humanist* (Cambridge, Mass., 1957).

_____, *The Religious Renaissance of the German Humanists* (Cambridge, Mass., 1964).

_____, "The Third Generation of German Renaissance Humaninsts," in *Aspects of the Renaissance*, ed. Archibald Lewis (Austin, 1967), pp. 105–121.

_____, "The Course of German Humanism," in *Itinerarium Italicum*, pp. 371–435.

Steinman, Jean, *Richard Simon et les Origines de l'Exegèse Biblique* (Brugge, 1960).

Strauss, Gerald, *Historian in an Age of Crisis: Johannes Aventinus, 1477–1534* (Cambridge, Mass., 1963).

_____, *Luther's House of Learning: Indoctrination of the Young in the German Reformation* (Baltimore, 1978).

Struever, Nancy L., *The Language of History in the Renaissance* (Princeton, 1970).

Stupperich, Robert, *Humanismus und die Wiedervereinigung der Konfessionen* (Leipzig, 1936).

_____, "Die Bedeuting der Lateinschule für die Ausbreitung der Reformation in Westfalen." *Jahrbuch für westfälische Kirchengeschichte* 44 (1952): 83–112.

_____, *Melanchthon* (Philadelphia, 1965); German original 1961.

Tedeschi, John., ed. *Renaissance Studies in Honor of Laelius Socinus*. (Florence, 1965).

Tracy, James D., *Erasmus: The Growth of a Mind* (Geneva, 1972).

_____, *The Politics of Erasmus: A Pacifist Intellectual and His Political Milieu* (Toronto, 1979).

_____, "Against the Barbarians: The Young Erasmus and His Humanist Contemporaries," *Sixteenth Century Journal* II (1980): 3–22.

Trinkaus, Charles, "Introduction," Lorenzo Valla's *Dialogue on Free Will*, in *The Renaissance Philosophy of Man*, ed. Ernst Cassirer, *et al.* (New York, 1948), pp. 147–154.

_____, "The Problem of Free Will in the Renaissance and the Reformation," *Journal of the History of Ideas*, 10 (1949): 51–62.

_____, *In His Image and Likeness: Italian Humanists on God and Human Dignity*, 2 vols. (Chicago, 1971).

_____, "Erasmus, Augustine, and the Nominalists," *Archiv fur Reformationsgeschichte* 67 (1976): 5–53.

Vasoli, Cesare, *La Dialettica e la retorica dell'Umanesimo* (Milan, 1968).

Vocht, Henri de, *History of the Collegium Trilingue Lovaniense*, 4 vols. (Leuven, 1951–1955).

Walker, D. P., *Spiritual and Demonic Magic From Ficino to Campanella* (London, 1958).

_____, *The Ancient Theology: Studies in Christian Platonism from the Fifth to the Eighteenth Centuries* (Ithaca, 1972).

Willehad, P. E., and Imhof, C. von, *Willibald Pirckheimer, Dürers Freund.* (Wienand, 1971).

Wittstock, O., *Johannes Honter, der Siebenbürger Humanist und Reformator* (Göttingen, 1970).

Winkler, Gerhard B., *Erasmus von Rotterdam und die Einleitungsschriften zum Neuen Testament* (Münster, 1974).

Woodward, W. H., *Erasmus Concerning the Nature and Aims of Education* (Cambridge, 1904).

Yates, Frances, *Giordano Bruno and the Hermetic Tradition* (London, 1967).

Martin Luther

Mark U. Edwards, Jr.

The year 1983 will see the quincentenary of Luther's birth (1483–1983), the meeting of the sixth International Congress of Luther Research in Erfurt and a veritable flood of commemorative *Festschriften*, biographies, and other books and articles on Martin Luther. Luther research is a scholarly "industry" that spans the globe and that reaches back into Luther's own times. Few areas of historical inquiry are as heavily populated with scholars and as copiously provided with scholarship. Even fewer areas are mined as zealously for "authoritative" pronouncements to use in twentieth century confessional controversies.[1]

Fortunately, few areas of historical inquiry are better provided for in terms of scholarly aids. Part I of this essay surveys the various aids to Luther research, including a listing of more than sixty literature reviews that have appeared since 1965. This section should orient the beginner and may even be of some use to seasoned scholars. Part II surveys current research and suggests directions it may (or should) take in the future. It is anything but comprehensive and bears the heavy imprint of my own interests and biases.

I
Biographies

Although dozens of biographies of Martin Luther have been written in the twentieth century, the nineteenth century biography by Julius Köstlin, revised by Gustav Kawerau and published in 1903, remains the most comprehensive. Heinrich Bornkamm's posthumously published *Martin Luther in der Mitte seines Lebens* (1979) should become the standard reference work for the period 1521 to 1530. Over twenty years ago Bornkamm (1958) pointed out the urgent need for a new comprehensive study of the older Luther, from 1532 to his death. This need remains unmet.

---

[1]See, for example, the literature review by Kohls (1977).

In English the affectionate biography by Roland Bainton, *Here I Stand!* (1950), remains the best introduction. H. G. Haile (1980) offers a portrait of the older Luther that is particularly strong in conveying Luther's literary gifts and style, his sense of humor, and the difficulties he faced in his last years. Bernhard Lohse (1981) offers a new and useful overview.

Bibliographic Aids and Literature Reviews

The *Lutherjahrbuch* describes itself as the "Organ of International Luther Research" and each year provides an extensive and extremely valuable "Lutherbibliographie."[2] It and the triannual *Luther* are publications of the Luther-Gesellschaft, whose membership spans the globe from Japan to Germany and many (often surprising) points in between.[3] Since 1972 the *Archive for Reformation History* has also brought out an annual *Literature Review*, an annotated bibliography on all aspects of "Reformation history" between 1450 and 1650, including a section on Luther.

In addition to these two annual bibliographies there is a vast number of literature reviews dealing with Luther research. I list in the bibliography more than sixty reviews of the literature, both general and on Catholic Luther research, that have appeared since 1965, and this list is not complete.[4]

Luther's Works

The standard scholarly edition of Martin Luther's works is the Weimar Ausgabe which began publication in 1883, the four-hundredth anniversary of Luther's birth, and which by 1983, the five-hundredth anniversary, will comprise more than one hundred volumes and still not be completed. There are numerous other editions and translations.[5] The major English translation is the fifty-five volume *Luther's Works: American Edition* (1955–1977), which is suitable for general readers and students, but cannot substitute for

[2]For a description of the bibliography's organization see Junghans (1975).
[3]For a history of the Gesellschaft, see G. Müller (1978). The address of the Gesellschaft's headquarters is Bei der Martinskirche 8, 2000 Hamburg 74, Federal Republic of Germany.
[4]Haikola (1966), Kantzenbach (1966), Lindberg (1966), Prenter (1966), Pesch (1966) (The preceding essays were also published in German; see Lutherische Rundschau [1966]), Lohse (1971), Green (1977), Kjelgaard-Pedersen (1977), Kohls (1977), Tokuzen (1977), Vercruysse (1977a, 1977b). See also the fine annotation review edited by Bigane and Hagen (1977).
[5]See the discussion of Aland, *Hilfsbuch*, below.

the Weimar Ausgabe in scholarly works. Another edition published in America between 1880 and 1910, the St. Louis edition of Walch (abbreviated W2), remains of value to scholars. The original Walch edition, published by Johann Georg Walch between 1740 and 1753, included many documents in addition to Luther's own writings, especially treatises by his Catholic and Protestant opponents, and presented a German translation of his Latin writings. The St. Louis editors added new material, new translations, and new commentary to the material compiled by Walch. The other documents are useful; the German translation of Luther's Latin can help with difficult passages (and are often used for this purpose by the editors of the Weimar Ausgabe); and the brief glossary in volume 17 of unusual or archaic words (W2 17:2240–2261) can supplement the other guides to Luther's Early High German.[6] Finally, the main subject index (W2 23:1–2131) to this edition is of use until the subject indices to the Weimar Ausgabe are completed.[7]

The Weimar Ausgabe is divided into four sections or *Abteilungen*. The largest comprises "writings" and is abbreviated as WA. Volumes in this section run from 1 to 58, with a number of split volumes (e.g., WA 10/1/1 and WA 10/2). The next section contains "letters" and is commonly abbreviated WABr with the Br standing for "Briefe." To date there are fifteen (soon to be sixteen) volumes. The third section is for "table talk" and is commonly abbreviated as WATR with the TR standing for "Tischreden." There are six volumes of "table talk" plus additions in WA 48. These jottings by students and other table companions must be used with special care.[8] Finally, the fourth section comprises Luther's German Bible translations and is abbreviated as WADB, with DB standing for "Deutsche Bibel."[9]

Hilfsbuch zum Lutherstudium

An invaluable tool in Luther research is Kurt Aland's *Hilfsbuch*

[6]See below.
[7]See below.
[8]See Kroker (1919) and the introduction in R. Buchwald (1938).
[9]Hans Volz (1978) has compiled a fitting companion piece to the WADB. In picture and text his volume examines the history of pre-Reformation German Bibles, the history of Luther's translations and their publications, the scholarly aids he employed, his co-workers, his printers in Wittenberg and elsewhere, the artists who provided illustrations, the spread of his Bible and its influence, and translations of his Bible into Low German and other languages. See also the modern reissue of the 1545 Bible [Volz (1972)].

zum Lutherstudium, 3rd revised edition (1970), compiled with the assistance of Ernst Otto Reichert and Gerhard Jordan. It is first and foremost a key to the various editions of Luther's works from the sixteenth to the twentieth centuries, but it also offers much more. It is divided into five parts:[10]

I. An alphabetical list of Luther's writings
II. Keys to the nineteenth and twentieth century editions of Luther's works
III. Keys to the major editions published in the sixteenth through the eighteenth centuries
IV. A chronological list of Luther's writings
V. Key to the Benzing bibliography of publications of writings by Luther through 1546.

In part I, main entries are numbered and alphabetized according to the main key word in each title. Each main, numbered entry gives the title of the writing; date of composition and, when different, date of publication; its location in the Weimar Ausgabe and in the other major scholarly editions; the point at which it is discussed in Köstlin and Kawerau; and its number(s) in Benzing's bibliography.[11] In addition to these main, numbered entries, the alphabetical list contains numerous secondary entries, almost a subject index, that refer the scholar to the appropriate main, numbered entries. This means that under headings such as "Dichtungen" or "Disputationes" or "Vorlesungen" or "Vorreden" the scholar will find listed with appropriate references all of Luther's poems, disputations, lectures, or forewords. There are also secondary entries for major subjects (such as "Taufe"), for individuals (such as Herzog Georg zu Sachsen), and for verses of the Bible (such as Gal. 3:23). There is a separate chronological listing for sermon collections (*Postillen*), a separate chronological listing of sermons, and a separate chronological list of letters with an accompanying alphabetical index of Luther's correspondents, a brief alphabetical subject index, and a key to German translations of Latin letters.[12]

Indices to Luther's Works

A complete scholarly index to Luther's works in the Weimar edi-

---

[10]For a detailed description, see Aland (1970), pp. 7–18.
[11]See below.
[12]The key for the *American Edition* of *Luther's Works* is incomplete, since the American Edition was itself incomplete at the time the *Hilfsbuch* was compiled. For a full listing of Luther's writings available in English (and not merely those in the *American Edition*), see Robbert (1965), Robbert (1970), Robbert (1978).

tion is still in preparation. Several partial indices are, however, already available. The Table Talk (*Abteilung Tischreden*) has its own indices to subject matter, names, and places, to Bible citations, and to citations of other works (WATR 6). For the Letters (*Abteilung Briefe*), an index of persons and places appeared in 1978 (WABr 15). An index of passages in the Letters dealing with Luther and his activities, an index of biblical passages, and an index of citations were scheduled to appear as one volume (WABr 16) in 1980.[13] A final volume containing a subject index should be nearing the end of the editorial process and should appear in the next several years.[14]

An index to Luther's treatises (*Abteilung Schriften*) has been in the works for decades.[15] To date, however, scholars have had to rely on several partial indices. In 1948 an index appeared as WA 58/1, composed largely by Georg Buchwald. It contains an index of references Luther made about himself as well as an index of persons and places. As useful as this index is, it is incomplete and inadequate. A number of the individual volumes of the WA contain their own partial indices.[16]

The indices for Luther's writings (*Abteilung Schriften*) have been in preparation since 1961, and some three million cards have been accumulated at the Institut für Spätmittelalter und Reformation in Tübingen. As of 1979, it was planned that an index to places and an index to persons, which would include authors cited by Luther, should be published in 1982.[17] Then, beginning in 1983, a volume of the Latin subject index should appear every two years. Five volumes are planned for this index. Beginning in 1993, the first of five planned volumes of the German subject index should appear. These indices will be selective, not exhaustive. When necessary, the interested scholar may consult the much fuller card index in Tübingen.

The Printing and Reprinting of Luther's Work

In considering Luther's influence on the Reformation movement and its spread and development, particular attention must be paid to the publication history of his various writings. Two bibliographies stand ready to assist the historian in this regard: Paul Pietsch's bibliography of all known publications through 1546 of Luther's

---

[13]I have not yet seen this volume.
[14]Lämmel (1979).
[15]See Mühlhapt (1977) and zur Mühlen (1979).
[16]The following list is taken from zur Mühlen (1979), p. 138n3. There are various indices in WA 10.1/2, 17/2, 21, 22, 24, 28, 32/2, 35, 40/3, 48, 51, 54, 56, 47/2, 57/3.
[17]zur Mühlen (1979).

High German Bible translation (WADB 2:201–704), and Joseph Benzing's (1966) bibliography of all known publications through 1546 of Luther's other writings.

Chronology of Luther's Life

Light can often be shed on a particular writing or event in Luther's life by considering what else he was doing or writing at the same time. Georg Buchwald's *Luther-Kalendarium* (1929) is a chronological table organized by year, month, and day, listing all known events in Luther's life. Buchwald chronicles Luther's correspondence, his disputations, his readings, his lectures, his ordination of others, his sermons, his trips, his writings, his conversation at meals, his illnesses, and numerous other odds and ends. In 1935 Bernhard Woerner brought out a series of indices to the Kalendarium that covered Luther's letters, trips, visitors (or those he visited), sermons, and disputations, reading, ordinations, and lectures. Research since 1929 has altered some of Buchwald's dates, and the *Hilfsbuch* by Aland should be consulted on such matters as the dating of letters and treatises.[18]

Linguistic Aids

At first glance Luther's German can look deceptively like modern High German. But at closer inspection it soon becomes apparent that his sentence structure and vocabulary differ in significant ways from today's usages. Herbert Wolf (1980) provides a handy introduction to Luther's German. Birgit Stolt (1979) offers a valuable survey of the linguistic aids available to the scholar. Unfortunately, as she points out, currently available lexicographic aids leave much to be desired. The many volume *Deutsches Wörterbuch* of the brothers Grimm remains the court of last resort, particularly when connotations as well as denotations for a particular word are sought. Much handier is Alfred Götze's *Frühneuhochdeutsches Glossar*, but it is incomplete and not always helpful, especially concerning nuances. Orthography also poses a problem when using Götze as well as other lexicons, since spelling in Luther's writings is not regular. Also handy and useful is the "Worterklärung zur Lutherbibel von 1545" and the accompanying "Zum Verständnis der Luthersprache" found in the appendix volume to Hans Volz (1972).

---

[18]For a very brief chronology, see Bornkamm (1961).

II
Current Research

In his *Luther's House of Learning: Indoctrination of the Young in the German Reformation* (1978), Gerald Strauss concludes on the basis of his survey of visitation records of rural parishes and small and middling towns that from the institution of the first evangelical visitation in 1527 to 1618 and the outbreak of the Thirty Years war, the common people continued to show a general ignorance of even the most elementary tenets of Lutheranism. Although these findings have not remained uncontested,[19] the challenge they pose Luther research seems clear. Luther research must turn more of its attention to the reception of Luther's theology, to its institutionalization, to its popularization.

In the remainder of this essay I can only address a few areas of current research that raise questions about the reception, institutionalization, and popularization of Luther's theology.

Initia Lutheri—Initia Reformationis[20]

The popular reception of Luther's theology is methodologically difficult to determine, especially for the first decade or so. Strauss (1978) has illustrated how visitation records can be used to test the knowledge (and perhaps the beliefs) of the rural population and some inhabitants of towns. But such reports first begin in 1527/28, and, in any case, do not deal with the Imperial cities, which showed the most enthusiastic popular support for the Reformation.[21] Bernd Moeller (1962; 1966; 1972) and Steven Ozment (1975) have suggested features in Luther's theology that may have attracted inhabitants of these free cities, but much research remains to be done to confirm or reject their suggestions.[22]

More manageable methodologically, but still in its infancy, is research on the popular presentation of Luther's theology in *Flugschriften* and other forms of popular literature[23] as well as in sermons. The older work by Maurice Gravier, *Luther et l'Opinion pub-*

---

[19]Reviews are still coming in. My own review-essay will appear in the *History of Education Quarterly*.

[20]This heading is borrowed from Oberman (1974).

[21]See Lau (1959) and Moeller (1962; 1966; 1972).

[22]See the report by Thomas Brady in this volume.

[23]For the relevant bibliography and a survey of current research, see Steven Ozment's contribution to this volume.

lique (1943), remains valuable, but does not go beyond some of the most famous publicists. Ozment (1975) based his argument in part on a reading of some of the *Flugschriften* literature. Körsgen-Wiedeburg (1976) and Marc Lienhard (1978a) have recently examined the picture of Luther presented in some of the pamphlet literature of the early Reformation period.[24] Substantial work on the popular presentation of Luther's *theology*, however, remains to be done.

Let me illustrate with three examples how current research on the young Luther might be widened to embrace questions of reception and popularization.

Controversy always swirls around attempts to establish lines of influence between individual theologians or theological "schools" of the late Middle Ages and the theology of the younger Luther. Most recently a number of scholars have been hard at work identifying a possible "Augustinian school" within the Augustinian order and tracing lines of influence between this "school" and Martin Luther.[25] Heiko Oberman, in his address to the Fourth International Congress for Luther Research in St. Louis, explored the possible linkages and summarized his argument as follows:

> Taking stock of this cumulative, admittedly circumstantial evidence, we can point to the *schola Augustiniana moderna*, initiated by Gregory of Rimini, reflected by Hugolin of Orvieto, apparently spiritually alive in the Erfurt Augustinian monastery, and transformed into a pastoral reform-theology by Staupitz, as the *occasio proxima*—not *causa!*—for the inception of the *theologia vera* at Wittenberg.[26]

David Steinmetz (1973) immediately raised questions about this line of argument and especially about Oberman's claims for a *via Gregorii* and for Staupitz's role in mediating this late medieval "Augustinian tradition." Oberman, in reply, conceded only that more research needs to be done in the sources and that critical editions of these sources need to be prepared.[27] Steinmetz (1980) has re-

---

[24]See also Ritter (1970), Brückner (1974), Ufer (1971; 1973), Crofts (1980), Lienhard (1978b; 1978c), Chrisman (1980), and the forthcoming Chrisman (1981).

[25]For a guide to the literature, see Gindele *et al.* (1977) and Steinmetz (1980). Trapp (1956) and Zumkeller (1964) are crucial for this debate. For a salutary caution on the issue of "influence," see Steinmetz (1980).

[26]Oberman (1974), p. 82.

[27]Oberman (1977a), p. 130n172. For an elaboration on his argument for the late medieval Augustinian school and its influence, see pp. 82–140. Oberman sets forth his program for research and for the preparation of needed critical editions in Gindele *et al.* (1977), pp. v–xiii.

newed his objections, questioning particularly whether Staupitz was the mediator to Luther of the *via Gregorii*.[28]

To this issue of the possible existence of an "Augustinian school" and its influence on Luther could be added questions about the reception of Luther's theology. For example, in light of the highly favorable reception of Luther's theology within his own German Augustinian Order, is it possible that an "Augustinian school" or "tradition" prepared others to receive (and perhaps initially to misperceive) Luther's new theology?

While the controversy over the posting (or non-posting) of the 95 Theses seems to have died down in recent years,[29] the scholarly argument over the correct dating of Luther's "breakthrough" to a new understanding of *iustitia dei*, as he described it in his 1545 Preface to his Latin writings (among other places), remains very much alive.[30] Its continued vitality is readily explained. A solution to the dating of Luther's "Reformation breakthrough" presupposes a definition of Luther's "Reformation" position, about which, for both historical and confessional reasons, there is no scholarly consensus. Secondly, the dating of the "Reformation breakthrough" has profound implications for the understanding of the Indulgence controversy and Luther's subsequent break with the Roman Catholic church. Put baldly, if the "breakthrough" comes before 1517, then one may argue that Luther's new understanding of justification led (inevitably?) to his criticism of indulgences and to his eventual break with the Roman Catholic church. On the other hand, if the "breakthrough" comes after 1517, then Luther's "Reformation" position must be seen within the context of, and perhaps even as a reaction to, the controversy over indulgences.

As I view the literature, this much seems clear. The development of Luther's theology occurs gradually through the period 1512 to 1520. Some aspects of his "mature" position emerge quite late (such

[28]Steinmetz (1980) also argues against the view that Luther was a disciple of Staupitz in his early hermeneutics or in his first articulation of his doctrine of justification. Oberman has also been challenged by Leif Grane (e.g., Grane [1968]; Grane [1975]), touching off a debate on the proper methodology to be employed in studying the development of Luther's theology (Grane [1974]; Oberman [1977b]; Grane [1977]).
[29]For a review of the literature, see Rublack (1970). The major contributions to the debate are Iserloh (1968), Honselmann (1966), Lau (1967), Bornkamm (1967), Bäumer (1968), Volz (1967), and Honselmann (1968).
[30]For a review and selections from the literature to 1968, see Lohse (1968). Subsequent contributions include Schäfer (1969), Bayer (1971), Kroeger (1971), Brecht (1977), Cargill Thompson (1980), and Steinmetz (1980).

as the distinction between law and gospel), while others are apparent quite early, although sometimes under a slightly different vocabulary from that which Luther would employ later.[31] Secondly, there are serious difficulties with both the early and late datings, difficulties that seem incapable of ever being fully resolved.[32] The early dating cannot satisfactorily deal with Luther's own late dating of his discovery, at the time of the second Psalms lectures, as set down in his 1545 Preface. The late dating cannot satisfactorily deal with Luther's own explicit statement that his "breakthrough" involved the passive understanding of *iustitia dei*, not his understanding of God's Word or Promise, as also set down in his 1545 Preface. Finally, given the gradual development of Luther's theology, perhaps his reported "breakthrough," while subjectively important to Luther, may be of less importance for our understanding of Luther's development as a theologian and leader of the Reformation than such quantities of research would suggest.

In any case, the debate over the posting of the 95 Theses and over Luther's "Reformation breakthrough" also suggests questions about reception and popularization. We are likely never to be able to determine whether the 95 Theses were actually posted. But we should be able to say more about what made them so appealing both to a number of German humanists, who were responsible for their wide circulation in the vernacular, and to the larger public, who bought and read them together with the even more popular *Sermon on Indulgences and Grace* (WA 1:243–46). Similarly, we may never reach a consensus on the exact content and dating of Luther's "Reformation breakthrough." But we should be able to determine to some extent what Luther's contemporaries, or at least his more prominent followers and, perhaps more important, those who acted as popular publicists for his cause, perceived to be central and *reformatorisch* in Luther's theology.

Institutionalization and Politicization

"Institutionalization and politicization" is an ugly heading, but it describes a real problem that faced the mature Luther. It is one thing to initiate a religious revolution; it is another to pass it on to future generations. There came a point when Luther's theology had

---

[31]See, for example, Steinmetz's (1980), pp. 68–95, lucid examination of humility and justification in Luther and Staupitz and his criticism of Bizer (1961).
[32]See Cargill Thompson (1980).

to be embodied in institutions. Moreover, the Peasants' War of 1525, the visitations of 1527 and 1528, the threatening recesses of the diets of 1529 and 1530, the formation of the League of Schmalkalden in 1531—these and similar events in the late 1520s and early 1530s were both cause and effect of a transition from a revolutionary movement made up primarily of ideologically committed individuals to a more conservative movement led by rulers of territories and city states. Political considerations, although never absent in the development of Luther's Reformation, came to exert an increasingly important role. Luther research needs to examine Luther's involvement in this process.

Several studies have recently appeared on Luther's role as a theological and political advisor to his Elector, to other Protestant rulers, and to the League of Schmalkalden. Trüdinger (1975) has examined the appropriate letters and opinions (*Gutachten*) dealing with several aspects of the internal development and spread of the Reformation. Wolgast (1977) has convincingly analyzed and placed in context the opinions penned by Luther and by the other Wittenberg theologians on external political matters. Kunst (1977), relying mainly on a close reading of Luther's correspondence, has focused on Luther's role as an advisor to his Elector on matters of public moment. Special attention has been devoted by Kunst, Wolgast, and others to Luther's changing position on the legitimacy, legal and theological, of armed resistance to the Emperor if attacked on account of the gospel.[33] We are now quite well informed about the older Luther's dealings with Protestant secular authorities, although more should be done, for example, on how Elector John Frederick, Landgraf Philip, and the League of Schmalkalden used Luther, his name, and his pen, to further their own, often largely political, designs.[34]

To understand properly the mature Luther and his influence on the course of the Reformation, scholars must also closely examine his influence on his colleagues at Wittenberg and, in turn, their influence on events, especially on the establishment of institutions. The most important and influential of these colleagues is certainly Philipp Melanchthon, who played a major role in the formation of confessional Lutheranism with his *Loci communes*, the *Augsburg Confession*, and the *Apology for the Augsburg Confession*, and who

---

[33]Recent titles include Scheible (1969), Dörries (1970), Wolf (1972), Ohlig (1974), Wolgast (1977), Kunst (1977), Skinner (1978), Shoenberger (1979), Cargill Thompson (1980). The classic study is Müller (1915). See also Günter (1976).

[34]This is suggested by Wolgast (1977). See also Kunst (1977).

frequently represented Luther and Electoral Saxony at Imperial Diets and at colloquies between Lutherans and Catholics. We very much need a thorough study of Melanchthon that picks up where Maurer's *Der junge Melanchthon* left off and takes the story to Melanchthon's death.[35] Second in importance to Melanchthon is John Bugenhagen, Wittenberg's pastor and sometime reformer of various northern German cities and territories, who was highly influential in the task of putting Luther's theology into practice. There is still no full modern biography or edition of his works. There is a similar lack for Justus Jonas and Nicholas von Amsdorf, two more close and influential friends of Luther.[36]

Even Luther's later polemics need to be reexamined in light of the institutional and political pressures of the later years.[37] For example, much of the scholarship on Luther's treatises on the Jews centers on whether a change in Luther's theology occurred between 1523, when Luther published a sympathetic appeal to the Jews, and 1543, when he published three such vulgar and harsh attacks that even some of his contemporaries were offended.[38] Luther's treatises need to be situated within the anti-Jewish currents of the period. Unfortunately, there is nothing on the anti-Jewish pamphlet literature analogous to Bohnstedt's (1968) study of the anti-Turkish *Flugschriften*. Yet Luther is not the only publicist who turned his pen to anti-Jewish tracts in the late 1530s and early 1540s.[39] Moreover, whatever his own motivation and intentions, Luther's tracts may have been used by Elector John Frederick and others in their battle with the Emperor over sovereignty; as "serfs of the Chamber of the Holy

[35]Maurer (1967–1969). For the literature on Melanchthon, see Hammer (1967, 1969), Fraenkel and Greschat (1967), and the *Lutherjahrbuch* annual bibliography. Scheible (1978) describes the new index to Melanchthon's letters. On relations between Luther and Melanchthon, see Mix (1901), Pauck (1961), Neuser (1961), Greschat (1965), and Maurer (1967–1969). On Melanchthon, Luther, and the Augsburg Confession, see Lohse (1980).

[36]On Luther's circle of friends, see Volz (1968/69) and Buchwald (1957). On Bugenhagen see the essays and bibliography in Rautenberg (1958); his letters are published in Vogt (1888). See also Bergsma (1966). On Jonas see the brief biography by Delius (1952); his letters were published by Kawerau (1884–85). On Amsdorf see the bibliography in Kolb (1978). Some of his treatises are published in Lerche (1938). Many of Luther's other colleagues deserve more attention.

[37]I hope soon to publish a study of the older Luther's polemics.

[38]In recent years the minority view, for example, that of Stöhr (1960), Siirala (1964), and Sucher (1977), is that a change did occur. The majority view, that of Maurer (1968) and Brosseder (1972), is that while a change did occur in Luther's practical suggestions for dealing with the Jews, there is a continuity in his underlying theological view of the Jews. For a review of the literature, see Brosseder (1972).

Roman Empire," the Jews may have been helpless victims and pawns in the struggle between the emperor and the princes, the *Reich* and the *Territorialstaaten*.[40]

Finally, as with the young Luther, more research needs to be done on the reception and interpretation of the mature Luther's theology, particularly as it is codified in confessions and catechisms,[41] institutionalized in church and school orders,[42] popularized in *Flugschriften*, and generally propagated by the printing press.[43] On this last point it should be noted that a study of *Flugschriften* contemporaneous with the older Luther's writings is greatly complicated by the fact that bibliographies of and monographs on German *Flugschriften* rarely go further than 1525. The visitation records themselves also deserve a systematic study.[44]

[39]For example:

anon. *Der Wücherer Messkram oder Jarmarckt. Ein Newer Pasquillus Ob der Wücher Sünde/ Ob vnd wo er verboten/ Vnd was seine gebürliche straff sey/ Auch Ob man sein zü erhaltung der nöttigen Kauffhendel entberen könte/ Und zü straffen sey* etc. (n.p., 1544);

_____. *Ein grausame/ erschrockenliche geschicht von einem vngotzförchtigem verrucktem vnnd verzweyfelten Christen man/ der sein eigen fleiss vnd blütt/ sein natürliches kind ein iunges kneblin den Seelosen/ Gottlosen/ Gottsverretterschen Juden verkaufft vnd zü kauffen geben hatt* . . . (n.p., 1544);

Bucerus, Martinus; Kymeus, Johannes; Melander, Dionisius; Lenyngus, Johannes; Winther, Justus; Niddanus, Johannes Pistorus; and Kauffungen, Caspar. *Ratschlag Ob Christlicher Obrigkeit gebüren müge/ das sie die Jüden/ vnter den Christen zu wonen guldē/ vnd wo sie zu gedulden/ welcher gestalt vnd mass* (Erfurt: Christoffel Holthammer, 1539);

Eck, John. *Ains Judenbüechlins verlegung: darin ain Christ/ gantzer Christenhait zü schmach/ will es geschehe den Juden vnrecht in bezichtigung der Christen kinder mordt* (Ingoldstat: Alexander Weissenhorn, 1542);

Margaretha, Anthonius. *Der ganz Jüdisch Glaub. Mit sampt einer gründlichen vnd warhafftigen anzeigunge/ aller satzungen/ Ceremoniē/ gebetten/ heymliche vnd öffentliche gebreüch/ derē sich die Juden haltē/ durch das gantz Jar* . . . (Frankfurt am Main, 1544).

[40]See Stern (1965).

[41]The recent anniversaries of the Book of Concord and the Augsburg Confession have produced a series of publications. See, for example, Green (1977), Lohff and Spitz (1977), Lohse and Pesch (1980). Catechisms have been collected and reprinted by Cohrs (1900–07; 1978), Moufang (1881; 1964), Reu (1904–35; 1976), Kohls (1971), among others. For a discussion of the literature and useful bibliographies, see Fraas (1971), Kohls (1971), and Strauss (1978).

[42]Church orders are being gradually brought out in Sehling (1902–13, 1955–). For an incomplete list of school orders, see Mertz (1902). Many of the school orders are reprinted in Vormbaum (1860). See the highly informative survey by Strauss (1978).

[43]See Ozment in this volume. Hortleder (1645) reproduces many sources from the period of the older Luther's life, including numerous *Flugschriften*. Two additional bibliographies worth mentioning are *Index Aureliensis* (1956–) and Klaiber (1978). Useful for identifying authors are Jöcher (1750–51) and Rotermund (1784–1819; 1961).

[44]See Strauss (1978), who uses the records impressionistically. For a partial list of published and unpublished records, see Zeeden and Molitor (1967).

Bibliography

Research Aids

Aland, Kurt, *Hilfsbuch zum Lutherstudium*, 3rd. rev. ed. (Witten, 1970).

Bainton, Roland, *Here I Stand! A Life of Martin Luther* (Nashville and New York, 1950).

Benzing, Josef, *Lutherbibliographie: Verzeichnis der gedruckten Schriften Martin Luthers bis zu dessen Tod* (Baden-Baden, 1966).

Bornkamm, Heinrich, "Martin Luther, Chronik seines Lebens," in *Das Jahrhundert der Reformation* (Göttingen, 1961), 11–36.

———, *Martin Luther in der Mitte seines Lebens. Das Jahrzehnt zwischen dem Wormser und dem Augsburger Reichstag*, ed. Karin Bornkamm (Göttingen, 1979).

Buchwald, Georg, *Luther-Kalendarium* (Leipzig, 1929).

Buchwald, Reinhard, *Luther im Gespräch. Aufzeichnungen seiner Freunde und Tischgenossen. Nach den Urtexten der "Tischreden" zum erstenmal übertragen* (Stuttgart, 1938).

Haile, H. G., *Luther: An Experiment in Biography* (New York, 1980).

Götze, Alfred, *Frühneuhochdeutsches Glossar*, 7th ed. (Berlin, 1967).

Köstlin, Julius and Kawerau, Gustav, *Martin Luther, sein Leben und seine Schriften*, 5th rev. ed. (Berlin, 1903).

Kroker, Ernst, "Luthers Tischreden als geschichtliche Quelle," *Lutherjahrbuch* 1 (1919): 81–31.

Lämmel, Klaus, "Die Register der Weimarer Lutherausgabe (Abteilung Briefe)," *Luther* 50 (1979): 145–47.

Lohse, Bernhard, *Martin Luther: Eine Einführung in sein Leben und sein Werk* (Munich, 1981).

Müller, Gerhard, "60 Jahre Luther-Gesellschaft," *Luther* 49 (1978): 99–108.

Pretsch, Paul. "Bibliographie der Drucke der Lutherbibel. Die Drucke des Jahres 1522 bis 1546," in *WADB* 2:201–704.

Robbert, George S., ed., "A Checklist of Luther's Writings in English," *Concordia Theological Monthly* 36 (1965): 772–92; 41 (1970): 214–220; *Concordia Journal* 4 (1978): 73–77.

Stolt, Birgit, "Germanistische Hilfsmittel zum Lutherstudium," *Lutherjahrbuch* 46 (1979): 120–35.

Volz, Hans, ed., *Martin Luther, Die gantze Heilige Schrifft Deudsch 1545.* 2 vols., (Munich, 1972).
_____, *D. Martin Luther, Die gantze Heilige Schrifft Deudsch 1545. Anhang und Dokumente,* (Munich, 1972).
_____, *Martin Luthers deutsche Bibel: Entstehung und Geschichte der Lutherbibel,* ed. Henning Wendland, introd. Wilhelm Kantzenbach (Hamburg, 1978).
Woerner, Bernhard, *Wegweiser in Buchwalds Luther-Kalendarium* (Leipzig, 1935).
Wolf, Herbert, *Luther: Eine Einführung in germanistischen Lutherstudien* (Stuttgart, 1980).
zur Mühlen, Karl-Heinz, "Die Register der Weimarer Lutherausgabe (Abteilung Schriften)," *Luther* 50 (1979): 138–44.

Literature Reviews

Atkinson, James, "Luther Studies," *Journal of Ecclesiastical History* 23 (1972): 69–77.
Baring, Georg, "Luther und die 'Theologia Deutsch' in der neuesten Forschung," *Theologische Zeitschrift* 23 (1967): 48–62.
Bigane, Jack and Hagen, Kenneth, *Annotated Bibliography of Luther Studies, 1967–1976* (St. Louis, 1977).
Bizer, Ernst, "Neue Darstellungen der Theologie Luthers," *Theologische Rundschau* 31 (1965/66): 316–49.
Boendermaker, Johannes P., *Tien Jaar Lutherstudie in Nederland* (Assen, 1969).
Brosseder, Johannes, *Luthers Stellung zu den Juden im Spiegel seiner Interpreten. Interpretation und Rezeption von Luthers Schriften und Äusserungen zum Judentum im 19. und 20. Jahrhundert vor allem im deutschsprachigen Raum* (Munich, 1972).
Duchrow, Ulrich; Hubner, Wolfgang; and Reith, Louis J., eds., *Umdeutungen der Zweireichelehre Luthers im 19. Jahrhundert* (Gütersloh, 1975).
Gieraths, P. G., "Das heutige Lutherbild. Bilanz und Ausblick." *Angelicum* 44 (1967): 409–48.
Green, Lowel C., "Luther Research in English-Speaking Countries since 1971," *Lutherjahrbuch* 44 (1977): 105–26.
Hagen, Kenneth G., "Changes in the Understanding of Luther: The Development of the Young Luther," *Theological Studies* 29 (1968): 472–96.

Haikola, Lauri, "Contributions in Finnish to Luther Research since the Second World War," *Lutheran World* 13 (1966): 288–90.

Hakamies, Ahti, *"Eigengesetzlichkeit" der natürlichen Ordnungen als Grundproblem der neueren Lutherdeutung. Studien zur Geschichte und Problematik der Zwei-Reiche-Lehre Luthers* (Witten, 1971).

Hornig, Gottfried, "Lutherforskning i Tyskland," *Tidsskrift for teologi og kirke* 38 (1967): 272–88.

Johnson, Roger, ed., *Psychohistory and Religion: The Case of Young Man Luther* (Philadelphia, 1977).

Junghans, Helmar, "Inhalt, Ordnung und Form der Lutherbibliographie," *Lutherjahrbuch* 42 (1975): 126–30.

Kantzenbach, Friedrich, "Luther Research as a Problem in Comparative Theology," *Lutheran World* 13 (1966): 257–71.

_____, "Lutherforschung als kontroverstheologisches Problem," in *Wandlungen des Lutherbildes*, ed. Karl Forster (Würzburg, 1966).

Kjelgaard-Pedersen, Steffen, "Die Lutherforschung in Skandinavien seit 1966," *Lutherjahrbuch* 44 (1977): 57–70.

Kohls, Ernst-Wilhelm, "Die Lutherforschung im deutschen Sprachbereich seit 1970," *Lutherjahrbuch* 44 (1977): 28–56.

Koch, Hans-Gerhard, *Luthers Reformation in kommunistischer Sicht* (Stuttgart, 1967).

Knoblauch, Bruno, "Bibliografia de Lutero. Bibliographie spanischsprachiger Lutherliteratur von 1942 bis 1965," *Lutherjahrbuch* 35 (1968): 173–76.

Lau, Franz, "Der Stand der Lutherforschung heute," in *Reformation 1517–1967. Wittenberger Vorträge*, ed. E. Kähler (Berlin, 1968).

Lindberg, Carter, "Luther Research in America, 1945–1965," *Lutheran World* 13 (1966): 291–302.

Loewenich, Walther von, "Wandlungen des evangelischen Lutherbildes im 19. und 20. Jahrhundert," in *Wandlungen des Lutherbildes*, ed. Karl Forster (Würzburg, 1966).

Lohse, Bernhard, "Die Lutherforschung im deutschen Sprachraum seit 1966," *Lutherjahrbuch* 38 (1971): 91–120.

Ludolphy, Ingetraut, "Der literarische Ertrag des Reformationsjubiläums in der Deutschen Demokratischen Republik," *Luther* 39 (1968): 60–75.

Müller, Gerhard, "Neuere Literatur zur Theologie des jungen Luther," *Kerygma und Dogma* 11 (1965): 325–57.

———, "Neuere Literatur zur Reformationsgeschichte," *Theologische* 42 (1976/77): 93–130.

Ohlig, Rudolf, *Die Zwei-Reiche-Lehre Luthers in der Auslegung der deutschen lutherischen Theologie der Gegenwart seit 1945* (Bern, 1974).

Pahl, Paul, "Some Recent English Publications on Luther (1969–1973)," *Lutheran Theological Journal* 7 (1973): 118–28.

Prenter, Regin, "Luther Research in Scandinavia since 1945," *Lutheran World* 13 (1966): 272–87.

Rublack, Hans-Christoph, "Neuere Forschungen zum Thesenanschlag Luthers," *Historisches Jahrbuch der Görres-Gesellschaft* 90 (1970): 329–43.

Sauter, Gerhard, ed., *Zur Zwei-Reiche Lehre Luthers* (Munich, 1973).

Schwarzwäller, Klaus, *Sibboleth. Die Interpretation von Luthers Schrift De servo arbitrio seit Theodosius Harnack. Ein systematisch-kritischer Überblick* (Munich, 1969).

Spitz, Lewis W., "Current Accents in Luther Study: 1960–1967," *Theological Studies* 28 (1967): 549–573.

———, "The Lutheran Reformation in American Historiography," in *The Maturing of American Lutheranism*, ed. H.T. Neve and B.A. Johnson (Minneapolis, 1968).

———, "Recent Studies of Luther and the Reformation," in *Luther, Erasmus, and the Reformation: A Catholic-Protestant Reappraisal*, eds. J.C. Olin, V.D. Smart, and R.E. McNally (New York, 1969), 134–150.

Stupperich, Robert, "Lutherforschung und Reformationsgeschichte: Ein Literaturbericht, II," *Archiv für Kulturgeschichte* 50 (1969): 300–22.

Tokuzen, Yoshikazu, "Die Lutherforschung in Japan seit 1967," *Lutherjahrbuch* 44 (1977): 89–104.

Vercruysse, Joseph E., "Kroniek van het Lutheronderzoek," *Bijdragen* 30 (1969): 184–200.

———, "Die Lutherforschung im niederländischen Sprachbereich seit 1969," *Lutherjahrbuch* 44 (1977): 71–74.

———, "Die Lutherforschung im romanischen Sprachbereich seit 1970," *Lutherjahrbuch* 44 (1977): 75–88.

Vinay, Valdo, "Lutherana," *Protestantesmo* 24 (1969): 79–94.

Walther, Christian, "Hat die Lehre von den zwei Reichen noch einen Sinn?" *Luther* 49 (1978): 15–24.

Wartenberg, Günter, "Bibliographie der marxistischen Luther-

Literatur in der DDR, 1945–1966," *Lutherjahrbuch* 35 (1968): 162–72.

Wolf, Gerhard P., *Das neuere französische Lutherbild* (Wiesbaden, 1974).

Zschäbitz, Gerhard, "Zum marxistischen Lutherbild," *Geschichtsunterricht und Staatsbürgerkunde* 9 (1967): 752–58.

zur Mühlen, Karl-Heinz, "Luther zwischen Tradition und Revolution," *Luther* 47 (1976): 61–76.

Literature Reviews: Catholic Luther Research

Bäumer, Remigius, "Die Erforschung der kirchlichen Reformationsgeschichte seit 1931," in *Die Erforschung der kirchlichen Reformationsgeschichte*, Remigius Bäumer and Hubert Jedin (Darmstadt, 1975).

Beyna, Werner, *Das moderne katholische Lutherbild* (Essen, 1969).

Bogdahn, Martin, *Die Rechtfertigungslehre Luthers im Urteil der neueren katholischen Theologie* (Göttingen, 1971).

Brandenburg, Albert, *Die Zukunft des Martin Luther: Luther, Evangelium und die Katholizität* (Münster/Kassel, 1977).

Brandmüller, Walter, *Damals geschehen heute diskutiert*. Vol. 2. *Der Beitrag der Kirche zum Werden Europas. Die Reformation Martin Luthers in katholischer Sicht. Ökumenismus vor dem Hintergrund der Geschichte* (St. Ottilien, 1979).

Crespi, Maris Lidia, "La storiografia contemporanea italiana di fronte a Martin Lutero," *La Scuola cattolica* 100 (1972): 134–57.

Fries, Heinrich, "Die Grundanliegen der Theologie Luthers in der Sicht der katholischen Theologie der Gegenwart," in *Wandlugen des Lutherbildes*, ed. Karl Forster (Würzburg, 1966).

Garcia-Villoslada, Ricardo, *Lutero visto por los historiadores catolicos del sigle XX* (Madrid, 1973).

Hasler, August, *Luther in der katholischen Dogmatik. Darstellung seiner Rechtfertigungslehre in den katholischen Dogmatikbüchern* (Munich, 1968).

Jedin, Hubert, "Wandlungen des Lutherbildes in der katholischen Kirchengeschichtsschreibung," in *Wandlungen des Lutherbildes*, ed. Karl Forster (Würzburg, 1966).

———, "Wandlungen des Lutherbildes in der katholischen Kirchengeschichtsschreibung," in *Martinus Luther. 450 Jahre Reformation* (Bad Godesberg, 1967).

_____, "Mutamenti dell'interpretazione cattolica della figura di Lutero e loro limiti," *Revista di storia della Chiesa in Italia* 23 (1969): 361–77.

Kooiman, Willem Jan, "Herdwaardering van Luther in de rooms-katholieke geschiedschrijving," *Rondoom het Woord* 10 (1968): 1–14.

Loewenich, Walther von, "Evangelische und katholische Luther-deutung der Gegenwart im Dialog," *Lutherjahrbuch* 34 (1967): 60–89.

_____, "Lutherforschung—auch im ökumenischen Zeitalter?" *Luther* 42 (1971): 97–109.

Lutz, Heinrich, "Zum Wandel der katholischen Lutherinterpretation," in *Objektivität und Parteilichkeit*, ed. R. Koselleck, W.J. Mommsen, and J. Rüsen (Munich, 1977).

Manns, Peter, *Lutherforschung heute—Krise und Aufbruch* (Wiesbaden, 1967).

Pesch, Otto H., "Twenty Years of Catholic Luther Research," *Lutheran World* 13 (1966): 302–16.

_____, "Aus der Lutherforschung: 453 Jahre Reformation," *Theologische Quartalschrift* 150 (1970): 417–32.

_____, *Ketzerfürst und Kirchenlehrer. Wege katholischer Begegnung mit Martin Luther* (Stuttgart, 1971).

Scheffczyk, Leo, "Eine Weiterführung katholischer Lutherforschung," *Münchener Theologische Zeitschrift* 27 (1976): 277–

Wicks, Jared, "Martin Luther through Catholic Eyes," *Chicago Studies* 8 (1969): 275–85.

Issues in Luther Research

Adelung, J. Chr. and Rotermund, H.R., eds., *Fortsetzungen und Ergänzungen zu Jöchers Allgemeines Gelehrten-Lexicon*, 6 vols., (Leipzig-Bremen, 1784–1819; Hildesheim, 1961).

Bäumer, Remigius, "Die Diskussion um Luthers Thesenanschlag—Forschungsergebnisse und Forschungsaufgaben," in *Um Reform und Reformation*, ed. August Franzen, (Münster, 1968).

Bayer, Oswald, *Promissio. Geschichte der reformatorischen Wende in Luthers Theologie* (Göttingen, 1971).

Bergsma, Johannes H., *Die Reform der Messliturgie durch Johannes Bugenhagen (1485-1558)* (Hildescheim, 1966).

Bohnstedt, John W., *The Infidel Scourge of God: The Turkish Menace as Seen by German Pamphleteers of the Reformation Era* (Philadelphia, 1968).

Bornkamm, Heinrich, *Thesen und Thesenanschlag Luthers— Geschehen und Bedeutung* (Berlin, 1967).

Brecht, Martin, "Iustitia Christ. Die Entdeckung Martin Luthers," *Zeitschrift für Theologie und Kirche* 74 (1977): 179–223.

Brückner, Wolfgang, ed., *Volkserzählung und Reformation: ein Handbuch zur Tradierung und Funktion von Erzählstoffen und Erzählliteratur im Protestantismus* (Berlin, 1974).

Buchwald, Georg, *Martin Luther als Kind, Vater und Freund* (Berlin, 1957).

Cargill Thompson, W.D.J., "Luther and the Right of Resistance to the Emperor," in *W.D.J. Cargill Thompson, Studies in the Reformation: Luther to Hooker*, ed. C.W. Dugmore (London, 1980).

————, "The Problem of Luther's 'Tower Experience' and its Place in his Intellectual Development," in W.D.J. Cargill Thompson, *Studies in the Reformation: Luther to Hooker*, ed. C.W. Dugmore (London, 1980).

Chrisman, Miriam Usher, "Lay Response to the Protestant Reformation in Germany, 1520–1528," in *Reformation Principle and Practice: Essays in Honour of A.G. Dickens*, ed. Peter N. Brooks (London, 1980).

————, *Lay Culture and the Culture of the Learned: Books, Men and Ideas in Strasbourg, 1480–1599* (New Haven, 1982).

Cohrs, Ferdinand, *Die evangelischen Katechismusversuche vor Luthers Enchiridion* (Berlin, 1900–07; Hildesheim, 1978).

Crofts, Richard, "Books, Reform, and the Reformation," *ARG* 71 (1980): 21–35.

Delius, Walter, *Lehre und Leben, Justus Jonas* (Berlin, 1952).

Dörries, Hermann, "Luther und das Widerstandsrecht," in *Wort und Stunde*, Vol. 3 (Göttingen, 1970), 195–270.

Fraas, Hans-Jürgen, *Katechismustradition. Luthers kleiner Katechismus in Kirche und Schule* (Göttingen, 1971).

Fraenkel, Peter and Greschat, Martin, *Zwanzig Jahre Melanchthonstudium. 6 Literaturberichte (1945–1965)* (Geneva, 1967).

Gindele, Egon; Geiter, Heinke; and Schuler, Alfred, eds., *Biblio-*

graphie zur Geschichte und Theologie des Augustiner-Eremi-tenordens bis zum Beginn der Reformation (New York, 1977).

Grane, Leif, "Gregor von Rimini und Luthers Leipziger Disputation," *Studia Theologica* 22 (1968): 29–49.

_____, *Modus loquendi theologicus. Luthers Kampf um die Erneuerung der Theologie (1515–1518)* (Leiden, 1975).

_____, "Lutherforschung und Geistesgeschichte. Auseinandersetzung mit Heiko A. Oberman," *ARG* 68 (1977): 56–109.

Gravier, Maurice. *Luther et l'Opinion publique. Essai sur la littérature satirique et polémique en langue Allemande pendant les années décisives de la Réforme (1520–1530)* (Paris, 1943).

Green, Lowell C., *The Formula of Concord: An Historiographical and Bibliographical Guide* (St. Louis, 1977).

Greschat, Martin, *Melanchthon neben Luther. Studien zur Gestalt der Rechtfertigungslehre zwischen 1528 und 1537*, vol. 1 of *Untersuchungen zur Kirchengeschichte* (Witten, 1965).

Günter, Wolfgang, *Martin Luthers Vorstellung von der Reichsverfassung* (Münster, 1976).

Hammer, Wilhelm, *Die Melanchthonforschung im Wandel der Jahrhunderte. Ein beschreibendes Verzeichnis*, 2 vols. (Gütersloh, 1967–68).

Honselmann, Klemens, *Urfassung und Drucke der Ablassthesen Martin Luthers und ihre Veröffentlichung* (Paderborn, 1966).

_____, "Die Urfassung der Thesen Luthers—Entgegnung zum Aufsatz von Hans Volz," *Zeitschrift für Kirchengeschichte* 79 (1968): 68–76.

Hortleder, F., *Handlungen und Ausschreiben . . . von den Ursachen dess Teutschen Kriegs Kaiser Carls dess V, wider die Schmalkaldische Bunds . . . ,* 2nd ed. (Gotha, 1645).

Index Aureliensis. Catalogus librorum sedecimo saeculo impressorum. (Baden-Baden, 1956–).

Iserloh, Erwin, *Luther zwischen Reform und Reformation-Der Thesenanschlag fand nicht statt*, 3rd ed. (Münster, 1968).

Jöcher, Christoph G., *Allgemeines Gelehrten-Lexicon*, 4 vols. (Leipzig, 1750–51).

Kawerau, Gustav, ed., *Der Briefwechsel des Justus Jonas*, 2 vols. (Halle, 1884–85).

Kohls, Ernst-Wilhelm, ed., *Evangelische Katechismen der Reformationszeit vor und neben Martin Luthers Kleinem Katechismus* (Gütersloh, 1971).
Kolb, Robert, *Nikolaus von Amsdorf (1483–1565): Popular Polemics in the Preservation of Luther's Legacy* (Nieuwkoop, 1978).
Klaiber, Wilbirgis, ed., *Katholische Kontroverstheologen und Reformer des 16. Jahrhunderts* (Münster, 1978).
Körsgen-Wiedeburg, Andrea, "Das Bild Martin Luthers in den Flugschriften der frühen Reformationszeit," in *Festgabe für Ernst Walter Zeeden zum 60. Geburtstag am 14. Mai 1976*, ed. Horst Rabe, Hansgeorg Molitor, and Hans-Christoph Rublack (Münster, 1976), 153–177.
Kroeger, Matthias, *Rechtfertigung und Gesetz. Studien zur Entwicklung der Rechtfertigungslehre beim jungen Luther* (Göttingen, 1971).
Kunst, Hermann, *Evangelischer Glaube und politische Verantwortung. Martin Luther als politischer Berater seiner Landesherrn und seine Teilnahme an den Fragen des öffentlichen Lebens* (Stuttgart, 1977).
Lau, Franz, "Der Bauernkrieg und das angebliche Ende der lutherischen Reformation als spontaner Volksbewegung," *Lutherjahrbuch* 26 (1959): 109–34.
———, "Die gegenwärtige Diskussion um Luthers Thesenanschlag Sachstandsbericht und Versuch einer Weiterführung durch Neuinterpretation von Dokumenten," *Lutherjahrbuch* 34 (1967): 1–59.
Lerche, Otto, ed., *Nikolaus von Amsdorff, Ausgewählte Schriften* (Gütersloh, 1938).
Lienhard, Marc, "Held oder Ungeheuer? Luthers Gestalt und Tat im Lichte der zeitgenössischen Flugschriftenliteratur," *Lutherjahrbuch* 45 (1978): 56–79.
———, "Mentalité populaire, gens d'Eglise et mouvement évangélique à Strasbourg en 1523," in *Horizons européens de la réforme en Alsace, Mélanges Jean Rott* (Leiden, 1978).
———, "Strasbourg et la querre des pamphlets," in *Les grandes figures de l'humanisme alsacien* (Strasbourg, 1978).
Lohff, Wenzel and Spitz, Lewis W., eds. *Discord, Dialogue, and Concord/Widerspruch, Dialog und Einigung.* Vol. 1 (Philadelphia, 1977), Vol. 2 (Stuttgart, 1977).
Lohse, Bernhard, ed., *Der Durchbruch der reformatorischen Erkenntnis bei Luther* (Darmstadt, 1968).

_____, "Luther und das Augsburger Bekenntnis," in *Das Augsburger Bekenntnis von 1530—Damals und Heute*, eds. Bernhard Lohse and Otto Hermann Pesch (Munich/Mainz, 1980).

Lohse, Bernhard and Pesch, Otto Hermann, eds., *Das Augsburger Bekenntnis von 1530—Damals und Heute* (Munich/Mainz, 1980).

Maurer, Wilhelm, *Der junge Melanchthon zwischen Humanismus und Reformation*, 2 vols. (Göttingen, 1967–1969).

_____, "Die Zeit der Reformation," in *Kirche und Synagoge. Handbuch zur Geschichte von Christen und Juden*, vol. 1, Karl-Heinrich Rengstorf and Siegfried von Kortzfleisch, eds. (Stuttgart, 1968).

Mertz, Georg, *Das Schulwesen der deutschen Reformation* (Heidelberg, 1902).

Mix, Gustav, "Luther und Melanchthon in ihrer gegenseitigen Beurteilung," *Theologische Studien und Kritiken* 74 (1901): 458–521.

Moeller, Bernd. *Imperial Cities and the Reformation*. ed. trans. by H. C. Erik Midelfort and Mark U. Edwards, Jr. (Philadelphia, 1972).
Originally: *Reichsstadt und Reformation* (Gütersloh, 1962); Revised edition: *Villes d'Empire et réformation*, trans. Albert Chenou (Geneva, 1966).

Moufang, Christoph, ed., *Katholische Katechismen des sechzehnten Jahrhunderts in deutscher Sprache* (Mainz, 1881; Hildesheim, 1964).

Müller, Karl, *Luthers Äusserungen über das Recht des bewaffneten Widerstands gegen den Kaiser* (Munich, 1915).

Neuser, Wilhelm H., *Luther und Melanchthon—Einheit im Gegensatz* (Munich, 1961).

Oberman, Heiko A., "Reformation: Epoche oder Episode," *ARG* 68 (1977): 56–109.

_____, "Headwaters of the Reformation: *Initia Lutheri—Initia Reformationis*," in *Luther and the Dawn of the Modern Era*, ed. Heiko A. Oberman (Leiden, 1974).

_____, *Werden und Wertung der Reformation: Vom Wegestreit zum Glaubenskampf* (Tübingen, 1977).

Ohlig, Rudolf, *Die Zwei-Reiche-Lehre Luthers in der Auslegung der deutschen lutherischen Theologie der Gegenwart seit 1945* (Bern/Frankfurt a.M., 1974).

Ozment, Steven E., *The Reformation in the Cities: The Appeal of*

Protestantism to Sixteenth-Century Germany and Switzerland (New Haven, 1975).
Pauck, Wilhelm, "Luther und Melanchthon," in *Luther und Melanchthon,* ed. Vilmos Vajta (Göttingen, 1961).
Rautenberg, Werner, ed., *Johann Bugenhagen. Beiträge zu seinem
400. Geburtstag* (Berlin, 1958).
Reu, Johann Michael, ed., *Quellen zur Geschichte des kirchlichen
Unterrichts in der evangelischen Kirche Deutschlands
zwischen 1530 und 1600,* 9 vols (Gütersloh, 1904–35; Hildesheim, 1976).
Ritter, Susanne, *Die kirchenkritische Tendenz in den deutschsprachigen Flugschriften der frühen Reformationszeit* (Tübingen, 1970).
Schäfer, Rolf, "Zur Datierung von Luthers reformatorischer Erkenntnis," *Zeitschrift für Theologie und Kirche* 66 (1969): 151–
170.
Scheible, Heinz, "Die neue Gesamtausagabe 'Melanchthons Briefwechsel'," *Wolfenbütteler Renaissance-Mitteilungen* 2
(1978): 75–80.
_____, *Das Widerstandsrecht als Problem der deutschen Protestanten, 1523–1546* (Gütersloh, 1969).
Sehling, Emil, ed., *Die evangelischen Kirchenordnungen des 16.
Jahrhunderts,* 5 vols. (Leipzig, 1902–13). Vols. 6ff. continued by the Institut für evangelisches Kirchenrecht der evangelischen Kirche in Deutschland zu Göttingen (Tübingen,
1955).
Shoenberger, Cynthia Grant, "Luther on Resistance to Authority,"
Journal of the History of Ideas 40 (1979): 3–20.
Siirala, Aarne, "Luther and the news," *Lutheran World* 11 (1964):
337–57.
Skinner, Quentin, *The Foundations of Modern Political Thought,*
vol. 2. *The Age of Reformation* (Cambridge, 1978).
Steinmetz, David C., "Luther and the Late Medieval Augustinians:
Another Look," *Concordia Theological Monthly* 44 (1973):
245–60.
_____, *Luther and Staupitz: An Essay in the Intellectual Origins of
the Protestant Reformation* (Durham, N.C., 1980).
Stern, Selma, *Josel of Rosheim: Commander of Jewry in the Holy
Roman Empire of the German Nation,* Trans. Gertrude
Hirschler (Philadelphia, 1965).

Stöhr, Martin, "Luther und die Juden." *Evangelische Theologie* 20 (1960): 157–82.

Strauss, Gerald, *Luther's House of Learning: Indoctrination of the Young in the German Reformation* (Baltimore, 1978).

Sucher, C. Bernd, *Luthers Stellung zu den Juden: Eine Interpretation aus germanistischer Sicht* (Nieuwkoop, 1977).

Trapp, Damasus, "Augustinian Theology of the 14th Century: Notes on Editions, Marginalia, Opinions and Book-Lore," *Augustiniana* 6 (1956): 147–265.

Trüdinger, Karl, *Luthers Briefe und Gutachten an weltliche Obrigkeiten zur Durchführung der Reformation* (Münster, 1975).

Ufer, Joachim, "Passion D. Martin Luthers," in *Der Reichstag zu Worms vom 1521: Reichspolitik und Luthersache*, ed. Fritz Reuter (Worms, 1971), 449–458.

_____, "Wie zeitgenössiche Flugschriften vom Reichstag zu Worms 1521 berichteten," *Blätter für pfälzische Kirchengeschichte und religiöse Volkskunde* 40 (1973): 196–209.

Vogt, Otto, ed., *Dr. Johannes Bugenhagens Briefwechsel* (Stetten, 1888).

Volz, Hans, "Die Urfassung von Luthers 95 Thesen," *Zeitschrift für Kirchengeschichte* 78 (1967): 67–93.

_____, "Luther und sein Freunde Kreis," *Tübinger Forschungen* 42/43 (1968/69): 6–.

Vormbaum, Reinhold, ed., *Die evangelischen Schulordnungen des sechszehnten Jahrhunderts* (Gütersloh, 1860).

Wolf, Gunther, ed., *Luther und die Obrigkeit* (Darmstadt, 1972).

Wolgast, Eike, *Die Wittenberger Theologie und die Politik der Evangelischen Stände. Studien zu Luthers Gutachten in politischen Fragen* (Gütersloh, 1977),

Zeeden, Ernst Walter and Molitor, Hansgeorg, eds., *Die Visitation im Dienst der kirchlichen Reform* (Münster, 1967).

Zumkeller, Adolar "Die Augustinerschule des Mittelalters: Vertreter und philosophisch-theologische Lehre," *Analecta Augustiniana* 27 (1964): 167–262.

Pamphlet Literature of
the German Reformation

Steven Ozment

What is a pamphlet? What types of information do pamphlets convey? These questions have become acute in recent years as new bibliographical aids and source editions have made pamphlets readily accessible to scholars in ever increasing numbers. In addition, the ever changing climate of scholarly opinion and interest has posed new questions to the literary sources of the Reformation. Whereas older historical scholarship drew on pamphlets largely to document the mainline narrative of the Reformation, especially as it related to the great theological and political conflicts of the age, newer research, inspired by interest in urban, social, cultural, and family history, has begun to explore pamphlet and tract literature for insights into the people and institutions of 16th century society—how their attitudes and beliefs were shaped, the techniques of communication and propaganda, the rise of new cultures, the inculcation of new values, the enforcement of new laws. While pamphlets continue to be studied for the light they shed on theological and political conflict, the broadening of historical curiosity about Reformation Europe has made the German pamphlet a source around which historians from many fields guided by different methods of study now gather.

What is a Pamphlet?

Because pamphlets exist in such large numbers and take such a variety of forms, defining the Reformation pamphlet is a complicated task. Probably more than 10,000 titles appeared in the first half of the 16th century. They range in size from two or three pages up to one hundred or more. Some are profound scholastic tracts, others almost puerile, nearly picture books.[1] Some are written in coarse popular language and filled with popular prejudices, while others are eloquently moving and fairminded. Hans-Joachim Köhler, leader of the pamphlet research project at the University of Tübingen, has proposed the following working definition, which stresses the pamphlet's character as an instrument of mass propaganda: "the pamphlet is an independent, non-recurring, unbound publication of more than one page whose purpose is to agitate (that is, move to action) and/or to propagandize (that is, influence opinion) and which is addressed to the masses or the public-at-large."[2]

This definition reflects the state of modern research on three counts. First, it treats the Reformation pamphlet as the product of literate, usually learned authors who were apologists for a cause. Earlier scholarship had tended to treat pamphlets, especially the many anonymous and pseudonymous ones,[3] too trustingly as objective reports of "popular opinion."[4] Secondly, this definition does not bog down in an attempt to distinguish pamphlets that express typical late medieval reform sentiments, especially those of an Erasmian and humanist nature, from pamphlets that contain the distinctively Protestant doctrines of justification by faith and the authority of Scripture alone.[5] The concern to classify pamphlets in this way makes a valid point, especially when we are dealing with pamphlets from the transition period of the early 1520s. Still, the search for the distinctively Protestant narrows the scope of the Reformation pamphlet, which could embrace as its own much arguably "unevangelical" criticism of church and society and many traditional reform ideals of a non-theological nature. Finally, Köhler's definition reminds us that the great majority of pamphlets were addressed to a non-specialized and often *non-literate* audience. Although Catholic and Protestant theologians conducted learned Latin satires and polemics by way of pamphlets, it was a mark of the Reformation pamphlet to address high and urgent matters in a language and style

[1]An example of such a picture book is *Geistlicher Blüthandel Johannis Huss/zu Constentz verbrannt A.D. MCCCXV am sechsten tag Juli. Mit gegen Vergleichung göttlicheren schrifft/und Bäpstlicher satzungen* [ed. by Ulrich von Hutten] (n.p., n.p.) [Oxford, Bodleian Library—henceforth: OX-BOD—Vet.Dle.118(6)].

[2]Köhler (1976), 50, 52, 54; Tompert (1978), 212–13.

[3]Perhaps as many as one-half of the Reformation pamphlets of the 1520s are anonymous or pseudonymous and give no place of publication. This was not only to ensure the safety of author and publisher, but also to convey the impression that the works expressed the will of the "public-at-large." Holborn (1942), 132.

[4]Ritter (1970), 4–16; Tompert (1978).

[5]Blochwitz (1930), esp. 176, 196–97, 206, 243–45. A more recent defense of this distinction is Scheible (1974).

ordinary people could identify with and understand—a language designed to succeed as well when *heard* as when read.[6] In this sense the Reformation pamphlet was a half-way house between elite and popular culture in the 16th century.

Köhler's definition excludes from the category of pamphlets all fictional and devotional literature, laws and ordinances, liturgical texts, scholastic and instructional texts, primarily aesthetic writings, texts which convey "purely" factual information without a recognizable polemical intent, and letters and sermons addressed to a specific audience.[7] If, however, agitation and propaganda are the key criteria, our definition must be flexible enough to embrace the variety of publications that speak to public issues at points in time when they have become controversial.[8] When, for example, Johann Diepold transformed St. John Chrysostom's simple biblical sermon on alms—a text that appears on the surface to be purely historical and instructional—into a German pamphlet, he placed this traditional work in the service of Protestant polemic against the medieval practice of tithing.[9] When a German translation of John of Paris's *Disputatio inter clericum et militem* (1296–98) circulated in Augsburg in 1522, it became Protestant criticism of clerical presumption to temporal rule.[10] A short catechetical work on baptism and the Eucharist—in appearance a purely devotional guide—urged its readers to refuse the last rites from the religious, who are said to have their minds set only on winning gifts and endowments, not consoling consciences at the hour of death.[11] Even straightforward political ordinances, circulated widely in short vernacular statements, sought to shape public attitudes. The Kitzingen common chest ordinance (1523), for example, praised needy local poor with good work records and blamed their impoverishment on forces beyond their control, while expressing outrage at the wandering poor who "fill

[6]Gravier (1942), 164.

[7]Köhler (1976), 50–51.

[8]As Köhler points out, a letter to a specific group on a specific occasion can be reprinted and disseminated as a "pamphlet" for the public-at-large. Köhler (1976), 54.

[9]*Ain Sermon Sancti Johannis Chrisostomi/von dem almussen/über die wort Pauli/in der ersten Epistel deren von Corinth. in latein von Joh. Oecolamp. anzaigt/und durch Joh. Diepold zu Ulm/verteütschitt* (1522) [Oxford, Bodleian Library, Tracts Lutheran —henceforth: OX-BOD T.L.—19.61].

[10]*Ain schöner dialogus zwischen ainem Priester und Ritter/von ainer steür/über die gaistlichenn etwan in Franckreich angelegt gehalten* [Augsburg, 1522] [OX-BOD T.L. 83.18].

[11]Justus Menius, *In was glauben und Meynung die kyndlein zur heiligen Tauff zu fordern seyn etc.* (1525) [British Museum—henceforth B.M.—3905.3.96].

the streets and churches and abuse charity in no small way" and whose plight is attributed to "their own idleness, drunkenness, gambling, or other such dishonorable activity."[12] One may agree with Maurice Gravier, who cites among the "pamphlets" of the 1520s "sermons, small popular brochures, works of piety, short parodies, large accounts of controversies, both simple and detailed allegories, brief historical reports, reeditions of ancient works, both Latin and German, both verse and prose"—all issued to establish dialogue and influence opinion on burning topics of the day.[13]

Pamphlets are our most direct access to the material and spiritual forces that moved people to reform and reaction in the first half of the 16th century. By means of pamphlets the fears and resentments, beliefs and values, self-interests and schemes that transformed German cities and towns were both expressed and aroused. The Reformation pamphlet did not only agitate; it also informed and instructed. It was an earnest lesson as well as propaganda, a careful justification of action as well as a call to arms.[14] The constructive, problem-solving side of pamphlets must not be lost amid their negative criticism. What has been said of the pamphlet dialogue can fairly by applied to the pamphlet literature generally:

> Here was true historical conflict, not fictional conflict, not the hypothetical problems of an exhausted spirituality or the harmless disputes over social rank that we find in medieval dialogues. The (Reformation) dialogue became instead *the* forum for resolving new, manifold, and true-to-life uncertainties that profoundly gripped peoples' lives. Here the new social conflicts of the age were fought through.[15]

Because Reformation pamphlets were tracts in defense of a cause, their trustworthiness as historical sources has understandably been questioned.[16] A dispassionate report was not the first concern of

---

[12]*Ein Christenliche Ordenung der Betler halben/uber den auffgerichten gemainen Kasten/in der Stadt Kitzingen zu Francken/am tag Martini angangen* (1523) [B.M. 8702.de.6].

[13]Gravier (1942), 174.

[14]Compare the pamphlets of the American Revolution: "For all their variety they have in common one distinctive characteristic: they are, to an unusual degree, *explanatory*. They reveal not merely positions taken but the reasons why positions were taken; they reveal motive and understanding: the assumptions, beliefs, and ideas that lay behind the manifest events of the time." *Pamphlets of the American Revolution 1750–1776*, I: 1750–65, ed. by Bernard Bailyn (Cambridge, 1965), vii.

[15]Lenk (1968), 13.

[16]As Ritter summarizes: "Seins- und Sollenszustand kann der spätere Betrachter nicht immer auseinanderhalten," Ritter (1970), 23.

pamphleteers. Their objective was to change (or preserve) society in certain fundamental ways. Care must be taken, therefore, to set each pamphlet within its historical context, to discover, so far as possible, the identity of its author and the circumstances of its publication. The difficult task before the student of pamphlets is to answer the following questions: Why at this particular time in this particular place did this particular individual or group write, publish, and/or circulate this particular pamphlet or series of pamphlets? As these questions are answered, we relive through pamphlets the arguments pro and con that helped prepare the way for (or frustrate) change at particular points in time.[17] In areas of Protestant success many pamphlets were the original forms of new secular laws and religious practices; as "propaganda" succeeded, it transformed itself into moral and religious ordinances whose enforcement brought about new patterns of behavior and created new institutions. As we succeed in locating pamphlets amid the events of their day, their initially troublesome self-interest and bias, far from disqualifying them as reliable historical sources, prove instead to reveal the essence of historical force.

Suspicion has also been cast on the usefulness of pamphlets as sources because of the high level of illiteracy in the 16th century. In Germany, where perhaps 95% of the population could not read, not only did pamphlets have a limited literate audience, but we cannot assume that those who did read them understood their message or, if they did, that they fully agreed with it.[18] This being the case, can we view pamphlets as revealing anything more than the minds of their authors?

Literacy may have been much higher throughout 16th century Germany than we have previously assumed.[19] Even so, illiteracy was not an insuperable obstacle to understanding the contents of vernacular pamphlets in an age still accustomed to communicate its *written* sources by proclamation and word of mouth in churches, on street corners, at the market place, and in pubs. Protestants urged their audiences to buy their own Bibles and advised the non-literate,

---

[17]"Les pamphlets nous mettent en contact immédiat avec les hommes et les faits. Ils nous donnent eux aussi l'impression d'une présence. Nous pouvons oublier les historiens et leur appreciations, les documents et les décisions impitoyables et injustes comme la lettre morte pour écouter les voix encore vivantes dans leurs appels chaleureux. . . . (Les pamphlets) traduisent avec fidelité les sentiments que nourrissait la foule allemande." Gravier (1942), 10.

[18]Scribner (1981).

[19]Strauss (1978), 200.

if need be, to hire students (usually for the fee of dinner) to read the Bible to them.[20] Also, the writing of pamphlets was not an idle pastime; local concerns and conflicts gave rise to their publication and, as we can confirm by such other contemporary sources as chronicles, letters, city ordinances, and popular broadsheets, pamphlets spoke to the needs and expectations of many in the communities in which they circulated.[21] In this sense pamphlets were commentaries on their times and reflections of the minds of their audience as well as agents of change.

This is not to deny that early modern communities were culturally and socially heterogeneous or to doubt that a pamphlet's audience was composed of active and critical readers. It is precisely the pamphlet's ability to penetrate such heterogeneity and individuality and discover the commonplaces within a community that makes it such an attractive source to the historian.

What Kind of Information do Pamphlets Convey?

What follows is a typology of pamphlets and the kinds of information they convey. In each case I have provided references to pamphlets that treat the topics in question and by their very titles in many instances focus the issues involved. For all but a few I have also given exact references to either a collection or library where these pamphlets may be found. While this information is intended to give the reader concrete and usable examples, what is here presented amounts to only a few hearty draughts from the great ocean of 16th century pamphlets.

A first category is pamphlets that address TRADITIONAL RELIGIOUS BELIEFS AND PRACTICES, both Protestant attacks upon them and Catholic defenses of them. This genre composes what might be called the "clamshells" of the pamphlet and tract literature of the early Reformation; they litter every shore of controversy in the 1520s, when religious issues seemed to rivet everyone's attention. From the Protestant side comes wave after wave of criticism attack-

---

[20]Johannes Römer concluded an anti-clerical dialogue with the advice: "Es ist mein radt/Welcher kein Bibel hat/Das er eyne überkum/Er sey latinisch oder ein stumm/ Unnd teglich darin lese." *Ein schöner Dialogus von den vier grözten Beschwernissen eines jeglichen Pfarrers* (1521) in Clemen (1907–11) III, 91.

[21]"Die spätmittelalterliche, deutschsprachige Kleinliteratur berücksichtigt die Disposition ihrer Adressaten, wenn sie in deren Bedürfnisstruktur und Erwartungshorizont hineinargumentiert, sich an deren Assoziationsspektrum orientiert und damit aktuelle Bewusstseinsinhalte der Zeit anspricht, aufnimmt und widerspiegelt," Tompert (1978), 211. See also Moeller (1981).

ing such traditional beliefs and practices as the sacrament of penance and confession,[22] indulgences,[23] confraternities,[24] masses, images, celibacy, fasting, saints, and religious holidays.[25] Catholic defenses of traditional beliefs and practices are far less numerous. This is due in part to the fact that the church did not initially take the Reformation with utmost seriousness; and, equally important, the orthodox position on these subjects was already known to the laity and tracts in its defense were not so interesting to them, hence less in demand and less financially rewarding to publishers. Still, pamphlets by Catholic apologists compose a sizable and still largely unanalyzed popular literature.[26]

A second category embraces the many varieties of ANTICLERICAL LITERATURE. One large, popular genre is the interrogation and correction of the clergy, especially monks, by earnest, Bible-wise

[22]Jacob Strauss, *Ein neüw wunderbarlich Beychtbüchlein/in dem die warhafft gerecht beycht und bussfertigkeit christenlichen gelert und angetzeygt wirt/und kürtzlichen alle tyranney erdychter menschlicher Beycht uffgehoben/zu seliger reüwe/frid und freüd der armen gefangen gewissenn* (1523) [OX-BOD T.L. 26.89].

[23]*Ein Dialogus oder Gespräch zwischen einem Vater und Sohn die Lehre Martini Luthers und sonst andere Sachen des Christlichen Glaubens belangend (1523)*, in Clemen (1907–11), 25–50.

[24]Jacob Strauss, *Underrict D. Jacob Straussen/wartzu die Bruderschaften nütz seyey/wie man sy bissher gehalten hat/und nun fürohin halten sol* (1522) [OX-BOD T.L. 22.107].

[25]The most comprehensive popular exposé of traditional religion from a Protestant point of view may be the series of eight pamphlet sermons by Heinrich von Kettenbach, published between 1522 and 1523, in Clemen, (1907–11). For range and consistency of such criticism compare the Protestant ordinance of Bern (6 pp.) with the reform program of Nürnberg's evangelical clerics (210 pp.): *Gemayn Reformation [der stat Bern]: und verbesserung der bisshergebrachten verwendten Gotsdiensten und Ceremonien/die neben dem wort Gottes/durch menschlich gutduncken nach und nach eingepflantzet/und durch des Bapstumbs hauffen tratzlich gehandthabet . . .* (1528) [B.M. 3906.bb.88]; *Ein Ratschlag/Den etliche Christenliche Pfarherren/Prediger/unnd andere/Götlicher schrifft verstendige/Einem Fürsten . . . gemacht haben* (Nürnberg, 1525) [OX-BOD Vet.Dle.138].

[26]On faith and works: Johann Dietenberger, *Der Leye. Obe der gelaub allein selig macht* (Strasbourg, 1524) [M.A. Pegg, *A Catalogue of German Reformation Pamphlets in the Libraries of Great Britain and Ireland* (Baden-Baden, 1973)—henceforth: Pegg—no. 6327], and Ulricus Burchardi, *Ain schöner lustiger Dialogus/von dem rechten waren glauben* (1525) [OX-BOD Vet.Dle.112(13)]; on penance and confession: Matthew Kretz, *Ain Sermon von der peicht* (1524) [OX-BOD T.L. 38.145]; on the priesthood; Johann Buchstab, *Das nit alle Christglöbige menschen gleich priester seyend* (Strasbourg, 1527) [Pegg, no. 386]; on the invocation of Mary and the saints: Johann Buchstab, *Von Fürbit der mutter gotesz Marie der lieben helgen und Englen Gottes* [Strasbourg, 1527] [Pegg, no. 390]; on purgatory: Matthew Kretz, *Ain Sermon/inhaltend etlich sprüch der schriff/von dem fegfewr* (1524) [OX-BOD T.L. 38.146]; on images, Hieronymus Emser, *Das man der heyligen bilder in den kirchen nit abthon soll* [Dresden, 1524] [Pegg. no. 752].

92 Reformation Europe

laity from all social ranks—peasants, burghers, and noblemen/ knights.[27] A related group of pamphlets compose the sometimes bitter, often hilarious satires on popes and clergy, a genre that includes so-called papal letters to and from the Devil; all-too-frank conversations between deceased popes now resident in hell; and caricatures which ascribe unflattering features of certain animals (especially wolves, foxes, and monkeys) to pontiffs both living and dead.[28] Then there are exposés of the cloistered life by actual and alleged renegade monks and nuns. Among the topics here debated is whether the nunnery really provided aristocratic and burgher women desirous of greater independence and power a more attractive option than a good marriage—not to mention the depiction of the home as a superior *religious* alternative to the cloister.[29] A final type of anti-clerical

[27]Hans Sachs, *Eyn gesprech von den Scheinwercken der Gaistlichen/und yhren gelubde* (1524), in *Flugschriften des frühen 16. Jahrhunderts, Microfiche Series 1978,* ed. by Han-Joachim Köhler (Zug, 1978)—henceforth: Tübingen Fiche—no. 592; Hans Staygmayer, *Ain schöner Dialogus oder Gesprech/von aynem Münch und Becken/wolcher die Oster ayer Samlen wollt* (Augsburg, 1524) [Tübingen Fiche, no. 981]; *Ayn freüntlichs gesprech/zwischen eynem Parfusser münch/auss der Provintz Osterreich/der Observantz/und einem Löffelmacher/mit namen Han Stöesser/gar lustig zu lesen* [1524] [OX-BOD T.L. 84.20]; *Eyn newer Dialogus oder gespräch/zwischen ainem verprenten/vertribnem Edelman und ainem Münch/Welchen am unrechsten geschech wann dieselben bayd vertriben/und die Münch Clöster auch verbrannt würden* [1524] [OX-BOD T.L. 83.197]; Han Herbst, *Eyn Brüderliche und Christenliche Heyliger geschrifft gegrundte ermanung/von einem unterthon und schefflin/Seynen Pastor oder pfarrhern zu geschickt/yn dem er jn seins pastor ampts erynnert/und seine schefflin mit dem wort gots zu weyden/und keyn taglöner an sein stadt zu stellen* (1524) [OX-BOD T.L. 37.142]; Wolfgang Zierer, *Ein Schöner Dialogus von einem Lantzknecht und prediger münich wie sy under wegen zu samen kommen synd und was sy mit einander geret haben* [1523] [B.M. T. 2209(14)]; *Beclagung eines Leyen genant Hanns Schwalb uber vil miszbrauchs christenlichs lebens* (1521), in Clemen (1907-11), 348-60.

[28]*Den grosmechtigisten Fürsten unnd herrn/herrn Luciffer/sampt gantzer Hellischer versamblung unsern gnadigisten herren/unnd Junckherrn* [Augsburg, 1521] [OX-BOD T.L. 10.114]; *Ain grosser Preiss so der Fürst der hellen genannt Lucifer yetzt den gaystlichen als Bäpst Bischoff Cardinel und der gleychen zu weysst und empeut . . .* [OX-BOD T.L. 10.115]; *Ein Kleglich gesprech Bapsts Leonis/und Bapsts Clementen/mit jrem Kemmerer/Cardinaln Spinola/in der Helle gehalten/den jetzigen Kirchenstand belangend* (1538) [OX-BOD T.L. 66.19]; Judas Nazarei, *Das Wolffgesang* (1522) [OX-BOD T.L. 28.108].

[29]Johann Eberlin von Günzburg, *Siben frum aber trostloss pfaffen klagen ire not, einer dem anderen . . .* (Basel, 1521) in *Eberlin von Günzburg, Sämtliche Schriften* II, 59-78; Johann Schevan, *Ein Sendbriff darinne er anzeigt aufs der Bibel und schrypfft/warumb er Barfusser orden des er etwan ym kloster zu Basell gewest verlassen* (Wittenberg, 1523) [OX-BOD T.L. 28.121]; *Anntwurt auf den sendbrieff/ainer vermainten gaistlichen klosterfrawen/der von Mariestain aussganngen/kloster leben und gelübdt/betreffende* (1524) [OX-BOD T.L. 38.159]; Johann of Schwartzenberg (and Andreas Osiander), *Ain schöner Sendtbrieff . . . Darinn (Johann of Schwartzenberg)*

pamphlet is the quasi-formal gravamina literature, which focuses a broad range of economic complaints against both high and low clergy.[30]

A third category of pamphlet literature embraces SOCIAL PROFILES AND COMMENTARY. Despite the often accompanying propaganda, polemic, and/or satire, pamphlets are also windows onto the social landscape of the 16th century. While much of the data here provided is also verifiable from other records, it can be argued that no other source gives so full and rich a picture of 16th century life. One rhymed social profile, for example, permits the following groups to complain about their lot (*stand*) in life: wives (about their husbands) and husbands (about their wives); prostitutes (about "secret whores", that is, housemaids and nuns); drunks (about the supply of wine); pilgrims; widows and orphans; subordinates (about their superiors); laity (about their canons); debtors (about the judge); workers; pastors (about their parishioners) and parishioners (about their pastors); workers (about merchants); Jews; and poets.[31] Hans Sachs, an unusually trustworthy commentator, details the moral and social problems of Nuremberg in pamphlets published in 1524. He describes the creation of monopolies; deceptive sales practices and pervasive use of false weights, measures, and accounting; the exploitation of workers by the commercial and publishing industries; high interest rates; the powerlessness of the poor before the law; and the greed of lawyers.[32] Eberlin von Günzburg

treffenliche und Christenliche ursachen anzaygt/wie und warum er seyn Tochter auss dem Closter daselbst (zum Hayligen Grab genannt) hinweg gefürt/und wider unter seyn vätterlichen schutz und ober handt zu sich genommen hat . . . (Nuremberg, 1524) [OX-BOD T.L. 38.170]; Bernard Rem, *Ain Sendtbrief an ettlich closterfrawen zu Sanct Katherina und zu Sanct Niclas in Augsburg* (Augsburg, 1523) [B.M. 3905.d.130]; *Antwurt zwayer Closter frawen im Katheriner Closter zu Augspurg/an Bernhart Remen/und hernach seyn gegen Antwurt* (Augsburg, 1523) [OX-BOD T.L. 31.183]; Florentina von Obern Weymar, *Ain Geschichte wie Got ainer Erbarn closter Junckfrawen aussgeholffen hatt* (Wittenberg, 1524) [OX-BOD T.L. 96.10]; Eberlin von Günzburg, *Ein vermanung aller christen das sie sich erbarmen uber die klosterfrawen*, in *Joh. Eberlin von Günzburg, Sämtliche Schriften* I, 25–30.

[30]*Teütscher nation beschwerd von den Geistlichen. Durch der Weltlichen Reichsständ/Fürsten und Herren Bapst Adriano schrifftlich überschickt nechst vergangenen Reichstag zu Nürenberg im xxii. jar angefangen und im xxiii. geendt* [1523] [OX-BOD T.L. 28.123]; *Beclagung teütscher Nation über die unbillichen beschwerd unnd bezwingknuss des Römischen stuls* [1526] [OX-BOD 47.50].

[31]*Clag etlicher stand/ganz kurtzweylig zulesen* [ca. 1520–21] [OX-BOD T.L. 83.9].

[32]*Ain Dialogus und Argument der Romanisten/wider das Christlich heüflein/den Geytz und ander offentlich laster betreffend* (Nürnberg, 1524) [Tübingen Fiche 592]. On Sachs' trustworthiness as a "historian," see Gravier (1942), 174.

describes the publishing industry's exploitation of religious conflict
and its often shoddy craftsmanship, providing a list of known books
to document his charges.[33] Pamphlet dialogues also discuss the social
consequences of Luther's teaching.[34]

Economic attitudes and practices also receive much direct commentary. A large pamphlet literature attacks "idleness," by which is
meant new forms of usurious loans and contracts, profiteering trade
and commerce, monopolizing and hoarding of staples like salt,
grain, and wine by shrewd purchase of futures, and generally all
business practices that permit individuals and groups, both clergy
and laity, to live off the sweat of others purely by economic manipulation.[35] The legality and propriety of paying tithes (and giving
alms) to clergy and magistrates is another much discussed pamphlet
topic in areas where the Reformation succeeded.[36] We also find
pamphlets proposing ways to justify the usurpation and redirection
of endowments originally given for Catholic masses, churches, and
monasteries—a problem not only for cities and territories in the
wake of the collapse of episcopal jurisdiction, but also for new Prot-

[33]*Mich wundert das kein gelt ihm land ist*, in *Sämtliche Schriften* III, 161–63.

[34]*Hüpsch argument red fragen und antwort Dreyer personen Nemlichen ains Curti-sanen aines Edelmans und aines Burgers. Nit allain kürtzweylig Sunder vast nutzlich zu lesen und zu heren Alles D.M.L. leer betreffent* [OX-BOD Vet.Dle.111(2)].

[35]Eberlin von Günzburg, *Mich wundert das kein gelt im land ist*, 158–60; Wilhelm Linck, *Von Arbeyt und Betteln wie man solle der faulheyt vorkommen/unde yeder-man zu Arbeyt ziehen* (Zwickau, 1523 [B.M.], *Von der falschen Betler büeberey/Mit einer Vorrede M. Luther* (Wittenberg, 1528) [OX-BOD T.L.102.6]—a description of 26 different species of undeserving "beggars"; Jacob Strauss, *Haubtstuck und Artickel Christenlicher leer wider den unchristlichen wucher* (1523) [OX-BOD T.L. 27.94] *Ein hupsch new gespräch/von den unersetlichen Hewschrecken . . . welcher zu dieser un-serer zeit/Stet/Land/Richs Arms/grüns und dürs/vil mehr den Pharaonis Hewschreck-en auffressen/und mit der wurtzeln verderbt* (1523) [B.M. 11515.aa.12].

[36]Caspar Hedio, *Von dem Zehenden zwu träffliche Predig* (1525) [OX-BOD T.L. 43.79]; Johannes Lansperger, *Ain nutzlicher Sermon: dem gemaynen volck/von der lieben Gottes/und des nächsten/nach rechtem verstand des nattürlichen gesetz/und der wort Christi/das jr wölt das euch die menschen thund/solt jr jnen auch thun Auch wie man den Zehenden gehen/und wer jn nemen soll . . .* (1524) [OX-BOD T.L.37.142]; Otto Brunfels, *Von dem Pfaffen Zehenden/Hundert unnd zwen und fyertzig Schluss reden* [Strasbourg, 1524] [OX-BOD T.L. 11.141]; Andreas Keller, *Von dem Zehen-den, Was darvon usz der schrifft zu halten sey* (1525) [B.M.]; Wilhelm Linck, *Ob die Geystlichen auch schuldig sein Zinsse, geschoss, etc. zugeben und andere gemeyne bürde mit zutragen* (Aldenburgk) [B.M.]; Andreas Osiander, *Ain schone, fast nutz-liche Sermon/uber das Ewangelion Matthei am 17. Da Christus den Zollpfenning bezalet* (Nuremberg, 1525) [OX-BOD T.L. 42.58]; *Hie mügt jr Christen wol verston/ wie man mit uns yetz umb ist gon/underm schein des Almusen zwar/hat man uns betrogen lange jar* [OX-BOD T.L. 83.1]; Casper Adler, *Von Allmosen geben/Eyn Ser-mon* (Nuremberg, 1533) [OX-BOD T.L. 60.13].

estants whose parents had written their last wills and testaments as good Catholics.[37]

Pamphlets also discuss a broad range of personal moral problems, among them gluttony and drunkenness; pride and presumption in dress (social climbing by apparently widespread transgression of sumptuary laws); profiteering in one's trade; and "fleshly" license.[38] An enormous literature discusses the personal and social evils of alcoholism, perhaps the most often condemned personal vice.[39] The dangers of dancing, especially by the young as a prelude to sexual immorality—what Melchior Ambach describes as sex-crazed dancing in which genitals are exposed[40]—receive attention. Although their extreme polemic and didacticism qualifies their usefulness, pamphlet "histories" and "newspapers" also abound to report the practices of "outgroups" like the Anabaptists of Münster.[41]

A fourth type of pamphlet is devoted to MARRIAGE AND FAMILY. Protestant pamphleteers not only defended clerical marriage against celibacy; they also esteemed the estate of secular marriage and defended it against the ridicule and even horror with which some contemporary authors depicted it.[42] By rejecting the legality of

[37]Wilhelm Linck, *Ein Christlich bedenckenn . . . Von den Testamenten der sterbenden Menschen. Wie di geschehen unnd voltzogen werden sollen noch götlichen gesetz* (Zwickaw, 1524) [B.M.].

[38]Michael Höfer, *Wes man sich in diesen gefährlichen Zeyten halten/und wie man dem zorn Gottes/so über die Welt entzünet ist/zuvor kommen soll/Auch was die ursach solches zorns sey* (1546) [OX-BOD T.L. 75.26].

[39]Sebastian Franck, *Vonn dem grewlichen laster der trunckenheit . . . was füllerey/sauffen und zutrincken/für jamer und unradt/schaden der seel und des leibs/auch armut und schedlich not anricht/und mit sich bringt . . .* (1528) [OX-BOD T.L. 57.23]; *Vormanung aus unsers gnedigsten herrn des Chürfursten zu Sachssen befehl/gestellet/durch die prediger zuvorlesen/widder Gotslesterung und füllerey* (Wittenberg, 1531) [OX-BOD T.L. 106.7]; Jacob Schenck, *S. Paulus Spruch . . . Sauffet euch nicht vol Weins/Daraus ein unordig wesen folget . . .* (Wittenberg, 1540) [OX-BOD T.L. 67.7]; Melchior Ambach, *Von Zusauffen und Trunckenheit/sampt iren schönen frücten . . .* (Frankfurt, 1544) [B.M. 3907.bb.10(2)]—a medley of biblical and patristic sources; *Von Zutruncken Laster unnd missbrauch die schentlichen darauss Erfolgen/Darmit yetz die gantz Teütsch Nation befleckt ist* (1523) [B.M.3906.g.41].

[40]Melchoir Ambach, *Von Tantzen/Urtheil/Auss heiliger Shrifft/und den alten Christlichen Lerern gestelt* (Frankfurt, 1544) [B.M.3907.bb.10(3)].

[41]Titles in Vogler, (1981).

[42]Thomas Stör, *Der Ehelich standt von Got mit gebenedeyung auffesetzt/soll umb schwärhait wegen der seltzsamen gaben der Junckfrawschafft yederman frey sein/und niemant verboten werden* (1524) [OX-BOD T.L. 37.122]; Leonard Culman, *Jungen gesellen/Jungkfrauwen und Witwen/so Ehelich wöllen werden/zu nutz ein unterrichtung/wie sie sich in ehelichen stand richten sollen* (Augsburg, 1568; first published, 1534) [B.M. 8416.22.34]; Caspar Gütell, *Uber das Evangelion Johannis . . . Eyn Sermon dem Ehlichen standt fast freudsam und nützlich* (1534) [OX-BOD T.L. 39.178].

clandestine marriages (the secret exchange of vows and sexual con-
summation at a couple's own or "God's" initiative) and requiring the
presence of credible witnesses and parental permission (at least up to
age 19) for a valid marriage, the Reformation placed marriage on a
surer legal foundation.[43] Protestant moralists also offered newly-
weds much advice and counsel on what constituted a good marriage
and family life. Pamphlets abound on the proper relationship between the spouses and between parents and children—what husbands owe wives, wives husbands, parents children, and children
parents.[44]

A fifth category of pamphlet embraces instructions by both magistrates and clergy on THE PROPER RELATIONSHIP BETWEEN
"CHURCH" AND "STATE," in particular the nature of civic duty
and the circumstances under which Christian subjects may resist
tyrannical higher authority. These were topics debated at length by
the jurists and theologians of Saxony and Hesse in the 1520s when
the Emperor threatened force against the Lutherans, and they were
rehashed in pamphlets and tracts with each recurring confrontation
down to the *Interim* (1548) and *Magdeburg Bekenntnis* (1550).[45]

---

[43]Johann Brentz, *Wie in Ehesachen/und inn den fellen/so sich derhalben/zu tragen/
nach Götlichen billichen Rechten/Christenlich zu handeln sey* (Wittenberg, 1531)
[OX-BOD T.L. 57.33].

[44]Justus Menius, *Erinnerung wass denen so sich inn Ehestand begeben zu bedencken
sey* (Wittenberg, 1528) [OX-BOD T.L. 51.13]; ibid., *An die hochgeborne Fürstin/
fraw Sibilla Herzogin zu Sachsen/Oeconomia Christiana/das ist von Christlicher Hauss-
haltung* (Nürnberg, 1530) [OX-BOD T.L. 106.21]; Wolfgang Russ, *Der Weiber
geschefft. Ausslegung des ain und dreissigten Capitels/der Spruchen Salomonis/was ein
redlich dapffer weib sey . . .* (1533) [B.M. 3165. ccc.41]; Caspar Cruciger, *Ausle-
gung/uber St. Paulus spruch zum Timotheo/Wie die Eheweiber selig werden . . .* (Erfurt, 1538) [OX-BOD T.L. 112.7]; Veit Dietrich, *Von der Kinder zucht . . .* (Nürnberg, 1546) in Oskar Reichmann, ed. *Etliche Schrifften für den gemeinen man/von
unterricht Christlicher lehr und leben/unnd zum trost der engstigen gewissen. Durch
V. Dietrich,* (Assen, 1972) 115–21.

[45]Scheible (1969); Wolfgang Kisswetter, *Eyn bevelhe des Churfurstenn von Sachssen
und Hertzog Johann Fridrichs/Wie sich die priesterschafft in yrn F.G. Furstenthumb
und landen halten solle/mit verkundung des heiligenn wort gottis* (1525) [OX-BOD
T.L. 43.90]; *Eyn Christenlicher Ratschlag unnd untterrichtung/welcher gestalt sich
alle Christenliche personen von Obern unnd unterthanen halten sollen* (1526) [OX-
BOD T.L. 47.42]—a Lutheran response to the Diet of Speyer; Philip Melanchthon,
*Das die Fürsten aus Gottes bevell und gebot schuldig sind/bey iren unterthanen abgöt-
terey unrechte Gottes dienst und false lehre abzuthun/und dagegen rechte Gottes dinst
und rechte Christliche lehr uff zu richten* (Wittenberg, 1540) [B.M. 1568/4319];
*Bekentnis, Unterricht und Vermanung der Pfarrherrn und Prediger der Christlichen
Kirchen zu Magdeburgk* (1550) in Friedrich Hortleder, *Handlungen und
Ausschreiben . . . des Teutschen Kriegs Karl V* (Gotha, 1615), IV/7; *Grundlicher
Bericht aus heiliger schrifft/wie ferne man den oberherrn/gehorsam schüldig/auch
wer/wie/unnd in welcherey fellen/man den verderblichen Tyrannen/möge widerstand
thun . . .* (1522) [B.M.3906.bb.91].

A sixth type of Reformation pamphlet was occasioned by PEAS-ANT PROTEST AND REVOLT in the mid-1520s. These pamphlets present both justifications and more frequently condemnations of the economic and political demands of German peasants. They are presently receiving a great deal of scholarly attention because of the intense interest of social historians and Marxists in such events.[46]

A final pamphlet category is CHRISTIAN MIRRORS, actually polemical catechisms for the laity that contain not only detailed theological and moral instruction, but also practical household advice. Such works grew in number and size after 1530 when successful Protestants began to consolidate their gains, and when confessional differences with Catholics as well as those between competing Protestant groups themselves hardened and became irreconcilable. Such "mirrors" exist both for adults[47] and for children.[48]

Although they do not represent a formal category, the illustrated title pages of pamphlets and the illustrations that occasionally appear within them also constitute an important source for art historians and historians with special interest in communication and propaganda. The related single broad sheet and cartoon, which often bear rhymed messages or ballooned comments, provide a still richer source.[49]

Aids for Pamphlet Research

German pamphlet research has been made easier by the new bib-

---

[46]Sebastian Lotzer, *Entschuldigung ainer Frummer Christlichen Gemain zu Memmingen* (1525), in *Sebastian Lotzers Schriften*, ed. by Alfred Goetze (Leipzig, 1902); *Ain nutzlicher Dialogus oder gesprechbüchlein zwischen ainem Münzerischen Schwermer und ainen Evangelischen frümen Bauern/Die straff der auffrürischen Schwermer zu Franckenhausen geschlagen/gelangende* (1525) [OX-BOD T.L. 44.95]; Laube and Seiffert (1975).

[47]Eberlin von Günzburg, *Ein schoner spiegel eins christlichen Lebens (1524)*, in *Sämtliche Werke* III, 98–106; Johann Spangenberg, *Vom Christlichen Ritter; Mit was Feinden er kempffen mus* (Wittenberg, 1543) [OX-BOD T.L. 117.10b]—a work so popular and effective that a Catholic "counter-catechism" was strategically written in imitation of it: Jaspar Gennep, *Catholischer Spangenbergischer Catechismus für die jungen Christen* (Cologne, 1561) [OX-BOD 1.C.252]; Antonius Corvinus, *Bericht/wie sich ein Edelman/gegen Gott/gegen seine elteren/weib/kinder/hausgesinde und seine untersassen halten sol/An den Merkischen/Lünenburgischen/Braunschweigischen/und allen Sechsischen Adel geschrieben* (Erfurt, 1539) [B.M. 698.e.22(5)].

[48]*Ain schöne Fräg und Antwurt den jungen kündern. Zu underweysen/got zuerkennen/auch in anruffen als ain vatter. Den jungen vast nützlich zu lernen* (1523) [B.M. 3504.c.6]—this is the so-called "Catechism of the (Bohemian) Brethren;" Johann Moeckard, *Ain Christliche einfältige/und zu dieser zeit seer notwendige ermanung/an die jugent/darinnen angezaigt wirdt was Kinder iren Eltern zuthun schuldig seind* (Augsburg, 1550) [OX-BOD T.L. 81.5].

[49]The possibilities are clear in Geisberg (1974), Hoffmann (1978), and Saxl (1957).

liographical aids and editions which appear below in the appended bibliographies. Two should be singled out as being especially helpful to the Anglo-American scholar. The first is the catalogue of pamphlets in the libraries of Great Britain and Ireland prepared by M.A. Pegg. Here one finds comparatively full titles, so that content can often be surmised, and actual, probable, or possible authors and places and dates of publication, in addition to each pamphlet's location in one or more libraries. Especially rich in German pamphlet literature is the Bodleian library, whose collection of well over two thousand pamphlets is available in volumes that usually contain five to ten pamphlets each, bound together according to year of publication and often by topic.

The second outstanding aid is the microfiche series presently being edited by Tübingen historians. To date this edition has published approximately 1500 pamphlets on microfiche and plans in coming years to make available all German and Latin pamphlets published in the Holy Roman Empire between 1501 and 1530—in excess of 5,000 pamphlets—with detailed bibliographical information including summaries of the contents of each pamphlet.[50] The project's publisher, the Swiss Inter-Documentation Company, also has in progress full collections of Dutch, Mennonite, and Reformed pamphlets (see bibliography below).

Bibliography

1. Pamphlet Collections and Editions

Augustijn, C., ed., *Dutch Pamphlets ca. 1486-1648. Section I: The Collection in the Royal Library, The Hague, on Microfiche* (Zug, 1979-).

Balke, Willem, et al., eds., *Reformed Protestantism: Sources of the Sixteenth and Seventeenth Centuries on Microfiche* (Zug, 1979-).

Berger, Arnold, ed., *Satirische Feldzüge wider die Reformation: Thomas Murner und Daniel von Soest* (Leipzig, 1933).

———, *Die Schaubühne im Dienste der Reformation*, I–II (Leipzig, 1935-36).

---

[50]Köhler, et al., *Bibliographie* (1978). Indexes accompany the microfiche.

———, *Lied-Spruch- und Fabeldichtung im Dienste der Reformation* (Leipzig, 1938).

———, *Die Sturmtruppen der Reformation. Flugschriften der Jahre 1520–25* (Darmstadt, 1964).

Clemen, Otto, ed., *Flugschriften aus den ersten Jahren der Reformation, I–IV* (Leipzig, 1907–11).

———, *Flugschriften aus der Reformationszeit in Faksimiledrucken. Neue Folge der Flugschriften aus den ersten Jahren der Reformation* (Leipzig, 1921–22).

Enders, Ludwig, ed., *Johann Eberlin von Günzburg. Sämtliche Werke*, I–III (Halle, 1896–).

Franz, Günther, ed., *Quellen zur Geschichte des Bauernkrieges* (Darmstadt, 1963).

Goedeke, Karl, ed., *Pamphilus Gengenbach* (Hannover, 1865).

Goetze, Alfred, ed., *Sebastian Lotzers Schriften* (Leipzig, 1902).

Greving, Joseph von, ed., *Corpus Catholicorum. Werke Katholischer Schriftsteller im Zeitalter der Glaubensspaltung*, I– (Münster i.W., 1919–).

Horst, Irvin B., ed., *The Radical Reformation Microfiche Project: Section I: Mennonite and Related Sources up to 1600* (Zug, 1977–).

Kaczerowsky, K., *Flugschriften des Bauernkrieges* (Hamburg, 1970).

Keller, A. von, & Goetze, E., eds., *Hans Sachs*, I–XXVI (Tübingen, 1870–1908).

Köhler, Hans-Joachim, ed., *Flugschriften des frühen 16. Jahrhunderts. Microfiche Serie 1978* (Zug, 1978–).

Kück, Eduard, ed., *Die Schriften Hartmuths von Cronberg* (Halle, 1899).

Laube, Adolf, & Seiffert, Hans W., *Flugschriften des Bauernkriegszeit* (Berlin, 1975).

Lenk, Werner, ed., *Die Reformation im Zeitgenössischen Dialog* (Berlin, 1968).

Reichmann, Oskar, ed., *Etliche Schrifften für den gemeinen mann . . . Durch V. Dietrich* (Assen, 1972).

Schade, Oskar, ed., *Satiren und Pasquille aus der Reformationszeit* I–III (Hanover, 1856–63).

Scheible, Heinz, ed., *Das Widerstandsrecht als Problem der deutschen Protestanten 1523–1546* (Gutersloh, 1969).

Schottenloher, Karl, ed., *Flugschriften zur Ritterschaftsbewegung des Jahres 1523* (Münster, 1929).

Schulz, Franz, & Bebermeyer, G., eds., *Thomas Murners deutsche Schriften* I–IX (Berlin/Leipzig/Strasbourg, 1918–31) [VI–VIII contain writings against the Reformation].

Zober, E., ed., *Spottlieder der evangelischen Stralsunder auf die romischkatholische Priesterschaft aus den Jahren 1524–27* (Stralsund, 1855).

2. Bibliographies of German Pamphlets and Tracts

Benzing, Josef, *Ulrich von Hutten und seine Drucker* (Wiesbaden, 1956).

――――, *Lutherbibliographie* (Baden-Baden, 1965).

Claus, Helmut, *Der deutsche Bauernkrieg im Druckschaffen der Jahre 1524–26: Verzeichnis der Flugschriften und Dichtungen* (Gotha, 1975).

Edmond, J.P., *Catalogue of a Collection of 1500 Tracts by Martin Luther and His Contemporaries 1511–1598* (New York, 1964).

Freys, E., and Barge, H., *Verzeichnis der gedruckten Schriften des Andreas Bodenstein von Karlstadt* (Niewkoop, 1965).

Geisenhof, Georg, *Bibliotheca Bugenhagiana. Bibliographie der Druckschriften des D. Johann Bugenhagen* (Nieuwkoop, 1963).

Hinz, James A., *A Handlist of the Printed Books in the Simmlerische Sammlung, Sixteenth Century Bibliography*, 6–7 (St. Louis, 1975).

Holzberg, Niklas, *Hans-Sachs-Bibliographie* (1976).

Hohenemser, Paul, *Flugschriftensammlung Gustav Freytag* (Hildesheim, 1966).

Köhler, Hans-Joachim, et al., *Bibliographie der deutschen und lateinischen Flugschriften des frühen 16. Jahrhunderts. Probedruck zur Erläuterung der Konzeption eines laufenden Forschungsprojekts* (Tübingen, 1978).

Köhler, W., *Bibliographia Brentiana* (Berlin, 1904).

Kuczynski, Arnold, *Thesaurus libellorum historiam Reformationis illustrantium. Verzeichnis einer Sammlung von nahezu 3000 Flugschriften Luthers und seiner Zeitgenossen* (Nieuwkoop, 1960).

Lorz, J., ed., *Bibliographia Linckiana. Gedruckte Schriften 1483–1547* (Nieuwkoop, 1977).

Pegg, M.A., *A Catalogue of German Reformation Pamphlets (1516–*

1546) in the Libraries of Great Britain and Ireland (Baden-Baden, 1973).

Panzer, Georg Wolfgang, *Annalen der älteren deutschen Literatur,* I–II (Hildesheim, 1961).

Ritter, Francois, *Repertoire bibiographique des livres imprime en Alsace,* 1–4– (Strasbourg, 1937–60).

Roloff, Hans-Gert, *Die, deutsche Literatur. Biographisches und bibliographisches Lexikon. II: Die deutsche Literatur zwischen 1450 und 1620* (Bern, 1978–).

Schottenloher, Karl, *Bibliographie zur deutschen Geschichte im Zeitalter der Glaubensspaltung 1517–85,* I–VII (Stuttgart, 1956–66).

Short-Title Catalogue of Books Printed in German-Speaking Countries and German Books Printed in Other Countries 1455–1600 Now in the British Museum (London, 1962).

Sixteenth Century Bibliography, 2: Early 16th Century Roman Catholic Theologians and the German Reformation: A Finding List of Center for Reformation Research Holdings (St. Louis, 1975); *12–19: The Center for Reformation Research Microfilm Holdings From All Periods: A General Finding List* (St. Louis, 1977–1979).

Stupperich, Robert, *Bibliographia Bucerana* (Gütersloh, 1952).

Weller, Emil, *Repertorium typographicum. Die deutsche Literatur im ersten Viertel des 16. Jahrhunderts* (Hildesheim, 1961).

———, *Der Volksdichter Hans Sachs und seine Dichtungen. Eine Bibliographie* (Wiesbaden, 1966).

Wolf, Gustav, *Quellenkunde der deutschen Reformationsgeschichte* I–III (Gotha/Stuttgart, 1915–23).

3. Secondary Studies

Balzar, Bernd, *Bürgerliche Reformationspropaganda. Die Flugschriften des Hans Sachs in den Jahren 1523–1525* (Stuttgart, 1973).

Baur, August, *Deutschland in den Jahren 1517–1525 betrachtet im Lichte gleichzeitiger anonymer und pseudonymer deutscher Volks- und Flugschriften* (Ulm, 1872).

Behrend, Fritz, "Die literarische Form der Flugschriften," *Zentralblatt für Bibliothekswesen* 34 (1917): 23–34.

Bezzel, Irmgard, "Das Verzeichnis der im deutschen Sprachbereich erschienenen Drucke des 16. Jahrhunderts. Ein bibliographisches Unternehmen in München und Wolfenbüttel," *Zeitschrift für Bibliothekswesen und Bibliographie* 21 (1974), 177–85.

Blochwitz, Gottfried, "Die antirömischen deutschen Flugschriften der frühen Reformationszeit (bis 1522) in ihrer religiössittlichen Eigenart," *ARG* 27 (1930): 145–254.

Böckmann, Paul, "Der gemeine Mann in den Flugschriften der Reformationszeit," *Deutsche Vierteljahrschrift für Literaturwissenschaft und Geistesgeschichte* 22 (1944): 187–230.

Bohnstedt, John W., *The Infidel Scourge of God: The Turkish Menace as Seen by German Pamphleteers of the Reformation Era* (Philadelphia, 1968).

Brunner, Horst, and Hirschmann, G., eds., *Hans Sachs und Nürnberg. Bedingungen und Probleme reichsstädtischer Literatur: Hans Sachs zum 400. Todestag* (Nürnberg, 1976).

Cohn, Henry, "Anticlericalism in the German Peasants War," *Past and Present* 83 (1979): 3–31.

Cole, Richard, "The Pamphlet and Social Forces in the Reformation," *Lutheran Quarterly* 17 (1975).

––––––, "The Reformation in Print: German Pamphlets and Propaganda," *ARG* 66 (1975): 93–102.

Dannenbauer, H., *Luther als religiöser Schriftsteller 1517–1520* (Tübingen, 1930).

Dickens, A.G., *The German Nation and Martin Luther* (London, 1974).

Febvre, Lucien, and Martin, H.-J., *L'apparition du livre* (Paris, 1974).

Fehr, Hans, "Massenkunst im 16. Jahrhundert-Flugblätter aus der Sammlung Wickiana," in *Denkmale der Volkskunst*, I (Berlin, 1924).

Geisberg, Max, *The German Single-Leaf Woodcut: 1500–1550*, I–IV, rev. and ed. by Walter L. Strauss (New York, 1974).

Goetze, Alfred, *Die hochdeutschen Drucker der Reformationszeit* (Strasbourg, 1905).

––––––, "Urban Rhegius als Satiriker," *Zeitschrift für deutsche Philologie* 37 (1905): 66–113.

Gravier, Maurice, *Luther et l'opinion publique. Essai sur la littérature satirique et polémique en langue allemand pendant les années decisives de la Réforme (1520–30)* (Paris, 1942).

Grossmann, Maria, "Wittenberg Printing, Early 16th Century" in

Sixteenth Century Essays and Studies (St. Louis, 1970).

Hirsch, Rudolf, *Printing, Selling, and Reading 1450–1550* (Wiesbaden, 1974).

Hoffmann, Konrad, "Typologie, Exemplarik and reformatorische Bildsatire," in *Kontinuität und Umbruch. Theologie und Frömmigkeit in Flugschriften und Kleinliteratur an der Wende vom 15. zum 16. Jahrhundert*, ed. by Josef Nolte, et al. (Stuttgart, 1978), pp. 189–221.

Holborn, Louise W., "Printing and the Growth of a Protestant Movement in Germany From 1517 to 1524," *Church History* 11 (1942): 123–37.

Huhndorf, G., *Publizistische Kleindrucke in England vor 1558* (Diss., Münster, 1959).

Humbel, Frida, *Ulrich Zwingli und seine Reformation im Spiegel der gleichzeitigen schweizerischen volkstümlichen Literatur* (Leipzig, 1912).

Jedin, Hubert, "Die geschichtliche Bedeutung der katholischen Kontroversliteratur im Zeitalter der Glaubensspaltung," *Historisches Jahrbuch* 53 (1933): 70–79.

Kalkoff, Paul, *Die Reformation in der Reichsstadt Nürnberg nach den Flugschriften ihres Ratsschreibers Lazarus Spengler* (Halle, 1926).

Köhler, Hans-Joachim, "Die Flugschriften. Versuch der Präzisierung eines geläufigen Begriffs," in *Festgabe für Ernst Walter Zeeden zum 60. Geburtstage*, ed. by Horst Rabe, et al. (Münster, Westf. 1976), 36–61.

———, "Fragestellungen und Methoden zur Interpretation frühneuzeitlicher Flugschriften. Forschungsergebnisse und -desiderate," in Hans-Joachim Köhler, ed., *Flugschriften als Massenmedium der Reformationszeit. Beiträge zum Tübinger Symposion vom März 1980 (Spätmittelalter und Frühe Neuzeit, 13)* (Stuttgart, 1981): 1–280.

Könneker, B., "Die deutsche Literatur im Zeitalter des Humanismus und der Reformation," in *Neues Handbuch der Literaturwissenschaft*, X, ed. by A. Buck (1972): 145–176.

Koloziej, Ingeborg, *Die Flugschriften aus den ersten Jahren der Reformation (1517–1525)* (Diss., Berlin, 1956).

Kramer, L., *Die Publizistik der alten Lehre während der Reformationszeit* (Diss., Berlin, 1941).

Laube, Adolf, "Zur Rolle sozialökonomischer Fragen in frühreformatorischen Flugschriften," in Köhler (1981): 205–24.

Legge, Theodor, *Flug- und Streitschriften der Reformationszeit in Westfalen (1523–83)* (Münster, 1933).

Lucke, Wilhelm, "Deutsche Flugschriften aus den ersten Jahren der Reformation," *Deutsche Geschichtsblätter* 9 (1908): 183–205.

Lucke, Peter, *Gewalt und Gegengewalt in den Flugschriften der Reformation* (Göppingen, 1974).

Moeller, Bernd, "Stadt und Buch. Bemerkungen zur Struktur der reformatorischen Bewegung in Deutschland," in Wolfgang J. Mommsen, ed., *Stadtbürgertum und Adel in der Reformation. Studien zur Sozialgeschichte der Reformation in England und Deutschland* (Stuttgart, 1979): 25–39; "Predigten in reformatorischen Flugschriften," in Köhler (1981): 261–68.

Münch, Jette, *Die sozialen Anschauungen des Hans Sachs in seinem Fastnachtspielen* (Diss., Erlangen, 1936).

Needon, Heinrich, *Technik und Stil der Reformationsdialoge* (Diss., Greifswald, 1922).

Niemann, Gottfried, *Die Dialogliteratur der Reformationszeit . . . Eine literarhistorische Studie* (Diss., Leipzig/Berlin, 1905).

Oberman, Heiko A., "Zwischen Agitation und Reformation—Die Flugschriften als 'Judenspiegel'," in Köhler (1981): 269–90.

Ozment, Steven, "The Social History of the Reformation: What Can We Learn From Pamphlets?" in Köhler (1981): 171–204.

Praschinger, I., *Beiträge zur Flugschriften literatur der Reformation und Gegenreformation in Wien und dem Lande Oesterreich unter der Enns* (Diss., Vienna, 1958).

Radlkofer, Max, *Johann Eberlin von Günzburg* (Nördlingen, 1887).

Riggenbach, Bernard, *Johann Eberlin von Günzburg und sein Reform-program* (Tübingen, 1974).

Ritter, Suzanne, *Die kirchenkritische Tendenz in den deutschsprachigen Flugschriften der frühen Reformationszeit* (Diss., Tübingen, 1970).

Saxl, Fritz, "A Spiritual Encyclopedia of the Later Middle Ages," *Journal of the Warburg and Courtauld Institutes*, 5 (1942): 82–142.

_____, "Illustrated Pamphlets of the Reformation," in *Lectures*, I (London, 1957).

Schafarschik, W., *Studien zu Dialogflugschriften der frühen Reformationszeit* (Diss., Tübingen, 1978).

Schaller, Heinrich, "Parodie und Satire der Renaissance und Reformation," *Forschungen und Fortschritte* 33 (1959).

Scharfe, S., *Religiöse Bildpropaganda der Reformationszeit* (Göttingen, 1951).

Scheible, Heinz, "Reform, Reformation, Revolution: Grundsätze zur Beurteilung der Flugschriften," *ARG* 65 (1974): 108–34.

Schottenloher, Karl, *Flugblatt und Zeitung. Ein Wegweiser durch das gedruckte Tagesschrifftum* (Berlin, 1922).

Schutte, Jürgen, 'Schympf red'. Frühformen burgerlicher Agitation in Thomas Murners 'Grossen Lutherischen Narren' (1522) (Stuttgart, 1973).

Scribner, Robert, "Flugblatt und Analphabetentum. Wie kam der gemeiner Mann zu reformatorischen Ideen?" in Köhler (1981): 65–76.

Stopp, F.J., "Reformation Satire in Germany," *Oxford German Studies*, 3 (1968): 53–68.

Strauss, Gerald, *Luther's House of Learning: Indoctrination of the Young in the German Reformation* (Baltimore, 1978).

Tompert, Hella, "Die Flugschrift als Medium religiöser Publizistik. Aspekte der gegenwartigen Forschung," in *Kontinuität und Umbruch. Theologie und Frömmigkeit in Flugschriften und Kleinliteratur an der Wende vom 15. zum 16. Jahrhundert*, ed. by Josef Nolte, et al. (Stuttgart, 1978).

Uhrig, Kurt, "Der Bauer in der Publizistik der Reformation," *ARG* 33 (1936): 70–125, 165–225.

Vogler, Gunther, "Das Taüferreich zu Münster im Spiegel der Flugschriften," in Köhler (1981): 309–52.

Volz, Hans, *Bibel und Bibeldruck in Deutschland im 15. und 16. Jahrhundert* (Mainz, 1960).

Weller, Emil, *Die ersten deutschen Zeitungen* (Hildesheim, 1962).

Wedler, Klaus, "Klassenkampf und Bündnisproblematik in den Flugschriften, Fastnachtspielen und Zeitgedichten des Hans Sachs," in G. Hertz, et al., eds. *Der Bauer im Klassenkampf. Studien zur Geschichte des deutschen Bauernkriegs* (Berlin, 1975), 203–32.

Werner, H., *Die Flugschrift Onus ecclesiae (1519) mit einem Anhang über sozial- und kirchenpolitischen Prophetien: Ein Beitrag zur Sitten- und Kulturgeschichte des ausgehenden Mittelalters* (Giessen, 1901).

The German Peasants' War

Robert W. Scribner

In the past decade, research on the German Peasants' War has made perhaps the most remarkable progress of any subject in sixteenth-century German history.[1] This was evident in work commemorating the 450th anniversary of the war in 1975, and some of the approaches advanced then and since are so innovative that they still require rigorous testing by further research.[2] In reviewing recent scholarship, we shall also be setting out questions and hypotheses that will shape studies in the coming decade.

A springboard for much recent work has been provided by two older interpretations. Günther Franz's general history of the Peasants' War, first published in 1933 and in its eleventh edition by 1977, has dominated Western scholarship for almost half a century, challenged only by the school of socialist historiography represented from the 1950s onwards by the historians of the German Democratic Republic.[3] Franz saw the Peasants' War essentially as a political struggle in which socio-economic grievance played little real role. It was caused by attempts to extend princely and seigneurial control over the peasantry by means of new or modified taxes, forms of tenure or servitude backed up by seigneurial law (*Herrschaftsrecht*).

---

[1] The literature on the German Peasants' War is now immense, and the references given here represent only a small sample of recent work. For works since 1974 consult Thomas (1976). Attention is also drawn to the following critical reviews of recent work on the Peasants' War: Midelfort (1978), Press (1975, 1978), Sabean (1976), Scribner (1977), Stalnaker (1975), and Scott (1979), by far the best of these.

[2] See the collections published to celebrate the anniversary: Bak (1975), Blickle (1975a), Moeller (1975), Oberman (1974), Wehler (1975), Wohlfeil (1975), Wollbrett (1975); from the GDR: Brendler and Laube (1977), Heitz et al. (1975), Steinmetz et al. (1976), Strobach (1975) and the special issue of *Jahrbuch für Regionalgeschichte* 5 (1975). A translated selection of the best of these is Scribner and Benecke (1979), the most effective introduction to the subject.

[3] For a bibliography of Marxist work since 1945, see Steinmetz (1980), Volz and Brather (1975), Wohlfeil (1972, 1975). For the best non-Marxist assessment of the GDR position, see Foschepot (1976) and Wohlfeil (1982), 169–199.

Peasant resistance took two forms: localised, spontaneous, and popular revolts appealing to traditional rights and customs (*altes Recht* or 'old law'); and organised, but far from popular, supraregional conspiracies, appealing to 'divine law' (*göttliches Recht*). Both types of revolt combined in the German Peasants' War, with the Reformation providing a mass basis for the previously limited appeal to 'divine law.'

By contrast, Marxist interpretations saw the conflict as socio-economic in origin, brought about by the clash between a declining feudal system and an emergent early capitalism. Over the years 1470–1520, class conflict rose to a peak, finding its ideological expression in the Reformation, which provoked the national crisis necessary to precipitate a revolution. This was essentially an "early bourgeois revolution" which failed because the disparate anti-feudal forces could not unite under a single, purposeful revolutionary leadership, as provided by Thomas Müntzer in Thuringia and Michael Gaismair in Tyrol.[4] For both interpretations, the defeat of the peasants in 1525–26 marked the end of their active political role in Germany until the modern era, the end also, for Marxists, of German revolutionary aspirations.

Let us now examine in turn the current state of debate about the origins, course, consequences, and broader significance of the Peasants' War, and what kinds of sources are available to the researcher.

Origins

Recent studies have shown that we can no longer ignore the socio-economic origins of the German Peasants' War. The most significant contribution has been that of Peter Blickle (1975b), who argues that it originated in a "crisis of feudalism" in southern Germany at the end of the Middle Ages, a crisis which was both socio-economic *and* political. It arose from attempts of both lords and peasants to cope with long-term structural changes during the fifteenth century, which saw the prolonged agrarian crisis of 1350–1450 followed after 1450 by a period of gradual recovery. Landlords attempted to compensate for their losses during the crisis period in two ways, by restricting freedom of movement of their tenants, and by exacting ad-

---

[4]For a succinct summary, see Steinmetz's theses in Scribner and Benecke (1979), 9–18, and at greater length in Steinmetz (1978) and Laube et al. (1974). But it would be wrong to see significant Marxist scholarship as confined to the GDR; important contributions have come from many other East European historians (see the bibliographies in note 3).

ditional dues. The first they achieved by reimposition of serfdom, which in turn facilitated the second.

Franz had argued for increased peasant well-being in the wake of the late fifteenth-century recovery, so that peasant grievances in 1525 were no reflection of their true economic situation. By contrast, Blickle contends that most peasants had suffered a decline in prosperity during the agrarian crisis, but, largely because of the political means adopted by their lords to cope with it, they were unable to share the benefits of the agrarian boom leading to recovery. The steady growth of population in the most densely settled areas such as Swabia also led to land shortage, increased impoverishment, and corresponding social tensions.

These developments are reflected directly in the Twelve Articles, the most widespread manifesto of 1525. All the means used by landlords to deal with the agrarian crisis are complained of there, above all, serfdom, the major tool of the lords' economic strategy. As Claudia Ulbrich (1979) has shown, serfdom was also a very useful political tool. As the sole right of lordship accepted across all territories, it could be used to amalgamate scattered lands through exchange of serfs, thus serving as a means of territorial rationalization and consolidation. It helped lords to transform feudal relations of "mutual dependence" into territorial subjection, a relationship of 'sovereign' to 'subject' (*Obrigkeit* and *Untertan*). But it also had far-reaching social effects, such as limitation of freedom of movement or choice of marriage partners, and loss of tenancy and inheritance rights.[5]

There are some obvious weaknesses in this line of argument. It relies heavily on studies of small territories in the South-west, such as those by Blickle, Ulbrich, and Sabean (1972), and we have been unable to test its general applicability by comparable findings from other areas which experienced the Peasants' War. Research on other parts of south Germany—lower Alsace by Rapp (1975), and Franconia by Endres (1971, 1973)—reveal considerable differences. In lower Alsace the peasantry was not overburdened with rents or taxes, and there was no pressure of overpopulation or shortage of land in either area. Moreover, in Franconia, Thuringia, and Tyrol the lynchpin of Blickle's argument, serfdom, was absent.[6]

There is clearly a major need for studies of the economic condi-

[5]On serfdom, see also Rabe (1977), Müller (1975).
[6]For these criticisms, see also Press (1978), 118, 120; Scott (1979), 702.

tions of the peasantry in areas outside upper Swabia, a need which even Marxist research of the past decade has done curiously little to meet.[7] However, the intending researcher will face a more difficult problem. The backdrop for Blickle's argument is provided by the analyses of Wilhelm Abel (1966, 1974) of long-term structural developments in pre-industrial Europe. Yet Abel's picture has been challenged on the basis of the theoretical model he employs: that he uses dubious neo-Malthusian assumptions about the effects of population change on economic growth or stagnation, and that he analyses an underdeveloped agrarian economy with models created for the analysis of modern industrial economies. It can be argued that he too sharply contrasts urban and rural economies, and that the rural economy was more resilient and differentiated than Abel allows.[8] The researcher undertaking empirical research must, therefore, be willing to test a number of different models of economic change more appropriate to the period under investigation.

Tom Scott (1979a) has foreshadowed a different approach which calls attention to the interpenetration of town and country, and the absence of rigid divisions between urban and rural economies. He argues that peasant agriculture became more specialised and market-orientated, enabling some peasants, at least, to profit from the revival in prices of primary products. Moreover, peasants were not hindered by urban guild restrictions from turning to rural craft production to supplement purely agrarian incomes. He suggests as a major field of investigation the nature and structure of markets and marketing, and their role in creating differentiation and adaptability in the rural economy.[9]

Scott also rightly insists that more attention should be given to the growth of an "early capitalist economy" during the later part of the fifteenth century. This penetrated deeply into the countryside and profoundly changed social and economic relations. Early capitalist wool farming in Thuringia led the lords to enclose common lands to graze large flocks, and deforestation caused by charcoaling and smelting for the mining industry was a constant source of grievance there. In the Swabian countryside, the effects of commodity production through the putting-out system is well attested. More broadly, early capitalist developments hastened the integration of the rural

[7]See the small amount of work listed in Steinmetz (1980) and Volz and Brather (1975), with Schwarze (1975) the most significant contribution.

[8]See Scott (1979a), 703, and Stalnaker, in Scribner and Benecke (1979), 30.

[9]See Scott (1979a), 958. For recent work on town-country relations, Maschke and Sydow (1974), Kiessling (1977), and Meynen (1979).

economy into a wider market system, enabling some peasants to take advantage of new market relations, while others fell victim to market exploitation.[10] It would greatly illuminate understanding of the economic state of the peasantry to pursue these questions within well-defined economic regions, taking account of features such as pasturage, dairying, viticulture, cereal production or market-gardening, and relating them to market relations and land tenure patterns.

With his study of anticlericalism in the Peasants' War, Henry Cohn (1979) called attention to another neglected but important field of economic research. The clergy possessed weapons not available to lay lords in the imposition of serfdom and the collection of dues. The peasants greatly resented ecclesiastical courts at least in part because they were an instrument of economic coercion, and the tithe was a major economic grievance. Yet we have virtually no extended studies of the economic role of the clergy, nor of the economic range and influence of individual monastic houses, chapters, orders, or prelates.[11]

Study of economic change also illuminates the social conflicts underlying the Peasants' War, for example, interfamilial conflict over inheritance rights caused by overpopulation, or the social effects of serfdom. Internal village conflict arose between better-off peasants able to exploit the emerging market economy and those unable to cope with its pressures (see Sabean, 1972, Endres, 1973, Rapp, 1975). Poorer peasants unable to produce an adequate surplus could be forced to work as wage-laborors for a better-off peasant. Common land could then be a point of tension as larger farmers attempted to tie usage rights to individual farms while the poorer wished to retain it for personal use. These developments can best be understood by close studies at village level.[12]

A useful theory here has been the concept of "peasant economy and society," formulated by Chayanov in 1925, and applied in several recent studies of the pre-industrial European peasantry.[13] It reconstructs economic relations from the viewpoint of the peasantry,

[10]See Scott (1979a), 958ff. On mining, the best study is Laube (1974); on grazing, see Quietzsch (1975); on deforestation in Thuringia, Scribner (1975), 38.

[11]Buck (1973) has examined the tithe in Nuremberg, but there has been nothing of the quality of Amman (1960, 1962); see, however, Baier (1934), Ochs (1934–36), and Ott (1969).

[12]For peasant stratification, see Blickle-Littwin (1977), reviewing Franz (1975).

[13]For examples of this approach, see Potter et al. (1967), Shanin (1971), Mendras (1976); also De Vries (1974), Parker and Jones (1975). For a fuller bibliography, see Schulze (1980), pp. 307–8 and Elbs (1980), 148–51 *passim*.

regarding the peasant family farm as an economic unit which consciously sought to achieve sufficiency by balancing inputs and outputs, if necessary using outside labor or cottage industry. A similar approach, inspired by the anthropological work of Redfield (1955, 1956) and Wolf (1966, 1971) reconstructs the peasant social world at village level. For our period these concepts have been tried out by Wunder (1975), Sabean (1979), and Elbs (1980). They are especially appropriate for studying areas of peasant tenant farming (*Grundherrschaft*), the norm for most of Germany, where production was based on the individual unit of the family farm. This unit was, as Schulze (1980, p. 70) points out, a precondition for political resistance by the pre-industrial peasantry, because it encouraged attempts to achieve economic autonomy unhindered by landlords, tax-gatherers, or urban middlemen.

Assessment of the impact of socio-economic changes cannot, however, ignore politics. Recent work by the Blickle school (see Blickle, 1980) emphasizes peasant resistance to the economic and political strategies of lords and rulers. Late-medieval peasant revolts were conscious acts of political protest, seeking to wrest from lords concessions which would be enshrined in written agreements and treaties. In the course of these struggles, the peasantry formulated clear conceptions of personal rights and freedoms in opposition to those of serfdom or subjection. Blickle (1979) also argues that such self-conscious forms of political struggle grew out of the experience of local government in the autonomous village community (*Gemeinde*). Peasant officials, carrying out local government functions, acquired the political experience and self-confidence to make demands of their social superiors. The importance of this experience was seen in the Peasants' War, when village officials provided so many rebel leaders. Here see also Blickle (1981).

Blickle's interpretation has not been unchallenged.[14] To take one example, he argues that such political consciousness challenged the legitimacy of the lords' claims within the framework of the existing political order. But it could be said that any heightened political awareness was merely a matter of an office-holding village elite. Preliminary findings indicate that village officials came not from the richest peasants, but from the middle stratum (see Blickle-Littwin, 1977), but it is equally likely that the lords could exploit internal village conflict by acting as arbitrators, and so reaffirming their legitimacy. These issues require a good deal more research, but the

---

[14]For an extended critique of Blickle, see Press (1975); and Scott (1979a).

most fruitful feature of this approach has been the attention paid to the development of political and legal concepts. Besides studies of "old law," "divine law," or the impact of Roman law, attention should be paid to changing notions of individual rights, emerging concepts of property, and the treatment of feudal rights as market commodities.

Another important political question is the relationship between peasant resistance and territorial state-building. Blickle (1979, 1980) advances two theses here. First, the peasants did not, as Franz suggested, simply react conservatively to princely demands. Rather, by the development of commons constitutions (*Landschaften*) they sought to improve political rights at territorial level.

Second, late-medieval rebellions reflect the structural characteristics of the territories in which they occur. The areas of widespread rebellion coincide geographically with those with well-developed *Gemeinde*, and there is also an observable difference between small and large territories. In the former there were more revolts against territorial rulers who were also landlords, in the latter rebels tended to appeal to their rulers over the heads of their landlords. Blickle further suggests that these differences can be related to the ways in which rulers of such territories dealt with the late-medieval agrarian crisis.

Many of the above suggestions are at present no more than hypotheses, but they indicate that the events of 1524–26 should be seen as the result of a complex interaction of economic, social, political, and ideological influences. This awareness has led some Western historians to see the Peasants' War as the result of a social system conflict, drawing on sociological conceptions of society as a functioning system susceptible to major conflicts through the appearance of dysfunctional elements.[15] This shares with Marxist approaches the advantage of studying the Peasants' War in terms of typical sociological processes, but also the weakness that historical change could be seen in an overly rigid and mechanical way. But if there is any consensus in recent research, it would indicate that the origins of the Peasants' War can be investigated only through an *histoire totale* which unites structures, events, and mentalities.

Course of the War

We are well supplied with narrative accounts of the events of

---

[15]See Bücking (1975), Press (1978), and Wohlfeil (1975), 280, all using rather different notions of a "system conflict."

1524–26 in most regions, although a number of recent studies of particular areas have shown how we can add to our knowledge, especially where they test the validity of fresh theoretical approaches.[16] Nonetheless, many of the leading questions remain open: how the revolt was at all possible on the unprecedented scale on which it occurred; why it took place in some areas and not in others; what were its forms of mobilization and organization; what were its stages of development; who were the leaders and bearers of the revolt; what was its ideological inspiration; how this ideology (if it existed) was related to the grievances, aims, and demands of the rebels; how the revolt was related to urban protest; what role was played by its opponents; and, above all, whether it was a revolution. On all of these questions, we are faced with a richness of suggestion, wide areas of controversy, and inconclusiveness in the empirical work carried out to date.

We can focus many of these questions through the most controversial thesis of recent years. In a modification of Franz's argument about 'divine law', Blickle (1975b) maintains that the Reformation unified otherwise disparate forms of protest. Its idea of Christian liberty confirmed and extended communitarian and anti-hierarchical ideas present in late-medieval popular protest, and its appeal to the Word of God as the infallible standard of Christian ethics provided a legitimating principle for a new idea of Christian social justice. Reformation propaganda of the years 1520–25 not only embodied these notions, but also placed them at the heart of the struggle for the Gospel, idealizing the "evangelical peasant" and the "common man" as its chief supporters. Response to this appeal was in fact wider than the peasantry—it encouraged protest by all disprivileged groups in town and country. 1524–26 was a "revolution of the common man." It was revolutionary because it seriously challenged hierarchical feudal society, for implementation of its principles of biblically-based social justice would have entailed a revolutionary reshaping of state and society. The dynamic of this revolt Blickle traces through the spread of the Twelve Articles, which transformed scattered protest into a revolution with a mass base and a unifying ideology.

The most trenchant criticism of this thesis has come from Scott (1979), who accuses Blickle of overestimating the power of ideology

---

[16]See, for example, Scott (1979b) or Rublack (1976); and from GDR historians, the contributions in the *Jahrbuch für Regionalgeschichte* 5 (1975).

to provoke revolt. Blickle's argument, however, is more complex than Scott admits. He sees popular "willingness to rebel" as the outcome of several interacting factors: economic burdens, social tensions, political expectations, and the force of legitimation upholding belief in the existing order. The more the last is challenged by alternative legitimations and its ideological grip loosens, the more the additive effect of the other factors increase readiness to rebel.[17] However, Scott is correct in that Blickle does not show how Reformation ideas were received among the peasantry, nor does he analyse specific instances of how they encouraged the revolt. Scott's alternative notion that the peasants pursued pragmatic goals and that wider ideological justifications emerged only later is questionable when it implies that the peasants had neither ideas nor ideals.[18] But for Blickle's argument to carry conviction it must show how popular biblicism operated at the level of the "common man" through the kind of empirical detail presented by Scott (1978-9) for Waldshut.

Blickle's thesis could be tested in a number of ways. One would be to examine the reception of Reformation ideas among the peasantry, not just as transmitted by print, but also through oral and visual means of communication. A model study is Ernst Schubert (1975), examining rumor and popular opinion in the late fifteenth century. Another would be a study of the impact of popular preachers, singly, in groups, or within a well-defined geographical area. A useful, if methodologically primitive, beginning here is Maurer (1979). A third is to study rural popular religion before the Reformation, especially attitudes to "holy men" and popular prophetic figures such as the Drummer of Niklashausen. Some of these attitudes were transferred to Luther, and the role of religious symbolism in the *Bundschuh* shows that religious legitimation for revolt did not originate with the Reformation.[19]

Folklore studies can contribute a great deal to such enquiry by extending our knowledge of symbolic aspects of peasant culture. GDR scholars have given a lead here with recent studies of the importance of bells, pipes, and drums in the Peasants' War (see Strobach, 1975).

---

[17]See Scott (1979a), 957, 962, and Blickle (1975b), 137.

[18]See Scott (1979b). Here his own conception is called a "structural analysis," although it is difficult to see what is structural about it. Its merit is that it is concerned not with structure, but with the dynamics of events.

[19]For pre-Reformation religious radicalism, see Hoyer (1970); on popular images of Luther, Scribner (1981), Ch. 2; on religious symbolism in the *Bundschuh*, Scribner, in Bak (1975), 36-38. On Niklashausen, see Arnold (1980).

As subjects for study we might also add popular ballads, proverbs, slogans, processions, festivals, and ceremonies.[20] All contribute to an understanding of how peasant opinion could be mobilized around religious ideas and symbols, and could best be studied at village level in conjunction with research into peasant social life.

The dynamics of revolt can be understood, as both Blickle and Scott agree, by investigating the sociological characteristics of rebellion through comparative analysis of the varying circumstances in which revolt broke out: how, when, and where grievances were discussed, or meetings and gatherings held; how leaders were chosen or demands prepared; how acts of rebellion were precipitated. Bierbrauer (1980) and Bücking (1975) have proposed typical stages of development which merit more rigorous testing. Thanks to work by GDR historians such as Hoyer (1975) and Bensing (1975), we are well-informed about peasant military organization, but more attention could be given to the counter measures and strategies of the authorities, for which Greiner (1974) and Sea (1975) are useful starting points. Understanding of why revolt broke out in some places and not in others would be greatly advanced by more studies of areas where there was no peasant revolt, to supplement the valuable studies by Buck (1971), Rankl (1975), and Vogler (1975).

Explanations of regional variations have concentrated so far on analysis of grievances and programs, and this has become further entangled with the problem of peasant strategies and tactics. Bücking (1975) argued that peasant political programs were an evolutionary response to changing circumstances, whereas Buszello (1975) and Blickle (1975b) regarded them more in political structural terms. In more fragmented territories the peasants sought more localized political and constitutional solutions; in larger territories they thought on a more territorial scale. But most historians agree that military activity was an essential dynamic element: once military conflict had broken out of the confines of individual territories the rebels expanded the scale on which they sought solutions. Overall, the rebels' political aspirations operated on three levels: desire for local autonomy for the individual village (and town); commons representation in territorial constitutions through autonomous communities; and, most radically, the abolition of all lordship except that of the Emperor.[21] How these levels are related to the different theatres of revolt remains controversial.

---

[20]These themes will be dealt with elsewhere in this volume.
[21]Buszello (1975), also in Scribner and Benecke (1979), 120ff.

The radicalism of such aspirations is another subject for debate. Buszello (1969, 1975) rejected the argument central to GDR interpretations that there was any notion of a unified and centralized nation state. The only program of this nature was the work of an isolated figure, Friedrich Wiegandt, and was not reflected in the aspirations of any actual peasant leader. Although Blickle argues the revolutionary implications of the Twelve Articles, it has been questioned whether anyone at the time saw them in that light. GDR historians regard them as a moderate program, and one church historian (Brecht 1974) even sees them as more theologically than politically inspired.[22] In general, the aims of the rebels are seen as either reformatory or pragmatic. It is now conceded that there were genuinely revolutionary programs such as Thomas Müntzer's revolutionary chiliasm, or Michael Gaismair's radically egalitarian Tyrolean constitution, but it is argued that they did not, except in the case of Müntzer, achieve any mass following.[23]

We are now moving towards a better understanding of Müntzer's role, with a wider appreciation both of his genuine revolutionary fervor and of his radical chiliasm. Inevitably Müntzer will appear peripheral to the main course of the Peasants' War as long as the weight of interest is directed towards south Germany. Perhaps for the same reason, overconcentration on the South, there has been a revival of interest in Michael Gaismair.[24] A proper evaluation of both of these genuinely radical figures, however, will be most effective when set against a broader in-depth study of peasant leaders. So far research into this subject has done no more than scratch the surface.[25]

The same might be said of another major theme, the relationship between urban and rural revolt. The urban disturbances of 1525 have attracted considerable attention, with some exemplary studies such as Rammstedt (1975) and Schilling (1975), while GRD scholarship has concentrated its attention most heavily on the urban dimensions of the Peasants' War.[26] But the trend of non-Marxist scholarship has been to play down the significance of links between urban

[22]On Wiegandt, *ibid.*, 120; on the GDR view of the Twelve Articles, see Laube and Seifert (1975), where they appear as part of the "moderate tendency."

[23]On this last point, see Scott (1979a), 719, 961.

[24]On Gaismair, see the further bibliography in Scott (1979a), 719; on Müntzer, *ibid.*, 720, and his article summing up the current research, forthcoming in *Journal of Ecclesiastical History.*

[25]We have not gone substantially beyond G. Franz, "Die Führer im Bauernkrieg," in Franz (1975), 1–15.

[26]On the latter, see the bibliography in Steinmetz (1980), 80.

and rural protest, perhaps out of scepticism about the thesis of the "early bourgeois revolution." Blickle's argument that the Peasants' War was a "revolution of the common man" has put the issue back on the agenda. The general response has been to question the concept of the "common man," or to argue that the grievances of townsmen were either different from, or essentially hostile to, those of rural dwellers. They shared some common ground in anti-clericalism and in opposition to the advance of territorial government, but most alliances between peasants and townsmen were matters of expediency. The widest possible area of agreement was most likely to be found at the level of ideals, around the slogans of the Gospel and divine justice, but it remains a matter for further investigation as to exactly how both social groups understood these slogans.[27]

This having been said, it is also true that we lack any comprehensive overview of how the towns responded to the challenge of the Peasants' War.[28] A proper analysis would include more sophisticated typologies of towns than just political or constitutional features (for example, socio-economic characteristics, local and regional functions). It would also include a more developed analysis of urban protest movements than we have seen so far in the study of the period, especially taking account of social stratification within towns and movements. We need to know more about those social groups which struck alliances with the peasants, and those which opposed or manipulated them. We have some useful discussions of the roles of miners,[29] but we require the same for other low-status groups such as market gardeners, wine-growers, day-laborers, hawkers and carriers, middlemen between town and country, and, above all, weavers. The last might be expected to be hostile to peasant demands because of the threat to their livelihood by cottage industry, but we know all too little about the social origins or migratory habits of weavers, and they may have had closer links with the countryside than we assume. Karl Czok (1975), has pointed out a fruitful line of inquiry with his study of suburbs as a point of transition between town and country which were also the gathering place of many urban underprivileged groups. His analysis of towns in Thuringia and Saxony deserves to be extended to other parts of Germany.

[27]See Lutz (1978), and on the latter point Wunder, in Bak (1975) and Becker in Blickle (1975a), 232–63.
[28]Sea (1979), the most recent attempt, is more limited in scope than its title suggests.
[29]See the bibliography in Steinmetz (1980), 86, and references in Scott (1979a), 964–5.

Finally, we should point to the importance of townsmen, both as preachers and as those educated leaders who wrote a good deal of the biblical legitimation for revolt into peasant programs and strategies. This raises the question of how far the ideology justifying the Peasants' War was in fact a "bourgeois ideology." The role of Zwinglian ideas in the south is accepted by some scholars, and it is recognized that Müntzer and Pfeiffer did succeed in forging a wider popular movement in Mühlhausen in Thuringia.[30] This shows that the GDR argument that the Peasants' War possessed an "early bourgeois" character deserves to be taken more seriously than has so far been the case among Western historians.

Consequences and wider significance

The consequences of the Peasants' War can be considered under the heading of short-term matters such as the immediate political repercussions and the tasks of pacification, punishment, and reparations; or under that of long-term consequences, whether political, social, economic, or demographic. In many of these fields, analysis has only just begun, but we know enough from recent work to refute arguments that it was a disaster for future peasant political activity and consciousness on the one hand, or that it had little or no long-term consequences on the other.[31]

On short-term matters we have already seen some fine studies on the impact of pacification and reparations. If viewed against a broader canvas, the ability of the peasantry to pay or not, and the ways in which the substantial sums in fines and reparations were raised should provide numerous insights into the functioning of rural economy and society.[32] The question of pacification leads into wider themes of Reformation history, especially the extent to which there was a real or imagined continuity between the rebels and the Anabaptist movements of the later 1520s and 1530s. Certainly, fear of renewed rebellion seems to have influenced the policies of ruling authorities on issues such as security, religious or social innovation, and the handling of any kind of dissent.

Fear proved, however, to be an instrument of progress. Vogler

[30]On Zwinglian ideas, Buszello (1969), 117, 120; Hoyer, in Scribner and Benecke (1979), 124ff. On Müntzer and Pfeiffer, Scott (1979a), 961.

[31]For the former, Franz (1977), Book II, Section H; for the latter, Klein (1975).

[32]See Sea (1975, 1977), Kintner (1971), and GDR works listed in Steinmetz (1980), 86.

(1977) has shown the considerable sympathy for peasant grievances
at the 1526 Reichstag of Speyer, which led to recommendations that
conditions should be ameliorated. Blickle (1973) has shown convincingly that the peasants made significant political gains at territorial level. In treaties of lordship, in territorial constitutions, in
the recesses of provincial diets, and in the continuing role of popular
territorial assemblies (*Landschaften*), peasants exerted an increased
political influence throughout the early modern period. Nor were
they cowed into submission by their defeat. Schulze (1980) has
shown this in his study of peasant resistance after 1525, even if there
was no uprising on quite the same scale. The peasants chose rather
to resist through exploitation of the legal instruments open to them,
through what Marxist historians have called "a lower form of class
struggle."[33]

Whether the Peasants' War marked the end of the Reformation as
a popular movement is still a central and unanswered question. Lau
(1959) argued that there were urban movements with popular elements and radical evangelical demands in the later 1520s and 1530s,
but that by no means settles the question. Essential elements of the
popular phase of the early 1520s are undeniably lacking after 1525:
the social radicalism of theological demands, the willingness of secular authorities to view religious radicalism with permissive tolerance, the readiness of Reformation theologians to speak out on matters of social justice. Above all, the air of prophetic and eschatological expectation is noticeably muted or regarded with suspicion.
There was a determined attempt by Reformation leaders, both political and theological, to distance themselves from the radical consequences of the early evangelical movements. Here the emergence of
the Müntzer legend as traced by Steinmetz (1971), with its profound
implications for our understanding of the progress of the Reformation post-1525, has yet to be fully evaluated.[34]

We also need more detailed studies of the policies of both Lutheran and Catholic authorities, especially for the period before the full
emergence of a politically-based Protestantism (1525–30), when fear
of renewed peasant upheaval was uppermost in the minds of secular
rulers. Also largely unexplored is the impact of the rebellion on the
mentality of the age, the theme being taken up only by historians of

---

[33]See Schulze (1980), 26–37, esp. 28.
[34]See also H. Kirchner, "Der deutsche Bauernkrieg im Urteil der frühen reformatorischen Geschichtsschreibung," in Oberman (1974), 95–125.

literature, such as Brackert (1975) and several GDR scholars.[35] There is a completely new field to plough here, perhaps through folklorist studies which would take the inquiry down to village level.

The wider significance of the Peasants' War has been pursued along two divergent lines of inquiry. GDR historians have investigated its importance in the transition from feudalism to capitalism, and comparatively in the context of peasant and bourgeois revolutions (see Heitz and Vogler, 1980). This interest is shared in common with Western scholars who are turning their attention to comparative studies of peasant revolts (see Schulze, 1980). The range of comparisons include near-contemporaneous revolts, such as that in 1514 in Hungary, or those in the Austrian lands and south-eastern Europe subsequent to the German Peasants' War, or the entire series of major and minor revolts in German-speaking lands up to the French Revolution.[36] Both schools attempt to relate peasant resistance to the development of the early modern state and the phenomenon of absolutism. Both have characteristic weaknesses: where Marxist scholars seem to hypostasize class and class-conflict, Western scholarship, especially in the Federal Republic of Germany, tends to hypostasize the state, seeing it as an entity above and separate from society. They have also made significant contributions in their characteristic ways, the one in challenging us to take seriously the importance of class and class conflict in pre-industrial societies, the other in reminding that there is a long-term structural history of politics that social historians should not ignore. Most scholars of all persuasions are agreed in seeing the German Peasants' War as some kind of turning point in early modern history, and as standing at the center of a wider circle of questions of great historiographical and methodological significance. The most challenging of these is how far it provides a model test case for the applicability of social science theory to historical analysis. On all of these questions debate will continue to be lively.

Sources

The sources available for study of this subject are manifold. They can best be described in terms of the different types of source material and by reference to leading examples of how the researcher might exploit them. On the narrower background, the immediate events

[35]See further references in Steinmetz (1980), 96.
[36]See further references in Scott (1979a), 972ff.

and general progress of the war itself, there are numerous published collections which show the typical documents from which the more traditional histories have been written: chronicles, contemporary narratives, official and private correspondence, minute books, financial records, interrogation protocols, and other legal records.[37] A much-neglected source are the *Kriegsakten* of the various authorities active in repressing the war, especially those of the Swabian League, whose value was demonstrated by Sea (1975). They contain much of importance besides the military history of the war.

That the older collections have not exhausted the stock of unpublished material is shown by the recent collection on Hesse by Struck (1975). For territories such as Tyrol, the French-German borderlands such as Alsace, Franche-Comté or Saar-Pfalz, as well as for central and parts of north Germany, a sizable amount remains unpublished. Central Germany remains very under-researched, and Lötzke and Kluge (1975) have sketched out the holdings of major archives in the GDR. Elsewhere much of value is likely to be found in small local archives such as those of individual towns, small territories or ecclesiastical lordships or institutions.[38]

There are innumerable untapped collections on the broader perspectives of the war, especially the socio-economic. These range from monastic and estate records, including individual contracts and agreements, mostly collected in *Urkundenbücher*; over feudal contracts and confirmations (*Lehnsbriefe und -reverse*); to lists of feudal dues or services recorded in *Zinsbücher*, *Zinsrodel* or *Kopialbücher*. Valuable material is often to be found in the account books kept by an estate bailiff or district official, and the same is true of the records kept by urban officials who dealt with rural districts. The correspondence of local officials, and of urban or princely authorities, either bundled up loosely or collected in *Missivbücher* or *Briefbücher* should not be overlooked, nor should the minute books of urban government or princely *Audienzbücher*. Records on trade and marketing are too numerous to be listed in the limited space here, but careful study of recent works on town-country relations will reveal the various kinds of source material of value for this field of inquiry.[39] Wider questions of demography and social structure can be tackled through valuable sources such as the Common Penny

[37]See, for examples, Franz (1935); further source collections in Schottenloher (1933) under *Bauernkrieg*.
[38]See, for example, the sources available for Leipzig, in Unger, (1975).
[39]See note 9.

returns (see Rowan 1977), the Turk Tax returns (see Schwarze 1975), the occasional census list or tax list for an episcopal enthronement, as well as the more numerous urban tax lists, which often provide a mass of information about the countryside.[40]

For an understanding of how to exploit the various sources required for study of the socio-economic dimensions of the Peasants' War, and of how to investigate rural economy and society at village level, one could not do better than to study the methodology set out in Macfarlane (1977). This also contains (pp. 39–41) a valuable summary of the major kinds of sources for community studies, which a researcher could easily adapt for German purposes. For an overview of the range of German equivalents, as well as examples of what can be achieved with such sources, see Sabean (1972), Ulbrich (1979), or Elbs (1980).

Legal and constitutional records can be used to study a whole range of topics from political-legal concepts through to peasant mentalities and social relations. Such records can be found at all levels of the legal process, from local, district, and county courts up to the proceedings of territorial assemblies and imperial diets. Besides the important proclamations and statutes concerning policing and administration, individual court cases can be enormously informative. Here the records of the *Reichskammergericht* have yet to be exploited to the full, although the procedures to be mastered are complex and the sheer volume of the proceedings exhaustingly tedious.[41]

A particularly important legal source which has been less than adequately evaluated are the collections of *Weistümer* extant for most parts of Germany. These are written records of customary law, usually originating at village level as a result of peasant initiative, and they provide a close view of legal, social and political relations in peasant communities. They overlap, and are sometimes identical with other legal forms such as *Urbare, Bauernbriefe,* and *Dorfordnungen.* The first collection of these rural legal records was published by Grimm (1840–78), and vast numbers have been published since then, while many others await discovery in archives.[42] They are just beginning to be evaluated more fully (see Blickle 1977, and

<hr>

[40]See, for example, Hans Eberhardt's introduction to Schwarze (1975) on Turk Tax; for towns, Batori (1979).

[41]For further literature, see Schottenloher (1933) under *Reichskammergericht.*

[42]For extensive listing of published *Weistümer,* see under this heading in Schottenloher (1933).

Arnold 1975, and the further literature cited there), and provide a major source for the new research of the years ahead.

Two other kinds of source deserve comment because their full potential has not yet been exhausted. First, there are the records of interrogations of the defeated peasants. These are too often regarded as biased and unreliable because of their compilation by prosecuting authorities, but if used with adequate methodological caution they can yield a good deal about the dynamics of the war and its ideological and psychological aspects. Many are in print, but many others await resurrection from the archives. Second, there are the numerous printed pamphlets, political manifestos and articles of grievance, of which GDR historians have made good use in recent years.[43] A thorough exploitation of this material will shortly be made possible by publication of the comprehensive catalogue of German pamphlets by Hans-Joachim Köhler of the University of Tübingen, mentioned elsewhere in this volume. This will allow more intensive research into printers, publishers, and printing history of Peasants' War tracts, and the preparation of useful editions such as that by Hoyer and Rüdiger (1975) or Laube and Seifert (1975).

Literary historians have shown what a wide range of aspects of the Peasants' War can be researched in and through contemporary printed pamphlets, ranging from political concepts, notions of violence and 'bourgeois ideology' through to the developing historiography of the Reformation and Peasants' War and their wider literary reception. Not to be overlooked in this context are the visual records in titlepages, broadsheets, paintings and drawings, alongside material artifacts.[44] It would be short-sighted, however, to use such valuable sources only as printed texts. They should be located in a wider context by comparison with unpublished and manuscript sources. A rigorous comparison of manuscript grievances with printed manifestos, or investigation of the development of grievances from peasant assembly to manuscript articles to printed tracts, for example, would enable these sources to be used to greater benefit than hitherto.

Finally, we should mention the archives where such materials are to be found. These are too numerous even to attempt a cursory listing here. A preliminary voyage of discovery can be undertaken in the invaluable handbook published by Minerva, *Archive im*

---

[43]See Steinmetz (1980), 84.
[44]See Scribner (1981) and further discussion by Christensen in this volume.

deutschsprachigen Raum (1974). This provides a summary overview of around 8,000 archives in German-speaking lands, giving for each archive the extent of its holdings, the time span covered by individual sections, and a bibliography. It also indicates whether there is a published catalogue (*Inventar, Bestandsübersicht, Repertorium*, occasionally *Findbuch*). Most of the major state archives in the Federal Republic of Germany and in the GDR have published such a *Bestandsübersicht*. For example, these exist for Darmstadt, Düsseldorf, Hannover, Karlsruhe, Münster, Osnabrück, and Wiesbaden in the Federal Republic; and for Altenburg, Dresden, Gotha, Greiz, Magdeburg, Meiningen, Lübben, Rudolstadt, and Weimar in the GDR. In all cases, titles for these should be sought under the relevant archive entry in the Minerva handbook.

A more limited overview of ecclesiastical archives is provided by the *Führer durch die Bistumsarchive der katholischen Kirche in der BRD* (1977), and by K. Dumrath, W. Eger, and H. Steinborg, *Handbuch des kirchlichen Archivwesens* (1977). For smaller, non-state archives, there are *Inventare nichtsstaatlicher Archive* for most of the states of the Federal Republic, the most extensive being those for Bavaria and the Rhineland. An invaluable handbook for north Germany is M. Hamann, ed., *Quellen zur ländlichen Sozialgeschichte im niedersächsischen Hauptstaatsarchiv in Hannover* (1975). For Austria, there is also a series of *Inventare österreichischer Archive*, and a similar series for Switzerland, although both are fairly incomplete.[45]

In conclusion, let me sum up the major emphases for research on the Peasants' War in the years ahead. First, it should be studied in its widest scope, as part of significant long-term changes in economy, society, and politics. Second, it should be viewed against the backdrop of typical historical processes as identified by social scientists: revolts, revolutions, the evolution of small communities, the processes of structural change. Third, there is need for research of narrower focus, which can locate these wider perspectives in the fine detail of closely-woven empirical research. Fourth, in all the fields discussed in this article, there is the need for a more sociologically aware "history of ideas," analysing intellectual, literary, legal, and political concepts in their wider social historical contest. Finally,

[45]For a fuller listing of these archive *Inventare* for Germany, Switzerland and Austria, see *Gesamtverzeichnis des deutschsprachigen Schrifttums* 1911–65, vol. 63 (Munich, 1978), 375–79.

there is a need to transcend the theoretically and methodologically primitive approaches that have marked many of our efforts so far, and to lift scholarship on the Peasants' War to the same level of sophistication now found in other areas of historical research.

I have spoken throughout of the incompleteness of much of the recent scholarship on the Peasants' War. To do so is not to underestimate its quality, but rather to pay tribute to its vitality and fertility. Even if recent scholars do not agree about the "revolution of 1525," few would dispute the revolution in modern studies of that event.

Bibliography

(An asterisk indicates that the work contains an extensive or especially useful bibliography.)

Abel, Wilhelm, *Agrarkrisen und Agrarkonjunktur. Eine Geschichte der Land- und Ernährungswirtschaft Mitteleuropas seit dem hohen Mittelalter* (Hamburg, 1966).
————, *Massenarmut und Hungerkrisen im vorindustriellen Europa* (Hamburg, 1974).
Amman, Hektor, "Klöster in der städtischen Wirtschaft des Mittelalters," *Argovia* 72 (1960): 102–33.
————, "Untersuchungen zur Wirtschaftsgeschichte des Oberrheinraums," *Zeitschrift für die Geschichte des Oberrheins* 110 (1962): 371–404.
Arnold, K., "Dorfweistümer in Franken," *Zeitschrift für bayerische Landesgeschichte* 38 (1975): 819–76.
————, *Niklashausen 1476. Quellen und Untersuchungen zur sozialreligiösen Bewegung des Hans Behem und zur Agrarstruktur eines spätmittelalterlichen Dorfes* (Baden-Baden, 1980).
*Bak, Janos (ed.), *The German Peasant War of 1525* (London, 1975).
Batori, Ingrid, "Ratsherren und Aufrührer. Soziale und ökonomische Verhältnisse in der Stadt Kitzingen zur Zeit des Bauernkriegs und der Reformation," in *Stadtbürgertum und Adel in der Reformation*, ed. W. J. Mommsen (Stuttgart, 1979).
Beier, H., "Des Klosters Salem Bevölkerungsbewegung, Finanz-,

Steuerwesen und Volkswirtschaft seit dem 15. Jht.," *Freiburger Diözesanarchiv* 62 (1934): 57–130.

Bensing, M., "Die 'Haufen' im deutschen Bauernkrieg," in *Der Bauer im Klassenkampf*, ed. G. Heitz et al. (Berlin, 1975).

Bierbrauer, Peter, "Bäuerliche Revolte im Alten Reich. Ein Forschungsbericht," in Blickle (1980).

Blickle, Peter, *Landschaften im Alten Reich* (Munich, 1973).

_____, ed. *Revolte und Revolution in Europa (Historische Zeitschrift,* Beiheft 4, Neue Folge, Munich, 1975). (a)

_____, *Die Revolution von 1525* (Munich, 1975). (b)

_____, ed., *Deutsche Ländliche Rechtsquellen* (Stuttgart, 1977).

_____, 'Peasant Revolts in the German Empire in the late Middle Ages,' *Social History* 4 (1979): 223–39.

_____, ed., *Aufruhr und Empörung? Studien zum bäuerlichen Widerstand im Alten Reich* (Munich, 1980).

_____, *Deutsche Untertanen. Ein Widerspruch* (Munich, 1981).

Blickle-Littwin, Renate, 'Besitz und Amt. Bemerkungen zu einer Neuerscheinung über bäuerliche Führungsschichten,' *Zeitschrift für bayerische Landesgeschichte* 40 (1977): 277–90.

*Brackert, Helmut, *Bauernkrieg und Literatur* (Frankfurt, 1975).

Brecht, Martin, "Der theologische Hintergrund der Zwölf Artikel der Bauernschaft in Schwaben von 1525," *Zeitschrift für Kirchengeschichte* 85 (1974): 30–64.

Brendler, G. and Laube, A., eds., *Der deutsche Bauernkrieg 1524/ 25. Geschichte – Traditionen – Lehren* (Berlin, 1977).

Buck, Lawrence P., *The Containment of Civil Insurrection: Nürnberg and the Peasants' Revolt, 1524–1525* (Ph.D. Dissertation, Ohio State University, 1971).

_____, "Opposition to Tithes in the Peasants' Revolt: A Case Study of Nuremberg in 1524," *Sixteenth Century Journal* 4 (1973): 11–22.

Bücking, Jürgen, "Der Bauernkrieg in den habsburgischen Ländern als sozialer Systemkonflikt, 1524–6," in *Der deutsche Bauernkrieg 1524–6*, ed. H. U. Wehler (Göttingen, 1975).

Buszello, Horst, *Der deutsche Bauernkrieg als politische Bewegung* (Berlin, 1969).

_____, 'Die Staatsvorstellung des "Gemeinen Mannes" im deutschen Bauernkrieg,' in Blickle, (1975).

Cohn, Henry J., "Anticlericalism in the German Peasants' War 1525," *Past and Present* 83 (1979): 3–31.

Czok, Karl, "Zur sozialökonomischen Struktur und politischen Rolle der Vorstädte in Sachsen und Thüringen im Zeitalter der deutschen frühbürgerlichen Revolution," *Wissenschaftliche Zeitschrift Karl-Marx-Universität Leipzig* 24 (1975): 53–68.

De Vries, Jan, *The Dutch Rural Economy in the Golden Age, 1500–1700* (New Haven, 1974).

Elbs, Eberhard, *Owingen 1584—der erste Aufstand in der Grafschaft Hohenzollern-Hechingen* (Constance, 1980).

Endres, Rudolf, "Probleme des Bauernkriegs im Hochstift Bamberg," *Jahrbuch für fränkische Landesforschung* 31 (1971): 91–138.

———, "Der Bauernkrieg in Franken," *Blätter für deutsche Landesgeschichte* 109 (1973): 31–68.

Foschepot, J., *Reformation und Bauernkrieg im Geschichtsbild der DDR* (Berlin, 1976).

Franz, Günther, *Der deutsche Bauernkrieg* (Munich, 1933). 11th ed. (Darmstadt, 1977).

———, *Der deutsche Bauernkrieg. Aktenband* (Munich, 1935).

———, ed., *Bauernschaft und Bauernstand 1500–1970* (Limburg/Lahn, 1975).

Greiner, Christian, "Die Politik des Schwabischen Bundes während des Bauernkriegs 1524/1525 bis zum Vertrag von Weingarten," *Zeitschrift des historischen Vereins für Schwaben* 68 (1974): 7–94.

Grimm, J., *Weisthümer*, 7 volumes (Göttingen, 1840–78).

*Heitz, G., Laube, A., Steinmetz, M., and Vogler, G., eds., *Der Bauer im Klassenkampf* (Berlin, 1975).

Heitz, G. and Vogler, G., "Agrarfrage und bürgerliche Revolutionen beim Übergang vom Feudalismus zum Kapitalismus," *Zeitschrift für Geschichtswissenschaft* 28 (1980), also published separately (Rostock, 1980).

Hoyer, Siegfried, "Hans Boheim—der revolutionäre Prediger von Niklashausen," *Zeitschrift für Geschichtswissenschaft* 18 (1970): 185–96.

———, *Das Militärwesen im deutschen Bauernkrieg 1524–6* (Berlin, 1975).

Hoyer, S. and Rüdiger, B., eds., *An die Versammlung gemeiner Bauerschaft. Ein revolutionäre Flugschrift aus dem deutschen Bauernkrieg* (Berlin, 1975).

Kiessling, Rolf, "Stadt-Land-Beziehung im Spätmittelalter," *Zeitschrift für bayerische Landesgeschichte* 40 (1977): 829–67

Kintner, P. L., "Memmingens 'Ausgetretene.' Eine vergessene

Nachwirkung des Bauernkrieges 1525-7," *Memminger Geschichtsblätter* (1971): 5-40.

Klein, Thomas, "Die Folgen des Bauernkriegs von 1525: Thesen und Antithesen zu einem vernachlässigten Thema," *Hessisches Jahrbuch für Landesgeschichte* 25 (1975): 65-116.

Lau, Franz, "Der Bauernkrieg und das angebliche Ende der lutherischen Reformation als spontaner Volksbewegung," *Luther Jahrbuch* (1959), 109-34.

Laube, Adolf, *Studien über den erzgebirgischen Silberbergbau von 1470 bis 1546* (Berlin, 1974).

Laube, A., and Seifert, H. W., eds., *Flugschriften der Bauernkriegszeit* (Berlin, 1975).

Laube, A., Steinmetz, M., and Vogler, G., *Illustrierte Geschichte der deutschen frühbürgerlichen Revolution* (Berlin, 1974).

Lötzke, H. and Kluge, R., "Quellen zur Geschichte des bäuerlichen Klassenkampfes in Deutschland in Staatsarchiven der DDR (16. Jht. bis 1789)," in Heitz (1975).

Lutz, R., *Wer war der gemeine Mann? Der dritte Stand in der Krise des Spätmittelalters* (Munich, 1978).

Macfarlane, Alan, *Reconstructing Historical Communities* (Cambridge, 1977).

Maschke, Erich, and Sydow, Jürgen, eds., *Stadt und Umland*, (Stuttgart, 1974).

Maurer, Justus, *Prediger im Bauernkrieg* (Stuttgart, 1979).

Mendras, Henri, *Sociétés paysannes* (Paris, 1976).

Meynen, Emil, ed., *Zentralität als Problem der mittelalterlichen Stadtgeschichtsforschung* (Cologne, 1979).

Midelfort, H. C. Erik, "The Revolution of 1525? Recent Studies of the Peasants' War," *Central European History* 11 (1978): 189-206.

Moeller, B., ed., *Bauernkriegs-Studien* (Gütersloh, 1975).

Müller, Walter, "Wurzeln und Bedeutung des grundsätzlichen Widerstands gegen die Leibeigenschaft im Bauernkrieg 1525," *Schriften des Vereins für die Geschichte des Bodensees und seiner Umgebung* 93 (1975): 1-41.

Oberman, Heiko A., ed., *Deutscher Bauernkrieg 1525*, special number of *Zeitschrift für Kirchengeschichte* 85, Heft 2 (1974).

Ochs, K., "Studien zur Wirtschafts- und Rechtsgeschichte des Klosters Beuron," *Hohenzollersche Jahreshefte* 1 (1934): 1-54; 2 (1935): 1-66; 3 (1936): 1-64.

Ott, H., *Die Klostergrundherrschaft St Blasien im Mittelalter* (Arbeiten zum historischen Atlas von Südwestdeutschland 4, Stuttgart, 1969).

Parker, W. N. and Jones, E. L., eds., *European Peasants and their Markets* (Princeton, N.J., 1975).

Potter, J. M., Diaz, M. N. and Foster, G. M., eds., *Peasant Society. A Reader*. (Boston, Mass., 1967).

Press, Volker, "Der Bauernkrieg als Problem der deutschen Geschichte," *Nassauische Annalen* (1975): 158–77. (a)

Press, Volker, "Herrschaft, Landschaft und 'Gemeiner Mann' in Oberdeutschland von 15. bis zum frühen 19. Jht.," *Zeitschrift für die Geschichte des Oberrheins* 123 (1975): 169–214. (b)

———, "Der deutsche Bauernkrieg als Systemskrise," *Giessener Universitatsblätter* 11 (1978): 114–35.

Quietzsch, Rudolf, "Der Kampf der Bauer um Triftgerechtigkeit in Thüringen und Sachsen um 1525," in *Der arm Man 1525: Volkskundliche Studien*, ed. H. Strobach (Berlin, 1975).

Rabe, H., *Das Problem Leibeigenschaft: Eine Untersuchung über die Anfange einer Ideologisierung und des verfassungsrechtlichen Wandels von Freiheit und Eigentum im deutschen Bauernkrieg (Vierteljahrschrift für Sozial- und Wirtschaftsgeschichte, Beiheft 64, Wiesbaden, 1977)*.

Rammstedt, Otthein, "Stadtunruhen 1525," in *Der deutsche Bauernkrieg 1524–1526*, ed. H. U. Wehler (Göttingen, 1975).

Rankl, Helmut, "Gesellschaftlicher Ort und strafrichterliche Behandlung von 'Rumor', 'Emporung', 'Aufruhr' und 'Ketzerei' in Bayern um 1525," *Zeitschrift für bayerische Landesgeschichte* 38 (1975): 524–69.

Rapp, Francis, "Die soziale und wirtschaftliche Vorgeschichte des Bauernkrieges im Unterelsass," in Moeller (1975).

Redfield, Robert, *The Little Community* (Chicago, 1955).

———, *Peasant Society and Culture* (Chicago, 1956).

Rowan, Steven W., "The Common Penny (1495–99) as a Source of German Social and Demographic History," *Central European History* 10 (1977): 148–64.

Rublack, Hans-Christoph, "Die Stadt Würzburg im Bauernkrieg," *Archiv für Reformationsgeschichte* 67 (1976): 76–100.

Sabean, David, *Landbesitz und Gesellschaft am Vorabend des Bauernkriegs* (Stuttgart, 1972).

———, "Der Bauernkrieg—ein Literaturbericht für das Jahr

1975," *Zeitschrift für Agrargeschichte und Agrarsoziologie* 24 (1976): 223–7.

_____, "Family and Land Tenure: a Case Study of Conflict in the German Peasant War 1525," in Scribner and Benecke (1979).

Schilling, Heinz, "Aufstandsbewegungen in der stadtbürgerlichen Gesellschaft des Alten Reiches. Die Vorgeschichte des Münsteraner Täuferreichs, 1525 bis 1534," in Wehler (1975).

Schottenloher, Karl, *Bibliographie zur deutschen Geschichte im Zeitalter des Glaubensspaltung 1517–1585*, 7 vols. (Leipzig, 1933–66).

Schubert, Ernst, " 'bauerngeschrey': Zum Problem der öffentlichen Meinung im spätmittelalterlichen Franken," *Jahrbuch für fränkische Landesforschung* 24/25 (1975): 883–907.

*Schulze, Winfried, *Bäuerliche Widerstand und feudale Herrschaft in der frühen Neuzeit* (Stuttgart, 1980).

Schwarze, E., *Soziale Struktur und Besitzverhältnisse der ländlichen Bevölkerung Ostthüringens im 16. Jht.* (Weimar, 1975).

Scott, Tom, "Reformation and Peasants' War in Waldshut and Environs: A Structural Analysis," *Archiv für Reformationsgeschichte* 69 (1978): 82–102, 70 (1979): 140–68. (b)

_____, "The Peasants' War: A Historiographical Review," *The Historical Journal* 22 (1979): 693–720, 953–74. (a)

Scribner, R. W., "Civic Unity and the Reformation in Erfurt," *Past and Present* 66 (1975): 29–60.

_____, "Is there a Social History of the Reformation," *Social History* 2 (1977): 483–505.

_____, *For the Sake of Simple Folk. Popular Propaganda for the German Reformation* (Cambridge, 1981).

*Scribner, R. W., and Benecke, Gerhard, *The German Peasants' War 1525. New Viewpoints* (London, 1979).

Sea, Thomas F., "Schwäbischer Bund und Bauernkrieg: Bestrafung und Pazification," Wehler (1975).

_____, "The Economic Impact of the German Peasants' War. The Question of Reparations," *Sixteenth Century Journal* 8 (1977): 74–97.

_____, "Imperial Cities and the Peasants' War in Germany," *Central European History* 12 (1979): 3–37.

Shanin, Teodor, *Peasants and Peasant Societies* (Harmondsworth, Middlesex, 1971).

Stalnaker, John C., "Auf dem Weg zu einer sozialgeschichtlichen

Interpretation des Deutschen Bauernkrieges 1525–1526," in Wehler (1975).

Steinmetz, Max, *Das Müntzerbild von Luther bis Engels* (Berlin, 1971).

———, *Deutschland 1476–1648*, 2nd. ed. (Berlin, 1978).

———, "Forschungen zur Geschichte der deutschen frühbürgerlichen Revolution," in *Historische Forschung in der DDR 1970–1980* (Berlin, 1980).

Steinmetz, Max, and Hoyer, Siegfried, eds., *Der deutsche Bauernkrieg und Thomas Müntzer* (Leipzig, 1976).

Strobach, Heinrich, ed., *Der arm Man 1525: Volkskundliche Studien* (Berlin, 1975).

Struck, Wolf-Heino, *Der Bauernkrieg am Mittelrhein und in Hessen: Darstellungen und Quellen* (Wiesbaden, 1975).

Thomas, U., *Bibliographie zum deutschen Bauernkrieg und seiner Zeit (Veröffentlichungen seit 1974)*, Fachdokumentation Agrargeschichte, 1976; Fortsetzung, 1977 (Stuttgart, 1976–77).

Ulbrich, Claudia, *Leibeigenschaft am Oberrhein im Spätmittelalter* (Göttingen, 1979).

Unger, Manfred, "Dokumente zur Geschichte des bäuerlichen Klassenkampfes aus dem 16.-18. Jht. im Staatsarchiv Leipzig," *Jahrbuch für Regionalgeschichte* 5 (1975): 239–48.

Vogler, Günter, "Ein Vorspiel des deutschen Bauernkrieges im Nürnberger Landgebiet 1524," in *Der Bauer im Klassenkampf*, ed. G. Heitz et. al. (Berlin, 1975).

———, "Der deutsche Bauernkrieg und die Verhandlung des Reichtages zu Speyer 1526," in *Herrschaftsverträge, Wahlkapitulationen, Fundamentalgesetze*, ed. R. Vierhaus (Göttingen, 1977).

Volz, Ingrid, and Brather, Hans-Stephan, "Der deutsche Bauer im Klassenkampf (1470 bis 1648). Auswahlbibliographie der Veröffentlichungen in den sozialistischen Staaten aus den Jahren 1945 bis 1972," in G. Heitz et. al. (1975).

Wehler, Hans Ulrich, ed., *Der deutsche Bauernkrieg 1524–1526* (Göttingen, 1975).

*Wohlfeil, Rainer, ed., *Reformation oder frühbürgerliche Revolution* (Munich, 1972).

———, (ed.) *Der Bauernkrieg 1524–26* (Munich, 1975).

———, Einführung in die Geschichte des deutschen Reformation (Munich, 1982).

Wolf, Eric R., *Peasants* (Engelwood Cliffs, N.J., 1966).

———, *Peasant Wars of the Twentieth Century* (London, 1971).

Wollbrett, Alphonse, ed., *La Guerre des Paysans 1525*, Société d'histoire et d'archéologie de Saverne et environs: Études alsatiques, numéro supplémentaire 93 (Saverne, 1975).

Wunder, Heide, "Zur Mentalität aufständischer Bauern," in Wehler (1975).

The Anabaptists

James M. Stayer

The historical picture of Anabaptism has been radically altered in the last two decades and particularly in the 1970s. There are probably few areas of Reformation research in which the watersheds can be marked so easily. Harold S. Bender, the venerable editor of the *Mennonite Quarterly Review* and the single individual most identified with the previous interpretation of Anabaptism, died in 1962. In the same year George H. Williams published *The Radical Reformation*, in many respects a *summa* of the findings of the "Bender school," but also the first major contribution to ending the isolation of Anabaptist studies from other fields of Reformation research. Ten years later Claus-Peter Clasen published his monumental *Anabaptism. A Social History*. In the decade since 1972 one major study has followed another. Many issues are still extremely controversial but the net effect of the new research has been to accomplish a major revision, which can be summarized as ending both the isolation of the Anabaptist field and the idealization of the Anabaptists.

The current agenda of Anabaptist research consists in breaking free from confessional partisanship and narrowness, recognizing the diversity and plurality of the Anabaptist movements, tracing their connections to the thought patterns of the medieval world, illuminating the importance of the hitherto overshadowed second generation, and working towards a method of social history appropriate to an undeniably and irreducibly religious phenomenon. These are the present concerns of Reformation research in general; they imply a thorough-going integration of Anabaptism into the historical and theological interpretation of the Reformation.

The previous generation of Anabaptist scholars demanded a very special position in Reformation studies for themselves and their historical characters. The work of these scholars can best be described as the "free church historiography". Many, but far from all of them, were affiliated, like Harold Bender, with the Mennonites, the lineal descendants of the Anabaptists. They were free churchmen writing about the first free church with the objective of seeing that it received the justice in the pages of church history that had been denied it by the events of the sixteenth century. In the sixteenth century Anabaptist dissenters, who insisted that baptism must be practiced exclusively upon mature believers, had been maligned, persecuted and killed. These Anabaptists were the fathers who kept the faith to the death, despite "dungeon, fire, and sword." Theirs was a religious tradition in which the martyrology was of almost equal significance with the Bible.

The historiographical outcome was to make the ugly duckling of the Reformation into its most beautiful swan. The "free church" was an ecclesiological ideal based on the term "sect" used in the religious sociology of Max Weber and Ernst Troeltsch. Weber and Troeltsch described the "sect" as a self-selecting elite religious congregation, as distinguished from the "church," a religious organization for all where everyone was welcome to partake of the goods of salvation insofar as he was capable.[1] Obviously governments with their general responsibilities preferred "churches" to "sects," so the "sect," traditionally a nasty term, could be renamed the "free church," a select church free from the state. State churches naturally preferred inclusive infant baptism ("the sociological sacrament"), while free churches insisted upon exclusive believers' baptism.

The first Anabaptists of the Reformation were seen as a group of pious Protestants under Conrad Grebel, who insisted on literal obedience to the Bible as opposed to the political compromises of the Zurich Reformer, Ulrich Zwingli.[2] In January 1525 they initiated the baptism of adult believers in defiance of the Zurich government and Zwingli, because they wanted the Christian church to be a voluntary community free of the state. They could not accept the moral compromises necessary for statesmen and politicians. Citing the Sermon on the Mount, they refused to allow their members to participate in government because they totally rejected violence, even in self-defense. One of the classics of the free church interpretation was a book by Franklin H. Littell which saw "Christian primitivism," the ideal of the restitution of the New Testament church, as the core of Anabaptism.[3] According to this view (both the view of Littell and

---

[1]Troeltsch (1912), 863; Weber (1906), 578.
[2]Bender (1950); Yoder (1958).
[3]Littell (1952).

the sixteenth-century Anabaptists), the Christian Church had un-
dergone a "fall" at the conversion of Constantine when it was amal-
gamated with the Roman state. The Anabaptists were the victims of
unremitting persecution by Catholic and Protestant governments
alike as they spread from Zurich through Switzerland, Germany,
Austria, and the Netherlands. Their expansion occurred as religious
exiles and wandering artisans set up small congregations of peaceful
Bible readers. The persecutions, which produced thousands of martyrs, took place simply because they would not conform to the officially sponsored religions and spoke out against evils such as war.
Roland Bainton, swept along on the wave of enthusiasm for Anabaptism, wrote that there was "a real possibility that Anabaptism, if
unimpeded by the sword of the magistrate, might have become the
prevailing branch of the church in Germany."[4] That abuses occurred in Anabaptist history, such as the sexual antinomianism of St.
Gall or the revolutionary communist and polygamous kingdom in
Münster, was not denied. However these aberrations were explained
in part by the general persecution. In any case, only sober, biblicist
Anabaptism survived; and when deviations arose they were quickly
condemned, just as Menno Simons condemned the Münsterites. The
real example of Anabaptist communalism was not to be found in
Münster but in tolerant Moravia, where thousands of Anabaptists
found refuge and set up the experiment in communal living and
sharing that still continues among the North American Hutterites.
The free church historians insisted that any religious group must be
judged by its ideals, not by instances of corruption and aberration.
By this standard the Anabaptists were the true biblical Christians of
the Reformation and the precursors of such modern values as religious toleration, pacifism, and the separation of church and state.

The free church historiography overreached itself when its idealization of Anabaptism became simply incredible. By the sixties even
shapers of the free church standpoint like Heinold Fast saw that the
rehabilitation of Anabaptism was so perfect that there was bound to
be a critical reaction to it.[5] The free church historians were most
vulnerable to the charge that they had artificially narrowed the
scope of Anabaptist studies by refusing to give serious attention to
Anabaptists who were not peaceful, biblicist, and holy, of whom
there were a significant number if one were disposed to look. Harold

[4]Bainton (1957), 321.
[5]Fast (1967), 25.

Bender and the Mennonite historians of Anabaptism were especially disposed to the narrowest possible focus of research, concentrating on "Anabaptism proper," "genuine Anabaptism," "normative Anabaptism," or "Evangelical Anabaptism," the last of which ultimately became the preferred term. Their objective was avowedly confessional, to isolate the Anabaptism which maintained an "unbroken course" from the sixteenth century to the Mennonite churches of their day, and not to permit their understanding of it to be confused by Thomas Müntzer, the Peasants' War, the revolutionary kingdom in Münster, or Spiritualists like Caspar Schwenckfeld and Sebastian Franck.[6] Partly because of the free church research strategy and partly because of other factors tending toward specialization, Thomas Müntzer, the Peasants' War, and the Spiritualist individualists were studied separately from the Anabaptists and from one another since the 1920s. One of the major thrusts of the research of the seventies was to break down the barriers between these related expressions of Reformation radicalism.

George Williams' *Radical Reformation* (1962) presented a panoramic Radical Reformation that included all radicals in Italy and Eastern Europe as well as Central Europe, and reconstructed some of the historical connections between the revolutionaries, the spiritualists, and the Anabaptists. On the one hand, his was an achievement of compilation, heavily indebted to the free church historiography; on the other, it foreshadowed a program of future research which transcended denominational history. In one respect, however, the researchers of the seventies have become wary of Williams' conception of a Radical Reformation. His efforts to formulate theological distinctions between the Radical Reformation and the Magisterial Reformation tend to obscure the dialectical relationship between the radicals and the major Reformers against whom they dissented. In general, it seems preferable to write of "the Reformation's radicals" rather than "the Radical Reformation."[7]

The new cross-fertilization between Müntzer studies and Anabaptist research was especially pertinent to the investigation of continuities between medieval religious consciousness and Anabaptism. Thomas Müntzer, as it has turned out, transmitted a good deal of medieval religious thought to South German Anabaptism. Hans-Jürgen Goertz's dissertation on the mystical structure of Müntzer's

[6]Bender (1944), 8.
[7]Cf. Goertz (1978), 7–20.

theology (1967) has had a major impact in the Anabaptist field. Goertz insisted that, rather than being a wayward pupil of Luther, Müntzer had preserved a pre-Reformation mystical theological tradition and adapted it to the soteriological concerns of the early Reformation. Moreover, as a Mennonite Goertz intended his work to have an application to the subject of Anabaptist origins. He regarded an understanding of Müntzer's theology as a necessary preliminary to grasping the theology of South German Anabaptists like Hans Denck.

This impulse was continued recently (1977) by the Canadian scholar Werner Packull, whose broad-ranging study of early South German and Austrian Anabaptism derived the movement from medieval mystical and apocalyptic beliefs transmitted by Müntzer to Hans Denck and Hans Hut. A few years earlier (1973) Steven Ozment had traced these same mystical ideas from the *German Theology* through Müntzer, Denck and Hut to Sebastian Franck, Sebastian Castellio and Valentin Weigel. He also elaborated another fundamental theme that appeared earlier in Goertz's study of Müntzer, the intrinsic connection of a traditional mystical theology with a sixteenth-century ideology of social protest. Christoph Windhorst's major study of Balthasar Hubmaier's baptismal theology (1976) stressed that it had important roots in medieval scholasticism as well as reflecting theological motifs from Luther and Zwingli. Another Canadian, Kenneth R. Davis, attempted to provide theological verification for the older theory of Albrecht Ritschl that Anabaptism was a continuation in laicized form of medieval monasticism. In many respects Davis's work, *Anabaptism and Asceticism* (1974), was the last blossoming of the Bender school, retaining Bender's category of Evangelical Anabaptism as a device for eliminating antinomian, spiritualist and revolutionary Anabaptists from his purview. However, Davis unabashedly accepted the moderate synergism of his protagonists, a prominent element in the theology of the Anabaptists studied by Packull and Windhorst as well. He continued in later writings to defend the category of Evangelical Anabaptism as a proper distinction between those Anabaptists whose ideal was the restitution of the New Testament church and figures like Müntzer and the Münsterites whose apocalyptic extremism led them to aim at "a superapostolic restoration hitherto unknown."[8] Davis' retention of a narrowly focused concept of Evangelical Anabaptism aside, these studies were united in their theological-intellectual history methodology and their denial of the previous general assumption that Anabaptism began on the theological ground of the Reformation.

That Anabaptism was far from monolithic in its belief system and its organization had been evident from the Reformation era itself when Sebastian Franck and Heinrich Bullinger both remarked upon the diversity of Anabaptist sects. The free church historians thought that the most fruitful way to deal with this empirical diversity was to identify an Anabaptist norm and then to take proper account of deviations from the norm. Otherwise, as Heinold Fast remarked during the 1975 meeting in Rüschlikon-Zurich commemorating the first believers' baptisms, we would be unable to say anything about the Anabaptists except that they were all different from one another. The assumption that Anabaptism must be more than a convenient and historically established name for the various groups practicing believers' baptism, that there must be an essence behind the name, lent vitality to the otherwise sterile debate on Anabaptist origins. If the Anabaptists began with Thomas Müntzer in Saxony, as older German Lutheran historians contended, they had one essence; if they began with Conrad Grebel in Zurich, as argued by the free church historians, they had another, entirely different essence.[9]

The challenge to this way of seeing the sixteenth-century Anabaptists began, as did much of the revision, within Mennonite circles themselves. Walter Klaassen demonstrated in his studies of the Anabaptist teaching on the Holy Spirit that there was a broad diversity of viewpoint on this subject among Anabaptist groups, and that the Anabaptist teachings overlapped substantially with the doctrines of the major Reformers.[10]

My *Anabaptists and the Sword* (1972) did the same thing as Klaassen's work, focusing on the very sensitive issue of political ethic. (The idea that Anabaptists were peaceful was one of the buttresses of Bender's characterization of genuine Anabaptism.) The book treats all Anabaptists, justifying this procedure by launching one of the first explicit polemics against the narrowness and distortions of the notion of "Evangelical Anabaptism." It discovered the key to its approach in the several historical groupings: the Swiss Brethren, Hut's movement, the Moravian *Stäbler*, the Marpeck brotherhood, the Central German Anabaptists, and the various Melchiorite sects.

[9]Cf. Bender (1953), 5.
[10]Klaassen (1963).

Each group developed a political ethic in accordance with its own needs. The central thesis of the book is that the variations in the teaching "on the sword" were not random but closely connected with the emerging identities of distinct, rival Anabaptist brotherhoods.

Bender's major book had been on Conrad Grebel and the beginnings of the Swiss Brethren. His idea that the Anabaptisms of South Germany and of the Netherlands were exported from Zurich rested on insecure foundations so long as Hans Hut and Melchior Hoffman, the major leaders of those two regional Anabaptisms, could not be explained as sound, Evangelical Anabaptists in the Swiss manner. The free church historiography had never successfully assimilated either of these charismatic, apocalyptic preachers into its categories.[11] The major biographies of Hut and Hoffman in the seventies established a very strong case for the plurality of Anabaptist traditions. Gottfried Seebass, a German Lutheran theologian, devoted a thorough *Habilitationsschrift* (1972) to Hut. He convincingly demonstrated how Hut carried Müntzer's apocalypticism and his mysticism into Anabaptism, and that Hut's missionary activity began in Franconia in 1526 with an appeal to veterans and fugitives from the Peasants' War.[12] But, instead of concluding in the manner of earlier Lutheran interpreters of Anabaptism that Anabaptism *per se* was revolutionary and Müntzerite, Seebass hypothesized that Hut's was "an entirely different Anabaptism" from that of the Swiss. Klaus Deppermann's biography of Hoffman (1979) fitted the emerging pattern. A social radical and a theocrat, Hoffman could not reasonably be freed from historical responsibility for the events in Münster, 1534–35. Furthermore, in organization and doctrine Hoffman clearly set up his own "Melchiorite" Anabaptism when he began to baptize adults in 1530.

"From Monogenesis to Polygenesis," the programmatic historiographical essay on Anabaptist origins which appeared in the 1975 *MQR* under the joint authorship of Deppermann, Packull (whose recently completed dissertation was in many respects a continuation of Seebass' study on a wider canvas), and myself, was an attempt to give form to the Anabaptist plurality so frequently confirmed in the research of the seventies. The point was that there were three historical "families" of Anabaptism, one going back to Grebel, a second

[11]Klassen (1959) was a weak Mennonite attempt to "explain" Hut.
[12]Seebass (1974).

to Hut and Denck, and a third to Melchior Hoffman and Jan Mat-
thijs (the father of the revolutionary episode in Münster). There
were some points of contact between the later Hut-Denck and Melchiorite branches and already established Anabaptist groups, but
the attempt to "derive" South German-Austrian or North German-
Dutch Anabaptism from the Anabaptism of Grebel in Zurich always
produced more confusion than clarity. Thus the stress on polygenesis
was a device to underscore the plural identity and plural religious
traditions of Anabaptism.

Calvin A. Pater's forthcoming book on Carlstadt and Anabaptism
challenges the polygenetic model.[13] Pater's work demonstrates that
Anabaptist studies have been impoverished by systematically ignoring Carlstadt's impact on the Anabaptists, pointed to by Walther
Köhler as long ago as 1925. Pater develops the intriguing argument
that after a brief Augustinian phase Carlstadt became the first anti-
predestinarian theologian among the Reformers, in this respect anticipating Hubmaier, Denck, Hoffman, and Menno. He sees the
Grebel group in Zurich, 1524 as a circle of Carlstadtians, and notes
that their critique of Müntzer was parallel to Carlstadt's. He also
underscores the extensive contacts between Carlstadt and Melchior
Hoffman. It sometimes seems as though Pater thinks that he has established a new "purely religious" Saxon monogenesis of Anabaptism in Carlstadt's nonviolent radicalism. However, there is strained
paradox in regarding Carlstadt, who never adopted believer's baptism, as the "father" of a movement centered around it, or in trying
to account for the continuously apocalyptic message of Hoffman in
terms of the unapocalyptic Carlstadt. Furthermore, the interpretations that stress the plural origins and character of Anabaptism have
devoted themselves to describing the structural evolution of the Anabaptist groups. They have assumed that Anabaptist ideas were socially transmitted. It would seem a regression to study this popular
religious phenomenon primarily in terms of intellectual influences, a
method appropriate, if at all, only with Protestant confessions dominated by school theologians.

The new Anabaptist social history, like much social history, has a
Marxist in its pedigree. Gerhard Zschäbitz, by all accounts the most
sensitive and flexible of the East German Marxist-Leninist historians
of the Reformation, wrote about Anabaptism in the late fifties and
early sixties as a part of the Early Bourgeois Revolution in Germany,

[13]To appear in 1982, based on Pater (1977).

the official East German rubric for the Reformation and Peasants' War. Focusing on Hans Hut and the Central German Anabaptists, he showed the oppositional bitterness often mixed with hopes for apocalyptic vengeance that imbued their statements. This was obviously, he argued, an expression of the social resentment occasioned by the suppression of the masses in the Peasants' War. The theory of the Early Bourgeois Revolution, with all its imperfections, provided a model of revolutionary upheaval, counter-revolutionary triumph, and sectarian withdrawal that could be tested on the several Anabaptist groups. The Marxist historiography first suggested that, despite its separatism, Anabaptism enjoyed no "purely religious" exemption from social process.

Claus-Peter Clasen applied a radically different social history methodology in his *Anabaptism: A Social History* (1972). He quantified all available published or unpublished source materials on Anabaptism in Switzerland, South and Central Germany and Austria. Although Clasen chose to exclude the Melchiorite sects of North Germany and the Low Countries, his book is undoubtedly the major research achievement of twentieth-century Anabaptist studies. It established the main contours of the social composition of non-Melchiorite Anabaptism, confirming and extending Paul Peachey's earlier study of the social structure of Swiss Anabaptism.[14] The preserved sources indicate that Anabaptism at first had a majority of its adherents in the cities and towns. In the late 1520s persecution removed educated and prosperous leaders from Anabaptist ranks, leaving the direction of the movement to craftsmen. As persecution was more effective in the towns than the rural districts, gradually peasants came to make up more than 60% of the Anabaptists. The relationship between rural and urban elements in the several phases of Anabaptist history continues to evoke lively disagreement, especially since a good number of current Anabaptist historians disagree with Clasen's blanket separation of Anabaptist beginnings from the Peasants' War. Clasen also advanced a series of important revisions. He showed that most Protestant magistrates, unlike those in Switzerland and Saxony, were averse to executing Anabaptists. Here he applied Ockham's razor to the mythology of the martyr church and offered some preliminary insights into the process by which the Anabaptist remnant was able to survive. Most important, he denied that Anabaptism was numerically significant, advancing the estimate that there were

[14]Peachey (1954).

only thirty thousand Anabaptists in the regions studied between the beginning of the movement and the Thirty Years War. Although Clasen provided a needed corrective to earlier notions which exaggerated the size and significance of the movement, he was overly assured about his quantitative methodology. His source material was necessarily incomplete. His ideals of a value-free social history led him to avoid dealing directly with Anabaptist religious thought; however, personal notions of social order and "common sense" colored Clasen's conclusions and descriptions in a manner of which he was unaware.

Albert Mellink, who applied a different variety of social history inspired by religious socialism, came to conclusions strikingly different from Clasen's in his study of Anabaptism in the Netherlands, a region omitted by Clasen. Here he discovered a revolutionary mass movement in the 1530s, and he asserted that the Anabaptists "had a very substantial following in the Netherlands for quite an extended time period" before the rise of Calvinism.[15] He criticized the absence of an ideal component in Clasen's social history.[16]

In 1973, the year after Clasen's book, Karl-Heinz Kirchhoff published his massive social analysis of the Münster Anabaptists, based particularly on a study of the records of confiscated properties following the Bishop's reconquest. His conclusions brought a disturbing anomaly into the social picture of Anabaptism. Whatever their other differences, Mellink, Zschäbitz, and Clasen had all agreed with the traditional notion by which Anabaptism was "the Protestantism of the poor." There were isolated protests before, as when the Dutch Mennonite historian, W. J. Kühler, asserted the considerable wealth of the Melchiorites who set out by ship from the Netherlands to Münster in 1534.[17] However, Kirchhoff's demonstration of the slightly above average prosperity of the native Münster Anabaptists and of the traditional social status of their leadership made the first important break with simplified class analysis of the sixteenth-century Anabaptists. Kirchhoff treated his work simply as a study in local history, but it is too thorough and convincing not to have wider reverberations.

Clasen was primarily interested in Anabaptism as a suitable proving ground for a method of social history which would answer all

---

[15]Mellink (1954), 325.
[16]Mellink (1979), 6–7.
[17]Kuehler (1921).

answerable questions in the manner of a positive science.[18] However, when one observes the discrepancies in the highly competent social histories of Clasen, Mellink, and Kirchhoff, it is clear that their partial and conflicting answers raise an agenda of new questions and that social history is no more "definitive" than earlier historical methodologies.

Umstrittenes Täufertum, 1525-1975, the volume marking the four hundred and fiftieth anniversary of Anabaptism, mirrored the clash between the free church historiography and the revisionists; but in number of contributions and in the sympathies of the editor, Hans-Jürgen Goertz, the revisionists were already in the superior position. Probably the most important new standpoint set forth in *Umstrittenes Täufertum* was a questioning of the venerable identification of Swiss Anabaptist origins with Troeltsch's "sect" type—in effect, it was denied that the original, conscious purpose of the believers' baptisms of 1525 had been to establish a "free church." Six years previously J.F.G. Goeters had devoted a very thorough, unpolemical investigation to the "prehistory" of Zurich Anabaptism, in which he showed how closely implicated the future Anabaptists were with the resistance of rural communities to the centralizing policies of the church and government of Zurich. At the time the essay drew only limited attention. In *Umstrittenes Täufertum* Martin Haas and I devoted complementary essays to describing a radical movement of 1522-25 that aimed at a "total Reformation" upon the independent initiative of rural Swiss communities. This mass movement was strongest in the eastern Swiss territories of Schaffhausen and St. Gall, where, as in Waldshut, it achieved a working alliance with the peasant uprisings of 1525. Haas concluded that it aimed at the purification of the cult in whole communities, not at the singling out of worthy individuals for a minority congregation. Conrad Grebel himself was closely involved with this mass Anabaptism. Sectarian withdrawal, separation from the world, was only fixed in Swiss Anabaptism with Michael Sattler's Schleitheim Articles of February 1527. The studies of Seebass and Packull, previously mentioned, produced a parallel challenge to the Troeltsch model, insofar as they denied that Hut's Anabaptism in South Germany and Austria had begun with the object of establishing "sects" or select, gathered congregations. According to this new research the very free church idea, centering on the individual decision of the believer, was a product of

---

[18]Hood (1981).

political and social history. Increasingly the historians of Anabaptism abandoned notions of ideal causation and of "purely religious" forces for a historical interdependence between ideal and social factors.

Such an interdependence between social processes and ideas was assumed in Goertz's *Die Täufer. Geschichte und Deutung* (1980), the first comprehensive interpretation of the Anabaptists written under the influence of the revisionist historiography of the seventies. Goertz committed himself to a pluralistic methodology joining theology, church history, intellectual history, and social history. He worked from the assumption of three substantially independent Anabaptist traditions: the Swiss Brethren, South German-Austrian Anabaptism, and North German-Dutch Anabaptism. As a theologian, he explicitly abandoned the quest for a historical and theological norm for Anabaptism: "There is no historical answer to the question of which among the many Anabaptist groups were the 'genuine' Anabaptists."[19] The Anabaptist theologies were products of a very different age which escapes us when we presume intimacy with it; at best modern theology can derive "impulses" from the theologies of the past. Goertz was most original when he combined his previous training as a theologian with his current commitment to social history. In his view the *Sitz im Leben*, the social context, for the Reformation generally, and for Anabaptism especially, was anticlericalism, here conceived not as a trivial idea but as a powerful social force. He demonstrated the diversity of the three Anabaptist traditions on a whole range of doctrinal issues once utilized for separating genuine from deviant Anabaptists: the role of the pastor, the use of Scripture, the process of salvation, baptismal theology, ecclesiology. Yet the anticlerical atmosphere of Reformation radicalism that was the common matrix of all Anabaptisms made them variations on a single soteriological and ecclesiological theme. The Anabaptists conceived of the salvation process as "betterment of life," and for the Christian collectivity this meant "to purify the church and to keep it pure."[20] Goertz assumes that there is an anticlerical root or common denominator for all of the abundant social *ressentiment* among Anabaptists. This is a very important idea for Reformation studies generally, one that those of us who have been trained as theologians or intellectual historians can too easily underestimate. Still, we need further clarification of anticlericalism, as to exactly what it means in

[19]Goertz (1980), 161.
[20]Ibid. 101.

the Reformation era and what it explains about the Reformation; as it stands, it is a concept rather too big and luxuriant, in need of pruning.

Anticlericalism was a medieval tradition—or at least a late medieval tradition. What explains its greater power in the Reformation than in the two or three previous centuries? Goertz assumes that the radicals of the Reformation era were, above all, radical anticlericals. These are subjects needing further investigation. How intense was the hatred of the clergy: how seriously are we to take statements like those of the proto-Anabaptist Simon Stumpf, that the Reformation could make no progress unless the priests were slain? The medieval tradition of anticlericalism was intertwined with the medieval rejection of wealth and of the rich; and, of course, community of property is a theme that recurs among Anabaptists. No one has been able until now (Reinhard Schwarz, with his tantalizing but insufficiently grounded book on Müntzer,[21] is no exception) to work productively with the Marxists' repeated suggestion of links between the fifteenth-century Taborites and popular currents in the Reformation. Yet it seems too early simply to abandon the notion of lingering Taborite influences among the Reformation's radicals. If there were such influences, they would surely be apocalyptic as well as communist and anticlerical. Especially with an Anabaptist leader such as Hoffman, who has a complex apocalyptic teaching (and one in which Jan Hus plays a prominent role!), the questions of how much he took over from medieval traditions, how much he drew directly from the Bible, how he reshaped what he received, seem definitely worth following.[22]

The place of medieval mysticism in the religious thought of radical leaders like Müntzer, Carlstadt, Hut, Denck, and Hoffman seems well established. Yet it is an elusive topic; the radicals seldom mention medieval mystical sources in their writings. Some previous interpreters see mystical intellectual frameworks, mystical soteriologies, among the figures just mentioned, while others insist that there is no more than a relatively superficial adoption of "mystical terminology." This debate is not over. A systematic study in comparative religious thought would be welcome, to probe the depth and importance of medieval mystical thought patterns among the Reformation's radicals. Neither is the persistence of the ascetic tradition

[21]Schwarz (1977).
[22]Werner O. Packull is working on this problem.

among Anabaptists a closed subject after Davis's book. There is fruitful research currently in progress on how specific monastic traditions affected particular Anabaptist leaders: for instance, C. Arnold Synder's work on Michael Sattler and the Benedictines, and George K. Epp's hypothesis that Menno Simons was educated by the Premonstratensians.[23]

To investigate the continuance of medieval religious thought in Anabaptism some sort of intellectual history methodology is required, but it is important to avoid simplistic assumptions about intellectual "influences." Particularly when the Anabaptists or other radicals were using the ideas of previous centuries, they did so only because of the needs of their present situation and they adapted the older ideas accordingly.

In Reformation studies generally the study of the second generation or of the late sixteenth century has tended to be most appealing to conservative scholars holding on to interpretations and methodologies established before the past two decades. This would make late sixteenth-century Anabaptism the natural preserve of researchers schooled in the free church tradition. Leonhard Gross's *The Golden Years of the Hutterites* (1980) would seem to fit this description and to foreshadow similar work in the future. For instance, the rooting of the Swiss Brethren in rural milieus in Bern, eastern France, and the Palatinate during the late sixteenth century probably marks the real transition from Anabaptist history to Mennonite confessional history. The persistence of the Swiss-South German Mennonite tradition under conditions of sporadic oppression is a promising research topic. Another similar "second generation" topic is the expansion of the Dutch-North German Mennonites, connected with the preaching of Leonard Bouwens.

Future research will continue to test the viability of the tripartite division of Anabaptism into the Swiss Brethren, South German-Austrian, and North German-Dutch movements. One relevant question is whether these movements which we now think of as different Anabaptisms produced different strains of religious thought. Certainly the idea of the heavenly flesh of Christ, to which Mary made no contribution, is a distinctively Melchiorite belief. What about eschatological-apocalyptic ideas? Do the eschatological differences between Sattler, Hut, and Hoffman justify the assumption of the research of the seventies that these are three different Anabaptisms? As

[23]Epp (1980).

Hans-Jürgen Goertz has said repeatedly, a full investigation of the different teachings on justification within Anabaptism is very important, since this was, after all, the central topic in Reformation theology. Were the early Swiss Brethren like Sattler fully on the soteriological ground of the Swiss-South German Reformation, as has often been claimed? It is a certainty that there were anti-predestinarian thinkers among the Anabaptists, who were more synergistic than the major Reformers. On the matter of distinguishing Anabaptist traditions, the biographies of Hut and Hoffman by Seebass and Deppermann have played a vital role. It needs only to be remarked that such central figures in Anabaptist group formation as Michael Sattler, Hans Denck, Melchior Rinck, Bernhard Rothmann and, above all, David Joris have not yet received adequate biographical treatment. A good regional study on Austrian Anabaptism remains to be written. Even such a fundamental issue as the comparative role of Swiss Anabaptists and the followers of Hut in the origins of Austrian Anabaptism is still unclarified. A complementary social history to Clasen's is needed for Anabaptism in North Germany and the Low Countries, the regions his study omitted.

Undoubtedly the unresolved issues in Anabaptist social history are the most important of all. One very big subject is the relation of Anabaptism and the Peasants' War. Claus-Peter Clasen's study of Württemberg Anabaptism found no connection between the two movements.[24] Gottfried Seebass's research on Hut's missionary work in Franconia suggests that his chiliastic message began with an appeal to disgruntled veterans and fugitives from the Peasants' War. Tantalizing connections between peasant upheaval and later Anabaptism have emerged from my research and Martin Haas's on Eastern Switzerland, and from Walter Klaassen's study of Michael Gaismair and his Tyrolian rebellion.[25] The links that Gerhard Zschäbitz and John Oyer have discovered between Central German Anabaptism and Müntzer's own peasant band are certainly substantial.[26] Still, none of the works that affirm the link between Anabaptism and the Peasants' War can match the methodological thoroughness of Clasen's with its negative result. Seebass has suggested, however, that there may be deficiencies in the source material that Clasen quantified. Peasants' War sources are far from completely edited

---

[24]Clasen (1965), 167–173.
[25]Klaassen (1978), 112–116.
[26]Zschaebitz (1958); Oyer (1964).

and Anabaptist source collections seldom inform us about an Anabaptist's life before his baptism.[27] Hence prosopographical studies in
each sensitive region seem to be called for.

However, whatever the results of further research into the Peasants' War-Anabaptist connection, it is certain that Anabaptism is a
decidedly smaller scale movement than the peasant risings. Here we
come to central issues about Anabaptism's social significance raised
by Clasen. Was Anabaptism intrinsically a network of small, with-
drawn sects as Clasen concluded, or is Clasen here taking over assumptions of the free church historiography by simply quantifying
source collections prepared at an earlier stage in Anabaptist research? An alternative research hypothesis would be that Anabaptism was but one distinctively profiled and historically durable expression of a broad spectrum of radicalism in the early Reformation.
This Reformation radicalism reached its crisis point in 1525, and included peasant and plebeian oppositions, spiritualist individualists,
and discontented scholars and artists. My present view is that both
Clasen's study and my own in 1972 were too narrowly and exclusively focused on Anabaptism to comprehend fully the movement's context in the earlier Reformation and the Peasants' War. Each of us
was still somewhat entrapped by the horizons of the "little Anabaptism" that the free church historians had created for their confessional objectives.

However valuable the idea of Anabaptism as a "radical" or "oppositional" movement may prove to be, it threatens to become a
modernizing anachronism. Some of the most stimulating recent interpretations of the Peasants' War may assist us in avoiding this.
John C. Stalnaker and David Sabean have argued that the Peasants'
War was the expression not of the downtrodden, but of a powerful,
although discontented, estate under its natural leaders. If we must
use a Marxist-Leninist anachronism the Peasants' War was "the
revolution of the kulaks"! With this analogy Kirchhoff's findings
about the elite leadership of Münster Anabaptism fit into a distinct
sixteenth-century radical, oppositional context. We should probably
be much more alert than hitherto in Anabaptist social history to
identify the Anabaptist social elites, the "natural leadership" of
Anabaptist groups, and how they functioned. Let us not too easily
accept the "progressive" notion that Anabaptist "opposition" meant
opposition to a tiered, hierarchical social structure. However sepa-

[27]Seebass (1974), 285.

rated the Anabaptists were from the sixteenth-century world of estates, they remained a part of it.

The present resources for Anabaptist research are still substantially a bequest of the earlier, free church historiography, and particularly of the Mennonites as the confessional descendants of the Anabaptists. Mennonite historical libraries, committed to possessing full holdings of the primary and secondary materials on Anabaptism, have been created at Goshen, Indiana, Bethel, Kansas, Harrisonburg, Virginia, and Waterloo, Ontario. The older European ancestor of these institutions is the library of the United Mennonite (*Doopsgezinde*) congregation at Amsterdam, now no longer a separate library but a collection housed in the Amsterdam University Library. Assembled over two and a half centuries, this collection contains 331 printed titles dating from the sixteenth-century on Anabaptism and related topics. Since 1977 these sixteenth-century sources have been available on microfiche from the Inter Documentation Company.[28]

Critical editions of Anabaptist sources have been published regularly since the thirties. In 1930 the first volume of the *Quellen zur Geschichte der Wiedertäufer* appeared under the editorship of the *Verein für Reformationsgeschichte*. Three volumes were published before the war, and when the series was continued in 1951 with American Mennonite financial support, "Täufer" was substituted for "Wiedertäufer" because of the polemical overtones of the latter term. In the postwar years independent series were devoted to Anabaptist sources in Switzerland and the Netherlands, and the Hessian Anabaptist documents were published as part of a multi-volume series for Hessian Reformation History.

The editors were of mixed backgrounds, reflecting the various inspirations of radical research. Archivists like Karl Schornbaum, Manfred Krebs, and Jean Rott have played a continuing prominent role in the publication of documents on Anabaptism. Secular historians like Leonard von Muralt, Martin Haas, Günther Franz, and Albert Mellink have set the tone of the Swiss, Dutch, and Hessian collections. Franz, the major historian of the Peasants' War, edited not only the Hessian *Täuferakten* but also the first nearly complete critical edition of the works of Thomas Müntzer (1968). Mellink, whose dissertation constituted a devastating critical assault upon the apologetic tendencies in the historiography of the Dutch Mennon-

[28]Horst (1977).

ites, has very recently edited the first two volumes of *Documenta Anabaptistica Neerlandica*, a series prominently supported by the Dutch Mennonites. Grete Mecenseffy, the editor of the Austrian sources, is a Protestant church historian. Gustav Bossert, Sr., the editor of the first volume in the main series, was a Lutheran pastor sympathetic to the Anabaptists. Lydia Müller, who began the editing of Hutterite documents, was a product of the post-World War I Renaissance in Luther scholarship, as was Robert Stupperich, primarily a Melanchthon scholar, who has edited the works of Bernhard Rothmann as well as the Catholic polemics against Münster Anabaptism.

The largest single contribution to the financing and editing of the source volumes came from the "free church historiography." Hans Hillerbrand's bibliography of Anabaptism (1962) was the result of a massive collective effort at the Mennonite Historical Library at Goshen, Indiana, a ripe fruit of the "Bender school" in the most precise sense. Robert Friedmann edited a volume of Hutterite documents; Walter Fellmann, editor of the Denck writings, is a Mennonite pastor; Gunar Westin and Torsten Bergsten, editors of the Hubmaier documents, are Swedish Baptists. The most exemplary volume in any of the series, that on Anabaptism in Eastern Switzerland (1973), was the achievement of Heinold Fast, Mennonite pastor in Emden, who is now in process of editing the devotional anthology of the Marpeck circle, the *Kunstbuch*. H. W. Meihuizen, Dutch Mennonite church historian, is at work on the first critical edition of the writings of Menno Simons, having already edited his focal *Fundamentboek*.

A number of Anabaptist source volumes are substantially finished and awaiting publication—the Bern documents, the sources pertaining to the career of Hans Hut, a volume on the Imperial cities in present-day Württemberg, and a third volume on Strasbourg. The publication of sources for Netherlands Anabaptism is only beginning. In some cases important Anabaptist source materials are available only in early pre-critical editions, like those of Christian Meyer and Friedrich Roth for Augsburg.[29] The works of Melchior Hoffman are probably too extensive to receive modern critical editing in their entirety; a selection will likely be necessary here, and certainly in the cases of David Joris' writings and the devotional literature of the Hutterites. The biggest gap of all, in an area once considered "mar-

[29]Meyer (1874); Roth (1900) and (1901).

ginal" to Anabaptist studies, is the absence of a critical edition of the writings of Andreas Carlstadt. Of his nineteen Latin and forty-nine German works, only ten are available in modern reprintings. Erich Hertzsch's edition of the eight very important anti-Lutheran writings of 1523–25 is little more than a reprinting.

In general, it seems that the various commissions engaged in the support of Anabaptist and radical source editions ought to improve their communications in search for a more comprehensive research strategy. The Bender school hoped for the achievement of a "definitive" history of sixteenth-century Anabaptism based on all pertinent primary sources. It soon became evident that a principle of selection was needed. Robert Friedmann complained about the emphasis upon court records as opposed to devotional writings in the *Quellen zur Geschichte der Täufer*. When the investigation of connections between Anabaptism and the Peasants' War came onto the research agenda, Gottfried Seebass remarked that the published source collections are badly suited for prosopographical study, as was noted previously.

Now that naive, positivist notions of definitive history are on the wane, it would be well to acknowledge that there will always be a dialectical relationship between the interpretations accepted at any given period and the source collections which then appear. Human and financial resources are not available to edit and publish all the sources; choices could be made, however tentatively, on the basis of some research strategy, in order to maximize the impact of the scholarly editions.

Bibliography

I. Interpretive Studies (first editions are indicated)
Armour, Rollin S., *Anabaptist Baptism* (Scottdale, 1966).
Bainton, Roland H., *David Joris* (Leipzig, 1937).
———, "The Anabaptist Contribution to History," in Hershberger (1957), 317–326.
Bauman, Clarence, *Gewaltlosigkeit im Täufertum* (Leyden, 1968).
Bender, Harold S., "The Anabaptist Vision," *Church History* 13 (1944): 3–24.
———, *Conrad Grebel, 1498–1526, The Founder of the Swiss Brethren, Sometimes called Anabaptists* (Goshen, 1950).

———, "The Zwickau Prophets, Thomas Müntzer and the Anabaptists," *Mennonite Quarterly Review* 27 (1953): 3–16.

Bergsten, Torsten, *Balthasar Hubmaier—Seine Stellung zu Reformation und Täufertum* (Kassel, 1961).

Blanke, Fritz, *Brüder in Christo* (Zurich, 1955).

Bornhäuser, Christoph, *Leben und Lehre Menno Simons'. Ein Kampf um das Fundament des Glaubens (etwa 1496–1561)* (Neukirchen, 1973).

Clasen, Claus-Peter, *Die Wiedertäufer im Herzogtum Württemberg und in benachbarten Herrschaften* (Stuttgart, 1965).

———, *Anabaptism. A Social History, 1525–1618* (Ithaca & London, 1972).

———, *The Anabaptists in South and Central Germany, Switzerland, and Austria* (Goshen, 1978).

Cornelius, Carl A., *Geschichte des Münsterischen Aufruhrs*, 2 vols. (Leipzig, 1855–1860).

Davis, Kenneth R., *Anabaptism and Asceticism, A Study in Intellectual Origins* (Scottdale, 1974).

———, "Anabaptism as a Charismatic Movement," *Mennonite Quarterly Review* 53 (1979): 219–234.

Deppermann, Klaus, Packull, Werner O., Stayer, James M., "From Monogenesis to Polygenesis. The Historical Discussion of Anabaptist Origins," *Mennonite Quarterly Review* 49 (1975): 83–121.

———, *Melchior Hoffman. Soziale Unruhen und apokalyptische Visionen im Zeitalter der Reformation* (Göttingen, 1979).

Epp, George K., "The Spiritual Roots of Menno Simons," in Harry Loewen, ed., *Mennonite Images: Historical, Cultural, and Literary Essays Dealing with Mennonite Issues* (Winnipeg, 1980): 51–59.

Fast, Heinold, *Heinrich Bullinger und die Täufer* (Weierhof, 1959).

———, "Die Sonderstellung der Täufer in St. Gallen und Appenzell," *Zwingliana* 11 (1960): 223–240.

———, "Europäische Forschungen auf dem Gebiet der Täufer- und Mennonitengeschichte, (1962–1967)," *Mennonitische Geschichtsblätter* 24 (1967): 19–30.

Friedmann, Robert, *The Theology of Anabaptism* (Scottdale, 1973).

Goertz, Hans-Jürgen, *Innere und äussere Ordnung in der Theologie Thomas Müntzers* (Leyden, 1967).

———, ed., *Umstrittenes Täufertum, 1525–1975. Neue Forschungen* (Göttingen, 1975).

_____, ed., *Radikale Reformatoren. 21 Biographische Skizzen von Thomas Müntzer bis Paracelsus* (Munich, 1978).

_____, *Die Täufer. Geschichte und Deutung* (Munich, 1980).

Goeters, J.F. Gerhard, "Die Vorgeschichte des Täufertums in Zürich," in *Studien zur Geschichte und Theologie der Reformation. Festschrift für Ernst Bizer* (Neukirchen, 1969): 239–281.

Gross, Leonard, *The Golden Years of the Hutterites* (Scottdale, 1980).

Haas, Martin, "Der Weg der Täufer in die Absonderung. Zur Interdependenz von Theologie und sozialem Verhalten," in Goertz, *Umstrittenes Täufertum*, 50–78.

Hershberger, Guy E., ed., *The Recovery of the Anabaptist Vision. A Sixtieth Anniversary Tribute to Harold S. Bender* (Scottdale, 1957).

Holl, Karl, "Luther und die Schwärmer," in *Gesammelte Aufsätze zur Kirchengeschichte*, I: *Luther* (Tübingen, 1923), 420–467.

Hood, Daniel, Review of Clasen (1978), *Sixteenth Century Journal* 12, 1 (1981), 105–106.

Horst, Irvin B., *The Radical Brethren: Anabaptism and the English Reformation to 1558* (Nieuwkoop, 1972).

_____, ed., *The Radical Reformation Microfiche Project: Section I: Mennonite and Related Sources up to 1600* (Zug, 1977-).

Kirchhoff, Karl-Heinz, *Die Täufer in Münster 1534–1535. Untersuchungen zum Umfang und zur Sozialstruktur der Bewegung* (Münster, 1973).

Klaassen, Walter, "Spiritualization in the Reformation," *Mennonite Quarterly Review* 37 (1963): 67–77.

_____, *Anabaptism: Neither Catholic nor Protestant* (Waterloo, 1973).

_____, *Michael Gaismair: Revolutionary and Reformer* (Leyden, 1978).

Klassen, Herbert C., "The Life and Teachings of Hans Hut," *Mennonite Quarterly Review* 33 (1959): 171–205, 267–304.

Klassen, William, *Covenant and Community* (Grand Rapids, 1968).

Köhler, Walther, "Die Zürcher Täufer," in *Gedenkschrift zum 400-jährigen Jubiläum der Mennoniten oder Taufgesinnten, 1525–1925* (Ludwigshafen, 1925), 48–64.

Krahn, Cornelius, *Dutch Anabaptism: Origin, Spread, Life and Thought, 1450–1600* (The Hague, 1964).

Kühler, W.J., "Het Anabaptisme in Nederland," *De Gids* 85–3 (1921): 249–278.

———, *Geschiedenis der Nederlandsche doopsgezinden in de zestiende eeuw* (Haarlem, 1932).

Littell, Franklin H., *The Anabaptist View of the Church* (New York, 1952).

Mellink, Albert F., *De Wederdopers in de Noordelijke Nederlanden, 1531–1544* (Groningen & Djakarta, 1954).

———, *De radikale Reformatie als thema van social-religieuze geschiedenis* (Nijmegen, 1979).

Meyer, Christian, "Zur Geschichte der Wiedertäufer in Oberschwaben," I: "Die Anfänge des Wiedertäuferthumbs in Augsburg," *Zeitschrift des Historischen Vereins für Schwaben und Neuburg* 1 (1874): 207–253.

Oyer, John S., *Lutheran Reformers against Anabaptists. Luther, Melanchthon and Menius and the Anabaptists of Central Germany* (The Hague, 1964).

Ozment, Steven, *Mysticism and Dissent. Religious Ideology and Social Protest in the Sixteenth Century* (New Haven & London, 1973).

Packull, Werner O., *Mysticism and the Early South German-Austrian Anabaptist Movement, 1525–1531* (Scottdale, 1977).

Pater, Calvin A., "Andreas Bodenstein von Karlstadt as the Intellectual Founder of Anabaptism," (unpub. Ph.D. diss. Harvard, 1977).

Peachey, Paul, *Die soziale Herkunft der Schweizer Täufer in der Reformationszeit, 1525–1540* (Karlsruhe, 1954).

Roth, Friedrich, "Zur Geschichte der Wiedertäufer in Oberschwaben," II, III: "Zur Lebensgeschichte Eitelhans Langenmantels von Augsburg," & "Der Höhepunkt der Bewegung in Augsburg und der Niedergang im Jahre 1528," *Zeitschrift des Historischen Vereins für Schwaben und Neuburg* 27 (1900): 1–45; 28 (1901): 1–54.

Schwarz, Reinhard, *Die apokalyptische Theologie Thomas Müntzers und der Taboriten* (Tübingen, 1977).

Seebass, Gottfried, "Müntzers Erbe. Werk, Leben und Theologie des Hans Hut," (unpub. Habilitationsschrift, Erlangen, 1972).

———, "Bauernkrieg und Täufertum in Franken," *Zeitschrift für Kirchengeschichte* 85 (1974): 284–300.

Stayer, James M., *Anabaptists and the Sword* (Lawrence, 1972).

The Anabaptists 157

——, "Die Anfänge des schweizerischen Täufertums im reformierten Kongregationalismus," in Goertz, *Umstrittenes Täufertum*, 19–49.

Troeltsch, Ernst, *Die Soziallehren der christlichen Kirchen und Gruppen* (Tübingen, 1912).

Vos, Karel, "Revolutionnaire hervorming," *De Gids* 84–4 (1920): 433–450.

Walton, Robert C., *Zwingli's Theocracy* (Toronto, 1967).

Weber, Max, " 'Kirchen' und 'Sekten' in Nordamerika," *Christliche Welt* 20 (1906).

Williams, George H., *The Radical Reformation* (Philadelphia, 1962).

——, *Reformation Radical*, tr. Antonio Alatorre (Mexico City, 1982).

Windhorst, Christoph, *Täuferisches Taufverständnis. Balthasar Hubmaiers Lehre zwischen traditioneller und reformatorischer Theologie* (Leyden, 1976).

Yoder, John H., "The Turning Point in the Zwinglian Reformation," *Mennonite Quarterly Review* 32 (1958): 128–140.

——, *Täufertum und Reformation im Gespräch* (Zurich, 1968).

Zeman, Jarold K., *The Anabaptists and the Czech Brethren in Moravia. A Study of Origin and Contacts* (The Hague, 1969).

Zschäbitz, Gerhard, *Zur mitteldeutschen Wiedertäuferb e wegung nach dem grossen Bauernkrieg* (Berlin, 1958).

——, "Die Stellung der Täuferbewegung im Spannungsbogen der deutschen frühbürgerlichen Revolution," in Gerhard Brendler, ed., *Die frühbürgerliche Revolution in Deutschland* (Berlin, 1961), 152–162.

II. Primary Sources (published since 1920)

Documenta Anabaptistica Neerlandica:

Vol. 1: *Friesland en Groningen, 1530–1550*, ed. Albert F. Mellink (Leyden, 1975).

Vol. 2: *Amsterdam, 1536–1578*, ed. Albert F. Mellink (Leyden, 1980).

Franz, Günther, ed., *Urkundliche Quellen zur hessischen Reformationsgeschichte*, vol. 4: *Wiedertäuferakten 1527–1626* (Marburg, 1951).

——, ed., *Thomas Müntzer, Schriften und Briefe* (Gütersloh, 1968).

Grosheide, Greta, ed., "Verhooren en Vonnissen der Wederdoopers, betrokken bij de aanslagen op Amsterdam in 1534 en 1535," in *Bijdragen en Mededeelingen van het Historisch Genootschap* 41 (1920), 1–197.

Hege, Christian, ed., "Pilgram Marbecks Vermahnung. Ein wiedergefundenes Buch," in *Gedenkschrift zum 400-jährigen Jubiläum der Mennoniten oder Taufgesinnten, 1525–1925* (Ludwigshafen, 1925), 178–282.

Hertzsch, Erich, ed., *Karlstadts Schriften aus dem Jahren 1523–1525* (Halle, 1956–57), 2 vols.

Loserth, John, ed., *Quellen und Forschungen zur Geschichte der oberdeutschen Taufgesinnten im 16. Jahrhundert. Pilgram Marpecks Antwort auf Kaspar Schwenckfelds Beurteilung des Buches der Bundesbezeugung von 1542* (Vienna & Leipzig, 1929).

Meihuizen, H. W., ed., *Menno Simons. Dat Fundament des Christelycken Leers* (The Hague, 1967).

Quellen zur Geschichte der (Wieder) Täufer:
Vol. 1: *Herzogtum Württemberg,* ed. Gustav Bossert (Leipzig, 1930).

Vol. 2: *Markgraftum Brandenburg (Bayern, I),* ed. Karl Schornbaum (Leipzig, 1934).

Vol. 3: *Glaubenszeugnisse oberdeutscher Taufgesinnter, I,* ed. Lydia Müller (Leipzig, 1938).

Vol. 4: *Baden und Pfalz,* ed. Manfred Krebs (Gütersloh, 1951).

Vol. 5: *Bayern, II,* ed. Karl Schornbaum (Gütersloh, 1951).

Vol. 6: *Hans Denck, Schriften,* ed. Georg Baring & Walter Fellmann (Gütersloh, 1955–1960).

Vol. 7: *Elsass, 1: Stadt Strassburg, 1522–1532,* ed. Manfred Krebs & Hans Georg Rott (Gütersloh, 1959).

Vol. 8: *Elsass, 2: Stadt Strassburg, 1533–1535,* ed. Manfred Krebs & Hans Georg Rott (Gütersloh, 1960).

Vol. 9: *Balthasar Hubmaier, Schriften,* ed. Gunnar Westin & Torsten Bergsten (Gütersloh, 1962).

Vol. 10: *Bibliographie des Täufertums, 1520–1630,* ed. Hans J. Hillerbrand (Gütersloh, 1962).

Vol. 11: *Österreich, I,* ed. Grete Mecenseffy (Gütersloh, 1964).

Vol. 12: *Glaubenszeugnisse oberdeutscher Taufgesinnter, II,* ed. Robert Friedmann (Gütersloh, 1967).

Vol. 13: *Österreich, 2,* ed. Grete Mecenseffy (Gütersloh, 1972).

Quellen zur Geschichte der Täufer in der Schweiz:
Vol. 1: *Zürich,* ed. Leonhard von Muralt & Walter Schmid (Zürich, 1974).

Vol. 2: *Ostschweiz*, ed. Heinold Fast (Zürich, 1973).
Vol. 3: *Drei Täufergespräche*, ed. Martin Haas (Zürich, 1974).
Die Schriften der Münsterischen Täufer und ihrer Gegner:
Vol. 1: *Die Schriften Bernhard Rothmanns*, ed. Robert Stupperich (Münster, 1970).
Vol. 2: *Schriften von katholischer Seite gegen die Täufer*, ed. Robert Stupperich (Münster, 1980).
Ziegelschmid, A. J. F., ed., *Die älteste Chronik der Hutterischen Brüder* (Ithaca, 1943).

Social History

Thomas A. Brady, Jr.

"Is there a social history of the Reformation?" Robert Scribner asked himself in 1976.[1] He replied that there is such a thing, albeit a paltry, confused, and undeveloped one. Reformation history continues to exert a remarkable resistance to methods and concepts that are commonplace in other fields, though there are many signs that this resistance is now crumbling. As the veil dissolves, the social historian can discover, or rather rediscover, the lines of inquiry that were broken off after World War I.

(1)
Varieties of Social History

Social history[2] is the study of the human past in terms of the groups through whose interrelations a given society gets its living and reproduces its structure and its culture. It is the historiographical counterpart to the advance of political emancipation during the past two hundred years. Social history develops two types or lines of inquiry. The first, which we may call the "analytical" or "descriptive" line asks, when applied to the Reformation: Who made the Reformation? What people, what kinds of people, took active parts for and against the movements, where, when, and why? The answers require the determination of persons by class, estate, sex, occupation, and family; they require fixing of geographical and temporal distinctions; they involve the analysis of motives; and they require the employment of the full range of social-historical methods, including quantitative ones.

The second line may be called the "interpretative" or "teleological" line: To whose benefit and to whose harm did the Reformation occur? What social developments were hindered, promoted,

---

[1]Scribner, (1976a), see Wohlfeil, in Hoyer (1980).
[2]See Hobsbawm (1971), Perrot (1976), Kocka (1977).

blocked, or shifted by the Reformation? The answers here presuppose a reasoned conception both of the place of Christianity in European history and of the social evolution of Europe from the Middle Ages to our own age. Here lie the roots and the breeding grounds of all current debates. Some historians feel this enterprise is futile or even harmful, arguing either that such notions are purely subjective or that—although few notions are sillier—the past should be studied "for its own sake"—as though a long-dead age still had a "sake." Most students of the Reformation, however, whatever their persuasions, have believed that the Protestant Reformation is one of the great central events of the history of our civilization, and that to understand it correctly is to come closer to understanding our own age.

The social history of the Reformation currently stands under the signs of two competing historical sociologies, which we may for convenience label "structuralism" and "Marxism." "Structuralist" social history[3] studies the relations and especially the conditions of superindividual processes, in preference to events and individuals. It emphasizes the enduring (the "longue durée" of the *Annales* school) institutions and habits of thought ("mentalités"), and pushes the state and political power to the edges of the historical picture. This school has developed the concept of "old status society" (German: *die altständische Gesellschaft*; French: *la société des ordres*)[4] for Europe between the twelfth and nineteenth centuries: a hierarchical society of legally defined status groups ("estates," "orders") distinguished from one another by functions, behavior, and notions of honor and prestige; the whole suffused by a patriarchal ethic and a static concept of the world. The distinction between "old status society" and "modern" or "industrial" society with its classes, class conflicts, and revolutions, tends to be drawn very sharply.

"Marxist history" is the currently fashionable name for historical materialism. Common to all its many forms is the belief that social structures and conflicts arise from the division of labor and control of production, and that class conflict is the basic dynamic force in history. Marxist historians treat the Reformation under the rubric of "the transition from feudalism to capitalism"[5] as the first adaptation of Christianity to the needs of a bourgeoisie which in the sixteenth century began its movement towards supplanting the feudal aristoc-

---

[3]Kocka (1977), 70–82.
[4]Conze (1967), Nicholas (1969/70).
[5]Hilton (1978).

racy as Europe's rulers. Two developments have enhanced Marxism's ability to analyze pre-capitalist societies and thus to meet the charge that it cannot account for the durability of human social institutions. The first is the idea of class as a set of relations rather than a quality or property of a social group,[6] which means that one must study whole social systems in order to understand their parts. The second development is the idea of "hegemony,"[7] the complex of leading ideas, through a sharing of which a society, except in revolutionary times, is bound together. These are two major steps on the way from social history towards the "history of society," that is, a comprehension of an entire society and its culture based on the interrelations of its principal groups. The relation between culture and society[8] is very fluid in much current Marxist historical writing.

The Reformation as Social History

The social history of the Reformation is thus not the study of certain topics or a particular aspect but an approach to the entire history of the Reformation. Its historical roots lie in the Germany of the 1840s, when Hegelian Protestant theology began to disintegrate in the direction of political and intellectual radicalism. Theologians began to interpret the different ages and forms of Christianity as products of different historical conditions, a tendency which was radicalized by Bruno Bauer (1809–1882) and fully secularized by Karl Marx and Friedrich Engels.[9] In keeping with its liberal and socialist roots the social history of the Reformation saw and sees in European Protestantism the dominant type of "modern" or "bourgeois" Christianity.

One line of social history of the Reformation developed in a relatively straightforward manner.[10] Friedrich Engels provided a classic interpretation in his *The Peasant War in Germany* (1850): the Peasants' War of 1525 and the Reformation mark the decline of feudal society. Engels later called the Reformation "revolution No. 1 of the bourgeoisie."[11] The German revolution was lost in 1525 when Luther led most of the bourgeois opposition (to feudalism) back into the arms of the feudal aristocracy against the revolutionary plebs

---

[6]Thompson (1964), Foreword.
[7]Bates (1975).
[8]Kocka (1977), 97–111.
[9]Wichelhaus (1965), 13–43.
[10]Vogler, in Wohlfeil (1972); Friesen (1974); Foschepoth (1976).
[11]Lösche, in Wohlfeil (1972), 165; Rammstedt, in Wohlfeil (1972), 235.

and peasantry. The failure of the revolution's goals—the opening of German society to capitalism and the formation of a national state—confirmed Germany's backwardness. Only in western Europe, in the Netherlands, France, and England, did Protestantism, in its Calvinist form, live up to its revolutionary calling. Engels' successors maintained but hardly extended his thesis, though several tried to build upon it a comprehensive interpretation of European culture from the Middle Ages to the Age of Revolution.[12] About 1960, building on work in the Soviet Union, scholars in the German Democratic Republic gave the thesis definitive form in the thesis of "the Reformation as early bourgeois revolution."[13]

Outside Germany, only England has an independent social history of the Reformation, and R. H. Tawney's *Religion and the Rise of Capitalism* (1926) is still the classic treatment of this theme. Tawney saw in the Reformation an adjustment of Christian doctrine to the needs of men who were determined that the Church should no longer fetter their economic lives through ethical norms. The writings of Christopher Hill, though limited to England, carry on Tawney's argument. English and American writers on the transition from feudalism to capitalism have in general shown little interest in the Reformation.[14]

The chief transmitters of the social history of the Reformation to American scholarship have been not the Marxists but Max Weber and Ernst Troeltsch. These two great figures of German sociology before World War One differed from their Marxist contemporaries chiefly in refusing to give a priori primacy to either material or spiritual causation in history. Like the Marxists, however, they saw the Reformation as a decisive turning towards the modern spirit and modern society. Weber, whose *Protestant Ethic and the Spirit of Capitalism* (1904/05) touched off the liveliest debate about the social consequences of the Reformation, saw in Protestantism the beginnings of a practical, rational way of regarding and managing life ("worldly asceticism"), which he found essential both to modern capitalism and to modern politics.[15] His doctrine of "ideal types" is sometimes invoked to bolster the structuralist social-historical theory of "old status society." It is true that Weber regarded the fact that the Reformation *preceded* capitalism as an argument against the no-

---

[12]Esp. Kofler (1974).
[13]Steinmetz (1960).
[14]As the works by Perry Anderson and Immanuel Wallerstein, both 1974.
[15]Schluchter (1979), 204–255; Delumeau (1965), 301–325.

tion of a *necessary* priority of the material over the spiritual. But unlike the structuralists, Weber saw the turn towards modernity in the sixteenth century, not in the nineteenth, and his notion of "transition to the modern"[16] cannot well be combined with the "longue durée."

The greatest sociologist of the Reformation, and of Christianity in general, was Weber's longtime Heidelberg colleague and friend, Ernst Troeltsch (1865–1923). In his masterpiece, *The Social Teachings of the Christian Churches* (1911; Engl. 1931), Troeltsch set out to distinguish the metahistorical heart of the Christian religion from the plethora of its historical forms; and he came to believe that Christian attitudes towards the world (the "social teachings" of his title) were not deductions from a changeless Christian message but responses to changing social and cultural conditions. Doctrines, institutions, laws, policies, and disciplines of the various Christian bodies in different ages were produced by forces immanent to history and not by interventions either of God or of His youngest assistant, the Hegelian "Idea." His scrupulous honesty made Troeltsch apply this approach even-handedly to Protestantism, which he divided into "Old" and "New" (roughly "orthodox" and "liberal"), as well as to early and medieval Christianity. German Lutheranism, he concluded, was mostly an ossified remnant of medieval ecclesiastical culture, while Calvinism and the sects had prepared the social-cultural ground for "modernity," which to Troeltsch meant individualism, spiritual religion, separation of church and state, tolerance, and democracy.[17]

Troeltsch, though he learned much from Marxism, also rejected it as a *consistent* approach to history. He saw in the lower classes the creative source of the major transformations of Christianity, and he believed that the Reformation was to a great extent an expression of the rise of the bourgeoisie.[18] His typology of the forms of Christian organization moved from spontaneous movements through closely organized, exclusive sects, to highly institutionalized, culturally comprehensive churches. This typology is the most commonly used —and abused—feature of *The Social Teachings*. The permanent value of his work on the Reformation lies in its social approach on a Europe-wide scale, and on this level it has no rival. He grappled

[16]Schluchter (1979), 202–203.
[17]Troeltsch (1928), 63.
[18]Troeltsch (1925), 65–66.

honestly with two questions. First: Where does the Reformation stand in the history of Europe? He answered that despite the failure of German Lutheranism, the Reformation as a whole represents the emergence of urban-bred forces and culture and the beginnings of their free development towards a secular modernity. The second question was: Why did the Reformation split into so many different forms? Troeltsch answered by placing social before national criteria: Lutheranism expressed the social backwardness of Germany; Calvinism, Anabaptism and Puritanism reflected the more maturely bourgeois culture of northwestern Europe.

These sociological interpretations of the Reformation still live. The "Weber Thesis" linking capitalism and Protestantism continues to inspire research.[19] Overtly sociological is Otthein Rammstedt's highly Weberian study of the Anabaptist kingdom at Münster in 1534/35.[20] Weber's vision of the Reformation has suffered badly, however, in that branch of neo-Weberian thought known as "modernization theory." In his massive *Kings or People* (1978), for example, Reinhard Bendix allows the Reformation a modest role as midwife to English nationalism but virtually ignores it in his treatment of Germany. A daring marriage of social theory and history is Erdmann Weyrauch's study of Strasbourg and the Augsburg Interim (1548) in the light of Nicholas Luhmann's "systems sociology."[21] Some historians resist, it is true, any use of sociological concepts in historical writing on the Reformation era; surely the most redoutable of them is Hugh Trevor-Roper.[22] Neither his dissent, however, nor the grumblings from other quarters against "sociologism,"[23] have had much braking effect on practice. The present state of research shows this clearly enough.

Achievements and Points of View

The following paragraphs focus on the German-speaking lands and on a few themes: the Reformation in the cities; the Reformation between town and land; and the Reformation as revolution. The concentration on Germany is dictated by the weight of the literature and by another consideration. Not only was "Germany"—here in its broadest sense—the homeland of the Reformation, it was also the

[19]Most recently, Crew (1978), though the title is misleadingly broad.
[20]Rammstedt (1966).
[21]Weyrauch (1978).
[22]Trevor-Roper (1967).
[23]Moeller, in Mommsen (1979), 29.

one area of Europe where the looseness of the structure of power permitted the revolt within the Church to penetrate the masses and allowed pressure for change to be exerted from below. In England, by contrast, the Reformation came from above, and "the broad mass of the population did not become involved before mid-century";[24] while in France the Reformation captured neither the court nor the rural masses.[25]

1. The Cities and the Reformation

The urban reform has become "a principal subject of interest to research on early modern Europe,"[26] in the words of Bernd Moeller, whose *Imperial Cities and the Reformation* (1962; Engl. 1972) sparked much of that interest. Moeller argues that the collision of Luther's theology with urban life powerfully affected both; and the victory of the movement in the South German free cities "can be definitively explained by the confrontation of the peculiarly 'urban' theology of [Huldrych] Zwingli and [Martin] Bucer with the communal spirit that flourished to a special degree in South Germany." The urban reformers "corrected Luther" by taking as their starting point the community, not the individual, and they thereby helped to revive and strengthen the old civic sense of the commune as a holy community of fortune. The fruition came, however, not in Germany but in Calvin's Geneva and, indirectly, in England and America.[27]

The urban reform for the moment takes its place beside the "Weber Thesis" as a central topos of the social history of the Reformation. "The Reformation was an urban event," A. G. Dickens has written in a much-cited passage.[28] He distinguishes an early, humanist-patriotic, popular reform in the cities from a later, authoritarian-Lutheran reform controlled by the princes; and he dates the transition to the mid-1530s. Heiko A. Oberman fixes the turning point at the restoration in Württemberg (1534), but he doubts that the urban movement was greatly different in character or that this shift is to be seen as a German tragedy.[29] Martin Brecht argues that

[24]Cohn, H.J., in Mommsen (1979), 309.
[25]Garrisson-Estèbe (1980), 335; and see Salmon (1975).
[26]Moeller (1978), 177; surveys by Rublack, in Moeller (1978), 9–27, and Greyerz (1980), 1–8.
[27]Moeller (1962), 54–55, 67, 76.
[28]Dickens (1974), 182.
[29]Oberman (1979).

Zwinglianism was only a political interlude in the southern free cities,[30] but most writers accept the thesis of the special character of the southern urban reform. The reform took on a different character when it happened late in the age of the Reformation as Kaspar von Greyerz has shown in his study of Colmar.[31] There are those, however, who deny in principle the special character of the urban reform.

One of them is Steven Ozment, whose *Reformation in the Cities* (1975) is a long plea against the view of a fundamental gulf between city and land and a peculiarly corporate character to urban religion. He argues for a unified view of the early Reformation as a movement of psychological-spiritual liberation of the individual, a kind of replication of Luther's own experience. Far from sacralizing the urban community (as Moeller would have it), Ozment's urban reformers faithfully transmit to the towns "Luther's original impulse to free individual and civic life from onerous religious beliefs, practices, and institutions."[32] This therapeutic reform had, apparently, nothing specifically to do with urban life, except that the townsfolk were more literate and, apparently, more burdened. It is difficult to determine what is specifically "social" about this interpretation, although Ozment's book is a sign of awareness that cities ought to be studied not as independent units but in the contexts of their social, political, and cultural surroundings.

There is much interest in the inner social dynamics of the urban reform. Investigations into the internal social tensions and struggles proceed along these lines. One is the study of the urban ruling groups, chiefly through prosopographical method, and their responses to the popular pressure for reform.[33] The other line studies the social character of the early reform movement itself through tax lists, guild records, grievance lists, and social topography, a multi-pronged method which has proved itself from the Saxon towns to Lyons to Kent.[34] Both the popular movements and the governmental responses to them are now seen as social phenomena, though there is still some argument about their dynamic relation to one another.

A central part of the study of the urban reformation is the study of

[30]Brecht (1977), and in Petri (1980).
[31]Greyerz (1980).
[32]Ozment (1975), 9.
[33]Birnbaum (1959); Jacob (1970); Rublack (1971); Scribner, (1976b); Brady (1978a).
[34]Davis (1975); Scribner (1975), and in Mommsen (1979); Wettges (1978); Broadhead, in Mommsen (1979); Clark, in Mommsen (1979); Rublack (1980).

propaganda and much work on the pamphlets is underway. Scribner reminds us, in response to Moeller's insistence on the centrality of printed propaganda—"no books, no Reformation"—that in view of the low levels of literacy, it is easy to overestimate the effectiveness of the printed word.[35]

With quantitative methods one can push beyond the study of movements to analyze whole urban social systems, as, for example, Helmut Bräuer's model study of Chemnitz (Karl-Marx-Stadt).[36] The project "Stadt in Spätmittelalter und Reformation"[37] at Tübingen aims to identify the "non-theological" factors which shaped the course and the consequences of the Reformation in ten German-speaking free and territorial cities, with emphases on pre-reformation ecclesiastical policy and on social stratification. In smaller cities nearly the entire surviving documentation is being processed with computer aid, and already important results are available on the political elites of several cities during this era, notably Kitzingen in Franconia and Colmar in Alsace.[38] In related work Hans-Christoph Rublack has thrown much new light on why the reform movement failed in some cities, particularly episcopal residential cities.[39] The Tübingen project has also yielded Erdmann Weyrauch's extremely important study "On Social Stratification," in which he surveys the literature on stratification and presents the project's own programming categories for social stratification.[40]

The North German cities present special problems, and not only through the relative lateness of their reforms. Franz Lau once tried to show that urban Lutheranism in the North was just as "popular" as urban religion in the South.[41] The master in this area is now Heinz Schilling, who in a series of studies on the Northwest German cities concludes that Lutheranism indeed emerged from below as a popular religion, that the urban elites were split between the old religion and the new, and that the success of Lutheranism strengthened the towns against the territorial princes—all in all, an important support for Moeller's fundamental insight.[42] Other studies confirm the coincidence of evangelical movements and political reform pressure

[35]Moeller, Scribner, in Mommsen (1979), 23–39, 44–45.
[36]Bräuer (1978).
[37]Zeeden and Bátori (1979).
[38]Bátori, Weyrauch, in Mommsen (1979).
[39]Rublack (1978), in Moeller (1978), and in Mommsen (1979).
[40]Weyrauch, in Bátori (1980).
[41]Lau (1959).
[42]Schilling, in Moeller (1978), and in Mommsen (1979).

from below in the northern cities.[43] Schilling is a prime example of a
consciously structuralist social historian, who sees the cities as balanced systems of social groups, for which internal struggles serve to
"let off steam."[44]

Study of the effects of the Reformation on urban institutions has a
classic topos in poor relief.[45] The new urban poor laws of the 1520s
(Nuremberg, Strasbourg, Ypres) used to be attributed to Luther's influence, which was thought to have made possible the secularization
and communalization of poor relief by attacking charity as a source
of merit. The recent literature shows, however, that there was in all
of Europe in the sixteenth century a trend towards stricter control
and greater supervision of the poor. Luther's theology, which al-
lotted these social tasks to the realm of the state, may well have reinforced this development in Germany.

2. The Reformation between City and Land

There is a definite tendency away from the city as an independent
organism and towards the theme of town-and-land. Schilling has
shown that relations with territorial princes played an important
role in the urban reforms in Northwest Germany; and Rublack,
Brecht and Sigrid Jahns, following the lead of Hans Baron, have laid
growing stress on the importance of Imperial politics to the free
cities of the South and to their reforms.[46] It has also been suggested
that some urban patriciates, notably of Strasbourg and Ulm, had
strong ties to the rural nobles and to rural society, and that not they
but the middling folk were the proper clientele for the Zwinglian-
Bucerian ideal.[47] At the other end of the social structure the concept
of "the common man" has come into use to unify the lower classes,
and sometimes the not-so-lower classes, of town and land.[48]

The heavy attention given the townsmen and, for Germany, the
peasantry, has left the nobles more or less in the shadows. The Reformation impinged on two problem areas for the nobles, a social
and a political one: embourgeoisement and competition from
urban-bred professionals; and maintenance of corporate privileges

[43]Postel, in Moeller (1978), and in Ehrbrecht (1980); Ehrbrecht, in Moeller (1978).
[44]Schilling, in Wehler (1975), 194–196, 235–236; Schilling, in Petri (1980), and in
Ehrbrecht (1980).
[45]Davis (1975), 60–65; Fischer (1979), with full literature.
[46]Schilling, in Mommsen (1979), 304; Baron (1937); Rublack (1980); Brecht (1977);
Jahns (1976).
[47]Brady, (1978a, 1978b).
[48]Blickle (1981); Lutz (1978).

against the crown.[49] Urban influence advanced on most fronts through most of the sixteenth century, and Blaschke has shown that even in Saxony the Reformation spread urban ideas to and influences on the nobles and the territorial regime. On the other hand, the Reformation came in some places—the Netherlands, France and Poland—as a godsent ideology for the defense of local and class privilege against centralizing monarchs, and it provided a cause around which nobles and urban bourgeois could unite.[50] In Germany, however, where the lesser nobles, after initial enthusiasm, only gradually and quite late (after mid-century) came to terms with the Reformation, the centers for noble-bourgeois rapprochement were not resistance movements but the princely courts.[51]

The Reformation as an expression of the intensifying urban domination of the land is one of the central concerns of the social history of the Reformation. In the city-state of Bern, for example, the Reformation accelerated the articulation of Bern's power over its territory.[52] Two recent, important books illustrate strikingly the urban character of Protestantism as it faced the land. Janine Garrisson-Estèbe's *Protestants du midi 1559–1598* (1980) stands nearly alone as a social study of the French Reformation.[53] She shows that Calvinism in the South was a party of castle and town, to which the peasantry was impervious. Radicalized by St. Bartholomew's Day, this party sought to establish a "United Provinces of the Midi" to defend traditional liberties against the crown; but unlike its Netherlandish counterpart, it could not rally the masses.

The theme of failure also runs through Gerald Strauss' remarkable *Luther's House of Learning* (1978), a study of the consequences of the Lutheran attempt to re-educate sixteenth-century Germans. Strauss establishes the clergy's goals from their programatic writings and then surveys church and school visitation records to test their success. He finds massive, successful resistance by the common folk, particularly the peasantry, to the introduction of a book-fed piety and a religion of social obedience. Lutheranism may be seen as one phase of urban Christianity's war on rural religion in the early modern era; and the successful popular resistance in Germany was likely

[49]Press, in Mommsen (1979), 333–336.
[50]Blaschke, in Moeller (1978); and see Kopitzsch, in Wohlfeil (1975), 199. On the Netherlands, see Smit (1970).
[51]Press (1970), in Mommsen (1979), and in Petri (1980).
[52]Walder (1980/81).
[53]Garrisson-Estèbe (1980).

bound up with the durability there of old-fashioned social and cultural forms. A study of urban Lutheranism might reveal a different level of clerical success, but only Strasbourg has comparable visitation records.

The Protestant clergy were natural agents of this cultural urbanization and social embourgeoisment. The condition of the clergy *before* the Reformation is the subject of Francis Rapp's superb book on the diocese of Strasbourg,[54] which shows that vested lay interests were so extensive and so powerful that no amount of good will could raise up a countervailing force for episcopal reform. What became of the clergy at the Reformation is treated both in studies on their new civic role and in prosopographical-social studies of the Rhine Palatinate, Ernestine Saxony, and Württemberg.[55] In this area the Reformation seems to have produced long-term social change through the transformation of the clergy into a solid professional sector of the bourgeoisie.

3. The Reformation as Revolution

Although revolution as a sharp, sudden political change with definite social implications is a modern idea, the consciousness of the possibility of such change reaches deep into the European Middle Ages.[56] Its theologized form, known as chiliasm or millenialism, was a constant presence in Christianity, and it was refurbished and intensified by the storms of the Reformation era.[57] The idea of the Reformation as revolution goes back at least to Hegel, who was perhaps the first to see in Luther the beginnings of a revolution which culminated in France in 1789. Today German-speaking Marxist scholars view the Reformation as part of the larger "early bourgeois revolution," though this idea is not widely accepted in other lands, and also not by other Marxist scholars.[58] Originally the Reformation in this conception was an assault on "ecclesiastical feudalism," which under Luther's leadership for a while became the vanguard of the anti-feudal movement. Once it parted company with the genuinely revolutionary forces, the urban plebs and the peasantry, the Refor-

[54]Rapp (1975).
[55]Moeller, (1972a, 1972b); B. Vogler (1976); Karant-Nunn (1979); Brecht (1969); Klaus (1969).
[56]Griewank (1969).
[57]N. Cohn (1970); Van Dülmen (1977), 367–370, who writes of "the chiliastic revolution"; Blickle (1981), 12–15, 282–287.
[58]See notes 10–11 above; Becker (1974); Hoyer (1980), 9–18; Oberman (1977).

mation became a prisoner of the princes. There has recently appeared a shift towards the ideological aspects of the Reformation and the role of Luther and his movement in breaking the *ideological* hold of feudalism and promoting a bourgeois world-view. Thus the entire question of a *social* revolution in sixteenth-century Germany has very much retreated towards the edge of the picture. The Reformation is no longer the instrument of the revolutionary social movement, but rather the reverse.[59]

A second concept of revolution connected with the Reformation is Blickle's "revolution of the common man," which, as it belongs properly to the topic of the Peasants' War, cannot be discussed in detail here. Blickle does argue that the events of 1525 were a struggle for the participation of the "common man" in the state and were not entirely unsuccessful.[60]

The Anabaptist kingdom at Münster in 1534/35 is the most plowed field of controversy about the revolutionary character of the Reformation. Here one must begin not with a book about Münster but with Claus-Peter Clasen's masterful quantitative study of Anabaptism.[61] He shows that persecution drove the movement from the cities, where it began, into rural insignificance, and that its small numbers do not justify the place Anabaptism has received in the literature. He holds their radicalism to have been genuine, if regrettable.

German Marxist scholarship has seen in Anabaptism a futile, poignant, highly theologized postscript to the lost revolution of 1525, and a protest against the princely reaction that followed.[62] Gerhard Brendler's book, which applied this idea to Münster, appeared in the same year as Otthein Rammstedt's analysis of Münster in a Weberian mode. Rammstedt sees Münster as a product of a true economic crisis and resultant social tensions, to which the charismatic Anabaptist leaders brought a prophetic message of hope. The Anabaptists came to power in Münster through the social struggle in the city, but their chiliasm expressed less one group's grasp at power than a renunciation of the world which gripped all classes. Rammstedt thus confirms Brendler's account on two points: that the movement arose from concrete economic and social conditions, and that

[59]Lösche, in Wohlfeil (1972), 178.
[60]Blickle (1981).
[61]Clasen (1972).
[62]Zschäbitz (1958); Brendler (1966); Rammstedt (1966); Kirchhoff (1973); Van Dülmen (1977).

the Anabaptist ideal at Münster was truly without hope, a utopia.

A third point of view is advanced by Karl-Heinz Kirchhoff, who studies only the *native* Anabaptists, of whom he can identify 1108 of some 7–8,000 Anabaptists at Münster. He concludes that the poor were not disproportionately represented in the commune, and that Münster Anabaptism was a movement "of a proud, self-conscious bourgeoisie."[63] Against Rammstedt, Kirchhoff asserts that a sociological explanation is not adequate for Münster. A still more recent view is Richard Van Dülmen's interpretation of Münster as the culmination of Anabaptism's "chiliastic revolution," itself an outgrowth of the events of 1525.

Münster has thus been analyzed in four different ways—by a Marxist, by two different kinds of Weberians, and by a structuralist —which makes it an object lesson for the beginner in this field. Such conflicts among historical sociologies are rooted in very different views of the relationships of that age to our own. Jürgen Kocka has put the central question like this:

> Is not a theory which, as a product of industrial-capitalist society, centers on and stresses socio-economic forces, stratification, and the causes of conflict, necessarily in danger of missing the central forces . . . when it is applied to the sixteenth century, an age whose conflicts were largely conditioned by religion and did not run along socio-economic cleavages?[64]

The structuralists believe so, and none more radically than Roland Mousnier, who denies not only the realities but also the *ideas* of class and revolution in the pre-industrial age.[65] Most historians believe, however, that there was some connection between that society and our own, and many believe that the connection rests on the evolution of the modern bourgeois from the premodern burgher. This question has been discussed on a theoretical level only once in the recent literature, by German Marxists in the *Zeitschrift für Geschichtswissenschaft* (1972–75), but without conclusive results.[66]

Some Shapes of Things to Come

While the theoretical debate rolls on, seemingly without firm con-

[63]Kirchhof (1973), 87.
[64]Kocka (1977), 103; and see Weyrauch, in Bátori (1980).
[65]See Brady, (1978a), ch. 1.
[66]See Foschepoth (1976), 70–80.

clusions, the social history of the Reformation gains empirical breadth and depth. Its methods are increasingly those of social history in general. There are signs of a growing influence of anthropological ideas, an approach whose great strength lies in the analysis of the ordinary life of ordinary people. "The common people of that day," as A. G. Dickens writes, "are now allowed to have minds and spirits. . . ."[67] The future will see a great deal more attention to non-bookish culture in town and land and, of course, to popular religion. Anthropologically inspired history has its limitations, however, particularly in dealing with politics and the State.

The social history of the pre-Reformation and Reformation churches cries out for investigation. Church property, its accumulation, uses, and appropriation by the laity at the Reformation ought to be the foremost topic. Then comes parish life, about which, despite the bulk of scattered, published material, we are badly informed. A third topic is the social effects of the dissolution of the monasteries, which have been studied only for England. Fourth, we need broadly designed studies of lay involvement and lay power in church life—patronage, endowments, Mass stipends. Why, in an era filled with evidence of strongly church-bound piety, did Johann Geiler (d. 1510) of Kaysersberg charge on behalf of his fellow-clergymen: "You laymen, you hate us!"[68] The current literature advances only hypotheses about the lay ruling classes' attachment to the old Church.

A second broad area is social theology, that is, the theological topoi which bore on social life—ecclesiology, ethics, political theology—the main stuff of Troeltsch's work. Among the major reformers, we are served fairly well for Zwingli, less so for Calvin, poorly for Bucer, and either too well or very poorly for Luther.[69] The study of Luther's social ideas has never recovered from its treatment at the hands of what Ernst Wolf called "the numerous representatives of the false guides of the 'Luther renaissance.' "[70] Luther was then praised as a prophet of social subordination and political obedience, now one hears of the democratic influence of his *sola fide*.[71] Among

[67]Dickens (1974), 210.
[68]Rapp (1975), 419. Fundamental is Kiessling (1971).
[69]Rother (1956), on Zwingli; Biéler (1959), on Calvin; and ever provocative on theology and society, Oberman (1979).
[70]Wolf (1965), 82n.
[71]Schilling, in Mommsen (1979), 302–303; Moeller (1978), 181–182.

the libraries of books on various aspects of his thought, there is no reliable treatment of his teachings on society, social groups, and social duties.

Thirdly, there are the social effects of the Reformation. Here we need the kind of studies, in which the literature on England is very rich, on the areas of life which might well have been shaped by the peculiarities of reformed church life: birth patterns,[72] family life, schooling, literacy. Such studies can have more than local significance, of course, only if they employ comparative method.

The two classic theses on the social history of the Reformation, the "early bourgeois revolution" and the "Weber thesis," are at the moment bogged down in inconclusiveness, and perhaps the time has come for a new approach, or rather the revival of an old approach, the Reformation as an adaptation of Christianity to the social evolution of Europe. If we begin from Troeltsch's notion of Protestantism as a city-bred religion, then the Reformation is a high-point in the *middle* of a great movement for the establishment of an orderly, self-conscious, person-centered piety for literate, free lay persons. Beginning in the towns of southern France and northern Italy in the High Middle Ages, at the Reformation it burst out in politically favorable parts of the North, spread into the land, and began to affect whole countries. This climax signals both the beginnings of the transformation of old city bourgeoisies into national ones, and movement of some affected states into the core positions in the infant, capitalistic world-economy. Something similar, though much weaker, happened in the Catholic lands: the Counter Reformation pressed Catholic life towards similar forms of piety and made war on the "superstition" of the old rural religion. The two confessional complexes of Europe did not really move apart, rather the driving forces shifted; and the Protestant North, in its desperate plunge from a world ruled by warriors and priests to one ruled by bankers and entrepreneurs, dragged the rest of Europe after it.

When the strident voices of the polemicists are still, when the grand systems of long-dead theologians fall away, when the sixteenth-century mutations of Christianity are seen entirely in historical context, then the Reformation will be regarded not only as Protestant and northern but also as Christian and European. Neither confessional nor racial-cultural explanations of the place of the Reformation in European history have survived the fire of historical criticism. Perhaps the social-historical explanation will.

[72]See Rublack (1976).

Bibliography

Series titles and some sub-titles have been omitted for the sake of space. Contributions to collective volumes are not listed separately.

Anderson, Perry, *Lineages of the Absolutist State* (London, 1974).

Baron, H., "Religion and Politics in the German Imperial Cities during the Reformation," *English Historical Review* 52 (1937): 405–427, 614–633.

Bates, T.R., "Gramsci's Theory of Hegemony," *Journal of the History of Ideas* 36 (1975): 351–366.

Bátori, I., ed., *Städtische Gesellschaft und Reformation* (Stuttgart, 1980).

Becker, W., *Reformation und Revolution* (Münster i. W., 1974).

Benedict, Philip., *Rouen during the Wars of Religion* (Cambridge, 1981).

Biéler, A., *La pensée économique et sociale de Calvin* (Geneva, 1959).

Birnbaum, N., "The Zwinglian Reformation in Zurich," *Past & Present* 15 (1959): 27–47.

Blickle, P., *Die Revolution von 1525*, 2nd ed. (Munich, 1981; Engl., Baltimore, 1982).

Brady, T. A., Jr. *Ruling Class, Regime and Reformation at Strasbourg, 1520–1555* (Leiden, 1978). (a)

———, "Patricians, Nobles, Merchants," *Social Groups and Religious Ideas in the 16th Century*, eds. M. Chrisman and O. Gründler (Kalamazoo, 1978): 38–45, 160–164. (b)

Bräuer, H., *Die Stadtbevölkerung von Chemnitz zwischen 1450 und 1600* (Karl-Marx-Stadt, 1978).

Brecht, M., "Herkunft und Ausbildung der protestantischen Geistlichen des Herzogtums Württemberg im 16. Jahrhundert," *Zeitschrift für Kirchengeschichte* 80 (1969): 163–175.

———, "Die gemeinsame Politik der Reichsstädte und die Reformation," *Zeitschrift der Savigny-Stiftung für Rechtsgeschichte*, kan. Abt. 49 (1977): 180–263.

Brendler, G., *Das Täuferreich zu Münster 1534/35* (Berlin, 1966).

Clasen, C.P., *Anabaptism. A Social History, 1525–1618* (Ithaca-London, 1972).

Cohn, N., *The Pursuit of the Millenium*, 3rd ed. (London, 1970).

Conze, W., "Social History," *Journal of Social History* 1 (1967): 7–16.

Crew, P.M., *Calvinist Preaching and Iconoclasm in the Netherlands, 1544–1569* (Cambridge, 1978).

Davis, N.Z., *Society and Culture in Early Modern France* (Stanford, 1975).

Delumeau, J., *Naïssance et affirmation de la Réforme* (Paris, 1965).

Dickens, A. G., *The German Nation and Martin Luther* (London, 1974).

Ehbrecht, W., ed., *Städtische Führungsgruppen und Gemeinde in der werdenden Neuzeit* (Cologne-Vienna, 1980).

Fischer, T., *Städtische Armut und Armenfürsorge im 15. und 16. Jahrhundert* (Göttingen, 1979).

Foschepoth, J., *Reformation und Bauernkrieg im Geschichtsbild der DDR* (Berlin, 1976).

Friesen, A., *Reformation and Utopia* (Wiesbaden, 1974).

Garrisson-Estèbe, J., *Protestants du midi 1559–1598* (Toulouse, 1980).

Greyerz, K. von, *The Late City Reformation in Germany. The Case of Colmar, 1522–1628* (Wiesbaden, 1980).

Griewank, K., *Der neuzeitliche Revolutionsbegriff*, 2nd ed. (Frankfurt a. M., 1969).

Hilton, R.H., ed., *The Transition from Feudalism to Capitalism* (London, 1978).

Hobsbawm, E.J., "From Social History to the History of Society," *Daedalus* 100, No. 1 (1971): 20–45.

Hoyer, S., ed., *Reform, Reformation, Revolution* (Leipzig, 1980).

Jacob, W., *Politische Führungsschicht und Reformation. Untersuchungen zur Reformation in Zürich 1519–1528* (Zürich, 1970).

Jahns, S., *Frankfurt, Reformation und Schmalkaldischer Bund* (Frankfurt a. M., 1976).

Karant-Nunn, S. C., *Luther's Pastors. The Reformation in the Ernestine Countryside*. Transactions of the American Philosophical Society, N.S. 69, pt. 8 (Philadelphia, 1979).

Kiessling, R., *Bürgerliche Gesellschaft und Kirche in Augsburg im Spätmittelalter* (Augsburg, 1971).

Kirchhoff, K.H., *Die Täufer in Münster 1534/35. Untersuchungen zum Umfang und zur Sozialstruktur der Bewegung* (Münster, 1973).

Klaus, B., "Soziale Herkunft und theologische Bildung lutherischer Pfarrer der reformatorischen Frühzeit," *Zeitschrift für Kirchengeschichte* 80 (1969): 22–49.

Kocka, J., *Sozialgeschichte. Begriff—Entwicklung—Probleme* (Göttingen, 1977).

Kofler, L., *Zur Geschichte der bürgerlichen Gesellschaft* 5th ed. (Darmstadt-Neuwied, 1974).

Lau, F., "Der Bauernkrieg und das angebliche Ende der lutherischen Reformation als spontane Volksbewegung," *Luther-Jahrbuch* 26 (1959): 119–134.

Lutz, R., *Wer war der gemeine Mann? Der dritte Stand in der Krise des Spätmittelalters* (Munich, 1978).

Moeller, B., *Reichsstadt und Reformation* (Gütersloh, 1962).

———, "Kleriker als Bürger," *Festschrift für Hermann Heimpel,* II (Göttingen, 1972): 195–224. (a)

———, *Pfarrer als Bürger* (Göttingen, 1972). (b)

———, ed., *Stadt und Kirche im 16. Jahrhundert* (Gütersloh, 1978).

Mommsen, W.J., ed., *Stadtbürgertum und Adel in der Reformation* (Stuttgart, 1979).

Nicholas, D.V., "New Paths of Social History and Old Paths of Historical Romanticism," *Journal of Social History* 3 (1969/70): 277ff.

Oberman, H. A., "Reformation: Epoche oder Episode?" *Archiv für Reformationsgeschichte* 68 (1977): 56–109.

———, *Werden und Wertung der Reformation,* 2nd ed. (Tübingen, 1979).

Ozment, S., *The Reformation in the Cities* (New-Haven-London, 1975).

Perrot, M., "The Strengths and Weaknesses of French Social History," *Journal of Social History* 10 (1976): 166–177.

Petri, F., ed., *Kirche und gesellschaftlicher Wandel in deutschen und niederländischen Städten der werdenden Neuzeit* (Cologne-Vienna, 1980).

Press, V., *Calvinismus und Territorialstaat* (Stuttgart, 1970).

Rammstedt, O., *Sekte und soziale Bewegung* (Cologne-Opladen, 1966).

Rapp, Francis, *Réformes et Réformation à Strasbourg. Eglise et société dans le diocèse (1450–1525)* (Paris, 1975).

Rother, S., *Die religiösen und geistigen Grundlagen der Politik H. Zwinglis* (Erlangen, 1956).

Rublack, H.-C., *Die Einführung der Reformation in Konstanz* (Gütersloh, 1971).

_____, "Konfession als demographischer Faktor?" *Festgabe für E.-W. Zeeden*, eds. H. Rabe, et. al. (Münster, i. W., 1976): 62–96.

_____, *Gescheiterte Reformation* (Stuttgart, 1978).

_____, "Nördlingen zwischen Kaiser und Reformation," *Archiv für Reformationsgeschichte* 71 (1980): 113–133.

Salmon, J. H. M., *Society in Crisis. France in the Sixteenth Century* (London-Tonbridge, 1975).

Schilling, Heinz, *Konfessionskonflikt und Staatsbildung* (Gütersloh, 1981).

Schluchter, W., *Die Entwicklung des okzidentalen Rationalismus* (Tübingen, 1979).

Scribner, R.W., "Civic Unity and the Reformation in Erfurt," *Past & Present* 66 (1975): 28–60.

_____, "Is there a social history of the Reformation?" *Social History* 4 (1976): 483–505. (a)

_____, "Why was there no Reformation in Cologne?" *Bulletin of the Institute for Historical Research* 49 (1976): 217–241. (b)

Smit, J.W., "The Netherlands Revolution," *Preconditions of Revolution in Early Modern Europe*, eds. R. Forster & J.P. Greene (Baltimore, 1970): 19–54.

Steinmetz, M., "Die frühbürgerlichen Revolution in Deutschland (1476–1535)," (1960) in Wohlfeil (1972): 42–55.

Strauss, G., *Luther's House of Learning* (Baltimore, 1978).

Tawney, R.H., *Religion and the Rise of Capitalism* (London, 1926).

Thompson, E.P., *The Making of the English Working Class, 1780–1950* (London, 1964).

Trevor-Roper, H.R., *Religion, the Reformation and Social Change* (London, 1967).

Troeltsch, E., *Deutscher Geist und Westeuropa*, ed. H. Baron (Tübingen, 1925).

_____, *Die Bedeutung des Protestantismus für die Entstehung der modernen Welt*, 5th ed. (Munich-Leipzig, 1928).

_____, *The Social Teachings of the Christian Churches*, trans O. Wyon, (London-New York, 1931).

Vahle, H., "Calvinismus und Demokratie im Spiegel der Forschung," *Archiv für Reformationsgeschichte* 66 (1975): 182–212.

Van Dülmen, R., *Reformation als Revolution* (Munich, 1977).

Vogler, B., *Le clergé protestant rhénan au siècle de la Réforme (1555–1619)* (Paris, 1976).

Walder, E., "Reformation und moderner Staat," *Archiv des historischen Vereins des Kantons Bern 65/66* (1980/81): 445–583.

Wallerstein, Immanuel, *The Modern World System. Capitalist Agriculture and the Origins of the European World Economy in the Sixteenth Century* (New York, 1974).

Wehler, H.-U., ed., *Der deutsche Bauernkrieg 1524–1526* (Göttingen, 1975).

Wettges, W., *Reformation und Propaganda* (Stuttgart, 1978).

Weyrauch, Erdmann, *Konfessionelle Krise und soziale Stabilität. Das Interim in Stassburg (1548–1562)* (Stuttgart, 1978).

Wichelhaus, M., *Kirchengeschichtsschreibung und Soziologie im neunzehnten Jahrhundert und bei Ernst Troeltsch* (Heidelberg, 1965).

Wohlfeil, R., *Reformation oder frühbürgerlicher Revolution?* (Munich, 1972).

———, *Der Bauernkrieg 1524–26* (Munich, 1975).

Wolf, E., *Peregrinatio*, II (Munich, 1965).

Zeeden, E.-W., and Bátori, I., "Spätmittelalter und Reformation. Die Arbeit im Sonderforschungsbereich 8 an der Universität Tübingen," *Jahrbuch der Historischen Forschungen* (1979): 50–54.

Zschäbitz, G., *Zur mitteldeutschen Wiedertäuferbewegung nach dem grossen Bauernkrieg* (Berlin, 1958).

Witchcraft, Magic, and the Occult

H.C. Erik Midelfort

It is no exaggeration to say that the biggest surprise of the last generation in studies of early modern European intellectual history has
been the rise of the occult sciences to positions of influence and even
respectability. No longer scorned or ridiculed, they now appear as
essential features of the quest for certitude, power, and coherence in
the sixteenth century. But what do we mean by an occult science?
Basic to its very definition was secrecy; these pursuits were hidden
from general view or depended on hidden, esoteric sources. Persuaded that truth was necessarily restricted to an elite few, these
seekers sometimes cultivated a gnostic sense of perfection, of separation from the common herd, of Nicodemite conformity to the outward requirements of any given religious establishment. This secrecy
was also due to two other fears: that translation of high mysteries into vernacular tongues would automatically corrupt them; and that
civil authorities might misconstrue the search for hidden wisdom as
an illicit dabbling with demons.

The occult Renaissance depended on at least three revivals: Lullism, Kabbalism, and Hermeticism. The teachings of Ramon Lull
(1234–1316) were based on an Augustinian Neoplatonism that saw
God's "dignities" or attributes infused throughout creation.[1] The
dignities were in turn connected to a set of relative qualities, such as
equality, minority, and agreement, to which various letters of the
alphabet corresponded. By manipulating the written language, the
alphabet, one could obtain answers to questions about the various
levels of creation. A true master of Lull's art could know everything
about the universe and also remember it all.[2] So impressive were
these claims that the University of Paris established a chair of
Lullism; Philip II's Escorial was planned along Lullist lines; even

---

[1]Secret (1964); Yates (1979); French (1972), 47.
[2]French (1972), 48.

Montaigne came under Lull's influence. During the Renaissance Lull's art of cognition and memory became fused with a revived Kabbalah, that Jewish art of mystical contemplation that found significance in the letters of the Hebrew alphabet.[3] In both Lullism and Kabbalah God was so thoroughly bound up in words and names that puny man could approach divinity as if there were a code to crack.

Hermeticism was a revival of the teachings of a supposedly ancient Egyptian theologian, Hermes Trismegistos (Thrice Great Hermes), then thought to be a contemporary of Moses and an inspired source for both the Hellenic tradition culminating in Plato and the Judaeo-Christian tradition, whose doctrines he seemed to anticipate. Hermes was only one of the *prisci theologi* or ancient theologians, whose number also included Orpheus, Zoroaster, Pythagoras, and Plato. Together they held out various kinds of hope to Renaissance intellectuals. They seemed to prove that God spoke extra-scripturally to great men of all ages and places, that truth in other words was not the closed-shop guild monopoly of logic chopping schoolmen. The ancient theologians also sanctioned a religious syncretism that might recognize the validity of all the ancient religions and the unity of mankind. Some of the Hermetic texts encouraged astrology, alchemy, and magic: pursuits that repudiated the Aristotelian method of science by emphasizing the importance of mathematics on the one hand and of personal operations with nature on the other. Experimentation and manipulation became basic values as they never had been in Aristotle's scheme of organic classification. Other Hermetic texts encouraged a gnostic piety that sought regeneration, intuition, or salvation through the discovery of the divine within oneself, a discovery linking man mystically with mankind and all of the cosmos. All of these doctrines depended on the interconnectedness of the universe, the awesome coherence of stars, planets, and man, of lead, gold, and psyche, of God, angels, and the human spirit.[4]

Much of the authority of the Hermetic tradition rested on its antiquity. Hermes was an example of extracanonical revelation only if his writings were as old as Moses's own. From the time of Tertullian and Lactantius down to the seventeenth century, this assumption inspired a constant or even growing enthusiasm for the Hermetic texts; when Marsiglio Ficino began the momentous task of providing

[3]Secret (1964), 1–21; Yates (1979), 9–15.
[4]French (1972), 69–72, 160–71.

translations into Latin of the works of Plato, he actually began not with Plato but with the *Corpus Hermeticum*, which had recently been recovered. Not only does this suggest the relative values of the two bodies of ancient wisdom, but the Hermetic texts permanently stained Ficino's understanding of Plato. Within 150 years one arm of the Renaissance chopped off the other as the methods of historical source criticism debunked the foundations of the Hermetic Renaissance. In 1614 the erudite philologist Isaac Casaubon proved that the Hermetic texts could not be as ancient as was generally supposed, that they must have been composed in the early Christian era (between 100 and 300 A.D.), under the diverse influence of Platonism, Stoicism, Jewish philosophy, and probably some Persian writings as well.[5]

No similar catastrophe overtook the Lullian and Kabbalist traditions, but the sixteenth century probably marks their peak of influence as well, for together with Hermeticism they blended to suggest not only that the world could be understood (which Aristotle had not doubted) but that man's place in the universe could be specified with literal and mathematical precision, that wisdom could give man operative control over himself and his environment, that all mankind could draw together in a spirit of acceptance rather than of mere toleration, that man could become like God.

The dimensions of this occult Renaissance are still unclear, but scholars of the last generation have demonstrated that its influence was everywhere. Starting with Ficino and Giovanni Pico della Mirandola, magic became a method of spiritual refinement, of manipulating spirits and maybe even angels to obtain health, insight, union with the ultimate forces of the cosmos. The famous German Hebraist, Johann Reuchlin, participated avidly in this quest, adding a profound familiarity with the Kabbalah to the magical enterprise. It is probable that his concern for the Hebrew language stemmed not from any general philosemitism and not from a thirst for the pure text of the Old Testament, but from a desire to purify and intensify the magic of Ficino and Pico.[6] The Benedictine abbot of Sponheim, Johannes Trithemius, was also fascinated by natural magic and came close enough to summoning spirits that he earned

[5]Yates (1964); Purnell (1976) has recently shown that the texts of Hermes were subjected to sharp critique as early as 1567, but these attacks remained relatively unknown.
[6]Zika (1976).

an unsavory reputation as a black magician.[7] Both Reuchlin and Trithemius contributed to the much more ambitious attempts of Heinrich Cornelius Agrippa of Nettesheim to set forth a practical and a religious magic that would tie man into all the forces and spirits of the cosmos.[8] Recently it has been shown that Agrippa was in close agreement with a number of radical religious reformers, especially in Strasbourg, and that his concern for secrecy in magic was similar to Nicodemite doctrines of religious secrecy.[9]

Inspired by these Kabbalist-Hermetic efforts, others attempted to put the new magic to use, whether as a source of tricks and intellectual showmanship, as in the case of the historical Doctor Faustus, or as a source of medical wisdom, as in the work of Paracelsus, who labored to teach the unity of spiritual, mental, and physical health.[10] Their works were doubly suspect in that they even tried to communicate their ideas in German, "casting their pearls before swine," as Trithemius said contemptuously to his errant student, Johann Steinemoel of Mechelin.[11]

Of course, it was not only in Germany that the occult sciences spread. In Italy, to name only a few of the savants, the Franciscan Francesco Giorgi of Venice (also known as Zorzi), published a large work in 1525, the *De harmonia mundi*, which laid out the musical connections between man and the universe. Kabbalah could be used, moreover, to prove the truth of Christianity, just as Reuchlin had thought. Even architecture should reflect the new-found harmonies between man the microcosm and the heavenly spheres of the macrocosm.[12] Geronimo Cardano developed the mathematical impulses of the Pythagorean philosophy and became thereby perhaps the leading mathematician of the whole sixteenth century. Giordano Bruno took the teachings of Hermes as a basis for a genuinely pagan revival of Egyptian religion in which all of Christendom could be reunited. Burned as a heretic in 1600, Bruno was once venerated as a martyr for science, for he had taught the Copernican system and had extracted the heretical conclusion that the universe was infinite. The researches of Frances Yates have shown that Bruno's heresies

[7]Arnold (1971) tries to downplay Trithemius' magic. For useful correctives see Brann (1977, 1979) and Evans (1979), 351–3.

[8]Nauert (1965); Walker (1958); Zambelli (1965, 1969, 1973, 1976).

[9]Zambelli (1976), 72–3, 86–7; Ginzburg (1970); Biondi (1974).

[10]Harmening (1973); Pagel (1958); Hemleben (1973).

[11]Harmening (1973), 68.

[12]Wittkower (1949); French (1972), 57–8, 150–3.

were not those of modern science but of the Hermetic tradition. But it is also becoming clear that the origins of modern science lie precisely in this murky world of numbers, mystery, and magic.[13] Nicholas Copernicus himself presented his heliocentric theory as one that accorded well with the teachings of Hermes Trismegistos,[14] and it is now well understood that Johann Kepler worked out his scheme of the universe under the obsession that he was thereby uncovering the magical harmonies of the spheres.[15] Even the sober Francis Bacon had deep roots in the magico-empirical tradition,[16] while Isaac Newton's mystical and alchemical writings far exceed his practical scientific works.[17]

In sixteenth-century England the most outstanding magus was John Dee, whom recent scholars have rescued from centuries of ridicule. Dee was active in an extraordinary number of fields: adviser to Queen Elizabeth, collector of the largest library of his time in England, apologist and promoter of English empire and exploration, foremost teacher of navigation and of mathematics, teacher of Sir Philip Sidney and center of his literary and philosophical circle (a circle that may have inspired Edmund Spenser as well), enthusiastic antiquarian and stimulator of research into British history, and all the while a devout student of the Lullian and Hermetic writings, and a worker of angel magic. What many of these pursuits share is an obsession with man's place in time, in geography or at sea, and in the cosmos. But more than just wanting to know where he was in all of these senses, Dee felt moved to provide the tools for active intervention. His magic, mathematics, poetics, and science were operational.[18]

In France, too, the occult Renaissance had a wide influence, especially in the artistic circle of the Pleiade, whose members, Pontus de Tyard, Antoine de Baif, and Guy Le Fevre de la Boderie, hoped to transcend the petty distinctions of scholastic theology in an eirenic and mystical religion based on the teachings of Hermes. One of the most outspoken of these eirenic thinkers was Guillaume Postel, the

[13]A dense literature has sprung up; see, e.g., Yates (1964, 1968); Debus (1977, 1978); Dobbs (1976); Drake (1970); Easlea (1980); French (1972); Koenigsberger (1979); Manuel (1968); Rossi (1968, 1975); Vasoli (1979); Westfall (1972). Westman (1977) provides a trenchant critique.
[14]Yates (1964), 153–5.
[15]Koestler (1964); Simon (1979).
[16]Rossi (1968).
[17]Dobbs (1976).
[18]French (1972).

renowned Kabbalist and orientalist who dreamed of a world united in the new faith. Even the Huguenot Phillipe Du Plessis-Mornay hoped for a reunion of faiths based on Hermes, who had taught that there was but one God.[19]

There is no doubt then that the occult sciences spread in countless directions, captivating even Shakespeare and Milton. Understandably, scholars have spent most of their efforts on the works of one or another magus. The result is that we are beginning to have solid studies of at least the most important of these figures. But the cost cannot be denied, the historical cost of coherence. Each hero appears on his author's stage, struggles with his contemporaries, thinks practical and eirenic thoughts, resists accusations of witchcraft, and dies. D. P. Walker recognized this danger when he undertook to survey the problem of distinguishing one form of magic from another in the sixteenth century, but even that work, for all its vigor and excellence, has a static quality, as if the problem were always the same.[20] The only broad surveys of the rise and fall of the Kabbalo-Hermetic tradition are those of Frances Yates, whose most recent speculations pit the bright but doomed forces of Hermeticism, toleration, and good will, against the implacable forces of Catholic obscurantism; the Renaissance against the witch hunters.[21] It is not a formulation of great persuasive power.

I think that we need new studies of what the occultists found wanting in their opposition; what was their serious critique of reason, whether pure or practical? And while we are at it, why did they seek a religious magic that always verged (when it did not converge) on heresy? What was their serious critique of grace, whether sacramental or sermonic? What did the more outspoken magicians expect to achieve with their operations? Eliza Butler showed long ago that a surprising amount of Renaissance magic was directed toward sordid, material ends.[22] When magic wasn't psychological, a giant metaphor for the mysteries of creativity, what were its goals?

Although many of the world's great libraries might support research into these questions, few would disagree that the best place for such work is London, and more specifically the Warburg Institute with its strong tradition of concern for the history of neo-

[19]French (1972), 157–58; Harris (1978); Bouwsma (1957); Copenhaver (1977, 1978).
[20]Walker (1958).
[21]Yates (1972, 1979).
[22]Butler (1949).

Platonism and the occult, and with the combined resources of its own library, the Wellcome Institute for the History of Medicine, and the British Library all close at hand.

It is a surprising but little-noticed fact that although the learned magi of the Renaissance were often, indeed routinely, accused of illicit demonolatry, they never paid the ultimate penalty on this account. Dee spent some months in prison on a charge of treason in 1555, Agrippa was not unacquainted with prison (for debt), and Pico repented and retracted his errors, but only Bruno was executed for his magical heresies, and even he was not accused of any pact with the devil, the standard charge against the witches. What was the difference? Why didn't the witches escape as easily as the learned? In answering this question we will need to review some of the most important advances in our understanding of witchcraft.

Twenty years ago the students of witchcraft were divided into two camps, the theologians and the Murrayites. Those who insisted on a theological definition and interpretation of witchcraft held that witchcraft was a peculiarly Christian offense, involving repudiation of one's baptism, a pact with the devil, witches' dances or sabbaths, and harmful magic.[23] While some of these elements could be found the world over (especially the belief in harmful magic, *maleficium*), the Christian features apparently made European witchcraft immune to cross-cultural comparisons: from this point of view witchcraft was basically a heresy. The followers of Margaret Murray clove to an equally uncompromising interpretation. They held that witches were the remnants of a prehistoric fertility cult, a popular religion so strong and pervasive that it was centuries before the church could attack it effectively. According to the Murrayites the great witch hunts of the late Middle Ages and the early modern period represent the final victory of Christianity over the paganism of the people.[24] During the last twenty years social historians have worked hard to erase the absurdities of these two extreme points of view.[25]

Among the more important investigations have been those that have concentrated on the patterns visible in the great witch hunt taken as a whole, temporal as well as geographic patterns. One of

---

[23]See Midelfort (1968) for literature; the attitude survives in Russell (1972).

[24]Murray (1921); see Midelfort (1968) for a list of Murrayites.

[25]Monter (1972); Henningsen (1980), 1–22; Larner (1981), chapters 1 and 2; Schormann (1977), 147–59.

the most important contributions has been the simultaneous but independent discovery by Norman Cohn and Richard Kieckhefer that
the documents on which historians had relied for their picture of
massive witch trials in fourteenth-century France were forgeries.[26]
This revelation had the effect of severing the assumed link between
inquisitorial proceedings against Albigensian heretics and the earliest witchcraft trials. It was a major blow to the witchcraft as heresy
school. It now appears that witch hunting began to increase only in
the fifteenth century, mainly in France, Switzerland, and southern
Germany. Moreover, it is plain that in these early trials at least the
common people had no concern with witchcraft as a sect of devil
worshippers. Villagers were worried about harmful witchcraft,
whether the result of charms and spells or the malignity of a sorcerer
or witch.[27] This conclusion dealt a fatal blow to the witch cult as
popular religion school, for it now seems certain that the witch cult
was a figment of the learned imagination.

   If witch hunting was not a direct offshoot of the hunt for heretics,
and if there was basically no organized cult to be rooted out in any
event, how shall we understand its extraordinary rise in the fifteenth
century? Some scholars have been tempted to link the rise of witchcraft prosecutions to a prevailing mood of anxiety or despair in the
late Middle Ages, perhaps prompted by adverse economic conditions.[28] The trouble with such a thesis has been that it is so vague
that it cannot be falsified; it does not seem to clarify why this region
or that town should have started hunting witches. More promising
have been those studies that have shown the connection between the
efforts of churchmen and learned judges to Christianize the rural
population and their shocked discovery that the common people
harbored an astonishing farrago of "demonic superstitions." Following the lead of Jean Delumeau, a number of scholars have asserted
that in one region or another witchcraft trials came in the wake of
stepped up efforts to convert the people.[29] Unfortunately, this attractive theory works best for the late sixteenth and early seven-

---

[26]Cohn (1975); Kieckhefer (1976).

[27]Kieckhefer has devised some useful tests of this conclusion. Horsley (1979a, 1979b)
calls attention to the usefulness of the traditional anthropological distinction between
sorcery (spells and charms that anyone can perform) and witchcraft (a capacity to
harm based not on actions but on a mysterious personal force). If his conclusions are
valid, folk fears need even more careful analysis than Cohn and Kieckhefer provide.

[28]Huizinga (1924) expressed this notion forcefully; Delumeau (1978), 232–53,
305–88, has recently attempted to give the thesis a measure of specificity.

[29]Delumeau (1977, 1978); Burke (1978); Muchembled (1978a, 1978b).

teenth centuries, when Tridentine and Reformed educational programs were going into place, and it also assumes not only that rural Europe was essentially pagan on the eve of the Reformation but that the ruling classes didn't know it. So we are back to contemplating the fifteenth century. In an outrageous work of multiple iconoclasm, Lionel Rothkrug has reminded us that the same authors who wrote the famous misogynist witch hunter's manual, the *Malleus Maleficarum* (1487), were also associated with the growing devotion to the Virgin Mary. Jacob Sprenger was one of the founders of the cult of the rosary.[30] This connection, if it is one, should lead to a new series of investigations into the status of women in the late Middle Ages. Witch hunting certainly looks from one angle like a war on women, especially when we consider that roughly eighty percent of the some 100,000 witches executed in Europe between 1400 and 1700 were women. Unfortunately until recently women's studies have been looking to witchcraft studies for help when it is evident that witchcraft studies need the benefit of demographic, psychological, and religious studies of women.[31]

Another approach to the problem of the beginnings of witch hunting has been the legal or procedural. It is evident that much of the "evidence" and most of the confessions obtained in witchcraft trials were dependent on rules of evidence that permitted, or even encouraged, torture and testimony from already convicted witches. It used to be argued that treating magic as if it were heresy was a fateful innovation of the later Middle Ages precisely because the frightful rules for pursuing heresy could then be applied. More recently, however, it has been shown that magic had always been considered heretical, from St. Augustine onwards. There was no late medieval innovation here.[32] Others used to argue that the revival of Roman Law allowed an inquisitorial procedure and the use of torture in ways that the Germanic codes did not. Although there is truth in this observation, the spread of torture and inquisition predate the fifteenth century by a couple of hundred years.[33] These may have been essential ingredients in the witch craze, but they were certainly not

[30]Rothkrug (1980), 82–3.
[31]Larner (1981) elaborates on witch hunting as a war on women. Some of the weaknesses of the attempted links between women's studies and witchcraft research are visible in Garret (1977). The attitudes of scholastic philosophers, theologians, physicians, and jurists towards women have been studied carefully in Maclean (1980).
[32]Peters (1978).
[33]For a quick survey of the literature see Langbein (1974), 141–55.

triggers. Recently the procedural argument has been refurbished for the German scene. It now appears significant that the imperial criminal code of 1532 (the *Carolina*) required ignorant local judges to consult their learned university colleagues in cases of witchcraft; in this way a dangerous link between local evidence and the fantasies of the theologically learned may have been forged.[34] The Spanish example also illustrates the extraordinary importance of legal procedure. From 1526 onwards the Spanish Inquisition was skeptical of evidence extracted from witches and skeptical also about the bizarre details of flight, demonic copulation, the witches' dance, etc. In fact, the largest witch hunt ever erupted only when this sober procedural skepticism was breached in 1609 in the Basque country of Navarre. With new procedures inviting accusations and confessions, the numbers of witches suddenly expanded and the number of suspects jumped to several thousand in just two years.[35] It is moreover widely recognized that reforms of legal procedures often brought witch trials to a halt, at least in their virulent, massive form.[36]

I am not sure that these studies have succeeded in explaining why Europeans began seeking out internal enemies in ever larger numbers, especially after 1450. There is much more work still to be done on this large puzzle, even if we can now see several of the larger pieces clearly.

The peak of witch hunting frenzy came across Western Europe between about 1560 and 1635, with significantly later peaks in Scotland, northwestern Germany, and Sweden, all three experiencing the worst panics in the 1660's.[37] Poland's peak came only after 1700, when over 5000 cases were prosecuted.[38] If we regard these areas as peripheral to the mainstream of European culture and therefore slower to contract the infection of witch hunting, we may be able to subsume the only North American panic under the same rubric. When the authorities at Salem, Massachusetts, executed nineteen witches in 1692 (plus one more for failure to plead), it was a surprisingly late epidemic by English standards, and it was held up to ridicule by English opponents of the Massachusetts experiment in godly

[34]Midelfort (1981).
[35]Henningsen (1980), 23.
[36]Midelfort (1972).
[37]Larner (1981); Schormann (1977); Ankarloo (1975); Heikkinen (1969).
[38]Baranowski (1952); see also the work on Russia by Zguta (1977a, 1977b).

rule.[39] From these late examples some historians have concluded that witchcraft trials died out as a result of rising disenchantment and enlightenment in Europe. With a new mechanical philosophy magistrates and the learned elites in general presumably found charges of witchcraft incredible.[40] The general difficulty with this explanation is that most of Europe got rid of chain reaction trials (and often the solitary trials as well) long before the faintest glimmer of the mechanical philosophy is visible in the minds of magistrates or the local elites. Spain had, as mentioned a moment ago, an elegant tradition of skepticism based on nothing more modern than a proper fear of the devil's deceptive powers, his ability to inspire false confessions and to implicate the innocent.[41] In southwestern Germany the largest wave of witch trials broke in the late 1620's; by the mid-1630's the worst was past for many regions. Surely it would be rash to posit a proto-early-Enlightenment in order to account for this pattern.

Rationalist historians used to claim that the high points of the witch craze corresponded with general religious fervor or more specifically with outbursts of religious warfare.[42] On this theory witch hunting was a religious war carried out by other means: instead of seeking out heretics and outspoken dissidents, the authorities are presumed to have sought out the hidden enemies of God. Although the timing of this explanation seems to work roughly for Germany and France, corresponding especially well to the surge of witch hunting during the years of Catholic triumph in the 1620's, the exact connection remains too vague. It cannot be shown that the persons trapped in witchcraft accusations were dissidents of any sort or that the authorities cared at all what they thought. It is possible, as Muchembled has argued, that Reformation and Counter-Reformation zeal for local piety was outraged to learn how thoroughly ignorant, or even contemptuous, villagers might be. To that extent the magisterial witch hunt can be seen as a further step in the continuing conflict of high culture with popular culture.[43]

In order to gain a firm grip on such questions social historians have recently worked witchcraft into the social fabric of village life,

---

[39]The best account is still Starkey (1950).
[40]Trevor-Roper (1968); Easlea (1980).
[41]Henningsen (1980), 22–23, 156–7, 349–50.
[42]Trevor-Roper (1968).
[43]Muchembled (1978, 1979); Burke (1978).

and it is no exaggeration to say that popular witchcraft beliefs are now the single best understood feature of popular religion in the early modern period. In England the researches of A. D. J. Macfarlane and Keith Thomas have emphasized the pervasiveness of magic and divining by the "cunning" men and women of the village. As a course of extra-ecclesiastical comfort in times of trouble, their efforts may have rivaled those of the ordained clergy in popularity if not in orthodoxy. And in the wake of the Reformation, with its attack on Roman Catholic magic, the local need for magic may actually have increased. Thomas and Macfarlane also concocted a psychological account of witchcraft accusations in which traditional demands for charity or alms ran into the rebuff of the newly reformed conscience (for alms giving came under attack as a form of popish good work); but these traditional demands could still trigger guilt among the refusers of charity, a guilt that then found expression in accusations of witchcraft aimed at alms seekers. It is an ingenious theory, but one that will carry us only so far, for it is plain that in the larger witchcraft trials such personally motivated accusations were swallowed up in tensions of a more general nature.[44] Perhaps the best study of the way that local problems could find expression in charges of witchcraft is the elegant book by Paul Boyer and Stephen Nissenbaum on Salem. They discovered that the lists of those accused of witchcraft (including their defenders) and of those bringing charges against the witches corresponded closely to a political and economic split in the village that went back for over a decade. This made it likely that charges of witchcraft were a final step in defending a traditional, autonomous form of village life increasingly threatened by the commercial nexus of the nearby port town.[45] Until this sort of study has been repeated in Europe we will not know how widely we may apply this model, but scholars have suspected for some time that political tensions might lie concealed within the folds of the witchcraft trial.[46] Another local study, from northern Italy, has pointed to the way that inquisitorial pressure between 1570 and 1640 transformed local superstitions into fully fledged confessions of witchcraft. The brilliant author, Carlo Ginzburg, misleadingly concluded that he had confirmed Margaret Murray's theory that witch-

---

[44]Macfarlane (1970); Thomas (1971); Macfarlane has recently retracted his earlier views on the way in which witchcraft accusations may have been connected to broad social changes, Macfarlane (1978), 1–2, 59–60.

[45]Boyer and Nissenbaum (1974).

[46]Midelfort (1972).

craft was simply the Christian interpretation of pagan fertility cults, but there is no doubt that his examination of folklore and popular heresy goes far to substantiate the idea that witchcraft accusations gave form to the fundamental conflict between popular and learned culture.[47] I have the impression that these local studies of witchcraft have only just begun to show their potential. The surviving records of these trials and investigations constitute, after all, the single largest body of direct evidence on the popular mentality. In witchcraft trials the common people might have their views of destiny and the devil, of village cohesion and social danger, recorded as they otherwise never were.

Another kind of pattern stands out in recent research: the geographical variety of Europe. England was essentially a land of isolated trials that stopped after one or two witches were convicted. Germany has recently been taken to be a land of massive, chain reaction trials that did not grind to a halt before scores of witches had been executed.[48] Working with these two stereotypes, which are both oversimplifications, E. William Monter has recently exposed a third type of trial, an intermediate form in which five to ten suspects might be disciplined.[49] Fully persuaded that witchcraft was a demonic cult, the magistrates of the Jura region of eastern France and western Switzerland nonetheless carried out their investigations so carefully that torture did not get out of hand and major panics did not develop. Monter has also observed that most of Europe's witchcraft trials came from such cultural borderlands: the Franco-Germanic frontier, the mountains of northern Italy, the Franco-Spanish Basque country.[50] It remains to be seen what we are to make of this observation, but it is worth noting perhaps that the most recent study of German witchcraft confirms an increasing severity as one moves westward from Lower Saxony into the culturally diverse region of the lower Rhine.[51] The recent study by Christina Larner has also begun the serious task of accounting for the major differences between Scotland and England, differences that may not all be mat-

[47]Ginzburg (1966, 1977).
[48]Midelfort (1972); Schormann (1977).
[49]Monter (1976).
[50]Monter (1980).
[51]Schormann (1977), 113–14, emphasizes the extraordinary place of Westphalia in the history of northwestern German witch trials. See also Dupont-Bouchat (1978), for interesting evidence that in Luxembourg the German regions were worse than the French.

ters of legal procedure. In particular, Larner suggests that witch-craft doctrine had political implications, a state-building function that Scottish authorities may have welcomed in the wake of the dis-ruptions of the sixteenth century.[52] So witchcraft may yet provide keys to the mind of the magistrates as well as that of the villager.

Getting at the mind of the magistrates was precisely what Robert Mandrou attempted in his book on French witchcraft. Charting the rise of a practical skepticism in the seventeenth century, he tried to show how French witch trials fell victim to the *révolution mentale* of the new naturalism.[53] His conclusions have not gone uncontested. Monter has argued that the judges of Burgundy gave up hunting witches long before they displayed any *crise de conscience*; and Al-fred Soman has shown that the Parlement of Paris exercised extraor-dinary care, even skepticism, as early as the sixteenth century.[54] It remains true, however, that France was the country of spectacular demonic possessions, especially in the seventeenth century, a feature of French religious life that has not yet found an adequate explana-tion.[55] Mandrou seems to have been right in arguing that the dra-matically possessed nunneries of France raised the issue of witch-craft and the devil's work to a national scandal, a level at which some statement of national policy became necessary. Louis XIV issued an edict in 1682 effectively decriminalizing witchcraft by declaring that only poisoners were worthy of death while other pretended witches were only charlatans. This move put a relatively early offi-cial end to French witchcraft trials. Although, as we have seen, Western Europe in fact stopped trying cases of witchcraft at about the same time, the authorities were much slower to remove witch-craft from the criminal code.

I have emphasized the important advances brought by social his-torians to the study of witchcraft, but it should be said at once that intellectual historians have made a number of exceedingly useful contributions as well. When one reflects on the fact that a large number of major political and intellectual leaders of Europe not on-ly expressed themselves on the issues surrounding witchcraft but contributed originally to the continuing debate, it is evident that

[52]Larger (1981).
[53]Mandrou (1968).
[54]Monter (1976); Soman (1977, 1978, 1981).
[55]See Ernst (1972); Certeau (1980); Walker (1981), for some notions of how to ex-plain the epidemic of French demon possessions.

witchcraft was more than just another unexamined part of their world picture. A problem that captivated Sylvester Prierias (the papal apologist of the 1520's), Jean Bodin, and King James I must be said to have unusual political resonances, and some of the best recent work has shown how witchcraft doctrines helped to crystallize a new view of political and religious authority.[56] Among skeptics, moreover, witchcraft was a proving ground for radical new ideas of religious experience and the limits of political coercion.[57]

There are still many important topics that need attention. No one has really undertaken to assess the impact of the *Malleus Maleficarum;* and although most scholars have been willing to assert that it was the most important single book in the field, a contention I have doubted elsewhere, there are no careful readings of the whole work.[58] In addition to this neglect, individual skeptics as eminent as Johann Weyer (whose *De praestigiis daemonum* was first published in 1563) and constructive scholastics as eminent as Martin Delrio (whose *Disquisitiones magicarum libri sex* first appeared in 1599/ 1600) have hardly provoked the scholarly attention they deserve.[59] So long as even the social historians are willing to concede that witch hunting proceeded from the fantasies and terrors of the learned, it is obvious that intellectual historians must play a major role in any forthcoming synthesis. The *culture des élites* may turn out to be every bit as mysterious as the recently discovered *culture populaire.*

In general, it can be said that witchcraft studies have gone into high gear in the last twenty years. One no longer reads the exaggerations that were once common currency even among cautious scholars. This fact does not at all mean that we are nearly agreed on the questions of origin, temporal pattern, geography, or decline. And some important questions have not been considered at all. In the book that I published in 1972 I tried to call attention to the dynamic within the largest witchcraft trials.[60] It seemed to me that in the midst of panic a pattern was visible, a process of self control that brought the domino chain of trials to a halt.[61] With all of the precise local studies, this broader question concerning the largest trials has

---

[56]Anglo (1976, 1977); Baxter (1977); Clark (1977); Larner (1981); Lange (1970).
[57]Walker (1958); Baxter (1977).
[58]Midelfort (1972); Anglo (1977) makes a beginning.
[59]Fisher (1975) marks a beginning with Delrio.
[60]Midelfort (1972).
[61]Midelfort (1979) sets forth a primitive model.

gone unduly neglected. There are also major theological questions left open by the witchcraft debate. What eschatological views would drive sixteenth-century Protestants to fear a crime hardly mentioned in the New Testament? European witchcraft was, in fact, a crime that was not strictly speaking discussed anywhere in the Bible: one searches in vain for the idea of a pact with the devil. This means that when biblical scholars of the early modern period sought to describe witchcraft in biblical terms, they were engaged in highly creative forms of exegesis. Yet, as noted with respect to the *Malleus Maleficarum*, careful theological studies have barely begun.[62] Was the fear of witchcraft connected to the fear of antinomianism? Were there theological schools or traditions that split over witchcraft? What of law and medicine? Were there fundamental principles that divided professionals? The reason for posing these questions is that too often scholars have been content to explain a man's attitude toward witchcraft by referring only to his character: was he humane and tolerant or cruel, bigotted, credulous, and intolerant? Surely the intellectual issues bear careful scrutiny.

Where should the aspiring scholar undertake witchcraft research? A great library is one consideration, and although both Yale and Harvard have excellent collections, two other libraries merit special attention. First, the A. D. White Library at Cornell University has an extraordinary collection of materials on witchcraft, carefully assembled in the nineteenth century by George Lincoln Burr. Second, the Henry Charles Lea Library of the University of Pennsylvania preserves the magnificent collection of books that Lea obtained while working on his never to be completed history of witchcraft. Aside from considerations regarding the library, students are best advised to go where their style of questioning will be appreciated. There are history programs so devoted to social history that the yearnings of an intellectual historian might wither. The reverse is less commonly true these days, but it has happened that even at the best schools a student will find it necessary to take counsel from whatever scholars he admires. Free advice is one of the last social graces of an academic world that threatens to become a business. Let us hope that students of magic and witchcraft may continue to share in the occult community of the magi even if they do not erect a cultic *communitas infidelium*.

---

[62]Oberman (1977), 201–36, marks only a beginning of the detailed work necessary.

Bibliography

Adriani, Maurilio, *Italia magica. La magia nella tradizione italica* (Rome, 1970).

Allen, Richard, *Crime and Punishment in Sixteenth-Century Reutlingen* (Ph.D. Dissertation, University of Virginia, 1980).

Alver, Bente Gullveig, *Heksetro og Troldom. Et studie i norsk heksewaesen* (Oslo, 1971).

Anderson, Alan and Raymond Gordon, "Witchcraft and the Status of Women: The Case of England," *British Journal of Sociology* 29 (1978): 171–84.

――――, "The Uniqueness of English Witchcraft," *British Journal of Sociology* 30 (1979): 359–61.

Anglo, Sydney, "Melancholy and Witchcraft: The Debate between Wier, Bodin, and Scot," in *Folie et déraison à la Renaissance* (Brussels, 1976), 209–22.

――――, *The Damned Art. Essays in the Literature of Witchcraft* (London, 1977).

Ankarloo, Bengt, *Trolldomsprocesserna i Sverige* (Stockholm, 1975).

Arnold, Klaus, *Johannes Trithemius, 1462–1516* (Würzburg, 1971).

Baranowski, B., *Procesy czarownia w. Poland w. XVII i XVIII wieku* (Lódź, 1952).

Baxter, Christopher, "Jean Bodin's *De la démonomanie des sorciers*," *Anglo* (1977): 76–105. (a)

――――, "Johann Weyer's *De praestigiis daemonum*," *Anglo* (1977): 53–75. (b)

Becker, G., *Aus der Zeit der Verzweiflung. Zur Genese und Aktualität des Hexenbildes* (Frankfurt, 1977).

Behrendt, R., "Abbot John Trithemius (1462–1516), Monk and Humanist," *Revue Bénédictine* 84 (1974): 212–29.

Ben-Yehuda, N., "The European Witch Craze of the Fourteenth to the Seventeenth Centuries: A Sociologist's Perspective," *American Journal of Sociology* 86 (1980); 1–31.

Bienmiller, D., and M. Millet, "Univers folklorique et sorcellerie à Dole aux XVIe et XVIIe siècles," *Cahiers Dolois* 1 (1977): 1–48.

Biondi, Albano, "La giustificazione della simulazione nel Cinquecento," in *Eresia e Riforma nell' Italia del Cinquecento*, ed. A. Biondi et al. (Florence-Chicago, 1974): 5–68.

Bouwsma, William, *Concordia Mundi. The Career and Thought of Guillaume Postel* (Cambridge, Mass., 1957).

Boyer, Paul, and Stephen Nissenbaum, *Salem Possessed. The Social Origins of Witchcraft* (Cambridge, Mass., 1974).

Brann, Noel L., "The Shift from Mystical to Magical Theology in the Abbot Trithemius (1462–1516)," *Studies in Medieval Culture* 11 (1977): 147–59.

———, "Conrad Celtis and the 'Druid' Abbot Trithemius: An Inquiry into Patriotic Humanism," *Renaissance and Reformation* N.S. 3 (1979): 16–28.

Burke, John, "Hermetism as a Renaissance World View," in *The Darker Vision of the Renaissance*, ed. Robert Kinsman (Berkeley, 1974): 95–117.

Burke, Peter, *Popular Culture in Early Modern Europe* (New York, 1978).

Butler, Eliza M., *Ritual Magic* (Cambridge, 1949).

Cardini, F., *Magia, stregoneria, superstizione nell' Occidente medievale* (Florence, 1979).

Caro Baroja, Julio, *The World of Witches* (Chicago, 1964).

———, *Vidas mágicas e Inquisición* (Madrid, 1967).

Ceard, Jean, "Folie et démonologie au XVIe siècle," in *Folie et déraison à la Renaissance* (Brussels, 1976): 129–48.

Certeau, Michel de, *La possession de Loudun*, 2nd ed. (Paris, 1980).

Charpentier, A., *La sorcellerie en Pays basque* (Paris, 1977).

Chaunu, Pierre, "Sur la fin des sorciers au XVIIe siècle," *Annales: Economies, Sociétés, Civilisations* 24 (1969): 895–911.

———, *Eglise, culture et société. Essais sur reforme et contre reforme (1517–1620)* (Paris, 1980).

Clark, Stuart, and J. F. J. Morgan, Religion and Magic in Elizabethan Wales: Robert Holland's Dialogue on Witchcraft," *Journal of Ecclesiastical History* 27 (1976): 31–46.

———, "King James' Daemonologie: Witchcraft and Kingship," *Anglo* (1977): 156–81.

———, "Inversion, Misrule and the Meaning of Witchcraft," *Past & Present* no. 87 (May 1980): 98–127.

Cohn, Norman, *Europe's Inner Demons. An Enquiry Inspired by the Great Witch Hunt* (New York, 1975).

Copenhaver, Brian P., "Lefèvre d'Etaples, Symphorien Champier, and the Secret Names of God," *Journal of the Warburg and Courtauld Institute* 40 (1977): 189–211.

———, *Symphorien Champier and the Reception of the Occultist Tradition in Renaissance France* (The Hague, 1978).

Crozet, R., *La sorcellerie en Auvergne* (Roanne, 1978).

Currie, Elliot P., "The Control of Witchcraft in Renaissance Europe," in *The Social Organization of Law*, ed D. Black and M. Mileski (London, 1973): 344–67.

Dawson, John P., *The Oracles of the Law* (Ann Arbor, 1968).

De' Antoni, D., "Processi per stregoneria e magia a Chioggia nel XVI secolo," *Ricerche di Storia Sociale e Religiosa* 7 (1973): 187–228.

Debus, Allen G., *Man and Nature in the Renaissance* (Cambridge, 1978).

———, *The Chemical Philosophy: Paracelsian Science and Medicine in the Sixteenth and Seventeenth Centuries* (New York, 1977).

Delumeau, Jean, *Catholicism between Luther and Voltaire* (London, 1977).

———, *La peur en Occident: XIVe–XVIIIe siècles* (Paris, 1978).

Dobbs, B. J. T., *The Foundation of Newton's Alchemy. The Hunting of the Greene Lyon* (Cambridge, 1976).

Döbler, H., *Hexenwahn. Die Geschichte einer Verfolgung* (Munich, 1977).

Drake, Stillman, "Renaissance Music and Experimental Science," *Journal of the History of Ideas* 31 (1970): 483–500.

Dukes, Eugene D., Magic and Witchcraft in the Writings of the Western Church Fathers (Ph.D. Dissertation, Kent State University, 1972).

Dunlap, R., "King James and Some Witches: The Date and Text of the Daemonologie," *Philological Quarterly* 54 (1975): 40–6.

Dupont-Bouchat, Marie-Sylvie, "La répression de la sorcellerie dans le duché de Luxembourg au XVIe et XVIIe siècles. Une analyse des structures de pouvoir et de leur fonctionnement dans le cadre de la chasse aux sorcières," *Prophètes et sorciers dans les Pays Bas. XVIe–XVIIe siècles*, ed. Marie-Sylvie Dupont-Bouchat, Willem Frijhoff, and Robert Muchembled (Paris, 1978).

Easlea, Brian, *Witch Hunting, Magic, and the New Philosophy. An Introduction to the Debates of the Scientific Revolution, 1450–1750* (Brighton, 1980).

Eliade, Mircea, "Some Observations on European Witchcraft," *History of Religions* 14 (1975): 149–72.

Ernst, Cécile, *Teufelaustreibungen. Die Praxis der katholischen Kirche im 16. und 17. Jahrhundert* (Bern, 1972).

Evans, R. J. W., *Rudolf II and His World* (Oxford, 1973).

———, *The Making of the Habsburg Monarchy, 1550–1700. An Interpretation* (Oxford, 1979).

Favret-Saada, Jeanne, *Deadly Words. Witchcraft in the Bocage* (Cambridge, 1980).

Fischer, Edda, *Die 'Disquisitionum Magicarum Libri Sex' von Martin Delrio als gegenreformatorische Exempel-Quelle* (Ph.D. Dissertation, Frankfurt, 1975).

Fournier, Pierre-Francois, *Magie et sorcellerie. Essai historique, accompagné de documents concernant la Magie et la Sorcellerie en Auvergne* (Moulins, 1979).

French, Peter J., *John Dee. The World of an Elizabethan Magus* (London, 1972).

Garrett, Clarke, "Women and Witches: Patterns of Analysis," *Journal of Women in Culture and Society* 3 (1977): 461–70.

Ginzburg, Carlo, *I benandanti. Stregoneria e culti agrari tra Cinquecento e Seicento* (Turin, 1966).

———, *Il nicodesimo* (Turin, 1970).

———, "Folklore, magia, religione," *Storia d'Italia*, ed. Giulio Einaudi, vol. 1 (Turin, 1972): 601–76.

———, "Folklore, magia e religione nelle campagne italiane," *Società, Chiesa e vita religiosa nell' 'Ancien régime'* (Naples, 1976): 427–42.

———, "Stregoneria, magia e superstizione in Europa fra medioevo ed età moderna," *Ricerche di storia sociale e religiosa* 11 (1977): 119–33.

Godet, A., "Hexenglaube, Rationalität und Aufklärung: Joseph Glanvil und Johann Moriz Schwager," *Deutsche Vierteljahrschrift für Literaturwissenschaft und Geistesgeschichte* 52 (1978): 581–603.

Göllner, C., *Hexenprozesse in Siebenbürgen* (Cluj, 1971).

Gorny, L., *La Kabbale: Kabbale juive et Cabale chrétienne* (Paris, 1977).

Harmening, Dieter, "Faust und die Renaissance-Magie: Zum ältesten Faustzeugnis (Johannes Trithemius an Johannes Virdung, 1507)," *Archiv für Kulturgeschichte* 55 (1973): 56–79.

Harrie, Jeanne, Francois Foix de Candale and the Hermetic Tradition in Sixteenth-Century France (Ph.D. Dissertation, University of California at Riverside, 1975).

———, "Duplessis-Mornay, Foix-Candale and the Hermetic Religion of the World," *Renaissance Quarterly* 31 (1978): 499–514.

Harris, Anthony, *Night's Black Agents: Witchcraft and Magic in Seventeenth-Century English Drama* (Manchester, 1980).

Heikkinen, Antero, *Paholaisen Liittolaiset. Noita- ja magiakäsityksiä ja -oikeudenkäynte jä suomessa 1600-luvun jälkipuoliskolla (n. 1640-1712)* (Helsinki, 1969), with English summary, pp. 374-94.

Hemleben, J., *Paracelsus: Revolutionär, Arzt und Christ* (Stuttgart, 1973).

Henningsen, Gustav, "Trolddom og hemmelige kunster. Heksefoflgelser," in *Dagligliv i Danmark 1620-1720*, ed. Axel Steensberg (Copenhagen, 1969), 161-96, 727-38.

———, *The Witches' Advocate. Basque Witchcraft and the Spanish Inquisition, 1609-1614* (Reno, 1980).

Horsley, Richard A., "Further Reflections on Witchcraft and European Folk Religion," *History of Religions* 19 (1979): 71-95. (a)

———, "Who Were the Witches? The Social Roles of the Accused in the European Witch Trials," *Journal of Interdisciplinary History* 9 (1979): 689-715. (b)

Huizinga, Johan, *The Waning of the Middle Ages* (London, 1924).

Jalby, R., *Sorcellerie, medecine populaire et pratiques medico-magiques en Languedoc* (Nyons, 1974).

Kelly, Henry A., *The Devil, Demonology and Witchcraft. The Development of Christian Belief in Evil Spirits* (Garden City, N.Y., 1968).

———, "English Kings and the Fear of Sorcery," *Medieval Studies* 39 (1977): 206-38.

Kieckhefer, Richard, *European Witch Trials. Their Foundations in Popular and Learned Culture, 1300-1500* (London, 1976).

Kneubühler, H. P., *Die Überwindung von Hexenwahn und Hexenprozess* (Diessenhofen, 1977).

Koenigsberger, D., *Renaissance Man and Creative Thinking. A History of Concepts of Harmony* (Atlantic Highlands, N.J., 1979).

Koestler, Arthur, *The Sleepwalkers* (London, 1964).

Kunstmann, Hartmut H., *Zauberwahn und Hexenprozess in der Reichsstadt Nürnberg* (Nuremberg, 1970).

Kunze, Michael, *Der Prozess Pappenheimer* (Ebelsbach, 1981).

Langbein, John, *Prosecuting Crime in the Renaissance: England, Germany, France* (Cambridge, Mass., 1974).

———, *Torture and the Law of Proof: Europe and England in the Ancien Regime* (Chicago, 1977).

Langdon, Rande Eve, Religion, Witchcraft and the Supernatural in

Elizabethan England (Ph.D. Dissertation, Harvard University, 1977).

Lange, Ursula, *Untersuchungen zu Bodins Démonomanie* (Frankfurt, 1970).

Larner, Christina, and Christopher Hyde Lee and Hugh McLachlan, *A Source Book of Scottish Witchcraft* (Glasglow, 1977).

_____, *Enemies of God* (London, 1981). (a)

_____, "Witch Beliefs and Witch Hunting in England and Scotland," *History Today* vol. 31 (Feb. 1981): 32–6. (b)

LeNail, J. F., Procédures contre les sorcières de Seix en 1562," *Bulletin annuel de la Société ariégeoise des sciences, lettres et arts* 31 (1976): 155–282.

Lenman, B., G. Parker, and V. Gatrell, eds., *Crime and the Law: The Social History of Crime in Western Europe since 1500* (London, 1980).

Leutenbauer, Siegfried, *Hexerei- und Zaubereidelikt in der Literatur von 1450 bis 1550* (Berlin, 1972).

Leutrat, P., *La sorcellerie lyonnaise* (Paris, 1977).

Lorini, F. E., and J. Bernabé, *La sorcellerie paysanne* (Brussels, 1977).

Macfarlane, A. D. J., *Witchcraft in Tudor and Stuart England* (London, 1970).

_____, *The Origins of English Individualism: The Family, Property and Social Transition* (Oxford, 1978).

Maclean, Ian, *The Renaissance Notion of Woman. A Study in the Fortunes of Scholasticism and Medical Science in European Intellectual Life* (Cambridge, 1980).

Magia, astrologia e religione nel Rinascimento. Convegno polacco-italiano, Varsavia 23–27 sett. 1972 (Accademia polacca d. scienze) (Wroclaw, 1974).

Mandrou, Robert, *Magistrats et sorciers en France au XVIIe siècle. Une analyse de psychologie historique* (Paris, 1968).

_____, *Possession et sorcellerie au XVIIe siècle: Textes inédits* (Paris, 1979).

Manuel, F., *A Portrait of Isaac Newton* (Cambridge, Mass., 1968).

Midelfort, H. C. Erik, "Recent Witch Hunting Research, Or Where Do We Go From Here?" *Papers of the Bibliographical Society of America* 62 (1968): 373–420.

_____, *Witch Hunting in Southwestern Germany, 1562–1684: The Social and Intellectual Foundations* (Stanford, 1972).

_____, "Were There Really Witches?" *Transition and Revolution*, ed. Robert Kingdon (Minneapolis, 1974): 189–233.

_____, "Witch Hunting and the Domino Theory," *Religion and the People: 800–1700*, ed. James Obelkevich (Chapel Hill, 1979): 277–88, 323–25.

_____, "Heartland of the Witchcraze: Central and Northern Europe," *History Today* vol. 31 (Feb. 1981): 27–31.

Miele, M., "Malattie magiche di origine diabolica e loro terapia secondo il medico beneventano Pietro Piperno (ob. 1642)," *Campania sacra* 6 (1975): 166–233.

Monter, E. William, "Inflation and Witchcraft: The Case of Jean Bodin," *Action and Conviction in Early Modern Europe*, ed. Theodore K. Rabb and Jerrold E. Seigel (Princeton, 1969): 371–89.

_____, "The Historiography of European Witchcraft: Progress and Prospects," *Journal of Interdisciplinary History* 2 (1972): 435–51.

_____, *Witchcraft in France and Switzerland. The Borderlands during the Reformation* (Ithaca, 1976).

_____, "French and Italian Witchcraft," *History Today* vol. 30 (Nov. 1980): 31–35.

Muchembled, Robert, *Culture populaire et culture des élites* (Paris, 1978). (a)

_____, "Sorcières du Cambrésis. L'acculturation du monde rural au XVIe et XVIIe siècles," in Dupont-Bouchat (1978), 155–261. (b)

_____, *La sorciere au village: XVe–XVIIIe siècles* (Paris, 1979).

Murray, A., "Medieval Origins of the Witch Hunt," *Cambridge Quarterly* 7 (1976): 63–74.

Murray, Margaret, *The Witch Cult in Western Europe: A Study in Anthropology* (Oxford, 1921).

Nauert, Charles G., *Agrippa and the Crisis of Renaissance Thought* (Urbana, 1965).

Nicholls, David, "The Devil in Renaissance France," *History Today* vol. 30 (Nov. 1980): 25–30.

Noize, M., "Le Grand Oeuvre, liturgie de l'alchimie chrétienne," *Revue de l'histoire des religions* 186 (1974): 149–83.

Oberman, Heiko A., *Masters of the Reformation* (Cambridge, 1981).

Pagel, Walter, *Paracelsus. An Introduction to Philosophical Medicine in the Era of the Renaissance* (Basel, 1958).

_____, *Das medizinische Weltbild des Paracelsus. Seine Zusammenhänge mit Neuplatonismus und Gnosis* (Wiesbaden, 1962).

Peters, Edward, *The Magician, the Witch and the Law* (Philadelphia, 1978).

Purnell, Frederick, "Francesco Patrizi and the Critics of Hermes Trismegistus," *Journal of Medieval and Renaissance Studies* 6 (1976): 155–78.

Raphaël, F., "Juifs et sorciers dans l'Alsace mediévale," *Revue des sciences sociale de la France de l'Est* 3 (1974): 68–106.

Reiss, W., "Die Hexenprozesse in der Stadt Baden-Baden," *Freiburger Diözesan Archiv* 91 (1971): 202–66.

Revel, J., "Superstizione e magia nell' eta moderna," *Ricerche di Storia Sociale e Religiosa* 11 (1977): 134–40.

Robbins, R. H., "Pandaemonium and the Sadducees," *Thought* 52 (1977): 167–87.

Roberts, G. J., Magic and Witchcraft in English Drama and Poetry from 1558 to 1634 (Ph.D. Dissertation, University of London, 1976).

Rossi, Paolo, *Francis Bacon: From Magic to Science* (Chicago, 1968).

———, "Hermeticism, Rationality and the Scientific Revolution," *Reason, Experiment and Mysticism in the Scientific Revolution*, ed. M. L. Righini Bonelli and W. R. Shea (New York, 1975): 247–73.

Rothkrug, Lionel, *Religious Practices and Collective Perceptions: Hidden Homologies in the Renaissance and Reformation. (Reflexions Historiques* 7, no. 1 (Spring 1980)).

Russell, Jeffrey B., *Witchcraft in the Middle Ages* (Ithaca, 1972).

Salimbeni, F., "La stregoneria nel tardo Rinascimento," *Nuova Rivista Storica* 60 (1976): 269–334.

Scholem, Gershom, *Ursprung und Anfänge der Kabbala* (Berlin, 1962).

Schormann, Gerhard, *Hexenprozesse in Nordwestdeutschland* (Hildescheim, 1977).

———, *Hexenprozesse in Deutschland* (Göttingen, 1981).

Schuler, R. M., "Some spiritual Alchemies of XVIIth-century England," *Journal of the History of Ideas* 41 (1980): 293–318.

Sebald, Hans, *Witchcraft. The Heritage of a Heresy* (New York, 1978).

Secret, F., *Les Kabbalistes Chrétiens de la Renaissance* (Paris, 1964).

Shumaker, Wayne, *The Occult Sciences in the Renaissance. A Study in Intellectual Patterns* (Berkeley, 1972).

Simon, G., *Kepler, astronome, astrologue* (Paris, 1979).

Singer, Gordon Andreas, "La Vauderie d'Arras," 1459–1491. An Episode of Witchcraft in Later Medieval France (Ph.D. Dissertation, University of Maryland, 1974).

Soman, Alfred, "Les procès de sorcellerie au Parlement de Paris (1565–1640)," *Annales: Economies, Sociétés, Civilisations* 32 (1977): 790–814.

_____, "The Parlement of Paris and the Great Witch Hunt, 1565–1640," *Sixteenth Century Journal* 9 (1978): 31–44.

_____, "Deviance and Criminal Justice in Western Europe, 1300–1800: An Essay in Structure," *Criminal Justice History: An International Annual* 1 (1980): 3–28.

_____, "La sorcellerie vue du Parlement de Paris au début du XVIIe siècle," *Actes du 104e Congres National des Societés Savantes. Bordeaux 1979. Section d'histoire moderne et contemporaine*, Tome II (Paris, 1981): 393–405.

Starkey, Marion, *The Devil in Massachusetts* (New York, 1950).

Stebel, H. J., *Die Osnabrücker Hexenprozesse* (Osnabruck, 1969).

Swales, J. K., and Hugh V. McLachlan, "Witchcraft and the Status of Women: A Comment," *British Journal of Sociology* 30 (1979): 349–58.

Tazbir, J., "Procès de sorcellerie," (in Poland) *Odrodzenie i Reformacja w. Polsce* 23 (1978): 151–77.

Thomas, Keith, *Religion and the Decline of Magic* (London, 1971).

Trevor-Roper, H. R., "The European Witch-craze of the Sixteenth and Seventeenth Centuries," in his *The Crisis of the Seventeenth Century. Religion, the Reformation and Social Change* (New York, 1968): 90–192.

Vasoli, C., "L'influence de la tradition hermetique et cabalistique," *Classical Influences on Western Thought*, ed. R. R. Bolgar (Cambridge, 1979): 61–75.

Victor, J.M., "The Revival of Lullism at Paris, 1499–1516," *Renaissance Quarterly* 38 (1975): 504–34.

Villeneuve, R., *Les procès de sorcellerie* (Verviers, 1974).

Villette, P., *La sorcellerie et sa répression dans le Nord de la France* (Paris, 1976).

Walker, D. P., *Spiritual and Demonic Magic from Ficino to Campanella* (London, 1958).

_____, *The Ancient Theology. Studies in Christian Platonism from the Fifteenth to the Eighteenth Century* (London, 1972).

_____, *Unclean Spirits: Possession and Exorcism in France and England in the late Sixteenth and early Seventeenth Centuries* (Philadelphia, 1981).

Walzel, Diana Lynn, The Sources of Medieval Demonology (Ph.D. Dissertation, Rice University, 1974).

Westfall, Richard S., "Newton and the Hermetic Tradition," *Science, Medicine and Society in the Renaissance. Essays to Honor Walter Pagel* ed. A. G. Debus (New York, 1972): vol. 2, 183–98.

Westman, Robert S., "Magical Reform and Astronomical Reform. The Yates Thesis Reconsidered," *Hermeticism and the Scientific Revolution* ed. R. W. Westman and J. E. McGuire (Los Angeles, 1977): 1–91.

Wittkower, Rudolf, *Architectural Principles in the Age of Humanism* (London, 1949).

Wolf, H. J., *Hexenwahn und Exorcismus. Ein Beitrag zur Kulturgeschichte* (Kriftel, 1980).

Wright, A. D., "The People of Catholic Europe and the People of Anglican England," *The Historical Journal* 18 (1975): 451–66.

Yates, Frances A., *Giordano Bruno and the Hermetic Tradition* (London, 1964).

_____, *The Art of Memory* (London, 1966).

_____, "The Hermetic Tradition in Renaissance Science," *Art, Science and History in the Renaissance*, ed. C.S. Singleton (Baltimore, 1968): 155–274.

_____, *The Theatre of the World* (London, 1969).

_____, *The Rosicrucian Enlightenment* (London, 1972).

_____, *The Occult Philosophy in the Elizabethan Age* (London, 1979).

Zambelli, Paola, "Cornelio Agrippa: scritti inediti e dispersi," *Rinascimento* 16 (1965).

_____, "Cornelio Agrippa, Erasmo e la teologia umanistica," *Rinascimento* 20 (1969): 1–59.

_____, "Il problema della magia naturale nel Rinascimento," *Rivista critica di storia della filosofia* 28 (1973): 271–96.

_____, "Magic and Radical Reformation in Agrippa of Nettesheim," *Journal of the Warburg and Courtauld Institutes* 39 (1976): 69–103.

Zguta, R., "Was There a Witch Craze in Muscovite Russia?" *Southern Folklore Quarterly* 41 (1977): 119–27. (a)

_____, "Witchcraft Trials in Seventeenth-Century Russia," *American Historical Review* 82 (1977): 1187–1207. (b)

_____, "Witchcraft and Medicine in pre-Petrine Russia," *The Russian Review* 37 (1978): 438–48.

Ziegler, W., *Möglichkeiten der Kritik am Hexen- und Zauberwesen im ausgehenden Mittelalter. Zeitgenössische Stimmen und ihre soziale Zugehörigkeit* (Cologne, 1973).

Zika, Charles, "Reuchlin's *De Verbo Mirifico* and the Magic Debate of the Late Fifteenth Century," *Journal of the Warburg and Courtauld Institutes* 39 (1976): 104–38.

_____, "Reuchlin and Erasmus: Humanism and Occult Philosophy;," *Journal of Religious History* 9 (1977): 223–46.

The Theology of Calvin and Calvinism

David C. Steinmetz

John Calvin is not a figure about whom we lack current biblio-graphical data.[1] Aside from the standard bibliographies of Niesel (1961) and Kempff (1975), which cover the period from 1901 to 1974, there are the annual bibliographies initiated by Tylenda (1971) and continued by De Klerk (1972–) in the *Calvin Theological Review* as well as the yearly surveys of recent Calvin studies in the *Literaturbericht* of the *Archiv für Reformationsgeschichte*. Further-more, Calvin College and Seminar in Grand Rapids, Michigan, have established a center for Calvin studies. The Calvin Library al-ready contains an enviable collection of early printings of Calvin's works, both in the original languages and in early translations. Probably even more important for the working historian than this collection of rare books is the still incomplete collection of articles, pamphlets, off-prints, books, and theses dealing with Calvin and Calvinism. The collection is important because it is undiscriminat-ing. Alongside the best studies of Calvin one can also find the very worst. The Library has not attempted to judge recent scholarship on Calvin; it has merely attempted to assemble and catalogue it. As a result, a scholar working in the Calvin Library can accomplish in a few days what would normally take an historian weeks to achieve, even in a great university research library. With such bibliographical aids and with such a developing research center, why should an at-tempt be made to write another bibliographical essay on John Calvin?

The justification—if any convincing justification at all can be given—lies less in a fresh chronicling of what has been done already

---

[1]Because of the length of the bibliography appended to this essay and because of the ease with which a reader can refer from the essay to the bibliography, I have at-tempted to keep the footnotes to an absolute minimum. I do want to thank, however, Ms. Susan E. Schreiner, candidate for the Ph.D. in Religion at Duke University, who assisted in the research for this essay.

(though a certain retelling of this story is unavoidable) than in suggesting what has been left undone. A new essay can point to lacunae in research or indicate projects which, while not entirely overlooked, have not been explored as fully as they might have been. Naturally, every historian will write a list of such projects from his or her own point of view. This essay, for example, is written from the point of view of an intellectual historian, one who admires the pioneering work of Robert M. Kingdon, Natalie Z. Davis, Nancy L. Roelker, and William Monter in the social and political history of early Calvinism, but who cannot usefully advise other historians how to imitate it. What I can do is suggest several clusters of intellectual problems which are worthy of further study and the kinds of literature in which solutions can be sought, beginning with Calvin's sermonic literature.

1. *The Sermons.* While Calvin's sermons were esteemed in Elizabethan England (indeed, Arthur Golding's translation of Calvin's 159 sermons on Job went through five editions in ten years), they have fared less well in more recent history. Although Denis Raguenier had transcribed 2,042 of Calvin's sermons (all of which were delivered ex tempore), the Genevan Library in 1805 disposed of 44 of the original 48 sermon manuscript volumes, pricing them according to their weight. Later, of course, the officials of the Library realized their mistake and attempted to recover the volumes which had been sold, but 35 volumes eluded recovery. Some had been purchased by the Bodleian, some by Bern, some by the Bibliothèque Nationale. Of the 2,304 sermons which we know were transcribed by Raguenier or others (including the 780 sermons published while Calvin was still alive), we have the text of 1,460. Over 800 sermons have simply disappeared.

The *Corpus Reformatorum* published 750 of Calvin's French sermons and 107 of his Latin, though without critical apparatus. The remaining sermons, the *sermons inédits*, are slowly being edited and provided with critical notes by an international team of scholars. Thus far the *Supplementa Calviniana* has published 87 sermons on II Samuel, 66 sermons on Isaiah 13–29, 28 sermons on Micah 1–7, 25 sermons on Jeremiah 14–18, and 2 sermons on Lamentations 1. Still to appear are further sermons on Isaiah, Ezekiel, Acts, I Corinthians and the Psalms.

The sermonic literature has not received the attention which the commentaries and the *Institutes* have attracted. The reasons for this neglect are not hard to explain. The sermons were directed toward the ear, not the eye. In comparison with the *Institutes* or the written commentaries they are repetitive, somewhat diffuse, less striking in their rhetorical effects, even at times rather commonplace in their style. Every sermon is evoked by an occasion, by a special relationship between preacher and audience which makes it possible for the preacher to leave certain things unsaid while it compels him to expand other topics at what appears to an outsider to be an unreasonable length. Yet at the same time these sermons show Calvin—in a way the commentaries, *Institutes* and polemical writings do not—at ease in the presence of a familiar and, on the whole, friendly audience, serving as a kind of broker or middleman between his technical theological interests and the popular religious concerns of the Genevans.

Ford Lewis Battles wrote some years ago of the need to bring the sermons into one uniform critically edited text (possibly as a continuation of the *Supplementa Calviniana*) and to translate the sermons into English for a generation of students largely unable to read the sixteenth-century French in which most of them were composed. Equally important is the need to study the sermons as literary, social, and exegetical documents. Perhaps the best studies since the Second World War devoted to this subject are the monographs by T. H. L. Parker and Richard Stauffer.

Parker attempted in his book to examine the rhetorical as well as the theological principles which underlay Calvin's homiletical method. He indicated briefly Calvin's place in the history of preaching (though without a detailed comparison of Calvin's preaching with his predecessors or contemporaries, particularly with preachers whose native tongue was French). He discussed the theological content of Calvin's preaching, although there were no surprises in this analysis for anyone familiar with the text of the *Institutes*. He even speculated on the influence of Calvin on the English pulpit in the 16th century. He did not discuss, though that is equally interesting, who read the many editions of Calvin's sermons published in Elizabethan England, why they esteemed them, and to what use they put them. This question is especially interesting in view of Trinterud's old thesis that the Rhineland reformers were far more influential in England than Calvin ever was.

Richard Stauffer examined what Calvin had to say about creation and providence in his sermons. It is striking that while the sermons do not contradict the teaching of the *Institutes*, it is also true that certain themes talked about in Calvin's academic theology are not brought up at all in his popular preaching or, if brought up, are given a somewhat different emphasis. For example, the rich theological tradition which supports the doctrine of the Trinity is not used at all by Calvin in his preaching, where he sticks strictly to biblical materials. Furthermore, only in his sermons does Calvin explain that there is a higher justice by which God would have been able to condemn the unfallen angels. This is God's secret justice which is distinct from his ordinary justice. And, whereas in the *Institutes* Calvin talks about the revelatory activity of God in nature and in history, he emphasizes in his sermons the self-manifestation of God in nature. Calvin as a preacher does not simply reiterate the teaching of his *Institutes* or commentaries but shapes his message to meet the religious needs and receptive capacities of his popular audience. What that reshaping of the message implies and to what extent it is paralleled by the emphases of other popularizers of the Calvinist Reformation are problems which have not as yet been sufficiently examined.

2. *Letters.* If Calvin in his preaching shows an aspect of his thought and personality which historians have all too frequently neglected, there are still other aspects of his character which can only be seen in his letters. Some letters were, of course, hardly letters at all. They were public essays intended to be read by as wide an audience as possible. In this category fall Calvin's apologetic letter to Francis I and his defense of Protestantism to Cardinal Sadoleto. But other letters, such as his request to a friend urging him to use Calvin's commentary on Seneca in his classes, or his touching letter to Viret on the death of his wife, Idelette, show Calvin with his guard down, human, vulnerable, and entirely sympathetic. Like John Wesley in a later age, Calvin is three-dimensional in his letters in a way that he is in no other genre of his writings, most moving when he is least concerned to move. The letters afford brief, candid glimpses into the private life of a very private man. No one, therefore, can assume that he is familiar with Calvin until he is familiar with the corpus of Calvin's letters.

Calvin's letters were collected by Charles de Jonviller, his last secretary, and edited by Theodore Beza, his principal successor. In the 19th century Jules Bonnet published a somewhat more comprehensive collection of letters which were translated by Constable and Gilchrist into English in 1858 and which still provide the English-speaking student with a valuable selection of 683 letters by Calvin. Because, however, of errors in the English translation, the Bonnet-

Constable-Gilchrist edition must be checked against the critical editions of Herminjard (198 letters from Calvin and 181 to him) and the *Corpus Reformatorum* (1,197 letters by Calvin, 1,571 letters to him and 1,503 about him or about Geneva) or compared with the more reliable German translation by Rudolph Schwarz. One could easily justify a new critical edition of the letters and a new annotated translation into English.

While the letters have always proven an important resource for the biographer of Calvin, as the latest biography of Calvin by T. H. L. Parker (1975) demonstrates so clearly, fewer historians have seen them as a resource for clarifying aspects of Calvin's theology or his vision of reform. There are signs, however, that this situation is changing. Jean-Daniel Benoit (1966) has used the letters to characterize Calvin's praxis as a pastor and spiritual advisor. John H. Bratt has found important clues in Calvin's letters which help to unravel Calvin's attitude toward the nature of women and their proper role in society. But, perhaps, the most ambitious attempt to make use of Calvin's correspondence is the monograph, *Calvinus Oecumenicus*, by Willem Nijenhuis.

Nijenhuis examines Calvin's activity as an ecumenical theologian and the theoretical foundation of his work as both are reflected in his letters. The letters show that, while Calvin is dedicated to the unity of the Church and is particularly distressed by the inability of the Lutherans and Reformed to give institutional expression to what Calvin regards as their essential unity, he gives priority to the question of truth over the question of ecclesiastical unity. Only confession of the truth can give a unity which will last. Therefore he cannot and will not paper over differences between himself and Rome or between himself and the anti-Trinitarian Biandrata. He cannot even bring himself to embrace vague or ambiguous doctrinal formulae which appeal to Melanchthon and Bucer but which from Calvin's point of view compromise essential convictions in the name of a very shaky unity. In other words, the letters show, in a way the *Institutes* really do not, both the passion of Calvin's ecumenical concerns and the theoretical boundaries which he is unwilling to violate, even if compromise achieves a temporary practical advantage.

3. *Commentaries.* I think it is no secret that the history of biblical exegesis in the sixteenth century represents one of the last, great, virtually unexplored frontiers of Reformation history. While the hermeneutics and, to a lesser extent, the biblical exegesis of Martin Luther have been explored (though we still lack a synthetic study of

Luther as an interpreter of Paul), no one has as yet done for the history of biblical interpretation in the sixteenth century what Beryl Smalley, P.C. Spicq, O.P., and Henri de Lubac have done for the history of exegesis in the Middle Ages. Even less has been done in relating the academic study of the Bible by theologians to the popular use of the Bible in poetry, story and song—to say nothing of its use by lawyers, politicians, exorcists and physicians.

In a sense, this lacuna is very puzzling. There was no book more important in the sixteenth century than the Bible. Cicero, Seneca, Aristotle, Plato, Quintilian, Augustine, Chrysostom and Jerome were all important authorities that intellectuals in the fifteenth century quoted with great regularity. But there was no book honored by intellectuals and ordinary people alike that received more attention, was better known, influenced more readers, was talked about or commented on more frequently, than the Bible. That is a shining and obvious fact. And yet the study of the history of the interpretation of the Bible in the sixteenth century is still an infant science.

In the preface to his commentary on Romans (1540), Calvin discusses his own exegetical method. While he confesses that he has learned an immense amount from reading the commentaries of Melanchthon and Bucer, he finds that he must develop an exegetical method somewhat different from theirs. Bucer, for example, discusses at length all the theological problems which he encounters in the text. The unhappy result of this procedure is that Bucer's comments are frequently much too long and stand between the student of Scripture and the biblical text. Melanchthon, on the other hand, only discusses the important themes or *topoi* in each chapter, omitting the discussion of many lesser—but to Calvin still important—details.

Calvin attempts to resolve the dilemma posed by the exegetical methods of Bucer and Melanchthon by commenting on each verse of a chapter (as distinct from Melanchthon) and by making those comments as brief as the nature of the text will allow (as distinct from Bucer). All lengthy discussions of theological topics are reserved for the pages of the *Institutes*, where they do not distract the reader from the immediate task of exegesis and where they can serve as a kind of general orientation to the structure and message of Scripture as a whole. Calvin called his exegetical method "lucid brevity," and it is one of his principal contributions to the intellectual heritage of the Reformation.

English-speaking students of Calvin are relatively fortunate in the ready availability of English translations of the commentaries. While no serious work can be done on Calvin's exegetical writings apart from the texts of them in the *Corpus Reformatorum*, beginning students do have access to a new reprint by Baker of the nineteenth century Calvin Society translation of Calvin's commentaries on the Old and New Testament as well as a modern and more reliable translation of the New Testament commentaries edited by T. F. and D. W. Torrance. What both sets of English translations lack, however, is a critical apparatus. Even the *Corpus Reformatorum* does not provide scholars with a guide to Calvin's Patristic sources. In that sense the commentaries, which are more accessible than the sermons, lag behind the *Supplementa Calviniana*, where one can find brief notes on the background of Calvin's sermonic exegesis.

The list of historians who have written on Calvin as an exegete is relatively short. T. H. L. Parker, who has written the most recent and most thorough study of this subject (1971), recommends as the best of older writers—Richard Simon, Friedrich August Gotttreu Tholuck, Edouard Reuss, and Philip Schaff—though he finds some help as well in Karoly Erdös, D.G. Escher, and Louis Goumaz. Goumaz, however, is primarily concerned with the *doctrina salutis* in Calvin's commentaries (as the title of his book plainly states) and consequently devotes far too little careful attention to the technical questions which trouble any student of commentaries. T. F. Torrance and Ronald S. Wallace also make use of the exegetical writings, but, like Goumaz, their interest is primarily in the theological content of those writings, not in the genre of commentary as such.

Parker does not himself attempt to talk about Calvin's Old Testament exposition but restricts himself to a study of the New Testament commentaries, though undoubtedly many of his conclusions are transferable to the Old Testament commentaries as well. Parker tries to trace the chronology of Calvin's New Testament commentaries and makes a brief effort to place Calvin in the history of biblical exegesis. Like Ganoczy, who has written on the impact of Paul on Calvin's method of interpretation (1976), Parker is interested in Calvin's hermeneutical principles, though F. L. Battles is probably correct when he observes that we still lack a definitive study of Calvin's hermeneutic. Parker leapfrogs over other historians who have examined Calvin's exegetical work in his careful establishment of the Greek text which Calvin used and in his comparison of the Latin version which Calvin provided with other existing Latin versions.

Obviously a critical work of this kind needs to be done for Calvin's
Old Testament commentaries as well.

It is difficult to single out one set of questions relating to Calvin's
commentaries which, more than any other, deserves immediate
study. Indeed, so little has been done on Calvin's exegesis that almost any kind of study will make some useful contribution to our
knowledge. Still there is at the moment particular need for studies
which will place Calvin's exegesis in the context of the history of biblical interpretation. How does Calvin's exegesis compare with the
biblical interpretation of the ancient Christian Fathers, the medieval Jewish and Christian commentators, the humanists, and, of
course, Calvin's Protestant and Roman Catholic contemporaries?

We know, of course, that while Calvin respected Augustine as a
theologian, he much preferred Chrysostom as an interpreter of
Scripture. Though John R. Walchenbach has examined the limited
question of the influence of Chrysostom on Calvin's interpretation of
I Corinthians, no one has as yet attempted to do for the broader
question of the relationship of Chrysostom to Calvin what Luchesius
Smits attempted in his study of the influence of Augustine on Calvin.
Even less has been done on the question of Calvin's relationship to
the tradition of biblical scholarship in humanism, the Middle Ages,
and early Protestantism. What we know about the pre-history of
Calvin's exegesis is largely guesswork and surmise.

4. *Institutes.* What has been studied most about Calvin, of
course, are his theological writings, particularly his *Institutes of the
Christian Religion.* An *institutio* is a manual which introduces the
basic principles of a subject to beginners who are learning for the
first time the terminology and structure of a new discipline. Because
Calvin continuously revised his manual from its first small edition of
1536 to the last definitive edition of 1559 and because he inserted in
the *Institutes* all the complex doctrinal discussions that he purposely
omitted from his commentaries, most students of Calvin have been
convinced that a knowledge of the *Institutes* is tantamount to a
knowledge of Calvin's thought in its entirety. As Imbart de la Tour
put it: "The whole of Calvinism is in the Institutes . . . "[2] While, as
we have already seen, that judgment is not wholly justified, nevertheless it is the case that the *Institutes* are central to the understand-

[2]Imbart de la Tour, *Les origines de la Reform, IV. Calvin et l'Institution Chrétienne* (Paris, 1935), 55.

ing of Calvin's thought in a way that no single book is central to the understanding of Luther.

Because the *Institutes* has been more highly valued by students of Calvinism than the sermons, letters, and commentaries, it has received the most critical attention. In addition to the older editions of Tholuck (1834–35) and the *Corpus Reformatorum* (1864) there is a modern critical edition of the 1536 and 1559 *Institutes* in the *Opera Selecta*. The work has been translated into English by Thomas Norton (1561), John Allen (1813), Henry Beveridge (1845), and Ford Lewis Battles (1960). The translation by Battles was edited by John T. McNeill and provided with invaluable footnotes and indices. More recently, Battles has translated and annotated the 1536 edition of the *Institutes*. Even the student who is limited to English is provided with reliable translations of Calvin's principal work and with a sophisticated critical apparatus.

A great deal of attention in the twentieth century has been devoted to the problem of the knowledge of God in Calvin's theology. In 1909 on the four hundredth anniversary of the birth of Calvin, *The Princeton Theological Review* published four articles on Calvin by Emile Doumergue, August Lang, Herman Bavinck, and Benjamin Warfield. Warfield's article represented the first attempt in English to deal in a scholarly and systematic way with the problem of the knowledge of God in Calvin, particularly in the *Institutes*. Warfield's article showed not only a careful study of the primary sources but also a wide familiarity with the secondary literature then available, particularly the studies of Julius Köstlin, Jacques Pannier, and J.A. Cramer. While the article was, on the whole, balanced and judicious, it did not treat Calvin's doctrine of faith as an integral part of his doctrine of the knowledge of God and so tended to overestimate the importance of Calvin's proofs for the credibility of Scripture.

The principal impetus for the study of this question, however, was provided, not by Warfield, but by a debate between Emil Brunner and Karl Barth in the 1930's. The debate opened with the publication of a little book, *Natur und Gnade* by Brunner. Brunner's essay was an apologetic for a "Christian natural theology," a revelation of God objectively present in creation, though not subjectively comprehensible to fallen human nature apart from Scripture. Brunner argued that the *imago Dei* had not been completely destroyed by the fall, but that remnants of it were still present in fallen human nature, forming a point of contact for the gospel. Furthermore, he maintained that the revelation of God in nature was not lost to the Christian, but rather that by the use of the spectacles of Scripture it could become possible again for the Christian to know God in and through his works. In all these contentions Brunner claimed Calvin as his principal authority.

Barth responded with a ferocious essay entitled *Nein: Antwort an Emil Brunner*. Barth agreed with Brunner that Calvin taught a *duplex cognitio Dei*, but denied that this doctrine was in any way related to Brunner's notion of a point of contact. On the contrary, Calvin constantly pointed his readers to the Bible as the true source of the knowledge of God.

> The possibility of a real knowledge by natural man of the true God, derived from creation, is, according to Calvin, a possibility in principle, but not in fact, not a possibility to be realized by us. One might call it an objective possibility, created by God, but not a subjective possibility, open to man. Between what is possible in principle and what is possible in fact there inexorably lies the fall. Hence this possibility can only be discussed hypothetically: *si integer stetisset Adam* (Inst., I, ii, 1).[3]

Since human beings have fallen, the content of their natural knowledge of God is only idolatry and superstition. Indeed, this is the possibility left open to them in fact. The revelation of God in nature, whatever its original purpose, serves only to render human beings inexcusable and to justify the wrath of God against them. There is no knowledge of God the Creator apart from knowledge of God the Redeemer. Peter Brunner and Gunter Gloede agreed with Brunner's reading of Calvin; Peter Barth and Wilhelm Niesel sided with Barth. Edward Dowey argued that the whole debate rested on a misunderstanding of what Calvin meant by the *duplex cognitio Dei*, while Parker (1959), who was sympathetic to Barth, suggested that the misunderstanding was probably Dowey's.

Interest in this issue declined in the 1960's as the fortunes of Neo-orthodox Protestant theology declined. At the same time Roman Catholic historians, stimulated in part by the ecumenical openness of the Second Vatican Council and the re-evaluation of the Protestant Reformation initiated by Joseph Lortz in 1939, began to examine in a fresh way the writings and career of John Calvin. Alexandre

---

[3]Barth (1946), 106.

Ganoczy (1966) in his important book on the young Calvin differed from Sprenger, who had attempted to cast light on Calvin's conversion by subjecting his language about it to minute scrutiny. Ganoczy believed it was impossible to understand Calvin's conversion apart from Calvin's self-estimate of his vocation as a Churchman and reformer.

Lucien Richard examined Calvin's spirituality and showed that it differed from the *Devotio moderna* in three important respects: (1) it was a spirituality directed toward service in the world; (2) it reinterpreted the old ecclesiological categories and by the use of a new epistemology laid the foundations for an individual spirituality with a different character and shape; and (3) it stressed the internal unity of theology and the Christian life. Heribert Schützeichel has reevaluated from a Catholic perspective Calvin's conception of faith and has compared the elements of Calvin's notion of faith with the older scholastic doctrines of *deus objectum fidei, fides informis, fides acquisita, fides implicita, coniectura moralis, spes proveniens ex gratia et meritis,* and *caritas prior fide ac spe.* Kilian McDonnell has done something of the same thing for Calvin's doctrine of the Eucharist, while Charles Boyer has re-opened the interesting question of the theological dependence of John Calvin on Martin Luther.

Apart from the influence of Neo-orthodox theology on Calvin studies in the first half of the twentieth century and of Catholic ecumenical theology in the sixties and seventies, no single dominant influence seems to be directing patterns of research in more recent Calvin studies. Nevertheless, there are four promising areas in which some work has been done but which have not been exhaustively mined.

A. *Relation of Calvin to earlier philosophical traditions.* Calvin is usually associated philosophically with Plato and with Stoicism. Ford Lewis Battles and André M. Hugo edited Calvin's commentary on Seneca's *De Clementia* and provided an introduction, translation, and notes. This critical edition of Calvin's philosophical commentary together with the author and source index of the McNeill-Battles translation of the *Institutes* provide a textual point of departure for any re-examination of the question of the relation of Calvin to earlier philosophical traditions.

Victor Nuovo in a Columbia University dissertation (1964) confirmed the judgment that, although Calvin's theology is biblical in its roots, it is nevertheless heavily dependent on classical antiquity. Nuovo described Calvin, particularly in his moral theology, as an eclectic who combined elements of Stoic and Platonic philosophy with other elements derived directly from the Bible. While Calvin repudiated ancient philosophy in its presuppositions and conclusions, he nevertheless believed that biblical theology achieved the goals which ancient philosophy had set for itself; namely, to lead men and women to a knowledge of God, immortality, and virtue.

Charles Partee in a more recent study argued against the tendency of historians to dismiss Calvin's relation to ancient philosophy. Calvin knew this philosophical tradition and his comments on it are an important element in his thought. Partee is not willing, however, to regard Calvin as a philosopher. His references to philosophy are too occasional to qualify him as a philosophical thinker. The book is full of important discussions and distinctions in which Partee attempts to establish not only Calvin's dependence on ancient learning, but also his criticism of it and his independence from it. While Calvin particularly attacks Aristotle and the Epicurean philosophers, he can reject Plato and the Stoics as well on certain questions. The essay of Egil Grislis on Calvin's indebtedness to Cicero, especially for his concept of *sensus divinitatis,* and the essay of William Bouwsma on the Stoic revival in the sixteenth century carry the debate on Calvin's use of the ancient philosophers in new and important directions.

Josef Bohatec and Jean Boisset were interested not so much in Calvin's direct relationship to ancient philosophy as in his indirect relationship to it mediated by French humanism. Bohatec concluded that, while Calvin was in every important sense of the term a humanist, he rejected the fascination of leading humanists with astrology, with the remnants of Stoic fatalism, with a kind of Epicurean "deism," and particularly with the doctrine of the immortality of the soul. Boisset attempted to define the relationship of Calvin to Platonism and humanism and to establish Calvin's independence of both. Calvin was too interested in the revelation of God in history to be merely Platonic, too intolerant of doctrinal deviations to be identified purely as a humanist.

B. *Relation of Calvin to earlier theological traditions.* It is surprising, especially considering Calvin's extensive conversation with the Christian past, that so little has been done to relate Calvin's theological position in the *Institutes* to the antecedent tradition of Christian theology. William Todd in a 1964 dissertation at Union Theological Seminary attempted to trace the evolution of Calvin's use of Patristic sources. Todd was of the opinion that Calvin's use of the Fathers in the 1532 commentary on *De Clementia* was dictated more by humanistic than by theological interests. Calvin began, however, in the *Psychopannychia* (1534) to select the Fathers for their theological and exegetical contributions to his position. Todd believes that the influence of Lutheran ideas led Calvin to see Augustine and the other Fathers in a new light and so rejects the thesis of Smits that Calvin was converted to the Reformation through the influence of Augustine. Todd also believes that it was Melanchthon who exercised the most important influence on Calvin in his reassessment of the theological role of the Fathers. Like Melanchthon, Calvin agreed with the humanistic idea that to go from false to true doctrine requires a movement back to historical origins.

E. P. Meijering extended this discussion by examining the relationship of Calvin to Irenaeus, Tertullian and Augustine on the question of curiosity; i.e., the desire of the human intellect to know what cannot be known under the conditions of human finitude and sin, especially about God. The question of how one distinguishes useful (and therefore presumably not speculative) knowledge from knowledge which is merely speculative (and therefore apparently useless) occupies the author in his first chapter. Meijering concludes that Calvin rejects many of the positions of medieval scholasticism—especially on the doctrines of God, creation, predestination, and Christology—for reasons which are not terribly dissimilar from the reasons put forward by the Fathers for the rejection of the views of the philosophers and heretics. Meijering lays such stress, however, on Calvin's biblicism, his desire to avoid theological speculation and to restrict theological inquiry to the text of Scripture, that he tends to underemphasize Calvin's passion to know everything which legitimately can be known about God through the text of Scripture.

Karl Reuter in 1963 attempted to analyze the basic themes in Calvin's thought and to trace these themes back to their classical and medieval roots. Reuter stressed the importance of Calvin's years at the Collège de Montaigu and argued that through John Major the young Calvin was influenced by Duns Scotus and Gregory of Rimini, especially by Scotistic "personalism" and by nominalist epistemology, an epistemology which led, in Reuter's opinion, to a "scriptural positivism." Reuter was also interested in the influence of Bernard and the *Devotio moderna* on Calvin's piety and of humanism on Calvin's theology of preaching. While Reuter's book is important and suggestive, he tends to rely, more heavily than a prudent historian should, on parallels or similarities in argument as proof of influence.

Armand LaVallee in his 1967 dissertation at Harvard examined all of Calvin's conscious and explicit references to scholastic theology in his commentaries and *Institutes*. LaVallee discovered that, although Calvin's direct references to particular scholastic theologians are rare—except for references to Peter Lombard—and although Calvin does not disclose the sources for his knowledge of medieval scholasticism, he was fully aware of it and developed his own theological position in a critical dialogue with it. LaVallee was inclined to believe that Calvin's perception of scholastic theology was shaped by his contact with late medieval nominalism and agreed with Reuter that John Major may have been the key figure in introducing Calvin to scholastic theology.

Other historians—such as, for example, Richard, McDonnell, Schützeichel, and Wendel—have talked about Calvin's relationship to medieval mystical and theological traditions, but what they have succeeded best in demonstrating is how little we know about this subject and how much remains to be done. We are still awaiting a definitive treatment of Calvin and late medieval Augustinianism or Calvin and Bernard or Calvin and Scotus or Calvin and Ockhamism or even Calvin and Thomas Aquinas. There are more topics in this area than there are qualified people to pursue them.

C. *Calvin and the natural order.* The doctrine of creation in and of itself has not received much attention in recent years. Bavinck and Kuyper discussed what they called "common grace," the goodness of God in preserving the created order, a goodness rooted in God's redemptive activity and yet not itself redemptive. But there has been very little consideration of the remnants of the original created order which survive the trauma of the Fall. There can be little doubt that there are such remnants. The succession of seasons, of days and nights, the order and movement of the stars were established by God before the apostasy of Adam. In spite of human sin God remains faithful to the world which he has created and preserves it from the full consequences of human disobedience. Calvin loves to celebrate the beauty of the stars and to marvel at the goodness of a God who created beauty above necessity. The role of natural law, of conscience, of the family, of nature as a source of the knowledge of God for the redeemed, of the restraint of nature "red in tooth and claw," of the perfection of nature in the eschaton—all of these themes are worthy of further study. The best recent book on the subject is the monograph by Richard Stauffer, while David Foxgrover has examined Calvin's views on conscience against the background of the earlier discussions by Gloede and Torrance. We still lack, however, a great book on Calvin's understanding of nature, one which would place his views in the context of his predecessors and contemporaries.

D. *Calvin and the emergence of Protestant scholasticism.* It has been the fashion ever since the middle of the 19th century to regard the development of Protestant scholasticism, especially the return of Protestant theologians to the study of the philosophy of Aristotle, as a fundamental betrayal of the original vision of the Protestant reformers. In this tradition Brian Armstrong, Walter Kickel, and Basil Hall have taken an essentially negative attitude toward the development of Reformed scholasticism. Armstrong, for example, argued that Calvinism under the influence of Aristotelian philosophy relied on speculative reason, became philosophically and metaphysically oriented, and abandoned the essentially biblical vision of Calvin himself. This negative assessment of Protestant Orthodoxy has been challenged by Bray, Raitt, Fatio, and Muller who take a more sanguine view of the transition from the purely biblical orientation of the reformers to the more philosophically oriented theology of the Reformed scholastics.

The history of Reformed orthodoxy has not engaged many historians in recent years, though Bizer, Faulenbach, Fatio, and Muller have begun to break new ground in the re-assessment of the period from 1550 to 1800. Still the names of such Reformed theologians as Polanus, Wollebius, Wendelin, Voetius, Witsius, Marckius, Sharpius, Turrettini, van Mastricht, and Pictet are virtually unknown, even to Church historians. Pietism, the Enlightment, the Evangelical Awakening, the growth of Liberal theology, and the Social Gospel have all conspired to put baroque theology in the shadows. But because a subject is not fashionable does not mean that it is inherently uninteresting, as the new debates over the transformation of Calvinism in the period of Protestant Orthodoxy demonstrate.

Some of the recent disagreements, however, seem to me to be traceable to the great ambiguity which characterizes the use of certain terms. Scholasticism, for example, is almost never defined, though one could argue that a scholastic is a teacher who treats theology by topic and who attempts to be as comprehensive as possible in the selection of the topics which he treats. Indeed, medieval scholasticism is not bound to any single philosophy, as the differences between Peter Lombard, Aquinas, Bonaventure, Scotus, and Ockham prove.

Stripped to its bare essentials, scholasticism is school theology. The problem which the scholastic faces and tries to solve is how knowledge can be transmitted from one generation to another, particularly in an environment in which competing visions (Roman Catholic, Lutheran, Socinian, Anabaptist, Arminian) are vigorously advocated. Students cannot be expected to read all the commentaries and treatises of the Protestant reformers and extract from them the essential theological points. But they can be expected to read the brief *Christianae Theologiae Compendium* of Wollebius or the relatively longer *Compendium Theologiae* of Marckius or the even longer (but, in comparison with the *opera omnia* of the Protestant reformers, relatively compact) *Theoretico-Practica Theologia* of Peter van Mastricht. In that sense, perhaps, even Calvin was a scholastic. He was interested in constructing a house of learning in the Church which was both Mother and School.

Calvin was not a scholastic in his rejection of the *quaestio* and *disputatio* as methods of argumentation, his concern with rhetorical clarity and force rather than with terminological precision, his extreme reluctance to speculate on theological topics outside the bounds of what he believes is warranted by revelation, and his contentment to leave unsaid what in his judgment cannot be said, even if it leaves his argument incomplete and his system unfinished. While the return to Aristotle marks a difference between Calvin and the later Calvinists, it is certainly not the only difference and it remains to be proven that it is the crucial one.

These problems are not the only issues in Calvin research which deserve further study. I am conscious as this essay draws to a close that we have not had time to discuss Milner on Calvin's doctrine of the Church, or Willis on the function of the *extra-Calvinisticum* in Calvin's thought, or Balke on Calvin and the Anabaptists, or Plath on Calvin's relationship to Basel, or Garside on Calvin's theology of music. The Calvin bibliography is very long and this essay of necessity is very short. But we have indicated some trends in Calvin research and suggested some possible lines for further research. These suggestions, however, are just that and nothing more. When all is said and done, the most important research problem for an historian is the problem which he or she finds absorbing, whether that problem is in fashion or out, trendy or eccentric, avant-garde or old-fashioned. A bibliographical essay is only a descriptive tool for the furtherance and enhancement of that free inquiry.

Bibliography

1. Bibliographies

Archiv für Reformationsgeschichte, Literaturbericht 1ff. (1972–).

De Klerk, Peter, "Calvin Bibliography," *Calvin Theological Journal* 7ff. (1972–).

Erichson, Alfred, *Bibliographia Calviniana*, reprint of the 1900 edition (Nieuwkoop, 1960).

Fraenkel, Peter, "Petit supplement aux bibliographies calviniennes, 1901–1963," *Bibliothèque d'Humanisme et Renaissance* 33 (1971): 385–414.

Kempff, Dionysius, *A Bibliography of Calviniana 1959–1974*, Studies in Medieval and Reformation Thought 15 (Leiden, 1975).

Niesel, Wilhelm, *Calvin-Bibliographie, 1901–1959* (Munich, 1961).

Tylenda, Joseph N., "Calvin Bibliography, 1960–1970," *Calvin Theological Journal* 6 (1971): 156–193.

2. Sources

Ioannis Calvini, Opera Quae Supersunt Omnia, 59 vols., eds. Wilhelm Baum, Eduard Cunitz and Eduard Reuss, Corpus Reformatorum 29–87 (Brunswick and Berlin, 1863–1900).

Joannis Calvini Opera Selecta, 5 vols., eds. Peter Barth and Wilhelm Niesel (Munich, 1926–1952).

Calvin, John, *Calvin's Commentary on Seneca's "De Clementia,"* with introduction, translation and notes by Ford Lewis Battles and André Malan Hugo, Renaissance Text Series 3, published for the Renaissance Society of America (Leiden, 1969).

Calvin, John, *Supplementa Calviniana*, sermons inédits (Neukirchen, 1936–).

Registres de la compagnie des pasteurs de Genèv au temps de Calvin, 3 vols., eds. R. M. Kingdon and J. F. Bergier (Geneva, 1962–69).

The Register of the Company of Pastors in the Time of Calvin, ed. and trans. P. E. Hughes (Grand Rapids, 1966).

Herminjard, Aimé-Louis, *Correspondance des Réformateurs dans les pays de langue francaise*, 9 vols. (Geneva, 1866–1897).

Johannes Calvins Lebenswerk in seinen Briefen, 2 vols., ed. and trans. Rudolf Schwarz (Tübingen, 1909).

Calvin, John, *Letters of John Calvin*, 4 vols., ed. Jules Bonnet, trans. David Constable and Marcus Robert Gilchrist (Philadelphia, 1858).

Calvin Translation Society, 47 volumes (Edinburgh, 1844–54). Includes the commentaries on the Old Testament. Reprinted Grand Rapids, 1948–1981.

Calvin's New Testament Commentaries, eds. D. W. and T. F. Torrance (Grand Rapids, 1959ff.).

Calvin: Commentaries, ed. J. Haroutunian, Library of Christian Classics 23 (Philadelphia, 1958).

Calvin: Theological Treatises, ed. J. K. S. Reid, Library of Christian Classics 22 (Philadelphia, 1954).

Calvin, John, *Institution of the Christian Religion (1536)*, ed. and trans. Ford Lewis Battles (Atlanta, 1975).

Calvin: Institutes of the Christian Religion, 2 vols., ed. John T. McNeill and trans. Ford Lewis Battles, Library of Christian Classics 20–21 (Philadelphia, 1960).

Calvin, John, *Sermons on Isaiah's Prophecy of the Death and Passion of Christ*, ed. and trans. T. H. L. Parker (London, 1956).

Calvin, John, *Sermons from Job*, ed. and trans. Leroy Nixon (Grand Rapids, 1952).

Calvin, John, *The Deity of Christ and other Sermons*, trans. Leroy Nixon (Grand Rapids, 1950).

Calvin, John, *Tracts and Treatises in Defense of the Reformed Faith*, 3 vols., trans. Henry Beveridge and historical notes by T. F. Torrance (Grand Rapids, 1958).

The Piety of John Calvin: An Anthology Illustrative of the Spirituality of the Reformer, selected, ed. and trans. Ford Lewis Battles (Pittsburgh, 1973).

Devotions and Prayers of John Calvin, ed. C. E. Edwards (Grand Rapids, 1960).

Calvin, John, *Catechism 1538*, trans. and annotated by Ford Lewis Battles (Pittsburgh, 1972).

3. Selected Secondary Works

Armstrong, Brian G., *Calvinism and the Amyraut Heresy: Protestant Scholasticism and Humanism in Seventeenth Century France* (Madison, 1969).

Balke, W., *Calvijn en de Doperse Radikalen* (Amsterdam, 1973).

Battles, Ford Lewis, "The Future of Calviniana," in *Renaissance,*

Reformation, Resurgence, ed. Peter De Klerk (Grand Rapids, 1976): 133–173.

Benoît, Jean-Daniel, *Calvin: directeur d'âmes; contribution á l'histoire de la piété Réformée* (Strasbourg, 1947).

Cramer, J.A. and H.U. Mayboom, *De apologeten* (Leiden, 1908–1920).

———, "Calvin the Letter-Writer," in *John Calvin,* ed. Gervase E. Duffield, Courtenay Studies in Reformation Theology 1 (Grand Rapids, 1966): 67–101.

Bizer, Ernst, "Die reformierte Orthodoxie und der Cartesianismus," *Zeitschrift für Theologie und Kirche* 55 (1958): 306–372.

Bohatec, Josef, *Budé und Calvin, Studien zur Gedankenwelt des französischen Frühhumanismus* (Graz, 1950).

Boisset, Jean, *Sagesse et sainteté dans la pensée de Jean Calvin* (Paris, 1959).

Bouwsma, William J., "The Two Faces of Humanism: Stoicism and Augustinianism in Renaissance Thought," in *Itinerarium Italicum: The Profile of the Italian Renaissance in the Mirror of its European Transformations,* eds. H. A. Oberman and T. A. Brady, Jr., Studies in Medieval and Reformation Thought 14 (Leiden, 1975): 3–60.

Boyer, Charles, *Calvin et Luther, Accords et différences* (Rome, 1973).

Bratt, John H., "The Role and Status of Women in the Writings of John Calvin," *Renaissance, Reformation, Resurgence,* ed. Peter De Klerk (Grand Rapids, 1976): 1–17.

Bray, John S., *Theodore Beza's Doctrine of Predestination* (Nieuwkoop, 1975).

Brunner, Emil, and Barth, Karl, *Natural Theology,* trans. Peter Fraenkel (London, 1946).

Davis, Natalie Z., "Strikes and Salvation at Lyons," *Archiv für Reformationsgeschichte* 56 (1965): 48–64.

Dowey, Edward A., *The Knowledge of God in Calvin's Theology* (New York, 1952).

Fatio, Olivier, *Méthode et théologie, Lambert Daneau et les débuts de la scholastique Réformée,* Travaux d'Humanisme et Renaissance 147 (Geneva, 1976).

Faulenbach, Heiner, *Die Struktur der Theologie des Amandus Polanus von Polansdorf* (Zurich, 1967).

Foxgrover, David Lee, "John Calvin's Understanding of Conscience," (Ph.D. dissertation, Claremont, 1979).

Ganoczy, Alexandre, *Le jeune Calvin, genèse et évolution de sa vo-cation réformatrice* (Wiesbaden, 1966).

———, "Calvin als paulinischer Theologe," in *Calvinus Theologus,* ed. W. H. Neuser (Neukirchen, 1976): 39–69.

Garside, Charles, *The Origins of Calvin's Theology of Music, 1536–1543,* Transactions of the American Philosophical Society 69 (Philadelphia, 1979).

Gloede, Günter, *Theologia Naturalis bei Calvin,* Tübinger Studien zur systematischen Theologie 5 (Stuttgart, 1935).

Goumaz, Louis F., *La doctrine de la salut (doctrina salutis) d'après les commentaires de Jean Calvin sur le Nouveau Testament* (Nyon, 1917).

Grislis, Egil, "Calvin's Use of Cicero in the Institutes I:1, A Case Study in Theological Method," *Archiv für Reformations-geschichte* 62 (1971): 5–37.

Hall, Basil, "Calvin against the Calvinists," in *John Calvin,* ed. Gervase E. Duffield, Courtenay Studies in Reformation Theology 1 (Grand Rapids, 1966): 19–37.

Kickel, Walter, *Vernunft und Offenbarung bei Theodor Beza* (Neukirchen, 1967).

Kingdon, Robert M., *Geneva and the Coming of the Wars of Religion in France, 1555–1563* (Geneva, 1956).

———, "The Economic Behavior of Ministers of Geneva in the Middle of the 16th Century," *Archiv für Reformations-geschichte* 50 (1959): 33–39.

———, "Social Welfare in Calvin's Geneva," *American Historical Review* 76 (1971): 50–69.

———, "The Control of Morals in Calvin's Geneva," in *The Social History of the Reformation,* eds. L. P. Buck and J. W. Zophy (Columbus, 1972): 3–16.

———, "The Control of Morals by the Earliest Calvinists," in *Renaissance, Reformation, Resurgence,* ed. P. De Klerk (Grand, Rapids, 1976): 95–106.

Köstlin, Julius, *Life of Luther* (New York, 1883).

Kuypers, Antoon, *Inleiding in de zielkunde,* 4. druk, paar de oor-spronkelijke uitgave van J.H. Bavinck (Kampen, 1963).

LaVallee, Armand Aime, "Calvin's Criticism of Scholastic Theolo-gy," (Ph.D. dissertation, Harvard University, 1967).

McDonnell, Kilian, *John Calvin, the Church and the Eucharist* (Princeton, 1967).

Meijering, E. P., *Calvin wider die Neugierde* (Nieukoop, 1980).

Milner, Benjamin Charles, *Calvin's Doctrine of the Church*, Studies in the History of Christian Thought 5 (Leiden, 1970).

Monter, E. William, *Studies in Genevan Government, 1536-1605*, Travaux d'Humanisme et Renaissance 62 (Geneva, 1964).

———, *Calvin's Geneva* (New York, 1967).

———, "Crime and Punishment in Calvin's Geneva, 1562," *Archiv für Reformationsgeschichte* 64 (1973): 281-287.

———, "The Consistory of Geneva, 1559-1569," in *Renaissance, Reformation, Resurgence*, ed. P. de Klerk (Grand Rapids, 1976): 63-84.

Muller, Richard A., *Christ and the Decree: Christology and Predestination in the Developing Soteriological Structure of Sixteenth Century Reformed Theology*, Studies in Historical Theology 2 (Durham, N.C., 1984).

Nijenhuis, Willem, *Calvinus Oecumenicus, Calvijn en de Eenheid der Kerk in het Licht van zijn Briefwisseling* (The Hague, 1959).

Nuovo, Victor L., "Calvin's Theology: A Study of its Sources in Classical Antiquity," (Ph.D. dissertation, Columbia University, 1964).

Pannier, Jacques, *L'église reformée de Paris sous Henri IV; rapports de l'église et et de l'état, vie publique et privée des protestants, leur part dans l'histoire de la capitale, le mouvement des idées, les arts, la société, le commerce.* (Paris, 1911).

Parker, T. H. L., *The Oracles of God, An Introduction to the Preaching of John Calvin* (London, 1947).

———, *Portrait of Calvin* (Philadelphia, 1954).

———, *Calvin's Doctrine of the Knowledge of God*, rev. ed. (Grand Rapids, 1959).

———, *Calvin's New Testament Commentaries* (Grand Rapids, 1971).

———, *John Calvin, A Biography* (London, 1975).

Partee, Charles B., *Calvin and Classical Philosophy*, Studies in the History of Christian Thought 14 (Leiden, 1977).

Plath, Uwe, *Calvin und Basel in den Jahren 1552-1556*, Basler Studien zur historischen und systematischen Theologie 22 (Zurich, 1974).

Raitt, Jill, *The Eucharistic Theology of Theodore Beza*, AAR Studies in Religion 4 (Chambersburg, 1972).

Reuter, Karl, *Das Grundverständnis der Theologie Calvins unter Einbeziehung ihrer geschichtlichen Abhängigkeiten*, Beiträge zur Geschichte und Lehre der Reformierten Kirche 15 (Neukirchen, 1963).

Richard, Lucien Joseph, *The Spirituality of John Calvin* (Atlanta, 1974).

Roelker, Nancy L., "The Appeal of Calvinism to French Noblewomen in the 16th Century: A Study in Psychohistory," *Journal of Interdisciplinary History* 2 (1972): 391–418.

_____, "The Role of Noblewomen in the French Reformation," *Archiv für Reformationsgeschichte* 63 (1972): 168–195.

Schützeichel, Heribert, *Die Glaubenstheologie Calvins*, Beiträge zur ökumenischen Theologie 9 (Munich, 1972).

Smits, Luchesius, *Saint Augustin dans l'oeuvre de Jean Calvin*, 2 vols. (Assen, 1957–58).

Sprenger, P., *Das Rätsel um die Bekehrung Calvins* (Neukirchen, 1960).

Stauffer, Richard, *Dieu, la création et la providence dans la prédication de Calvin*, Basler und Berner Studien zur historischen und systematischen Theologie 33 (Bern, 1978).

Todd, William Newton, "The Function of the Patristic Writings in the Thought of John Calvin," (Ph.D. dissertation, Union Theological Seminary, New York, 1964).

Torrance, Thomas F., *Calvin's Doctrine of Man* (Grand Rapids, 1957).

Walchenbach, John R., "John Calvin as Biblical Commentator: An Investigation in Calvin's Use of John Chrysostom as an Exegetical Tutor," (Ph.D. dissertation, University of Pittsburgh, 1974).

Wallace, Ronald S., *Calvin's Doctrine of Word and Sacrament* (Edinburgh, 1953).

_____, *Calvin's Doctrine of the Christian Life* (Grand Rapids, 1961).

Warfield, Benjamin B., "Calvin's Doctrine of the Knowledge of God," in *Calvin and Augustine*, ed. Samuel G. Craig (Philadelphia, 1956): 29–130.

Wendel, Francois, *Calvin: The Origins and Development of his Religious Thought* (New York, 1963).

Willis, E. David, *Calvin's Catholic Christology*, Studies in the History of Christian Thought 1 (Leiden, 1966).

Pamphlet Literature
of the French Reformation

Robert M. Kingdon

France witnessed a significant outpouring of pamphlet literature during the period of the Reformation. That part of this literature which has attracted the most interest to date was published in the second half of the sixteenth century and was explicitly political in content. It thus accompanies in both time and topic the ferocious wars of religion which ravaged France, beginning with the massacre of Vassy in 1562, reaching one climax after the St. Bartholomew's massacres in 1572, a second during the siege of Catholic Paris from 1591 to 1594, and ending only with the promulgation of the Edict of Nantes in 1598. Of these political pamphlets the most widely studied were written by Protestants during the beginning of the wars of religion in the 1560's and after the St. Bartholomew's massacres in the mid-1570's. The Protestant pamphlets provoked by these massacres developed particularly sophisticated arguments for armed resistance to tyrannical government that were designed to attract support for Protestant-led revolts against the French royal government. There was an even greater number of Catholic political pamphlets, however, and they are attracting increasing interest. Catholic pamphlets written during the siege of Paris also developed arguments for armed resistance to a tyrannical government, but were designed to justify the Catholic League's revolts against the French royal government. Their arguments often parallel those advanced by Protestants. Together these two series of pamphlets have long been recognized as having articulated a body of political ideas of continuing importance in justifying resistance to tyranny, and as having considerable historical significance in explaining the great revolutions which led to modern forms of government in England, America, and France.

The concentration of scholars upon pamphlets that are political in content can thus be explained in part by the interest and significance of the political ideas which many of them contain. But it can also be explained in part by the fact that a great many French pamphlets of the period concentrated on specific political issues as well. This poses a problem of interest to historians. The most obvious explanation can be found in the political history of France during the Reformation period. A royal government which had arguably been the richest and most powerful in Europe early in the sixteenth century was torn by the most vicious forms of political rivalry and warfare late in the century. These tensions grew in part from a pronounced weakness in the monarchy itself, stemming from a series of royal minorities following the accidental death of Henry II in 1559 as three of his weak sons succeeded him in turn. These periods of rule by boys or young men provoked crises inherent in the royal form of government as powerful aristocrats competed for effective control of governmental machinery either as regents or in less obvious positions at court. These tensions also grew in part from the increasingly bitter controversy among religious factions. The rapid spread of militant Calvinism in France after 1550 and of militant forms of Catholicism after 1560 boiled over into political rivalry. The political explosions provoked by these two sets of reinforcing tensions created a natural appetite among the literate public for political news. They also created an understandable appetite among the more reflective for fresh ideas about the nature of the state, the functions of the state, and the legitimacy of resistance to the state. Political pamphlets fed both appetites.

A second explanation for a concentration by the French upon pamphlets political in content, however, may well be found in the dynamics of the printing industry. In periods of peace and prosperity most printers tended to concentrate their resources on selected widely selling staples: editions of the classics for the scholarly market; Bibles and service books and summaries of theology for the religious market; collections of laws and commentaries on these collections for the lawyers' market; other standard references for a number of other, and usually smaller, markets. In times of war and economic uncertainty, however, a number of printers tended to divert resources to the publication of topical pamphlets. Hans Joachim Bremme has demonstrated that this was true of Geneva in the decades after Calvin died when Protestantism was fighting for its life in France. Such religious staples as Calvin's books tended to remain in publishers' inventories, and printers switched to publishing contemporary histories and political pamphlets.[1] Denis Pallier has demonstrated that this was also true of Paris in the decade when the Catholic League dominated its politics. The religious and legal staples that sustained most Parisian printers sold poorly and printers switched to publishing political pamphlets.[2] These switches may be explained in part by a shift in the tastes of the market for printed matter. They should also be explained, Pallier argues, by the economics of the publishing industry. Warfare tended to disrupt seriously the trade in printed matter. Fairs, networks of peddlers, and other channels of distribution were unable to do their normal work of relaying standard books to their usual purchases. In desperation, printers on the edge of bankruptcy turned to grinding out small and inflammatory topical works that required little investment of capital and that could be sold quickly and easily in local markets.

It would be misleading to conclude that French printers produced only political pamphlets, or that their political pamphlets contain nothing of religious, economic, or social interest. Salvo Mastellone (1972) demonstrated that many suggestive conclusions about the social relationships and economic positions of French aristocrats can be gleaned from political pamphlets of the late sixteenth century.[3] And Donald R. Kelley provides significant new insights into the family, the congregation, the university, and the legal profession, in addition to fresh observations on confessional and political parties, in his book (1981) based on these pamphlets.[4] It is nevertheless fair to conclude that most of the French pamphlets of the Reformation period are obviously political in content and that most of the attention paid to this literature by scholars has focused upon its political content. This essay, consequently, is primarily about French political pamphlet literature of the Reformation period.

Where We Are

A useful introductory guide to the political pamphlets produced in France during the Reformation period can be found in Hauser (1906–1915). Although this overview is old, compiled well before the triumph of the school of the *Annales* within France and its de-

[1]Bremme (1969), 89–93.
[2]Pallier (1976), 119–130.
[3]Mastellone (1972). In some respects this is a sequel to Caprariis, (1959) which is also based on French political pamphlets. Mastellone, however, adopts a significantly broader perspective.
[4]Kelley (1981).

mands for "total history," its very age makes it useful. For Hauser's generation history was still primarily political history: dates, kings, and diplomacy were important. Thus he is careful to direct his readers to sources of political significance. Within the scope of his reference work, it was possible to hit only the high spots, but he was conscientious and shrewd, and his comments are thus usually useful and reliable. They include remarks about a number of the more interesting single pamphlets and guidance to a number of widely circulated composite works which were in reality collections of contemporary pamphlets.

More specific, if somewhat technical, information on specific pamphlets can be gained from the works of descriptive bibliographers. Some of this information is scattered through works of more general reference. Some of it has been focused more specifically upon pamphlets. These bibliographical studies are normally devoted to specific printers or publishers, sometimes gathered within a specific publishing center. Of the publishing centers then producing books in French, Paris, of course, was by far the largest and most important, for it was several times larger than any other French city, housing both the capital of the French royal government and the largest and most important French university. Paris thus supplied the largest single market for reading matter in French. The French royal government deliberately tried to increase the centralization of publishing in Paris with subsidies and laws in order to bring the industry more closely under government control. Many technical studies of individual Parisian printers and publishers have been written, though there is still more to be done on many of them. Masses of fresh information on their business activities is hidden in the manuscript notarial records of legal transactions deposited in the *Minutier Central* of the National Archives in Paris, and is in the process of being extracted and examined by dozens of scholars. The most important of the reports on this research are being published under the name of Philippe Renouard, based on notes he gathered before his death some time ago, which are now being checked, completed, and published by teams of modern scholars. These include a general *Répertoire des imprimeurs Parisiens, libraires, fondeurs . . . jusqu'à la fin du XVIe siècle* (Geneva, 1965), complemented by an ongoing series of volumes supplying more specific information on individual printers and publishers, arranged alphabetically (Geneva 1965–). This series is only beginning.

Lyon was the second largest French center of publication. While the city may not have been larger than Rouen, there were no other French cities of the second rank after Paris that were much larger. Lyon also possessed massive commercial and financial ties with Italy, complemented by significant if probably less important ties with Germany through Switzerland. The city was also sufficiently far from Paris to be free to carve out a somewhat independent market. The standard work of reference on early printing and publishing in Lyon is Baudrier (1895–1921), with a supplementary volume of index tables (1965).

Geneva was the third largest center of publication in French, but only in the later part of the sixteenth century. It became important because of the establishment of the Calvinist Reformation there. Calvin succeeded in luring to Geneva many of the most eminent printers of Paris and Lyon to join him in organizing an ambitious and strenuous attempt to win all of France to the Reformed religion. Of these emigrating printers, the most prominent were Robert Estienne, the royal printer in Paris, and Antoine Vincent, a particularly successful printer of Lyon, but they were accompanied by many others. The Genevan printing industry has been studied by Chaix (1954) and Bremme (1969), complemented by a useful general bibliography compiled by Chaix, A. Dufour, and G. Moeckli (1966).

These three centers were all large and flourishing, devoted to the publication of many kinds of books. While they published the majority of pamphlets printed in French, they published even more books of a larger and more continuing utility. Studies of these centers and their printers necessarily cannot focus solely upon pamphlets. There were other minor centers of French publication, however, that published little other than pamphlets. Bibliographical studies of their production, therefore, necessarily make more direct contributions to our knowledge of literature in pamphlet form.

The great pioneer in the technical study of French pamphlets of the Reformation period was Eugénie Droz, perhaps better known for her work in launching and directing the most important modern publishing house devoted to the scholarly study of French culture during the periods of the Renaissance and Reformation. Until her death at an age near ninety Mlle. Droz found time from her business and editorial career to pursue her own bibliographical studies, many of which she published in her own house. Her highly technical analyses of specific pamphlets or specific printers are scattered about in articles published in the *Bibliothèque d'Humanisme et Renaissance*, gathered in a series of four post-retirement collections (1970–1976), and elsewhere. Probably the most important of these studies is a three-volume set Mlle. Droz prepared jointly with Louis Desgraves (1960). This work is simply an extended list of pamphlets published in La Rochelle by the printers Berton, Haultin, and Portau, but it is several times longer than any previous list of La Rochelle printings. During the wars of religion the port of La Rochelle became a key military center for the Protestant effort to conquer France. Its few printers supported this effort energetically by publishing inflammatory pamphlets, most of them political in content, designed to advance the Protestant cause and undermine Catholic political reaction to that cause. Because of their inflammatory content, most of these pamphlets were clandestine, with either no indication of printer and place of publication or with false addresses. Sometimes the false addresses were in Protestant centers beyond the reach of French royal power, like Basel; sometimes they were in good Catholic centers, like Paris. The printers of La Rochelle clearly felt that only clandestine pamphlets had much chance of circulating widely in a country that remained largely Catholic in government and that tried to impose strict censorship to prevent circulation of works regarded as subversive. For modern scholars to connect these pamphlets to the printers of La Rochelle requires great technical expertise, including the ability to examine closely decorative matter and individual letters to establish the printer who actually used that material in the sixteenth century. Precisely these skills were developed by Droz and Desgraves to establish the origins in La Rochelle of these many pamphlets. Their skills are fully displayed in this joint study, which is accompanied by copious photographic reproduction of the materials upon which their attributions are based. Both scholars used the same skills elsewhere to identify the origins of other French Protestant political pamphlets, Desgraves most notably in his book on Eloi Gibier (1966) of Orléans, which reconstitutes the production of another provincial printer of pamphlets, Droz most notably in a series of articles on individual French pamphlets published outside of France in such places as Geneva, Basel, and Heidelberg.

Few of these technical studies, however, can be completely satisfactory to most general historians. They are extremely useful works of reference, indispensable for identifying specific pamphlets and for establishing the context in which they were produced, but they tell us relatively little of the content of these pamphlets or of the markets for which they were intended.

Greater guidance on matters of this sort is provided by a group of scholars stimulated by the *Annales* school which dominates contemporary French historiography. The most seminal of these scholars was a man who helped found the school, Lucien Febvre. Among the many desiderata he presented to the scholarly community of types of historical study which could broaden our knowledge of the past beyond traditional political chronologies to an understanding of past cultures in the totality, was a suggestion for a new history of the book. Febvre wanted this subject to be studied not just by establishing lists of individual works and printers but by reconstructing the entire book industry, placing it in its social, economic, and political context and examining the markets that it created and served. Febvre prepared a sketch of this study late in his own life, then turned his notes and outline over to a younger scholar, Henri-Jean Martin. The result was an essay published as their joint work (1958) and translated into English without any change or updating (1976). It remains the most thoughtful and sensible single general survey of the development of the printing industry and its impact on society throughout Europe between 1450 and 1800. Martin then proceeded to develop a distinguished career as the world's greatest authority on early modern French publishing. He laid a particularly persuasive claim to this status with his monumental dissertation on the seventeenth-century Parisian publishing industry (1969), based on decades of massive archival research in Paris. Martin also stimulated, encouraged, and patronized a number of additional monographic studies on aspects of early modern French printing. A number of these studies have appeared in a series of publications sponsored by the fourth section of the École Pratique des Hautes Études in Paris, under the general title *Histoire et civilisation du livre*, published by the Librairie Droz in Geneva.

Many of these studies, to be sure, do not deal with the Reformation period, and even those that do are not limited to use of pamphlets. But some do, the most notable of which is probably Pallier (1976). This meticulous study is in part an exhaustive list with descriptions of more than 870 pamphlets published in Paris during the years of great political tension from 1585 to 1594 including many written while the city was under siege. Most of them are by more or less fanatical Catholics, railing against Protestantism and against any government inclined either to include Protestants within its ranks or even to tolerate Protestants within the country. But Pallier goes well beyond his simple list to provide a great deal of fresh infor-

mation on the printers who produced these pamphlets, on how they
were organized and related to the political and ecclesiastical leaders
of the city, and on the publics to which they sold their wares.

   Even a study as fresh and as detailed as Pallier's, however, cannot
exhaust its subject. Many of these pamphlets contain highly individual, even idiosyncratic arguments developed in an intricate, ingenious, or erudite manner. The more interesting or influential of
them deserve intensive separate study.[5] Baumgartner (1976), has
undertaken this task in his unpretentious analysis of several of these
pamphlets. He pays particular attention to just two of them, Jean
Boucher's *De justa abdicatione*, and the anonymous *De justa reipub-
licae christianae authoritate*. A number of studies have been devoted
to the particularly radical and interesting *Dialogue d'entre le
maheustre et le manant*, another anonymous product of the Paris
Catholic League, attributed to François Cromé. This pamphlet has
been skillfully edited by Peter M. Ascoli (Geneva, 1977), and is the
subject of thoughtful though sharply differing analyses in articles by
Ascoli and J. H. M. Salmon.[6] Salmon finds in this treatise, and particularly in its very first edition, a whiff of authentic democratic
radicalism. Ascoli finds in it a more traditional set of popular Catholic objections to compromise with Protestantism.

   Some of the earlier French Protestant political pamphlets, particularly those labelled "monarchomach" because of their calls for
armed resistance to royal government, have been subjected to even
more intensive examination. Thus François Hotman's *Franco-
Gallia*, with its stirring appeal to a peculiar view of French constitutional history in order to justify resistance, has been published in a
splendid variorum Latin edition by Ralph E. Giesey with an English
translation by J. H. M. Salmon, encased in a magnificent critical
apparatus (Cambridge, 1972). By including texts of the changes
made in this pamphlet through several editions, Giesey and Salmon
demonstrate how Hotman adjusted his arguments to fit changing
political circumstances between 1573 and 1586. Similarly Theodore
Beza's *Du droit des magistrats*, which combines legal, historical,
and Biblical arguments to justify resistance to the French crown and
which was written by Calvin's successor as leader of the internation-

[5]For a good general and recent introduction to the content of those French pamphlets of special interest to historians of political thought, see Skinner (1978) *passim*,
especially chs. 7–9.
   [6]Ascoli (1974), 3–22; Salmon (1972), 540–576.

al Reformed movement but published anonymously to win non-Protestant support to the cause of resistance, has been presented in modern critical editions: of the Latin version by Klaus Sturm (Neukirchen—Vluyn, 1965) and of the French version by Madeleine Marabuto (Saint-Julien-l'Ars, 1968) and Robert M. Kingdon (Geneva, 1971). The anonymous *Vindiciae contra tyrannos* has similarly been subjected to intensive study, perhaps most notably by Ralph E. Giesey, who has demonstrated its striking and innovative use of arguments drawn from Roman private law.[7].

Where We Seem to be Going

As in so many fields, the positions in which we find ourselves help indicate where we are going. There is clearly room for further useful development of all the approaches to French pamphlet literature of the Reformation period already sketched. The highly technical study of pamphlets issued by individual printers, demanding a sure control of descriptive bibliography, has much to teach us still. It can give us a surer knowledge of the geography of the publication of these often incendiary and clandestine pamphlets. My own recent studies have convinced me, for example, that there were more French political pamphlets published in London than has previously been realized. Some were printed in French, some in Latin, some in English translation. Some were surreptitiously sponsored by the English crown and even distributed in France through diplomatic channels.[8] Others may not have been inspired directly by officials of the Elizabethan government, but were still the products of a printing industry very closely supervised by the crown including many printers with personal ties of friendship and patronage to government leaders. Their publishers often worked in close collaboration with printers in La Rochelle and elsewhere on the continent.

A similar story of the publication of pamphlets outside of France to support precise political goals within the kingdom can be put together for the city of Geneva and probably also for such German cities as Basel, Strasbourg, and Heidelberg. A first step toward doing so, however, must be the discovery of just which pamphlets were published where. This often requires the technical skills of the bibliographer.

More study is needed of the production of pamphlets within the

[7]Giesey (1970), 41–56.
[8]Woodfield (1973), 24–33.

economic, social, and political context of the French publishing industry. The primary materials to make possible studies of this kind exist in the unpublished sets of notarized legal documents preserved in most French departmental and municipal archives. Most of these sets are not yet fully catalogued, and their use has necessarily been somewhat haphazard and random. Documents detailing the business careers of printers and publishers, to be sure, have probably been collected more extensively than those of practitioners of other trades, but there is more to be gathered on them and even more to be gathered on their business associates—the merchants who supplied publishers and printers with supplies, or the professional men who supplied publishers with their most lucrative markets. A few inventories of the private libraries of professional men prepared after their deaths, for example, have already provided rich suggestions about the markets for various kinds of books, including pamphlets.[9]

Finally, analysis of individual pamphlets of interest or influence is needed. The most popular of the "monarchomach" pamphlets provoked by the St. Bartholomew's massacres, for example, was probably the anonymous *Reveille-matin*. It is less interesting as a work of political theory than the pamphlets that have already been edited. But it went through many more editions at the time, and there is evidence that it had an inflammatory effect on groups of French noblemen considering resumption of war against the crown. It poses great problems of interpretation. Its lines of argument are somewhat inconsistent and suggest the possibility that it is actually a combination of pieces written by at least two polemicists,[10] and parts of it are needlessly offensive to certain segments of the natural audience for pamphlets of this type. It contains some nasty remarks about the religious policy of the English government, for example. These no doubt explain why it was never translated into English or published in London. The evidence of its contemporary influence, however, suggests that it deserves more intensive attention than it has as yet received.

In addition to the continued exploitation of existing ways of studying French political pamphlets, we can also expect the development of new approaches. As the works of Mastellone (1972) and Kelley (1981) suggest, there may well be further attempts to extract new types of information from these sources. Politics in the sixteenth

---

[9]E.g. Doucet (1956).
[10]Suggested by Salmon (1959), 19, n.7. Cf. Kelley (1981), 301 and ff.

century involved rivalry of tightly-knit extended aristocratic families supported by sizable groups of organized clients. Political pamphlets thus can tell us something about the structures and loyalties of aristocratic families. Politics also involved the dispersal of considerable sums of money, often under the ultimate control of royal treasuries. Political pamphlets can thus tell us something about the finances of royal governments and the economies upon which they draw.

Yet more speculative possibilities are suggested by the provocative and stimulating study by Elizabeth L. Eisenstein (1979). This fascinating exploration into the impact upon European culture of the revolution in communications accomplished by the development and institutionalization of printing deliberately omits consideration of the impact of printing upon politics. Yet surely this impact must have been considerable, in France as elsewhere. The kings of France were quick to see political advantage in the invention of printing. They poured substantial subsidies into the publication of works of humanist scholarship, no doubt in part to gain the respect and support of the scholarly community. They used the press to disseminate the texts of laws, and thus to gain greater knowledge of and respect for royal law. And they were particularly sensitive to the use of pamphlets to manipulate public opinion in the court, in aristocratic circles, and in wider parts of the community. The theologians of the Sorbonne and the governments of Paris and Lyon were encouraged to keep a close watch on pamphlet literature and to move quickly to suppress those who published or disseminated pamphlets with subversive or heretical ideas. The royal court itself was aware of the circulation of political pamphlets offensive to its interests and occasionally instructed ambassadors to file protests with foreign governments for permitting the publication of individual pamphlets. I have found record of the filing of such protests by French ambassadors to both the court of England and the federated Swiss cantons.[11] The invention of print and its use by alert governments no doubt should be an important ingredient in explaining the general increase in the power of many governmental units in the Reformation period. Further studies of how governments supported and used printers

[11]For an example of a complaint to the English court, in 1571, see Hector de la Ferrière, ed., *Lettres de Catherine de Médicis*, IV (Paris, 1891), 92–93, complemented by *Correspondance diplomatique de Bertrand de Salignac de la Mothe Fénélon*, IV (Paris and London, 1840), 301, 305. For examples of complaints to the Swiss, see the sources cited by Bremme (1969), 83–86.

or sought to control and muzzle them could be very revealing. Among these governments, the French royal government and the municipal governments of Paris and Lyon should certainly be included, as should the de facto governments created by great aristocrats who dominated the extreme Protestant and Catholic factions within France in defiance of royal authority. These aristocrats also hired printers, issued manifestoes designed for publication, and sought to manipulate and control the press in other ways as did various local governments. The publishing industry was also exploited by governments outside of France that had vital interests in the kingdom, such as in the Rhenish Palatinate, and England.

How We Get There

Obviously the most important raw materials for the study of French pamphlets during the Reformation are the pamphlets themselves. There are thousands of them scattered widely throughout the world. The most important of these collections are in Paris, above all in the *Bibliothèque Nationale*, but also in the *Arsenal, Mazarine,* and *Sainte-Geneviève* libraries, and in the library of the *Société de l'histoire du protestantisme français*. There are also important collections elsewhere in France and in cities ringing France. The *British Library* in London and the *Bibliothèque publique et universitaire* in Geneva possess important collections as do libraries in such cities as Basel. There are even important sets of French pamphlets in research libraries scattered through the United States. Effective bibliographical control of this mass of material, however, is far from satisfactory. Many of the libraries possessing these pamphlets, particularly the older ones in Europe, have over the centuries bound together in large volumes groups of vaguely connected pamphlets. Indexes or catalogues to these libraries often provide very incomplete and misleading guides to these volumes, and thus to the library's total holdings of pamphlets. There can, therefore, be no substitute for spending hours in rare-book libraries, calling up volume after collective volume, and carefully inspecting each to discover its full content of pamphlets.

There are, nevertheless, certain bibliographical guides of some value. The printed catalogues of the *British Library* and *Bibliothèque Nationale* note the presence of a number of pamphlets, as so do the often unpublished catalogues of other libraries. For scholars working in America there is a useful introductory guide compiled by Lindsay and Neu (1969). It supplies a short-title list of the pamphlets contained in some fifteen American research libraries, arranged chronologically with an index of authors and titles. It is far from perfect. Several additional American research libraries possess significant numbers of these pamphlets, and even the libraries inventoried for this catalogue contain pamphlets which are not listed, sometimes because they were purchased more recently, sometimes because they had not been fully catalogued locally—perhaps because they had been purchased in bound collective volumes of the sort one finds commonly in Europe—at the time Lindsay and Neu visited these libraries. Still, this catalogue supplies a very useful preliminary guide to pamphlet collections in the United States. Monographs using this catalogue as a starting point have already been published.

For the English speaking world a useful supplementary guide to the location of some pamphlets is supplied by the superb *Short-Title Catalogue of Books Printed in England, Scotland & Ireland, and of English Books Printed Abroad, 1475–1640* (London, 1926), now being revised by Katharine F. Pantzer, in part with materials gathered by W. A. Jackson and F. S. Ferguson (London, 1976). It is, of course, only of peripheral use to the student of French pamphlet literature, including only the few French pamphlets published in Britain and a few translations into English or Latin of pamphlets originally printed in French.

More useful are a number of catalogues and lists for specific printers, authors, and places. They range from old classics compiled in the nineteenth century to such modern bibliographies as the lists of Chaix, Droz, Desgraves, and Pallier mentioned above. The old classics, incidentally, should not be neglected. There is still no better guide to the printings of the house of Estienne, which worked in Paris for several kings of France and in Geneva for John Calvin and his successors, than Renouard (1843). Few of the Estienne printings were pamphlets, to be sure, but some of them certainly were.

Those who would like to explore some of the more technical ways of studying pamphlets of the sixteenth century, should learn some descriptive or analytical bibliography. There are a number of good guides to this discipline. A reliable classic is McKerrow (1927). It can be supplemented by Gaskell (1972). Gaskell's main contribution, however, is to the study of books printed after 1800 and the introduction of machine presses. Although Gaskell slightly updates and corrects McKerrow here and there, McKerrow remains adequate for most students of the sixteenth century. Both these surveys are intended primarily for the students of books produced in England, but the printing technology they describe and the types of book they analyze were virtually the same in France and, for that matter, elsewhere on the continent. It is possible to develop even greater technical expertise in this field by following the paths indicated by great technicians such as Fredson Bowers. Most historians will not want to go that far. They tend not to be much concerned with such problems as those posed by the minor variations among various states within a single edition.

Those who would like to examine the economic context in which printers of sixteenth-century pamphlets operated should use studies of the Plantin press in Antwerp, particularly as summarized by Voet (1969, 1972). The Plantin press, thanks to encouragement and subsidy from King Philip II of Spain, became the largest and most prosperous publishing house in all of Europe in the late sixteenth century. Plantin was originally French, continued to trade with France after his establishment in Antwerp, and produced a few French pamphlets himself. He made his greatest profits, however, from printing the Catholic service books whose use was mandated by the Council of Trent. He used these profits and Spanish subsidies to erect a large building in downtown Antwerp which still stands. It continued to be used as the headquarters of a publishing empire for nearly three centuries after Plantin's death by his heirs of the Moretus family. Then it was turned into a museum with all its equipment and records intact. The equipment includes ancient hand presses, foundries, and fonts of type. The records include accounts detailing Plantin's running expenses for labor and supplies as well as his sales to wholesale houses, to patrons, and to retail customers. With them one can reconstruct the precise cost and market of an individual book, including an individual pamphlet. And since the technology and organization of the sixteenth-century publishing industry seems to have been fairly uniform, one can extrapolate informed guesses on the probable costs and sales of pamphlets elsewhere. One can also find precise information on the few French pamphlets Plantin printed himself, usually in support of the royal Catholic cause. He printed, for example, a pamphlet containing the royal excuses for the Saint Bartholomew's massacres, in which King Charles IX takes full responsibility for the butchery, but claims it was necessary to avert a plot against his life.[12]

---

[12]*"Discours sur les causes de l'execution faicte es personnes de ceux qui avoyent conjuré contre le roy et son estat.* En Anvers, de l'imprimerie de Christophe Plantin, 1572." From the bibliography of Plantin works compiled by C. Ruelens and A. de Backer, *Annales Plantiniennes, 1555–1589* (Paris, 1866), 126–127.

Those who wish to speculate must depend on their own general knowledge of the period, their own imaginations, and the daring example of such scholars as Elizabeth Eisenstein. Whatever the approach, however, there remains much to be done with French pamphlets of the Reformation period. They provide evidence available nowhere else of the rather volatile states of public opinion in sixteenth-century France. They provide even stronger evidence of the ways in which leaders of French society sought to manipulate that opinion.

Bibliography

Ascoli, Peter M., "A Radical Pamphlet of Late Sixteenth Century France: le Dialogue d'entre le maheustre et le manant," *Sixteenth Century Journal*, V/2 (1974): 3–22.

Baudrier, Henri, *Bibliographie lyonnaise*, vols. 1–12 (Lyon, 1895–1921); Index (Paris, 1965).

Baumgartner, Frederic J., *Radical Reactionaries: The Political Thought of the French Catholic League* (Geneva, 1976).

Bremme, Hans Joachim, *Buchdrucker und Buchhändler zur Zeit der Glaubenskämpfe: Studien zur Genfer Druckgeschichte, 1565–1580* (Geneva, 1969).

Caprariis, Vittorio de, *Propaganda e pensiero politico in Francia durante le guerre di religione, 1559–1572* (Naples, 1959).

Chaix, Paul, *Recherches sur l'imprimerie à Genèva de 1550 à 1564* (Geneva, 1954).

_____, Dufour, Alain, and Moeckli, Gustave, *Les livres imprimés à Genèv de 1550 à 1600* (Geneva, 1966).

Desgraves, Louis, *Éloi Gibier, imprimeur à Orléans* (Geneva, 1966).

Doucet, R., *Les bibliothèques parisiennes au XVIe siècle* (Paris, 1956).

Droz, Eugénie, *Chemins de l'hérésie* (Geneva, 1970–76).

_____, and Desgraves, Louis, *L'Imprimerie à La Rochelle* (Geneva, 1960).

Eisenstein, Elizabeth L., *The Printing Press as an Agent of Change* (Cambridge, 1979).

Febvre, Lucien, and Martin, Henri-Jean, *L'apparition du livre* (Paris, 1958); English translation, *The Coming of the Book* (London, 1976).

Gaskell, Philip, *A New Introduction to Bibliography* (Oxford, 1972).

248 *Reformation Europe*

Giesey, Ralph E., "The Monarchomach Triumvirs: Hotman, Beza, and Mornay," *Bibliothèque d'Humanisme et Renaissance*, XXXII (1970): 41–56.

Hauser, Henri, *Les sources de l'histoire de France, XVIe siècle*, vols. 1–4 (Paris, 1906–1915).

Kelley, D.R., *The Beginning of Ideology: Consciousness and Society in the French Reformation* (Cambridge, 1981).

Lindsay, Robert O., and Neu, John, *French Political Pamphlets, 1547–1648: A Catalog of Major Collections in American Libraries* (Madison, 1969).

Martin, Henri-Jean, *Livre, pouvoirs, et société à Paris au XVIIe siècle* (Geneva, 1969).

Mastellone, Salvo, *Venalità e Machiavellismo in Francia, 1572–1610* (Florence, 1972).

McKerrow, Ronald B., *An Introduction to Bibliography, for Litarary Students* (Oxford, 1927).

Pallier, Denis, *Recherches sur l'imprimerie à Paris pendant la ligue, 1585–1594* (Geneva, 1976).

Renouard, Ant. Aug., *Annales de l'imprimerie des Estienne* (Paris, 1843).

Salmon, J. H. M., *The French Religious Wars in English Political Thought* (Oxford, 1959).

———, "The Paris Sixteen, 1584–1594: the Social Analysis of a Revolutionary Movement," *Journal of Modern History*, XLIV (1972): 540–576.

Skinner, Quentin, *The Foundations of Modern Political Thought*, vol. 2, *The Age of Reformation* (Cambridge, 1978).

Voet, Leon, *The Golden Compasses, A History and Evaluation of the Printing and Publishing Activities of the Officina Plantiniana*, vols. 1–2 (Amsterdam, 1969, 1972).

Woodfield, Denis B., *Surreptitious Printing in England, 1550–1640* (New York, 1973).

Reformation and Art

Carl C. Christensen

In 1526 when Erasmus gave Hans Holbein the Younger a letter of introduction to take with him to the Netherlands, he wrote by way of explanation concerning the artist's departure from Reformation Basel: "Here the arts are cold; he goes to England in order to scrape together a few angelots."[1] The notion that the evangelical movement created a frigid atmosphere for the arts can claim a long history and continues to provide one topic for discussion.[2] Although modern scholars have examined the relationship of art and Reformation from a number of other perspectives as well, much remains to be done. The purpose of the present essay is threefold: (1) to survey the scholarly literature of the past couple of decades, (2) to offer some suggestions as to the likely course of future investigation, and (3) to indicate source materials useful for research. The scope is restricted for the most part to topics dealing with the relationship of art and the Protestant Reformation. Further, the emphasis is placed primarily—though not exclusively—on the German-speaking lands of Europe.

Recent Literature

Theology and Art: We may begin with the relationship of theology and art, a problem that formed the point of departure for much of the discussion during the Reformation era itself. Recent scholarship on this topic may be said to date from the publication in 1957 of a pair of influential essays by Hans von Campenhausen.[3] Von Campenhausen sought to repair what he saw as an important omission in previous literature: neglect of the image debate of the sixteenth cen-

---

[1]Stechow (1966), 131.
[2]For art decline in Germany, see Christensen (1979), 164–80; also Baxandall (1980), 75–78.
[3]Campenhausen (1957a); (1957b).

tury. Acknowledging that Martin Luther's views, at least, had received some previous scholarly attention, von Campenhausen proceeded to offer a penetrating comparison of the Wittenberg reformer with his counterpart in the early Swiss reform, Huldreich Zwingli of Zurich.

The Zurich reformer was the subject of the first major study to follow von Campenhausen, an excellent book by Charles Garside.[4] Garside's monograph is a landmark work because it contains the first full-scale investigation of Zwingli's teachings and policies on church art. No previous author had ever presented such a detailed examination of the genesis of the Zurich reformer's views or related them so closely to the historical context. The result is a finely drawn picture of the interaction of ideas and events which had for its final outcome a complete removal of all paintings and statues from Zurich's churches in 1524.

The topic of Zwingli is taken up yet again in Margarete Stirm's book on the image problem in the Reformation.[5] This time, however, the Zurich reformer plays a secondary role, receiving considerable less attention than either Luther or John Calvin. The longest portion of Stirm's substantial volume is devoted to Luther. While the author deals briefly with historical and art historical problems, the main strength of her presentation lies in its detailed doctrinal analysis. The radical teachings of Andreas Karlstadt also receive some consideration, although they serve primarily as a foil to the description of Luther's more moderate position.

A further discussion of Karlstadt, the pioneer iconoclastic theologian of the evangelical movement, is offered in my own recent book, which also provides an alternative interpretation of the development and nature of Luther's views on religious images.[6]

Doctoral dissertations have added significantly to our knowledge of theology and art in the sixteenth century, especially with respect to the teachings of certain of the lesser known or later writers of the period. Carlos Eire has studied Martin Bucer and Heinrich Bullinger from this perspective, while the interaction of Protestant and Catholic views on images in the Netherlands has been examined in some detail by David Freedberg and Keith Moxey.[7] Although further re-

---

[4]Garside (1966).
[5]Stirm (1977).
[6]Christensen (1979), 23–35; 42–65.
[7]Eire (1979), 136–48; Freedberg (1972), 32–104; Moxey (1977), 139–228.

search undoubtedly will be done in theology and art, it appears that the neglect lamented by von Campenhausen twenty-five years ago no longer characterizes the topic.

Iconoclasm: To a certain extent, the same thing may be said concerning the state of scholarship on Reformation iconoclasm. Until rather recently the topic has been somewhat slighted,[8] but in the past couple of decades it has experienced a notable expansion of research. While much undoubtedly remains to be learned, the gains in knowledge have been substantial.

Our increased understanding has partly resulted from scholars wisely paying heed to the widely varying circumstances in which art destruction occurred in the sixteenth century. As a consequence of detailed local research there has emerged a more adequate sense of the different patterns displayed in iconoclastic activity. Charles Garside made an important contribution in this regard.[9] In his work on Zurich he provided evidence of a rapidly executed governmental policy of image removal accomplished with a minimum of tumult and violence. By the resolute but orderly manner in which they proceeded, the evangelical rulers of the city established one model of Reformation iconoclasm.

Subsequent studies of iconoclasm in other communities have revealed other models or patterns. For instance, I found in Lutheran Nuremberg an example of official protection of most existing church art, whereas in Basel we have an illustration of how the failure of city authorities to act promptly could permit the build-up of enormous popular resentment against idols which finally erupted in large-scale iconoclastic riots.[10]

Recent research also has revealed a range of different scholarly methods or approaches to the study of iconoclasm. Some relate more directly to art than others. For example, image destruction can be evaluated in terms of lost aesthetic monuments and the resulting impoverishment of mankind's cultural heritage.[11] Or, iconoclasm's effect on subsequent artistic creativity—both quantitatively and qualitatively—may serve as a focus of attention, as in studies by David Freedberg and Keith Moxey on the Netherlands.[12] Other lines of in-

---

[8]Cf. Freedberg (1977b), 165.

[9]Garside (1966), 158–60.

[10]Christensen (1979), 66–78, 93–102; for iconoclasm in Geneva, see Eire (1979), 190–235.

[11]See Christensen (1979), 107–109.

[12]Freedberg (1972); Freedberg (1977a); Moxey (1977), *passim.*

quiry pertain more to religious or political history. Some researchers have been examining episodes of image destruction for what they reveal about the process of religious and political change—questions of reform leadership, reform tactics, and the like.[13] And still others have emphasized the element of social class conflict.[14]

Whether the results of all these investigations can be harmonized is difficult to say. It is true that a comprehensive history of the topic has not yet appeared.[15] But at least much more of the preliminary research for such a synthesis has been completed now than was the case a couple of decades ago.

Art Works and Iconographical Themes: The Reformation not only caused the destruction of countless works of art, it also influenced —more or less directly—the creation of numerous others. This impact upon artistic creativity can be discussed under several possible subheadings. We shall proceed here with reference to the following: ecclesiastical art, propaganda art, and individual iconographical themes.

Probably the most interesting questions relating to ecclesiastical art in the Reformation are the following: Was there a specifically Protestant church art and, if so, what were its characteristics? Due to the hostile attitudes of both Zwingli and Calvin toward the use of images in churches one is forced to turn to an examination of early Lutheranism for an answer to these questions. A major contribution to our knowledge of this topic was made by Oskar Thulin's 1955 book on the Cranach altars of the Reformation.[16] That Lucas Cranach the Elder and his sons painted altarpieces with evangelical subject matter has long been known. Thulin's monograph compellingly focused attention on that fact by providing a series of iconographically detailed and profusely illustrated discussions of a half-dozen of these works.

A briefer but at the same time more comprehensive description of early Lutheran church art appeared shortly after Thulin's work in a book by Hans Carl von Haebler.[17] Analysis of sixteenth-century monuments forms only one portion of this partly art historical, partly theological volume. Nonetheless, the work proved most valuable,

---

[13]Cf. Crew (1978); Eire (1979), 159ff and 236ff.

[14]See Warnke (1973).

[15]As Freedberg (1977a), 28, much research remains to be done on French, Scandinavian, and Eastern European iconoclasm. For England, see Phillips (1973).

[16]Thulin (1955).

[17]Haebler (1957).

both for its often highly suggestive comments and for its numerous illustrations, many depicting little known paintings and carvings.

One of the temptations facing students of early Lutheran art has been to confine their investigation too exclusively to works in the Cranach or Wittenberg tradition. If von Haebler's book helped to correct that bias, the same may be said of a somewhat later study by Walter Hentschel discussing a school of Dresden sculptors in the sixteenth and seventeenth centuries.[18] Hentschel treats a number of closely related stone carvers many of whose commissions consisted of epitaph monuments and altar retables for placement in Protestant churches. Both text and illustrations provide evidence for the popularity of the *Last Supper* motif in evangelical altarpiece iconography—a phenomenon further examined in other recent studies, including my own.[19]

Until very recently one of the most inadequately researched topics of Reformation art was the use of visual imagery, particularly woodcuts, as a vehicle of popular propaganda. The importance of the graphic arts for disseminating evangelical ideas has often been commented upon in the past but there existed no adequate scholarly investigation of the matter. Fortunately, this gap finally has been filled with a ground-breaking study by R. W. Scribner.[20] Scribner's book is notable on a number of counts, not least of all for its scope and comprehensiveness. Even more noteworthy, however, is the methodology employed. Although the author has produced what he describes as an essentially historical study, the approach is really interdisciplinary in nature. Extensive use has been made of the tools of art history, folklore, sociology, and semiology or the science of signs. By applying such methods Scribner is able to make important contributions to a number of different areas of study—for example, to the growing body of scholarship on popular culture. The book also nicely achieves its author's purpose of demonstrating the value of visual sources as evidence in analyzing popular mentalities. In a variety of ways this pioneering study must be judged a major addition to our knowledge.

There remains one topic to be considered in this context, that is research on the significance of the Reformation for the development of individual iconographic themes. There are two distinct phenome-

[18]Hentschel (1966).
[19]Oertel (1974) and Christensen (1979), 148–54.
[20]Scribner (1981).

na to be observed here: the impact of reform ideas on the use and interpretation of existing visual symbols, and the creation of new artistic subject matter under the influence of the evangelical movement.

A well known example of the former process may be found in a
still influential article published by Christine Kibish in 1955 examining a group of paintings by Cranach on the subject of *Christ Blessing
the Children.*[21] For a more recent instance from the Low Countries
we can refer to a study by Grace Vlam on the *Calling of Saint Matthew* in sixteenth-century Flemish painting. Vlam finds that in the
historical context representations of the Calling were meant to be
understood as a summons to Reformation, and as a "tool for the expression of reformatory ideas."[22]

More wide-ranging than either of the above-mentioned studies is
the book by Craig Harbison on the *Last Judgment* in sixteenth-
century northern art.[23] It has been said of Harbison's work that it is
"the first to attempt an overview of the development of a religious
image in reaction to changing Protestant theologies over the space of
a century."[24] There is no opportunity here to summarize all of Harbison's findings. Suffice it to say that one result of his research has
been to show how the *Last Judgment* motif sometimes assumed an
altered significance when portrayed in Protestant art, a consequence
of the fact that "for Luther, Christ's judgment often became not so
much a means of dispensing God's justice as of displaying God's
love."[25]

One of the most valuable sections of Harbison's book is that in
which he discusses the inclusion of the *Last Judgment* motif in a very
influential class of new Protestant compositions entitled *The Law
and the Gospel* or *Allegory of Law and Grace.*[26] The existence of this
Law and Gospel subject in evangelical art, to be sure, is no original
discovery. Thulin included a most useful chapter on the topic in his
Cranach monograph, and quite appropriately so, since the Wittenberg artist generally is credited with the invention of the theme.[27] In
subsequent years increasing attention has been devoted to this popular subject which probably contained the most complete expression

[21]Kibish (1955).
[22]Vlam (1977), 563, 569.
[23]Harbison (1976b).
[24]Andersson (1978), 553.
[25]Harbison (1976b), 92.
[26]Harbison (1976b), 94–102.
[27]Thulin (1955), 126–48.

of Lutheran doctrine to be found anywhere in sixteenth-century art.[28]

Dürer and Cranach: It is not possible to discuss individually all the artists whose work may have been affected by the Reformation. However, I have chosen to single out two German painters whose importance for our topic is unusually great: Albrecht Dürer and Lucas Cranach the Elder. The most significant milestone in recent Dürer scholarship was provided by the five-hundredth anniversary of the artist's birth, celebrated in 1971. The occasion was marked by several exhibitions—including a particularly impressive one in Nuremberg, Dürer's native city—as well as by the publication of numerous books and articles. Many of these writings were admirably critiqued in a review article by Wolfgang Stechow and thus I may keep my comments to a minimum.[29] Of special interest to Reformation scholars are the following: (1) the Nuremberg exhibition catalog containing a discussion of the artist's links to early Protestantism; (2) a scholarly essay by Gottfried Seebass on Dürer's place in the Reformation movement; and (3) a massive volume of Dürer bibliography.[30] Since the anniversary year, other publications of note have appeared. One might mention, for example, the detailed discussion of the artist's theological views in a book by Gerlinde Wiederanders.[31] There also have been studies on the relationship of individual Dürer works to the evangelical reform: (1) Donald Kuspit's analysis of the late portraits; (2) Craig Harbison's article on the *St. Philip* engraving; and (3) essays by Gerhard Pfeiffer, Peter Strieder, and myself[32] on the famous *Four Apostles* painting.

The five-hundredth birth anniversary of Lucas Cranach the Elder followed by one year that of Albrecht Dürer. This event, too, was observed with art exhibitions and scholarly presentations. From among the latter I call attention especially to the papers given at a conference in Wittenberg, several of which deal with Reformation themes.[33] None of the Cranach exhibitions staged in 1972, however, can compare in importance with the one held in Basel in the summer

---

[28]See Poscharsky (1963), 153–65; Ehresmann (1966–67), *passim;* Christensen (1979), 124–30; Andersson (1981), 51, 72–74; Scribner (1981), 216–18.

[29]Stechow (1974).

[30]*Albrecht Dürer 1471–1971* (1971), 199–212; Seebass (1971); Mende (1971).

[31]Wiederanders (1975).

[32]Kuspit (1975); Harbison (1976a); Pfeiffer (1972), 271–96; Strieder (1973); Christensen (1979), 181–206.

[33]Published in Feist, Ullmann, and Brendler (1973).

of 1974. From the standpoint of scholarship, the most important consequence was the superb two-volume catalog issued to accompany the exhibition. As in the case of the Dürer catalog mentioned above, we have here a work of major significance which includes a section on the artist's works depicting Reformation themes.[34]

In the same year as the Basel exhibition a monumental new Cranach study was published in East Germany by Werner Schade. Fortunately, a translation of this scholarly and well illustrated book has now been published in America.[35] It would be no exaggeration to state that with the latter publication we have the first substantial monograph in English on the Wittenberg artist and his workshop.

Our discussion of recent Cranach publications may fittingly conclude with a reference to the newly revised, English edition of the great Friedländer and Rosenberg catalog of paintings.[36] One may hope that the availability of this fundamental work, plus other writings mentioned here, will elevate interest in the Wittenberg artist to new heights in the Anglo-Saxon world.

Future Research Opportunities

Although scholarship has been quite active in the past few decades, there remains much to be done. For purposes of discussion we may divide our treatment of future research into two main categories: (1) that which focuses on art and artists as the primary topic, and (2) that which employs art as evidence in the study of other historical questions.

With regard to art itself one may safely predict, first of all, that research will continue in the field of iconographic studies. We are becoming increasingly aware of the extent to which the Reformation influenced the choice and interpretation of subject matter in sixteenth-century art. In some instances new artistic themes were invented, but more frequently a novel set of meanings was read into visual motifs already at hand. Because of their use of familiar imagery, examples of the latter type are not always easily recognizable. Intensive research into both visual and written sources may be required to uncover the message conveyed by these compositions in their Reformation setting.[37]

---

[34]Koepplin and Falk (1976), 498–522.
[35]Schade (1974) and (1980).
[36]Friedländer and Rosenberg (1978).
[37]One aspect of this problem is mentioned by Saunders (1978–79), 59.

Obviously, it is impossible to state precisely where future iconographical discoveries will be made. One example may be mentioned, however, of an older theme which perhaps deserves more
study, the *Prodigal Son* motif. Craig Harbison has suggested that "it
is in the depiction of the actual return of the Prodigal Son . . . that
we most clearly find the contemporary religious meaning of this
theme. . . . For the welcome given to him by his father stresses,
above all, the factor of faith. . . . Only his faith in his father's mercy and love gained him the grace and forgiveness which, according
to Luther, all Christians must seek in God."[38]
In addition to research on individual iconographic themes there
also is needed further examination of certain broader groups of subject matter. In the case of Reformation art, one such category consists of stories from the Old Testament. There seems little doubt that
the Hebrew Scriptures acquired greater prominence in European art
because of Luther and the evangelical movement. Some years ago
Erwin Panofsky observed that "the Protestant inclination to go back
to the sources . . . [led Protestants to regard] the Old Testament as
a revelation *sui iuris*, instead of as a mere prelude to, or even a pre-
figuration of, the New."[39] Panofsky demonstrated his point with
comparative data on art works by two seventeenth-century masters,
Rubens and Rembrandt. Subsequently, other studies have provided
examples from a time closer to the Reformation. In my own book I
presented evidence that the tendency begins as early as the Lutheran
altar panels of Cranach the Elder.[40] In an essay on Maarten van
Heemskerck Eleanor Saunders has noted that the Netherlandish artist concentrated on depicting Old Testament stories in a fashion un-
paralleled among earlier print designers working outside the realm
of traditional scriptural illustration.[41] David Freedberg, on the
other hand, reports a greater emphasis on the Old Testament also in
post-Reformation Catholic art.[42] The whole topic invites further investigation.
Iconographic research sometimes is employed in the analysis of a
class of art works defined by format or function. One area of Reformation art where such an approach might prove fruitful is that of

[38]Harbison (1969), 33. In general, on the theme, see Kirschbaum (1972), cols.
172–74.
[39]Panofsky (1969), 10.
[40]Christensen (1979), 161.
[41]Saunders (1978–79), 62.
[42]Freedberg (1972), 251–52.

German Lutheran altarpieces. To be sure, the individual monuments have been inventoried and the creations of prominent artists discussed in art historical literature. But this body of art works as a whole seems never to have been subjected to a thorough, systematic investigation. We possess no detailed, yet comprehensive evaluation comparable to that devoted to Lutheran pulpit art by Peter Poscharsky.[43] Whether anyone will attempt to apply Poscharsky's painstaking methodology to altarpiece art is impossible to say.

In addition to Lutheran altarpieces there are other categories of Reformation art that merit further study. Despite the longstanding scholarly preoccupation with the pictures in Luther's Bibles and, to a lesser extent, in his catechisms, certain aspects of early Protestant book illustration remain inadequately discussed in the modern literature.[44] For instance, one might mention the woodcuts adorning various editions of Luther's prayer book.[45] To the best of my knowledge, this class of images still awaits careful evaluation and comparison with the visual material in other evangelical publications of the period.

Research in the future undoubtedly will concern itself with artists as well as art works. A more intensive examination of the personal reactions of painters, sculptors, and printmakers to the religious crisis of the Reformation would, as Craig Harbison notes, provide a fascinating study. Both in Germany and the Netherlands the range of responses was quite broad.[46] One is tempted to inquire whether any meaningful patterns can be found among these variations. Questions like the following come to mind: (1) what percentage of artists in a given area actively supported the Reformation and, among those who did, how important was religious commitment as a motivating force? (2) to what extent were factors such as socioeconomic status a determinant of behavior? (3) how much of an issue was the threat of iconoclasm or loss of art commissions?[47] The scholar seeking answers to these questions may find it helpful to consult studies on the reaction of other groups (e.g., the humanists) to the evangelical movement.

Let us turn now to our second category of future research possibilities: the use of art works as source material in the investigation of

---

[43]Poscharsky (1963).
[44]For Bible illustrations, see Oertel (1977).
[45]Christensen (1979), 170.
[46]Harbison (1976c), 78.
[47]For a recent study of socioeconomic status, see Brady (1975).

historical questions. The serious exploitation of visual evidence by historians is a quite recent development. Norman Cantor and Richard Schneider explained this earlier neglect of nonverbal sources as "partly due to the self-restraining principle that institutional history had to be the hard foundation of historical knowledge and therefore was to be built up first, and partly due to scholars' personal inclination and taste."[48] Be that as it may, a greater appreciation for the importance of visual evidence has begun to manifest itself.

I believe that most historians today would agree that a sensitive study of art works can enhance our knowledge of several aspects of the past. To begin, let us take a topic of religious history. Pre-Reformation piety has left a vast deposit of evidence in the pictorial imagery of the time. Granted, the beliefs and devotional practices found reflected there normally will not prove to be altogether unknown from written documents. Nonetheless, these visual materials are capable of augmenting the verbal record in a variety of ways.

One potential contribution from such art works derives from their capacity to furnish interesting corroboratory detail. A case in point is the supporting testimony gleaned from stained glass and ecclesiastical statuary by A. N. Galpern in his recent analysis of popular religion in a selected area of sixteenth-century France.[49] In the future, failure to consult visual evidence in this type of study perhaps will be considered a serious scholarly omission.[50]

Sometimes a proper appreciation of even a single vivid image can add an extra dimension of emotional empathy to our otherwise excessively cerebral understanding of past religious experience. Peter Strieder's fine essay on a *Sacred Heart* votive print provides a model for further investigation along these lines.[51]

Turning to the Reformation movement, the problem of explaining religious change obviously becomes a major concern. What moved people to abandon the old faith and adopt the new? In answering such questions visual evidence will continue to prove a helpful source of knowledge. My comments above concerning Scribner's study of art as propaganda illustrate the importance of this type of investigation. Scribner's research marks a giant step forward but, as he himself acknowledges, by no means exhausts the topic. He lists as

[48]Cantor and Schneider (1967), 80.
[49]Galpern (1976), 13, 17, 20, 45, 56, 90, 95–97.
[50]For examples of regional research on art and the Reformation, see Wandersleb (1968–70) and Reingrabner (1978).
[51]Strieder (1976).

other promising areas of inquiry the use of popular propaganda in sixteenth-century France and the Netherlands, and its role in the Counter Reformation.[52] I suspect that even for Germany more evidence will be forthcoming regarding the printing and distribution of polemical pictures, their impact on the populace, and so on. Certainly enough work now has been done to confirm the great value of this type of nonverbal documentation.

Moving from religious to social history, it is becoming apparent that a variety of uses can be found in this field also for visual evidence. For example, further analysis of the manner in which different groups in society are portrayed in the pictorial media no doubt will prove illuminating. A few pioneering studies have been devoted to examining the treatment of the peasant in German art. The results are intriguing for questions they raise about the social impact of the Reformation as well as its social context. For it may be, as R. W. Scribner in another work has suggested, that "the Reformation brought new ways of looking at the peasant," changes affecting both his self-esteem and the evaluation placed upon him by members of other classes.[53] As a fascinating example of research on peasant imagery currently underway, there might be mentioned a doctoral dissertation being written in art history at Columbia University. The author, Alison Stewart, is investigating the depiction of peasant festivals in German graphic art during the 1520's and 1530's. Her topic, while obviously bearing on art and social history, also intersects with the religious history of the Reformation in the sense that contemporary attitudes toward peasant life were much influenced by Luther and other theologians of the time.[54]

In a somewhat similar vein, it seems likely that we may learn more about the status of women in Reformation Europe from a careful look at art works of the era. An examination of epitaphs, for example, poses interesting questions about the manner in which women are portrayed on funerary monuments—most typically as members of a deceased male's family rather than as the main subject of the composition. It is intriguing also to note that women figure prominently in two of the themes popular in evangelical circles around Lucas Cranach: *Christ and the Adulteress,* and *Christ Bless-*

[52]Scribner (1981), 249. He also lists the depiction of social conflict in visual evidence.
[53]Scribner (1976), 30. See also Zschelletzschky (1975), 298–359; and Karl-Heinz Klingenburg (1973), 145–49 and 214–16.
[54]I owe this information to the kindness of Ms. Stewart.

ing the Children. A link from these compositions to views on marriage and family has been established by Christiane Andersson but I suspect that more remains to be said on the matter.[55] And what is the historian to make of Cranach's notorious nudes? Even his friend Luther once was provoked to exclaim: "Master Lucas is a coarse painter. He might have spared the female sex because they are God's creatures and because of our mothers."[56] The responsibility for these provocative pictures may rest with Cranach's princely patrons rather than the artist himself, but in either case the manner in which women are portrayed calls for further comment.

Sources and Research Tools

Source materials for the study of Reformation and art may be broadly classified under two headings, visual and verbal. I shall discuss examples of both categories here. In addition, I shall mention some research tools useful for finding still other sources plus the information necessary to interpret them correctly when found.

Let us consider first visual evidence. As much as possible, the researcher will want to examine the art objects at first hand, and this means visiting the museums, libraries, churches, or other places where they are situated. Art works owned by public museums usually are among the most accessible of visual artifacts, not least of all because such institutions normally issue catalogs of their holdings containing valuable technical and scholarly data as well as photographic illustrations which may themselves serve as useful visual evidence. There is some indication of a recent trend toward assembling bibliographical information on this class of publications. For example, the scholar wishing to locate descriptions of catalogs for collections in West Germany will find his task simplified by the appearance of a new series of handbooks being prepared for this purpose.[57]

The locating and interpreting of art works situated in churches may be greatly facilitated by the use of geographically arranged inventories of art and architectural monuments. Published inventories of this sort have been issued in various countries of Europe. They exist in an especially complete and detailed form for the German lands, where they have been assembled—region by region, locality by locality—in vast multi-volume sets. Indeed, a modern art bibli-

---

[55]Andersson (1981), 45, 55–56.
[56]Quoted from Fleming (1973), 351; for the original text, see Lüdecke (1953a), 174.
[57]See Ehresmann (1979), no. 200, 60.

ography requires a dozen pages simply to list them all.[58] The inventory volumes include photographs and diagrams as well as written descriptions of art works and are extremely useful for doing certain kinds of research.[59]

Reference has been made to reproductions of art objects and these, of course, will prove of great utility even to the scholar who has access to the original works. Art reproductions in most instances are easy enough to locate when one is studying a particular artist, especially if he is well-known. More apt to be overlooked are collections illustrating the works of more than one master. I should now like to discuss a few of these publications, concentrating on examples from the graphic arts in Germany.

We may begin with Walter Strauss' newly revised edition of Max Geisberg's collection of German woodcuts from the period 1500–1550.[60] This four-volume publication makes available for the first time in a format suitable for general study a famous group of prints originally assembled by Geisberg in the 1920's. Geisberg issued the woodcut reproductions in forty-three large loose-leaf folios. The set proved difficult to use. Accessibility was improved somewhat by the publication in 1930 of an illustrated index volume to the collection. The illustrations in the index volume, however, were very small and thus of limited value. Therefore, the appearance of a new edition was most welcome, especially insofar as Strauss took the opportunity to include many additional woodcuts. The prints reproduced in the revised Geisberg illustrate a wide range of subject matter and portray numerous scenes of great interest to the social and cultural historian as well as the Reformation scholar.

Walter Strauss followed up his edition of Geisberg with the publication of a new three-volume collection of his own, containing German woodcuts from the years 1550–1600.[61] Many woodcuts of this later period are of a lower artistic quality than typical works from the first half of the sixteenth century. However, this does not lessen their value for the historian.

Broader in scope than either Geisberg or Strauss is F. W. H. Holl-

---

[58]Ehresmann (1979), 239–51.

[59]For examples of studies utilizing inventory materials, see Poscharsky (1963) and my essay on "The Significance of the Epitaph Monument in Early Lutheran Ecclesiastical Art (ca. 1540–1600)" in Buck and Zophy (1972), 297–314.

[60]Geisberg (1974).

[61]Strauss (1975).

[62]Hollstein (1954ff).

stein's vast publication of German graphic art.[62] In volume one of this work Hollstein announced his intention of providing "illustrations of some eight thousand of the more important prints of the German School, including about five thousand which have never yet been reproduced."[63] Unfortunately, Hollstein died when only five volumes had been published.[64] The series eventually was continued under different editorship, but it became necessary to reduce the number of reproductions in the later segments. Since the work is organized by last names this means that the richness of illustration depends somewhat upon where a particular artist falls in the alphabet. Despite these limitations, Hollstein remains a helpful source of visual material, particularly when used in conjunction with Geisberg and Strauss.

As mentioned above, the second broad category of sources consists of verbal or written evidence. This includes both handwritten (archival) and printed materials. Both exist in great abundance for the Reformation period. There can be no question of entering into a discussion here of sixteenth-century verbal documentation as a whole. Instead, I shall limit myself to treating a few printed editions of primary sources which are of special relevance to the researcher working on art related topics. Once again, the emphasis will be on the German lands.

Collections of documents have been published pertaining to the art history of a region or locality as well as to individual artists. Two examples of the former type shall be mentioned. First, there is a three-volume set by Hans Rott embracing southwest Germany and German-speaking Switzerland in the fifteenth and sixteenth centuries.[65] This forms an extremely valuable publication reproducing selected archival documents from a large number of communities including Strasbourg, Basel, Zurich, Constance, Ulm, Memmingen, Nördlingen, and St. Gall. The documents are grouped first by locality and then into sections dealing chronologically with the practitioners of the different art forms. A lengthy general index of artists also is subdivided according to the medium in which the various masters worked.

One of the great German art centers conspicuously—if understandably—absent from the Hans Rott collection is the free imperial

[63]Hollstein (1954ff), 1: "Introduction."
[64]Hollstein (1954ff), 9:5.
[65]Rott (1933–38).

city of Nuremberg. Fortunately, we have other publications providing documents from that community. Among them the most important perhaps is a three-volume work by Theodor Hampe which reproduces city council decrees relating to the arts during the period 1474–1618.[66] When consulted with other types of primary materials the Hampe collection is an exceedingly valuable resource for research pertaining to Albrecht Dürer's native town.

Dürer's own writings represent an outstanding example of the kind of evidence which can be used to supplement official governmental records. Dürer was a rarity among northern European artists in that he expressed himself so well in verbal form. Theoretical treatises, letters, autobiographical writings, poems, a travel diary, and inscriptions and notations of various kinds all have been preserved for posterity. Fortunately, we now possess them in a magnificent three-volume critical edition by Hans Rupprich.[67] The inclusion of other contemporary writings mentioning Dürer further enhances the usefulness of this superb collection. Only a fraction of the Dürer corpus has ever been translated into our language, most of it contained in a book first published in the nineteenth century by the English scholar, William Martin Conway. The appearance in 1958 of a second, American edition of Conway has helped make these selections more widely available.[68]

In the case of Cranach the Elder, we have much less surviving literary evidence than exists for Dürer. What written materials we possess from the Wittenberg master's own hand consist largely of business letters and other practical notations, i.e., bills, receipts, and the like. Further, according to Werner Schade, "the archive documents for the life and work of the Cranach family of artists have not yet been completely collected."[69] Schade himself, however, provides a most helpful chronological listing of Cranach sources, as well as their locations.[70] In recent years, moreover, selections of Cranach documents have been published by Walther Scheidig, Heinz Lüdecke, and Johannes Jahn.[71]

At various points reference has been made to publications that we

[66]Hampe (1904).
[67]Dürer (1956–69).
[68]Dürer (1958).
[69]Schade (1980), 401.
[70]Schade (1980), 401–53.
[71]Walther Scheidig in Lüdecke, ed., (1953a); Lüdecke, ed., (1953b), *passim;* Jahn (1972), 587–662.

may categorize as research tools. Certainly among the most valuable of all such scholarly aids are bibliographies, which for the field of art history come in numerous forms. Leading examples of the major types, including the indispensable serial bibliographies, are well described in Ehresmann's excellent handbook.[72] For recent literature on art and Reformation, however, one should also consult the annual *Supplement: Literature Review* volume of the journal *Archive for Reformation History*.

In conclusion, it seems appropriate to take note of a new series of largely topical critical bibliographies on northern European art now in preparation. Some of the individual volumes, when completed, undoubtedly will prove useful to readers of the present essay. The series is under the general editorship of Professor Craig Harbison of the University of Massachusetts and will be published by G. K. Hall of Boston. A partial listing as of the moment includes the following titles: Peter and Linda Parshall, *Art and the Reformation*; Lloyd Benjamin, *Art and Religious Devotion in the 15th Century*; Charles Minott, *Germany, 1500–1550*; James Snyder, *Dutch Art, 15th & 16th Centuries*; Thomas Kaufman, *Central Europe, 1550–1620*; James Mundy, *Bruges, 1480–1550*; and Larry Silver, *Antwerp, 1480–1550*. These bibliographies currently are scheduled to begin appearing in print in about 1983.[73]

Bibliography

Works Cited

Andersson, Christiane D., Review of Craig Harbison, *The Last Judgment in Sixteenth Century Northern Europe: A Study of the Relation Between Art and the Reformation*, *The Art Bulletin* 60 (1978): 553–55.

———, "Religiöse Bilder Cranachs im Dienste der Reformation," *Humanismus und Reformation als kulturelle Kräfte in der deutschen Geschichte*, ed. Lewis W. Spitz (Berlin, 1981): 43–79.

---

[72]Ehresmann (1979), esp. nos. 27, 28 (28–29). For German regional art bibliographies, Ehresmann's list should be supplemented with that in Besterman (1971), 44–47. 44–47.

[73]I owe this information to the kindness of Professor Harbison.

Baxandall, Michael, *The Limewood Sculptors of Renaissance Germany* (New Haven, 1980).

Besterman, Theodore, *Art and Architecture: A Bibliography of Bibliographies* (Totowa, 1971).

Brady, Thomas A. Jr., "The Social Place of a German Renaissance Artist: Hans Baldung Grien (1484/85–1545) at Strasbourg," *Central European History* 8 (1975): 295–315.

Buck, Lawrence P. and Zophy, Jonathan W., eds., *The Social History of the Reformation* (Columbus, 1972).

Campenhausen, Hans Frhr. v., "Die Bilderfrage in der Reformation," *Zeitschrift für Kirchengeschichte* 68 (1957): 96–128. (a)

———, "Zwingli und Luther zur Bilderfrage," *Das Gottesbild im Abendland*, ed. Günter Howe (Witten and Berlin, 1957): 139–72. (b)

Cantor, Norman F. and Schneider, Richard I., *How to Study History* (New York, 1967).

Christensen, Carl C., *Art and the Reformation in Germany* (Athens, Ohio and Detroit, 1979).

Crew, Phyllis Mack, *Calvinist Preaching and Iconoclasm in the Netherlands 1544–1569* (Cambridge, 1978).

Dürer, Albrecht, *Dürer: Schriftlicher Nachlass*, ed. Hans Rupprich, 3 vols. (Berlin, 1956–69).

———, *The Writings of Albrecht Dürer*, trans. and ed. William Martin Conway (New York, 1958).

———, *Albrecht Dürer 1471–1971: Exhibition Catalog of the German National Museum in Nürnberg* (Munich, 1971).

Ehresmann, Donald L., "The Brazen Serpent: A Reformation Motif in the Works of Lucas Cranach the Elder and his Workshop," *Marsyas* 13 (1966–67): 32–47.

———, *Fine Arts: A Bibliographic Guide to Basic Reference Works, Histories, and Handbooks*, 2nd ed. (Littleton, Colo., 1979).

Eire, Carlos M.N., "Idolatry and the Reformation: A Study of the Protestant Attack on Catholic Worship in Germany, Switzerland and France, 1500–1580" (Ph.D. Dissertation, Yale University, 1979).

Feist, Peter H., Ullmann, Ernst, Brendler, Gerhard, eds., *Lucas Cranach: Künstler und Gesellschaft* (Wittenberg, 1973).

Fleming, Gerald, "On the Origin of the Passional Christi and Antichristi and Lucas Cranach the Elder's Contribution to Reformation Polemics in the Iconography of the Passional," *Gutenberg Jahrbuch 1973* (1973): 351–68.

Freedberg, David A., "Iconoclasm and Painting in the Netherlands, 1566–1609" (Ph.D. Dissertation, Oxford University, 1972).

———, "The Problem of Images in Northern Europe and its Repercussions in the Netherlands," *Hafnia: Copenhagen Papers in the History of Art 1976* (Copenhagen, 1977): 24–45. (a)

———, "The Structure of Byzantine and European Iconoclasm," *Iconoclasm*, ed. Anthony Bryer and Judith Herrin (Birmingham, 1977): 165–77. (b)

Friedländer, Max J. and Rosenberg, Jakob, *The Paintings of Lucas Cranach*, rev. ed. (Ithaca, N.Y., 1978).

Galpern, A.N., *The Religions of the People in Sixteenth-Century Champagne* (Cambridge, Mass., 1976).

Garside, Charles Jr., *Zwingli and the Arts* (New Haven, 1966).

Geisberg, Max, *The German Single-Leaf Woodcut: 1500–1550*, 4 vols., rev. and ed. Walter L. Strauss (New York, 1974).

Haebler, Hans Carl von, *Das Bild in der evangelischen Kirche* (Berlin, 1957).

Hampe, Theodor, ed., *Nürnberger Ratsverlässe über Kunst und Künstler im Zeitalter der Spätgotik und Renaissance*, 3 vols. (Vienna, 1904).

Harbison, Craig, "Introduction to the Exhibition," *Symbols in Transformation* (1969): 15–34.

———, "Dürer and the Reformation: The Problem of the Re-dating of the *St. Philip* Engraving," *The Art Bulletin* 58 (1976): 368–73. (a)

———, *The Last Judgment in Sixteenth Century Northern Europe: A Study in the Relationship between Art and the Reformation* (New York, 1976). (b)

———, "Reformation Iconography: Problems and Attitudes," *Print Review* 5 (1976): 78–87. (c)

Hentschel, Walter, *Dresdner Bildhauer des 16. und 17. Jahrhunderts* (Weimar, 1966).

Hollstein, F. W. H., *German Engravings, Etchings and Woodcuts: ca. 1400–1700* (Amsterdam, 1954ff).

Jahn, Johannes, *Lucas Cranach d. Ä. 1472–1553: Das gesamte graphische Werk* (Munich, 1972).

Kibish, Christine O., "Lucas Cranach's *Christ Blessing the Chil-*

dren: A Problem of Lutheran Iconography," *The Art Bulletin* 37 (1955): 196–203.

Kirschbaum, Engelbert, ed., *Lexikon der christlichen Ikonographie,* Vol. 4 (Rome, 1972).

Klingenburg, Karl-Heinz, "Die Wandlung des Bildes vom gemeinen Manne als Ausdruck der gesellschaftlichen Rangerhöhung der unteren Volksschichten," Feist, Ullmann, Brendler (1973): 145–49 and 214–16.

Koepplin, Dieter and Falk, Tilman, *Lukas Cranach: Gemälde, Zeichnungen, Druckgraphik,* 2 vols. (Basel and Stuttgart, 1974, 1976).

Kuspit, Donald B., "Dürer and the Lutheran Image," *Art in America* 63 (1975): 56–61.

Lüdecke, Heinz, ed., *Lucas Cranach der Ältere: Der Künstler und seine Zeit* (Berlin, 1953). (a)

———, ed., *Lucas Cranach der Ältere im Spiegel seiner Zeit: Aus Urkunden, Chroniken, Briefen, Reden und Gedichten* (Berlin, 1953). (b)

Mende, Matthias, *Dürer-Bibliographie* (Wiesbaden, 1971).

Moxey, Keith P.F., *Pieter Aertsen, Joachim Beuckelaer, and the Rise of Secular Painting in the Context of the Reformation* (New York, 1977).

Oertel, Hermann, "Das protestantische Abendmahlsbild im niederdeutschen Raum und seine Vorbilder," *Niederdeutsche Beiträge zur Kunstgeschichte* 13 (1974): 223–70.

———, "Das Bild in Bibeldrucken vom 15. bis zum 18. Jahrhundert," *Jahrbuch der Gesellschaft für niedersächsische Kirchengeschichte* 75 (1977): 9–37.

Panofsky, Erwin, "Comments on Art and Reformation," *Symbols in Transformation* (Princeton, 1969): 9–14.

Pfeiffer, Gerhard, "Albrecht Dürer's *Four Apostles:* A Memorial Picture from the Reformation Era," Buck and Zophy (1972): 271–296.

Phillips, John, *The Reformation of Images: Destruction of Art in England, 1535–1660* (Berkeley, 1973).

Poscharsky, Peter, *Die Kanzel: Erscheinungsform im Protestantismus bis zum Ende des Barocks* (Gütersloh, 1963).

Reingrabner, Gustav, "Zur Kunst der Reformation in Österreich," *Jahrbuch der Gesellschaft für die Geschichte des Protestantismus in Österreich* 94 (1978): 7–66.

Rott, Hans, *Quellen und Forschungen zur südwestdeutschen und schweizerischen Kunstgeschichte im XV. und XVI. Jahrhundert*, 3 vols. (Stuttgart, 1933–38).

Saunders, Eleanor A., "A Commentary on Iconoclasm in Several Print Series by Maarten van Heemskerck," *Simiolus* 10 (1978–79): 59–83.

Schade, Werner, *Die Malerfamilie Cranach* (Dresden, 1974).

———, *Cranach: A Family of Master Painters*, trans. Helen Sebba (New York, 1980).

Scribner, R. W., "Images of the Peasant, 1514–1525," *The German Peasant War of 1525*, ed. Janos Bak (London, 1976): 29–48.

———, *For the Sake of Simple Folk: Popular Propaganda for the German Reformation* (Cambridge, 1981).

Seebass, Gottfried, "Dürer's Stellung in der reformatorischen Bewegung," *Albrecht Dürers Umwelt: Festschrift zum 500. Geburtstag Albrecht Dürers am 21. Mai 1971* (Nuremberg, 1971): 101–31.

Stechow, Wolfgang, ed., *Northern Renaissance Art 1400–1600: Sources and Documents* (Englewood Cliffs, N.J., 1966).

———, "Recent Dürer Studies," *The Art Bulletin* 56 (1974): 259–70.

Stirm, Margarete, *Die Bilderfrage in der Reformation* (Gütersloh, 1977).

Strauss, Walter L., *The German Single-Leaf Woodcut 1550–1600: A Pictorial Catalogue*, 3 vols. (New York, 1975).

Strieder, Peter, "Albrecht Dürers 'Vier Apostel' im Nürnberger Rathaus," *Festschrift Klaus Lankheit*, ed. Wolfgang Hartmann (Cologne, 1973): 151–57.

———, "Folk Art Sources of Cranach's Woodcut of the Sacred Heart," *Print Review* 5 (1976): 160–66.

Symbols in Transformation: Iconographic Themes at the Time of the Reformation, Exhibition Catalog (Princeton, 1969).

Thulin, Oskar, *Cranach-Altäre der Reformation* (Berlin, 1955).

Vlam, Grace A. H., "The Calling of Saint Matthew in Sixteenth-Century Flemish Painting," *The Art Bulletin* 59 (1977): 561–70.

Wandersleb, Martin, "Luthertum und Bilderfrage im Fürstentum Braunschweig—Wolfenbüttel und in der Stadt Braunschweig im Reformationsjahrhundert," *Jahrbuch der Gesellschaft für niedersächsische Kirchengeschichte* 66 (1968): 18–80; 67 (1969): 24–90; 68 (1970): 208–72.

Warnke, Martin, "Durchbrochene Geschichte? Die Bilderstürme

der Wiedertäufer in Münster 1534/1535," *Bildersturm: Die Zerstörung des Kunstwerks*, ed. Martin Warnke (Munich, 1973): 65–98, 159–67.

Wiederanders, Gerlinde, *Albrecht Dürers theologische Anschauungen* (Berlin, 1975).

Zschelletzschky, Herbert, *Die "drei gottlosen Maler" von Nürnberg: Sebald Beham, Barthel Beham und Georg Pencz. Historische Grundlagen und ikonologische Probleme ihrer Graphik zu Reformations- und Bauernkriegszeit* (Leipzig, 1975).

The English Reformation

Paul Seaver

A long generation ago it was still possible for the Regius Professor of Modern History at Oxford to write without indulging in undue scholarly caution that "the one definite thing which can be said about the Reformation in England is that it was an act of State."[1] Other things had been and would be said about the English Reformation, many asserted with great conviction, but it was precisely to escape from such partisan dogmatism that Maurice Powicke sought to focus on the constitutional act rather than on its religious significance. Both traditions, the religious partisan and the constitutional, found powerful voices in the 1950s: Philip Hughes's magisterial *The Reformation in England*, the three volumes of which appeared between 1951 and 1954, was a work which in the aftermath of Vatican II now seems to smack more of Trent than of our own era; and G.R. Elton's *England under the Tudors*, which appeared in 1953, gave a new life to the old and honorable tradition of constitutional history and presented a new interpretation of the Henrician Reformation which left it almost devoid of religious meaning. Thomas Cromwell, who along with Thomas Wolsey was one of the traditional villains of the piece, emerged as the great architect of the royal supremacy in the Church, the creator of the unitary State and the supremacy of statute, and although this product of Elton's "younger and more reckless days" has been subjected to almost continuous revision and refinement, not least by Elton himself, the politics of the Henrician Reformation and the role of Thomas Cromwell have not lost their centrality.[2]

Nevertheless, in the course of the past twenty years the tidy picture of religious reform as part of a larger, government sponsored

[1]Powicke (1941), 1.
[2]The judgment is Elton's (1977), V; for Cromwell's enforcement of the Reformation and for his role as a reformer of Church and State, see Elton (1972) and (1973).

transformation has been infinitely complicated by other concerns and questions. As Christopher Haigh recently noted in an acute reflection on the different problems facing historians of the German and English Reformations, "while . . . scholars working on the German Reformation were trying to establish why their Reformation was as it was, specialists on the English Reformation still had not decided what their Reformation was actually like."[3] Nevertheless, one suspects that few would be prepared to argue that the loss of clarity and simplicity has been an unmitigated intellectual tragedy, for the 'act of state' model of the Reformation painted a picture of England that was an anomaly in Western Europe, a passive society composed of a largely ignorant and indifferent laity and a demoralized clergy unable or unprepared to resist the impress of the successive Tudor Reformations—Henrician, Edwardian, Marian and finally Elizabethan.

The end of the age of heroic simplicities and the beginning of the modern age of rich confusion was signalized by the publication in 1964 of A.G. Dickens' *The English Reformation*. While giving due attention to Crown initiatives and parliamentary statutes, Dickens nevertheless insisted that

> so far as the new beliefs are concerned, it must be acknowledged that, irrespective of his relations with Rome, Henry VIII could not have frozen the English in their religious posture of the year 1530. Even during the last seven years of his reign, when he was attempting to check Protestantism, it was spreading more rapidly than ever before, and it captured the government immediately upon his death. When we are tempted to underestimate its expansive capacities, we should recall that in the Netherlands, in Scotland and elsewhere, it soon played havoc with the plans of kings and governments.[4]

Religious change, rather than the acts of government, was seen as central, and the Reformation in England, while lacking the charismatic leadership of a Luther, was seen as taking place within the context of larger European changes of attitude and conviction. Secondly, Dickens saw the laity as anything but passive. "Protestantism was emphatically never limited to the clerical group which acknowledged the leadership of Cranmer or to the knot of 'advanced' courtiers under Edward Seymour. . . . " "Amongst the substantial

[3]Haigh (1979), 88.
[4]Dickens (1964), 108.

classes, and even amongst the populace of London, the Home Counties and East Anglia, these opinions were making still more rapid progress during the last decade of Henry VIII."[5] Thirdly, as befitting a Yorkshireman, Dickens was well aware of the depth of provincial divisions with traditional English society and recognized that, while the growth of Protestantism in Essex might be attributable to indigenous forces, the conversion of Newcastle and Hull was largely the consequence of a deliberate campaign of evangelical preaching.[6]

For all the richness of its detail and the incisiveness of its analysis, Dickens' *The English Reformation* proved to be important less perhaps as a new synthesis than as an agenda for the future. Although he followed the traditional chronological framework, beginning with the reign of Henry VIII with backward glances at late medieval Lollardy and the *devotio moderna* and ending with the Elizabethan Settlement, the central place he gave to religious change, to the conversion of ordinary Englishmen to the new evangel, inevitably raised the question whether the Reformation should not be seen as a long process, beginning perhaps with the Lollard manifesto of 1395—"we pray God of his endless goodness reform our Church, all out of joint, to the perfecting of the first beginning"[7]—and ending a century and a half later with the penetration of "the Dark Corners of the Land" in the course of what Michael Mullett, following Dickens, has recently called "the second English Reformation."[8] Secondly, Dickens not only opened up the question of the traditional chronological framework but also that of the speed of change, for although Dickens had pictured Protestantism as a potent force already by the end of the 1540s, his emphasis on the centrality of religious change and his recognition of provincial differences raised the possibility of distinctively local rates of change. His own recent article on Robert Parkyn, who died in 1569 and whom Dickens called "the last medieval Englishman," suggests in fact how much change may have depended on the passing of a generation whose formative experiences antedated both Edwardian Protestantism and Tridentine Catholicism.[9]

Dickens' seminal work suggested other dimensions to the problem

[5]Ibid., 193.
[6]Ibid., 235.
[7]Cross (1976), 9.
[8]Hill (1974); Mullett (1980), 4.
[9]Dickens (1975).

besides the chronological. First, his work raised the vexed and perhaps unanswerable question of the relative importance of Crown
and Councillior initiative on the one hand and of popular evangelism on the other. And secondly, by dealing with the Reformation
not only as doctrinal change but also as manifest in changing attitudes and social relations, his interpretation suggested the need to
examine the relationship of religion and popular lay culture. As
Thomas Brady recently noted in another context, Reformation history has been bifurcated between " 'traditionalists,' who study the
historical context in order to illuminate the Reformation, and 'mod-
ernists,' who study the Reformation in order to illuminate the society in which it occurred."[10] Without necessarily accepting the pejo-
rative implications of such nomenclature, it is nevertheless the case
that the "modernist" approach has led to work on the impact of religious change on social institutions and attitudes and to studies of the
consequences of the Reformation on popular culture and mentality.
Curiously, although Keith Thomas' equally seminal *Religion and
the Decline of Magic* was published a decade ago (1971), and although the importance of its anthropological approach was recognized immediately, it has had few imitators so far. Nevertheless, the
consequence has clearly been to give lay society and lay attitudes
and initiative an importance they never had before, and it is surely
no accident that the most recent textbook on the Reformation mani-
fests the newer broad chronology and has as its main theme "the triumph of the laity in the English Church."[11]

The newer themes presented by the social history of the Reformation and by the role of the Reformation in English social history have
not replaced older concerns. Rather, Reformation studies are presently being pursued on all fronts. What follows is a necessarily incomplete picture, taken, as it were, in mid-flight and largely confined to the past half-dozen years. Some of the salient features appear clearly enough, but the rapid motion has left others blurred
and indistinct.

First of all, it now seems evident that the late medieval movement
of reform associated with Wyclif can no longer simply be seen, at
best, as preparing a kind of seed-bed for sixteenth-century Protestantism, a lower-class readership for Tyndale's New Testament, or,
at worst, as discrediting Biblically based reform as abberrant ex-

[10]Brady (1979), 90–91.
[11]Cross (1976).

tremism and, hence, as making the reception of Protestantism or indeed of any reform of the Church more difficult.[12] Lollardy, if Michael Wilks is correct, must now be seen as two quite distinct, although connected, movements: a government-sponsored reformation launched as the culmination of a long conflict with the papacy in the later fourteenth century, as the outcome in fact "of the effective seizure of ecclesiastical sovereignty by the monarchy of Edward III;" and, secondly and much later, a popular movement which remained after "its political power drained away and its adherents became detectable."[13] According to this view, "Wyclif had from the beginning considered himself to be the spokesman *par excellence* for the king and the court. The gospel of reform was something to be carried out from the central government by lay magnates and university-trained ecclesiastics after the fashion of the Carolingian *missi dominici* as part of the day to day duties of administering the realm, whilst Wyclif himself acted like a latter-day Alcuin at the center advising them in how to do it."[14] This "autonomous national church" was then destroyed by a successful reassertion of the hierocratic point of view in the Lancastrian period, by the defeat of the so-called "Lollard knights," the remnant of the Wycliffite court party, and by the repression of the popular movement this new national church had begun to generate.

Most research recently has focussed on what might be called the sectarian history of Lollardy. It seems evident that by the 1420s Lollardy was largely a lay heresy, but, if the sermons preached against it can be counted as evidence, nevertheless still a formidable one.[15] Although never more than a small minority, these "known" men and women survived in a handful of communities—London, Bristol, Coventry, the Chilterns, Kent, Essex, etc.—, nurtured their religious life in conventicles for Bible reading (it now seems beyond dispute that Wyclif was not responsible for the translation), and apparently experienced little difficulty in maintaining a viable existence for over a century without significant clerical leadership.[16] Although

---

[12]An interpretation sympathetic to this earlier view of K. B. McFarlane's is to be found in Dickinson (1979), 315–335, esp. 334. Despite its date of publication, Dickinson was not able to use Lambert (1977), Hudson (1978), or Wilks (1978).

[13]Wilks (1978), 68–69.

[14]*Ibid.*, 67.

[15]Haines (1972).

[16]Cross, (1978b); (1975); Brockwell (1980); Wilks (1975); Aston (1977), which has much to say about both the means to literacy and the appeal of literacy in a largely illiterate society.

Emma Mason has recently argued that "radical reform, in the guise of Wyclif, offered little scope for the pretensions of ordinary laymen," it is hard to square that with the assertion of a Suffolk Lollard "that every true man and woman being in charity is a priest," a notion which was to have a long, popular future ahead of it.[17] Women in particular found, not for the last time, that "unorthodoxy offered women outlets for religious activity that were not to be found in the established church," and Claire Cross has assembled considerable evidence for the fact that women seized their opportunity.[18]

What remains unclear is the ultimate fate of Lollard communities. Christopher Hill has pointed to the continuity of a number of ideas and practices stretching from the Lollards to the Civil War radicals, but should a communal continuity be posited as well?[19] Whether late Lollardy should be seen as an inchoate, largely leaderless lay movement, focusing on Bible reading and exegesis and easily absorbed into the new Protestantism, or whether late Lollardy with its lay assertiveness should be seen rather as leading to the misleadingly termed "anabaptist" heresies—to the sacramentaries of Henry VIII's late years, to the "free-willers" of Edward's and Mary's reigns, and to such "mechanic preachers" as Christopher Vitel who came to lead the English Familists in Elizabeth's reign—has not been definitively answered and perhaps cannot be. Nevertheless, Hill is not the only one to be struck by the geographical coincidence of old Lollardy and new Protestant heresy and heterodoxy.[20]

If Lollardy was the remnant of a failed Reformation, what can be said for the reforming impulse within the Church itself? For if a recent critique of the traditional view has any substance, rather than an unresponsive, essentially moribund "medieval" Church, we should picture instead a complex but vital institution still capable of change and renewal until overwhelmed by rising expectations the institution itself had nourished.[21] Late medieval monasticism has

[17]Mason (1976); Aston (1980), 452.
[18]Aston (1980), p. 441; Cross, (1978a).
[19]Hill (1978).
[20]Cross (1975), 278; see also Cross (1978b); Loades (1978) and (1979). Contrary to Loades' view, Patrick Collinson found evidence of popular heresy and organized conventicles in the mid-sixteenth century at Cranbrook and Tenterden in Kent, both old Lollard centers: (1980), 117–178. For recent work on Henry Hunt and the Free Will men and Christopher Vitel and the Familists, see Martin (1976), (1979), (1978); Moss (1975) and (1978).
[21]Duggan (1978).

traditionally been pictured as the weakest link in the chain of traditional ecclesiastical institutions, long since having lost its hold on lay charity and further emasculated by declining religious vocations. Yet a recent study of Glastonbury in its last years argues that "renaissance and renewal are words not too strong to characterise some aspects of that great community," and another study of Marmaduke Huby's abbacy at Fountains argues that his long years of leadership produced a "vigorous, prosperous monastic community, well-governed at every level, growing in numbers, and giving its recruits a thorough training, both within the house and at the schools. . . ."[22] The late medieval universities have had an equally bad press, but a recent study of fifteenth-century Oxford, while admitting that it was in "one of its less expansionist and exciting periods," nevertheless points to the "promotion of university theology as a spiritual, evangelical and deliberately anti-heretical cure for the ills of fifteenth-century society" as one of its few successes: "the Reformation was to succeed in an England which possessed more senior graduates in traditional medieval theology than at any time in its previous history."[23] Episcopal leadership was responsible for this emphasis on theological training, and John Morton's archiepiscopate has been recently characterized as "reform by centralization," which, if it led to too many and too visible jurisdictional battles, nevertheless was a policy that had been successful under Ximenes in Spain and might have proved so in England as well, but for the accidents of Wolsey's character and Henry's dynastic difficulties.[24] Although the evidence is still fragmentary, it suggests institutional recovery. "The Reformation may suggest that the Church did not move fast enough in anticipating the religious needs of the new men of the Renaissance, but the [episcopal] registers indicate that at least the Church made a serious effort along traditional lines to offer the people of late medieval England a better parish life than that of their ancestors."[25]

It may be that we have posed the question badly. It is at least arguable that no reform of ecclesiastical structures either before or after the Reformation could answer all the criticisms levied against the Church by its lay and clerical critics nor accommodate all the

[22]Dunning (1977), 214; Baker (1977), 209.
[23]Dobson (1978), 215.
[24]Harper-Bill (1978), 20.
[25]Frankforter (1977), 224.

demands or pressures put upon it. For example, the demand for an educated, preaching parochial clergy was voiced from one end of the sixteenth-century to the other, from Chancellor William Melton's exhortation to the York ordinands in 1510 to the Puritan surveys of the clergy collected in the *Seconde Parte of a Register* in the 1580s. The number of graduate ordinands had been rising at the end of the fifteenth century; it was still rising at the end of the sixteenth; but "in 1584 only 14 per cent of the clergy of Coventry and Lichfield diocese were graduates . . . , and by 1602/3 the percentage had only risen to 24 per cent."[26] In any event, too many remained indifferent preachers or "dumb dogges," and the laity experimented with hired lecturers and such innovatory structures as the London and Norwich Feofees for Impropriations.[27] On the other hand, some institutions of the late medieval church retained their vital popularity until destroyed by the Reformation. Although the last miraculous cure attributed to Becket's shrine took place in 1474, more than 300 miracles were recorded in connection with Henry VI's tomb at Windsor in the last decades of the century; as Finucane concludes, "pilgrimage, then, especially to the 'new' shrines, was still important to many . . . in the later Middle Ages and sixteenth century, in spite of the growing criticisms by reformers."[28] Similarly, in his recent study of chantries, Kreider noted that "on the eve of the Reformation chantries were still being founded in all parts of the realm, even in London. . . . For many Englishmen from all parts of the realm the Reformation was therefore to be an intensely painful experience."[29] Joyful and liberating for some, the Reformation was painful, as all revolutions are, for many, and resisted actively or passively far more widely than the usual description of the magisterial Reformation allows for.[30] Chantries and pilgrimages were clear targets for Protestant reformers; Kreider's and Finucane's studies remind us of how little we still know about late medieval popular belief and practice and about the survival of such ideas, attitudes and

[26]O'Day (1979), 132.

[27]Seaver (1970), but see Collinson (1975).

[28]Finucane (1977), 194–195, 202.

[29]Kreider (1979), 91–92; see also Kitching (1977), 130. This latter article presents a valuable survey of what is presently known and what questions remain to be answered about the dissolutions and their impact.

[30]One of the reasons Elton (1972) is so important a work is that it gives us a glimpse of the widespread foot-dragging and resentment present even in the early stages of the Henrician Reformation.

habitual practices into the increasingly hostile world of sixteenth-century Protestant England.[31]

In the history of the Reformation in England pride of place is still given to the 1530s, to Cromwell's decade, and the fact that the centrality of those years seems beyond dispute is no small testimony to the continued dominance of the views of G.R. Elton. However, if we continue to see the period largely in his terms, or in reaction to his views, it is nevertheless the case that his views have changed substantially in recent years. Whereas he formerly saw an abrupt break occuring when Thomas Cromwell gained the king's ear in 1532 and put an end to the years of drift which had followed Wolsey's fall in 1529, Elton now sees the 30s as a culmination of several decades of development during which the call for the reform of the commonwealth became increasingly insistent, found a voice in governing circles in the writings of Edmund Dudley and Sir Thomas More among others, but failed to be translated into effective policy until Cromwell recognized that reform of the commonwealth was only possible under the aegis of the sovereign, centralized state. Henry's desperate need for a divorce became, then, the occasion rather than the cause of the breach with Rome and the Royal Supremacy a means of articulating the central character of the new polity. However, rather than a secularly minded *politique* who would, "as the world stood, believe even as his master the king believed," Elton now sees Cromwell as a Protestant whose "sincere devotion to the Bible . . . supplied one of the driving forces to an essentially political temperament, the principled undertone and transcendental justification of labours that concentrated upon reforming the earthly existence of men by reconstructing the state." In fact, Cromwell had "become convinced that only a form of Protestantism could serve the polity he was building."[32] Further, Elton still insists that "one feature . . .

[31]For example, Phythian-Adams has shown how vital the Corpus Christi pagents were to the civic culture of Coventry, even in the face of the crisis the city experienced in the 1520s and 1530s: (1979), 264. Much pagentry disappeared with the abolition of gilds and chantries, but the Corpus Christi pagents survived until 1579. Why did it survive so long, and what did it mean to the citizens of that increasingly Protestant town?

[32]Elton (1977), 172. Given Elton's apparent conviction that Cromwell saw some form of Protestantism as necessary to the "polity he was building," it may be a mistake to formulate Elton's current thesis, as Brendan Bradshaw does in an acute review, as holding that "Cromwell appears as a politically minded protestant who determined to construct a sovereign state as a means to the purification of religion and the renewal of society, to reform the commonwealth, body and soul." Bradshaw (1979), 462. At least at times Elton still seems to see Cromwell as viewing reformed religion as a necessary means, not as an end in itself.

above all others distinguishes the reformation in England and sets it apart from its fellows in the Protestant camp, even in such regions of monarchical reforms as Denmark and Sweden, and that is its political structure. The newly established royal supremacy and the preservation of an old system of episcopal government are the most notable hallmarks of the Church of England in the sixteenth century and after. They came first, before the genuine reformation had even begun, and they were the deliberate achievement of the founders, Henry VIII and Thomas Cromwell."[33]

Rather than offering a new consensus and synthesis, Elton's *Reform and Reformation* seems instead to have signalized the renewal of interest now manifest in the early years of the Reformation. Recent studies by J. J. Scarisbrick and by J. A. Guy of Cardinal Wolsey suggest that that paradoxical prelate may not have been as much a stranger to reform in Church and Commonwealth as has sometimes been suggested,[34] which doubtless helps to explain why the likes of Sir Thomas More and Thomas Cromwell accepted him as patron.[35] Nothing succeeds like success: what is needed perhaps is someone to undertake the melancholy task of chronicling the Reformation of the 1520s, the Catholic Reformation that failed. By then even those bastions of the establishment, the Inns of Court, had been infected with heresy, and Gordon Rupp sees in Fisher's 1526 sermon against heretics, delivered at St. Paul's, a symbol of a regime now on the defensive and about to be overwhelmed by "an immense flood of quite unstoppable ideas."[36]

The initial stages of the Henrician Reformation proper have come to seem increasingly complex. Pursuing a line first suggested by Scarisbrick, Steven Haas has recently argued that there was "a specific theory of divine-right absolutist sovereignty already in wide circulation by 1529 which Henry knew well and acted upon in 1530–32" before an effective propaganda campaign against the papacy was launched on behalf of Henry's schismatic policies in the years after 1532; further, he has suggested that the Boleyns had in 1529 brought William Tyndale's work on Christian obedience to the

[33]Elton (1979), 15.

[34]Scarisbrick (1978); Guy (1977). Contemporaries had as much trouble as we do in seeing this side of Wolsey, for which Wolsey himself was largely to blame. See, e.g., Fisher (1978).

[35]For Thomas More's relationship to the great Cardinal, see Scarisbrick (1977), and Guy (1980a).

[36]Fisher (1977); Rupp (1980), 18.

attention of the king who not only gave it an "enthusiastic reception" but at least briefly sought to recruit that difficult theologian for service in his campaign against the Pope.[37] Several years ago Scarisbrick suggested that an important collection of draft bills which offered a comprehensive program of reform of Church and State, and which Elton had supposed was a product of the Cromwellian reformers in 1534, might in fact have been the last product of Sir Thomas More's reforming efforts as Lord Chancellor in 1531; J. A. Guy has now argued for the date 1530 and for the authorship of the common lawyer, Christopher St. German.[38] Whatever its provenance, it now seems increasingly obvious that Cromwell was much more successful as the architect of the Royal Supremacy and the sovereign state than as a reformer of Church and Commonwealth.[39] How authoritarian a twist the Cromwellians gave to their reform is symbolized in a sense by Starkey's treatment of the concept of adiaphora, traditionally an area of Christian liberty.[40] In all fairness, it must be granted that the difficulty in obtaining obedience, to say nothing of active support, was a major one, recognized from the outset in the efforts to promote Lutheran notions of a divine kingship. As John Yost has recently noted, "we need to give more attention than has been customary in recent research to the importance of disestablishing the old order as a necessary first step in developing a new order;"[41] Elton's *Policy and Police*, published almost a decade ago (1972), remains the one major attempt to explore this complex of problems.

Despite the initial dependence on Lutheran ideas of divine kingship, it is now clear that even Tyndale, perhaps the most Lutheran of the early reformers, had by 1530 "emerged from Luther's shadow."[42] Lutheran teachings on justification were shared by all protestants, but Tyndale, Cranmer, and Latimer all broke with the Lutherans on the divisive doctrine of the Real Presence.[43] The crucial

[37]Haas, (1979), 353, and (1980), esp. notes 9 and 10; see also Alsop (1980).

[38]Scarisbrick (1977); Guy (1980b).

[39]See, e.g., Slavin (1977); Block (1977), and Bowker (1977); for the failure of commonwealth reform, see Bradshaw (1979), esp. 466–469.

[40]Mayer (1980), esp. 47. On the other hand, Yost has argued that "the greatest religious change in the early English Reformation was a more sensitive moral and social consciousness that stressed the responsibility of the Christian in regard to the problem of the present world." Yost (1975), 202.

[41]Yost (1978), 446.

[42]Cargill-Thompson (1979), 32; see also Williams (1975).

[43]Hall (1979).

connection with Bullinger's Zurich began as early as 1536, a connection to Switzerland and the Rhineland which was not only due to the importance of the great Strassburg reformers, Bucer and Martyr, in the early years of Edward's reign, but also, as Claire Cross has shown, to a steady if small influx of Swiss students to the two English universities.[44]

If the doctrinal position of the nascent English Reformation was characterized more by movement than by clear definition for the first two generations at least, the political side—the definition and use of the new royal supremacy—was not much less confused. How episcopal authority was to be exercised in the light of the new Supremacy was a problem raised by Cranmer's initial metropolitical visitation, and, as Margaret Bowker has cogently argued, "the danger of leaving the question open was that the royal supremacy would effectively be lost to the bishops, and particularly to the archbishop, who would visit with the king's support but on the authority of his episcopal office held and exercised by divine authority."[45] Even the dissolution of the monastic church now seems rather haphazard what with a handful of refoundations taking place in 1536–37 and the final decision for outright destruction occuring only in late 1537 or 1538.[46]

On the whole there has been more revisionist work recently on the politics of the 1540–1560 era than on the various religious settlements of those years. M. L. Bush, Barrett L. Beer and Dale Hoak have given us a new and rather unattractive Somerset and a partially rehabilitated Northumberland, but they have given scant attention to the Edwardian religious Reformation.[47] On the other hand, the hopes and expectations that Cardinal Pole had for the Marian reaction have finally come into clear focus, largely due to the work of R. H. Pogson, who argues convincingly that the Catholic revival was not so much doomed by the impossibility of the task as by the

---

[44]Cross (1979a); both reformed theological traditions have recently received treatments useful to historians: Kendall (1979), and Baker (1980).

[45]Bowker (1975), 234; for later developments in the working out of this complex relationship, see Cross (1977).

[46]Hallam (1978); for a survey of what is known about the disposal of monastic and chantry property, see Kitching (1977).

[47]Booty has recently argued that in the Prayer Books, Homilies and Articles, "Cranmer and others were attempting to deal with England's social/economic plight and the resultant unrest, particularly amongst the commons." (1976), 67. The hypothesis is interesting, but the evidence offered, while suggestive, is too sketchy to be conclusive.

"brevity and political misfortune of the reign."[48] The Elizabethan Settlement, too, has appeared in a new guise. Thirty years ago J. E. Neale saw it as the product of a compromise between an embattled queen and the radical Protestants in the House of Commons, cheered on by their friends among the returning Marian exiles. Instead Winthrop S. Hudson argues that "a conspicuous feature of the Elizabethan regime at its outset was the harmony that prevailed between the queen, the council, the Commons, and the forces of Protestant reform. . . . In spite of the confusion and delay in reaching a religious settlement occasioned by a recalcitrant house of lords and by disconcerting changes of signals in the lower house, for almost a year after Elizabeth's accession there were few signs of any fundamental disagreement between the queen and those who constituted the core of her support."[49] If short-lived, this unity was real and based, Hudson shows, on what he calls the Cambridge connection, common associations among the architects of the Settlement stretching back in some cases to the mid-1530s.

Although frequently taken as the *terminus ad quem* of the English Reformation, what was remarkable about the Settlement was how little it settled. Fundamental issues such as the doctrine of predestination and the nature of the Eucharist, which had divided English Protestants in the mid-century, remained unresolved.[50] There was not even agreement on what pure and primitive church the reformers hoped to restore.[51] Certainly the episcopal leadership saw itself not as entering into some kind of Protestant Promised Land, but rather as resuming the task of conversion and reform, scarcely underway a decade earlier, and doing so under formidable handicaps both of clerical ignorance and diminished economic resources.[52] Even as late as 1575 "the godly and well-affected" hoped that Grindal's appointment as archbishop would permit the reforming of "some parts of these Romish dregs remaining."[53] However, if we use

[48]Pogson (1980), 126; see also Pogson (1975), and (1974). "Bloody" Bonner, who has always had a bad press, has finally received his just deserts (the reality is not much more attractive than the myth) in Alexander (1975). Thorp (1978) has recently suggested convincing reasons for seeing Wyatt's rebellion, contrary to David Loades, as having religious as well as political motivations, a position reached independently by Clark (1977), 87–98.
[49]Hudson (1980), p. 147.
[50]Hargrave (1978); Brink (1979).
[51]Luoma (1977).
[52]Booty (1979); Collinson (1979a), 85–106.
[53]Quoted in Collinson (1979b), 42.

the hopes of the "godly and well-affected" as our criteria, if we see the English Reformation as still an ongoing process until the godly lost their hope for the reform of Church and State and turned inward to their congregations and their own souls, we will find ourselves incorporating into a single process what Dickens with some reason has dubbed "the second Reformation" of the mid-seventeenth century.[54]

What is now clear is that, if attention is paid not simply to the religious settlements of kings, queens and Parliaments, but also to the creation of communities of Protestant clergy and laity, the process of the Reformation was a varied one, occuring at different dates and in some communities not at all or only in the form of resurgent Catholicism. In Canterbury and Sandwich Peter Clarke has shown that a Protestant group was already in existence in the early 1530s and had established a strong position in city government by the end of the decade, aided and abetted by the patronage of both Cranmer and Cromwell.[55] At Hull, on the other hand, Protestantism did not begin to gain converts in numbers until the 1570s when a lectureship was founded by the corporation with Grindal's encouragement, and at York a powerful clerical establishment backed by a sympathetic corporation insured continuity with the pre-Reformation past, a continuity broken only by the passing of a generation and by outside pressure exerted by the Earl of Huntingdon, who forced the magistrates to hire a town preacher in 1580.[56] County communities show a similar variation. In Suffolk a potent alliance between Protestant ministers and magistrates had been cemented by the 1570s; in Lancashire, despite the dedicated preaching of a generation of Puritan ministers, an indifferent when not hostile gentry and an active and effective Catholic mission had prevented any substantial Protestant success even by the end of the sixteenth century.[57] It is clearly a mistake to assume that the new evangel had only to be preached to be ac-

[54]Dickens (1964), 336. As Collinson notes, "the ultimate failure to bring to creative fruition what Grindal would have recognized as a Church rightly reformed was not forseen in 1583. Indeed, the vision of a godly church and commonwealth was as bright in the 1640s as at any time in the early history of the Reformation." (1979a), 284.

[55]Clark (1979b); (1977), ch. 2; cf. also Collinson (1980). Gloucester seems to have anticipated the official sanction of the government, generating "an active protestant following in the city" in the 1530s: see Clark (1979a), 181. See also Sheils (1977).

[56]Cross (1979b), and (1980).

[57]For Suffolk, see Collinson (1977); see also Seaver (1977). For Lancashire, see Haigh (1975), and (1977). For Durham, see James (1974); for the diocese of Chester, see Manning (1976).

cepted; as Christopher Haigh notes, "at the local level the Reformation was not a walkover for the Protestants, it was a real contest."[58]

Further, it is now evident that it was a contest waged by a clerical
establishment subject to rising expectations and falling resources, to
new professional standards coupled with new pressures from the
family obligations of married clergy, to new demands for a godly
discipline accompanied by a declining respect for the church courts.
The probing investigation of this institutional framework has been
one of the major developments in recent Reformation historiography, and the researches of a group of younger historians has now
produced a number of important articles and three substantial
monographs: Felicity Heal's on episcopal incomes, Ralph Houlbrooke's on ecclesiastical jurisdiction and courts, and Rosemary
O'Day's on the professionalization of the Protestant clergy.[59] The
episcopal leadership, castigated by Latimer for "their lording and
loitering," now appear in some respects more sinned against than
sinning. Forced into the unhappy role of tax collector, subjected to
the unremitting rapacity of crown and aristocracy, it is nevertheless
fair to say, as Houlbrooke does, that "for the first time . . . there
was established in England a body of bishops who were nearly all
normally resident in their dioceses, regular in their visitation and as-
siduous in preaching."[60] Although the anomalous medieval system of
patronage survived, minus the system of monastic titles, the standards of the parochial clergy had been transformed by the end of the
century, at least if a university education is taken as an adequate cri-
terion.[61] The disciplinary machinery of the church, unreformed if
by no means moribund at the outset of the Reformation, still contributed little to it: the Word was preached, the sacraments rightly
administered, but a godly discipline failed to materialize, and the
only jurisdictions that remained popular were those like probate
that served the interests of the laity.[62] It is hard to avoid the conclusion that the survival of so much of the medieval framework of the
ecclesiastical structure, largely unreformed into the sixteenth cen-

[58]Haigh (1979), 105.

[59]Heal (1980); Houlbrooke (1979); O'Day (1979).

[60]Houlbrooke (1977), 98; for taxation and the clerical economy generally, see Heal
(1976), and (1977); cf. Haigh (1976), and Hembry (1978). It is not clear that Protestant
bishops, burdened by family responsibilities, were more ruthless in exploiting their
temporalities than their Catholic colleagues, if Edmund Bonner was at all typical of
the latter: see Alexander (1978). For the wider consequences of episcopal impoverishment, see Sheils (1976).

[61]O'Day (1977), and (1976).

[62]Lander (1976); Houlbrooke (1976); Kitching (1976).

tury, was responsible in great measure both for the peculiar shape of
the English Reformation and for the ultimate frustration of the reforming impulse.

For all the great strides that have been made in our understanding
of the Reformation Church, what the laity made of all these actions
of priests and prelates, crowned heads and councillors, is much less
clear. David Palliser and Imogen Luxton, following Keith Thomas's
lead, have sketched some of the elements of the shift from ritual observance and local cults and traditions to a literate, Bible-based religious culture, a popular Reformation which Palliser notes had much
vaguer chronological boundaries than the official Reformation.[63]
The spiritualized household and the work ethic have recently been
the subject of revisionist treatments, although these constitute little
more than footnotes to previous work by Christopher Hill, and Lawrence Stone has commented briefly on the impact of the Reformation on the development of the companionate marriage as a social
and religious ideal.[64] Recent work on American Puritan sabbatari-
anism and attitudes toward death sheds light on English antecedents.[65] R. L. Greaves' forthcoming study of Elizabethan social
thought should tell us much about the new cultural norms the Reformation attempted to create, but only studies of individual expression, of families and small communities will tell us how Englishmen
experienced the upheaval of the Reformation and what type of reli-
giosity, what spiritual style, they came to adopt in consequence.[66]
Customs and traditions and the habits of mind that give them life
are relatively inaccessible, but even popular literature which historians have readily at hand has been largely neglected, with the notable exception of Bernard Capp's important study of almanacs.[67] We
have had three recent studies of apocalyptic thought in the English
Reformation, but we know virtually nothing about its impact.[68]
Were Puritanism and Protestant sectarianism the only two forms
popular lay piety took in the English Reformation? Did the "godly"
in one way or another encompass all Protestant Englishmen who responded positively, with "a sovereign and reviving joy" as Milton
put it, to the Reformation, and, if not, how shall we define the alter-

[63]Palliser (1977), and Luxton (1977).
[64]Todd (1980); O'Connell (1976); Seaver (1980); Stone (1977), esp. 135–142.
[65]Solberg (1977); Stannard (1977).
[66]Greaves (1981); Prest (1978), and Wrightson and Levine (1979) are exemplary of
what I mean.
[67]Capp (1979). Catechisms, on the other hand, have yet to receive systematic study.
[68]Ball (1975); Christianson (1978); and Firth (1979).

native styles pious Englishmen discovered in that period of spiritual renewal and discovery?[69] Until such questions can be answered, Christopher Haigh's comment that historians of the English Reformation have still not decided "what their Reformation was actually like" remains a compelling judgment.[70]

Bibliography

Alexander, Gina, "Bonner and the Marian Persecutions," *History* 60 (1975): 374–391.

———, "Victim or Spendthrift? The Bishop of London and His Income in the Sixteenth Century," in *Wealth and Power in Tudor England*, eds. E. W. Ives, R. J. Knecht, and J. J. Scarisbrick (London, 1978): 128–145.

Alsop, J. D., "Cromwell and the Church in 1531: the Case of Waltham Abbey," *Journal of Ecclesiastical History* 31 (1980): 327–330.

Aston, Margaret, "Lollardy and Literacy," *History* 62 (1977): 347–371.

———, "Lollard Women Priests?" *Journal of Ecclesiastical History* 31 (1980): 441–461.

Bainton, R. H., "Feminine Piety in Tudor England," in *Christian Spirituality*, ed. Peter Brooks (London, 1975): 183–201.

Baker, Derek, "Old Wine in New Bottles: Attitudes to Reform in Pre-Reformation England," in *Renaissance and Renewal in Christian History. Studies in Church History*, v.14, ed. Derek Baker (Oxford, 1977): 193–211.

Baker, J. Wayne, *Heinrich Bullinger and the Covenant* (Athens, Ohio, 1980).

Ball. B. W., *A Great Expectation: Eschatological Thought in English Protestantism to 1660* (Leiden, 1975).

Block, Joseph, "Thomas Cromwell's Patronage of Preaching," *Sixteenth Century Journal* 8/1 (1977): 37–50.

Booty, J. E., "Church and Commonwealth in the Reign of Edward IV," *Anglican Theological Review*, Suppl. Series, 7 (1976): 67–79.

———, "The Bishop Confronts the Queen: John Jewel and the

---

[69]Roland Bainton's all-too-brief discussion of the varieties of piety displayed by the four daughters of Anthony Cooke suggests that such a task is not impossible (1975).
[70]Haigh (1979), 88.

Failure of the English Reformation," in *Continuity and Discontinuity in Church History*, eds. F. F. Church and T. George (Leiden, 1979): 215–231.

Bowker, Margaret, "The Supremacy and the Episcopate: the Struggle for Control, 1534–1540," *Historical Journal* 8 (1975): 227–243.

_____, "The Henrician Reformation and the Parish Clergy," *Bulletin of the Institute of Historical Research* 50 (1977): 30–47.

Bradshaw, Brendan, "The Tudor Commonwealth: Reform and Revision," *Historical Journal* 22 (1979): 455–476.

Brady, Thomas A., Jr., " 'Social History of the Reformation.' 'Sozialgeschichte der Reformation.' A Conference at the Deutsches Historisches Institut London, May 25–27, 1978," *Sixteenth Century Journal* 10/1 (1979): 89–92.

Brink, J. R., " 'Fortes of Fathers': An Unpublished Sixteenth-Century Manuscript Relating to Patristic Writing on the Eucharist," *Sixteenth Century Journal* 10/1 (1979): 83–87.

Brockwell, Charles W., Jr., "Answering 'the Known Men': Bishop Peacock and Mr. Richard Hooker," *Church History* 49 (1980): 133–146.

Capp, Bernard, *Astrology and the Popular Press. English Almanacs 1500–1800* (London, 1979).

Cargill-Thompson, W. D. J., "The Two Regiments: The Continental Setting of William Tyndale's Political Thought," in *Reform and the Reformation: England and the Continent c. 1500–c.1750*. Studies in Church History, Subsidia 2, ed. Derek Baker (Oxford, 1979): 17–33.

Christianson, Paul, *Reformers in Babylon: English Apocalyptic Visions from the Reformation to the Eve of the Civil War* (Toronto, 1978).

Clark, Peter, *English Provincial Society from the Reformation to the Revolution: Religion, Politics and Society in Kent, 1500–1640* (Hassocks, Sussex, 1977).

_____, " 'The Ramoth-Gilead of the Good': Urban Change and Political Radicalism at Gloucester 1540–1640," in *The English Commonwealth 1547–1640*, eds. Peter Clark, Alan G. T. Smith, and Nicholas Tyacke (Leicester, 1979): 167–187. (a)

_____, "Reformation and Radicalism in Kentish Towns c.1500–1553," *Stadtbürgertum und Adel in der Reformation / The*

Urban Classes, the Nobility and the Reformation, eds. W. J. Mommsen, et al. Pubs. of the German Historical Institute, London, v.5 (Stuttgart, 1979): 107–127. (b)

Collinson, Patrick, "Lectures by Combination: Structures and Characteristics of Church Life in 17th Century England," *Bulletin of the Institute of Historical Research* 48 (1975): 182–213.

_____, "Magistracy and Ministry: A Suffolk Miniature," in *Reform, Conformity and Dissent*, ed. R. Buick Knox (London, 1977): 70–91.

_____, *Archbishop Grindal 1519–1583* (London, 1979). (a)

_____, "The Downfall of Archbishop Grindal and its Place in Elizabethan Political and Ecclesiastical History," in *The English Commonwealth 1547–1640*, eds. Peter Clark, Alan G. R. Smith, and Nicholas Tyacke (Leicester, 1979): 39–57. (b)

_____, "Cranbrook and the Fletchers: Popular and Unpopular Religion in the Kentish Weald," in *Reformation Principle and Practice*, ed. Peter Newman Brooks (London, 1980): 171–202.

Cross, Claire, "Popular Piety and the Records of the Unestablished Churches, 1460–1660," in *The Materials, Sources and Methods of Ecclesiastical History.* Studies in Church History, v.11, ed. Derek Baker (Oxford, 1975): 269–292.

_____, *Church and People, 1450–1660: the Triumph of the Laity in the English Church* (Hassocks, Sussex, 1976).

_____, "Churchmen and the Royal Supremacy," in *Church and Society in England, Henry VIII to James I*, eds. F. Heal and R. O'Day (London, 1977): 15–34.

_____, " 'Great Reasoner in Scripture': the Activities of Women Lollards, 1380–1530," in *Medieval Women.* Studies in Church History, Subsidia 1, ed. Derek Baker (Oxford, 1978): 359–380. (a)

_____, "Religious and Social Protest among Lollards in Early Tudor England," in *The Church in a Changing Society: Conflict, Reconciliation or Adjustment* (Uppsala, 1978): 71–75. (b)

_____, "Continental Students and the Protestant Reformation in England in the Sixteenth Century," in *Reform and Reformation: England and the Continent, c.1500–c.1750.* Studies in Church History, Subsidia 2, ed. Derek Baker (Oxford, 1979): 35–57. (a)

_____, "Parochial Structure and the Dissemination of Protestant-
ism in Sixteenth Century England: A Tale of Two Cities," in
The Church in Town and Countryside. Studies in Church
History, v.16, ed. Derek Baker (Oxford, 1979): 269–278. (b)
_____, "Priests into Ministers: the Establishment of Protestant
Practice in the City of York," in *Reformation Principle and
Practice*, ed. Peter Newman Brooks (London, 1980): 203–
225.
Dickens, A. G., *The English Reformation* (London, 1964).
_____, "The Last Medieval Englishman," in *Christian Spiritual-
ity*, ed. Peter Brooks (London, 1975): 141–181.
Dickinson, J. C., *An Ecclesiastical History of England: The Later
Middle Ages from the Conquest to the Eve of the Reforma-
tion* (London, 1979).
Dobson, Barrie, "Oxford Graduates and the So-Called Patronage
Crisis of the Later Middle Ages," in *The Church in a Chang-
ing Society: Conflict, Reconciliation or Adjustment* (Uppsa-
la, 1978): 211–216.
Duggan, Lawrence G., "The Unresponsiveness of the Late Medieval
Church: A Reconsideration," *Sixteenth Century Journal* 9/1
(1978): 3–26.
Dunning, Robert W., "Revival at Glastonbury 1530–9," in *Renais-
sance and Renewal in Christian History.* Studies in Church
History, v.14, ed. Derek Baker (Oxford, 1977): 213–222.
Elton, G. R., *Policy and Police. The Enforcement of the Reformation in the Age of Thomas Cromwell* (Cambridge, 1972).
_____, *Reform and Renewal. Thomas Cromwell and the Com-
monweal* (Cambridge, 1973).
_____, *Reform and Reformation: England 1509–1558* (London,
1977).
_____, "England and the Continent in the Sixteenth Century,"
in *Reform and Reformation: England and the Continent
c.1500–c.1750.* Studies in Church History, Subsidia 2, ed.
Derek Baker (Oxford, 1979): 1–16.
Finucane, R. C., *Miracles and Pilgrims: Popular Beliefs in Medi-
eval England* (London, 1977).
Firth, K. R., *The Apocalyptic Tradition in Reformation Britain
1530–1695* (Oxford, 1979).
Fisher, Rodney M., "Reform, Repression and Unrest at the Inns of
Court, 1518–1558," *Historical Journal* (1977): 783–801.
_____, "Simon Fish, Cardinal Wolsey and John Roo's Play at

Gray's Inn, Christmas 1526," *Archive for Reformation History* 69 (1978): 293–298.

Frankforter, A. Daniel, "The Reformation and the Register: Episcopal Administration of Parishes in Late Medieval England," *Catholic Historical Review* 43 (1977): 204–244.

Greaves, R. L., *Society and Religion in Elizabethan England* (Minneapolis, Minn., 1981).

Guy, J. A., *The Cardinal's Court* (London, 1977).

——, *The Public Career of Sir Thomas More* (New Haven, 1980). (a)

——, "The Tudor Commonwealth: Revising Thomas Cromwell," *Historical Journal*, 23 (1980): 681–687. (b)

Haas, Steven, "Henry VIII's *Glasse of Truthe*," *History* 64 (1979): 353–362.

——, "Martin Luther's 'Divine Right' Kingship and the Royal Supremacy: Two Tracts from the 1531 Parliament and Convocation of the Clergy," *Journal of Ecclesiastical History* 31 (1980): 317–325.

Haigh, Christopher, "Finance and Administration in a New Diocese: Chester 1541–1641," in *Continuity and Change: Personnel Administration of the Church of England 1500–1642*, eds. R. O'Day and F. Heal (Leicester, 1976): 145–166.

Haigh, Christopher, *Reformation and Resistance in Tudor Lancashire* (Cambridge, 1975).

——, "Puritan Evangelism in the Reign of Elizabeth I," *English Historical Review* 42 (1977): 30–58.

——, "Some Aspects of the Recent Historiography of the English Reformation," *Stadtbürgertum und Adel in der Reformation/The Urban Classes, the Nobility and the Reformation*, eds. W. J. Mommsen, et al. Pubs. of the German Historical Institute London, v.5 (Stuttgart, 1979): 88–106.

Haines, Roy M., " 'Wilde wittes and wilfulnes': John Swetstock's attack on those 'poymongers', the Lollards," in *Studies in Church History*, v.8, eds. G. J. Cuming and Derek Baker (Cambridge, 1972): 143–154.

Hall, Basil, "The Early Rise and Gradual Decline of Lutheranism in England (1520–1600)," in *Reform and Reformation: England and the Continent, c.1500–c.1750*. Studies in Church History, Subsidia 2, ed. Derek Baker (Oxford, 1979): 103–131.

Hallam, Elizabeth, "Henry VIII's Monastic Refoundations of 1536–

37 and the Course of the Dissolution," *Bulletin of the Institute of Historical Research* 51 (1978): 124–131.

Hargrave, O.T., "The Predestinarian Controversy Among the Marian Protestant Prisoners," *Historical Magazine of the Protestant Episcopal Church* 47 (1978): 131–151.

Harper-Bill, Christopher, "Archbishop John Morton and the Province of Canterbury, 1486–1500," *Journal of Ecclesiastical History* 29 (1978): 1–21.

Heal, Felicity, "Clerical Tax Collection under the Tudors: the Influence of the Reformation," in *Continuity and Change: Personnel and Administration of the Church of England 1500–1642*, eds. R. O'Day and F. Heal (Leicester, 1976): 97–122.

––––––, "Economic Problems of the Clergy," in *Church and Society in England, Henry VIII to James I*, eds. F. Heal and R. O'Day (London, 1977): 98–118.

––––––, *Of Prelates and Princes. A Study of the Economic and Social Position of the Tudor Episcopate* (Cambridge, 1980).

Hembry, Phyllis, "Episcopal Palaces, 1535 to 1660," in *Wealth and Power in Tudor England*, eds. E. W. Ives, R. J. Knecht, and J. J. Scarisbrick (London, 1978): 146–166.

Hill, Christopher, "Puritans and 'the Dark Corners of the Land'," in *Continuity and Change in Seventeenth-Century England* (London, 1974): 3–47.

––––––, "From Lollards to Levellers," in *Rebels and Their Causes*, ed. Maurice Cornforth (London, 1978): 49–67.

Houlbrooke, Ralph A., "The Decline of Ecclesiastical Jurisdiction under the Tudors," in *Continuity and Change: Personnel and Administration of the Church of England, 1500–1642*, eds. R. O'Day and F. Heal (Leicester, 1976): 239–258.

––––––, "The Protestant Episcopate 1547–1603: the Pastoral Contribution," in *Church and Society in England, Henry VIII to James I*, eds. F. Heal and R. O'Day (London, 1977): 78–98.

––––––, *Church Courts and the People During the English Reformation, 1520–1570* (Oxford, 1979).

Hudson, Anne, ed., *Selections from English Wycliffite Writings* (Cambridge, 1978).

Hudon, Winthrop S., *The Cambridge Connection and the Elizabethan Settlement of 1559* (Durham, North Carolina, 1980).

James, M. E., *Family, Lineage and Civil Society: A Study of Society, Politics and Mentality in the Durham Region 1500–1640* (Oxford, 1974).

Kendall, R. T., *Calvin and English Calvinism to 1649* (Oxford, 1979).

Kitching, Christopher, "The Prerogative Court of Canterbury from Warham to Whitgift," in *Continuity and Change: Personnel and Administration of the Church of England 1500–1642*, eds. R. O'Day and F. Heal (Leicester, 1976): 191–214.

_____, "The Disposal of Monastic and Chantry Lands," in *Church and Society in England, Henry VIII to James I*, eds. F. Heal and R. O'Day (London, 1977): 119–136.

Kreider, Alan, *English Chantries: the Road to Dissolution* (Cambridge, Mass., 1979).

Lambert, M. D., *Medieval Heresy: Popular Movements from Bogomil to Hus* (London, 1977).

Lander, Stephen, "Church Courts and the Reformation in the Diocese of Chichester," in *Continuity and Change: Personnel and Administration of the Church of England 1500–1642*, eds. R. O'Day and F. Heal (Leicester, 1976): 215–238.

Loades, D. M., "Protestant Sectarianism in England in the Mid-Sixteenth Century," in *The Church in a Changing Society: Conflict, Reconciliation or Adjustment* (Uppsala, 1978): 76–81.

_____, "Anabaptism and English Sectarianism in the Mid-Sixteenth Century," in *Reform and Reformation: England and the Continent, c.1500–c.1750*. Studies in Church History, Subsidia 2, ed. Derek Baker (Oxford, 1979): 59–70.

Luoma, J. K., "Restitution or Reformation? Cartwright and Hooker on the Elizabethan Church," *Historical Magazine of the Protestant Episcopal Church* 46 (1977): 85–106.

Luxton, Imogen, "The Reformation and Popular Culture," in *Church and Society in England, Henry VIII to James I*, eds. F. Heal and R. O'Day (London, 1977): 57–77.

Manning, Roger B., "The Making of a Protestant Aristocracy: the Ecclesiastical Commissioners of the Diocese of Chester," *Bulletin of the Institute of Historical Research* 49 (1976): 60–79.

Martin, J. W., "English Protestant Separatism at its Beginnings: Henry Hart and the Free-Will Men," *Sixteenth Century Journal* 7/2 (1976): 55–74.

_____, "Elizabethan Familists and other Separatists in the Guildford Area," *Bulletin of the Institute of Historical Research* 51 (1978): 90–93.

_____, "Christopher Vitel: An Elizabethan Mechanick Preacher," *Sixteenth Century Journal* 10/2 (1979): 15–22.

Mason, Emma, "The Role of the English Parishioner, 1100–1500," *Journal of Ecclesiastical History* 27 (1976): 17–29.

Mayer, Thomas F., "Starkey and Melanchthon on Adiaphora: A Critique of W. Gordon Zeeveld," *Sixteenth Century Journal* 11/1 (1980): 39–49.

Moss, J. D., "The Family of Love and English Critics," *Sixteenth Century Journal* 6/1 (1975): 35–52.

_____, "Variations on a Theme: The Family of Love in Renaissance England," *Renaissance Quarterly* 31 (1978): 186–195.

Mullett, Michael, *Radical Religious Movements in Early Modern Europe* (London, 1980).

O'Connell, Laura S., "Anti-Entrepreneurial Attitudes in Elizabethan Sermons and Popular Literature," *Journal of British Studies* 15 (1976): 1–20.

O'Day, Rosemary, "The Reformation of the Ministry, 1558–1642," in *Continuity and Change: Personnel and Administration of the Church of England 1500–1642*, eds. R. O'Day and F. Heal (Leicester, 1976): 55–76.

_____, "Ecclesiastical Patronage," in *Church and Society England, Henry VIII to James I*, eds. F. Heal and R. O'Day (London, 1977): 137–155.

_____, *The English Clergy: Emergence and Consolidation of a Profession, 1558–1642* (Leicester, 1979).

Palliser, D. M., "Popular Reactions to the Reformation during the Years of Uncertainty 1530–1570," in *Church and Society in England, Henry VIII to James I*, eds. F. Heal and R. O'Day (London, 1977): 35–56.

Phythian-Adams, Charles, *Desolation of a City. Coventry and the Urban Crisis of the Late Middle Ages* (Cambridge, 1979).

Pogson, Rex H., "Revival and Reform in Mary Tudor's Church: A Question of Money," *Journal of Ecclesiastical History* 25 (1974): 249–265.

_____, "Reginald Pole and the Priorities of Government in Mary Tudor's Church," *Historical Journal* 18 (1975): 3–20.

_____, "The Legacy of Schism: Confusion, Uncertainty and Change in the Marian Clergy," in *The Mid-Tudor Polity c.1540–1560*, eds. Jennifer Loach and Robert Titler (London, 1980): 116–136.

Powicke, Maurice, *The Reformation in England* (Oxford, 1941).

Prest, Wilfred R., "The Art of Law and the Law of God: Sir Henry Finch (1558–1625)," in *Puritans and Revolutionaries*, eds. Donald Pennington and Keith Thomas (Oxford, 1978): 94–117.

Rupp, Gordon, "The Battle of the Books: the Ferment of Ideas and the Beginning of the Reformation," in *Reformation Principle and Practice*, ed. Peter Newman Brooks (London, 1980): 1–19.

Scarisbrick, J. J., "Thomas More, the King's Good Servant," *Thought* 52 (1977): 249–268.

_____, "Cardinal Wolsey and the Common Weal," in *Wealth and Power in Tudor England*, eds. E. W. Ives, R. J. Knecht and J. J. Scarisbrick (London, 1978): 45–67.

Seaver, Paul, *The Puritan Lectureships* (Stanford, 1970).

_____, "Community Control and Puritan Politics in Elizabethan Suffolk," *Albion* 9 (1977): 297–315.

_____, "The Puritan Work Ethic Revisited," *Journal of British Studies* 19 (1980): 35–53.

Sheils, W. J., "Some Problems of Government in a New Diocese: the Bishop and the Puritans in the Diocese of Peterborough," in *Continuity and Change: Personnel and Administration of the Church of England 1500–1642*, eds. R. O'Day and F. Heal (Leicester, 1976): 167–187.

_____, "Religion in Provincial Towns," in *Church and Society in England, Henry VIII to James I*, eds. F. Heal and R. O'Day (London, 1977): 156–176.

Slavin, Arthur J., "Cromwell, Cranmer and Lord Lisle: A Study in the Politics of Reform," *Albion* 9 (1977): 316–336.

Solberg, Winton U., *Redeem the Time: The Puritan Sabbath in Early America* (Cambridge, Mass., 1977).

Stannard, David E., *The Puritan Way of Death. A Study in Religion, Culture, and Social Change* (New York, 1977).

Stone, Lawrence, *The Family, Sex and Marriage in England 1500–1800* (New York, 1977).

Thorp, Malcolm R., "Religion and the Wyatt Rebellion of 1554," *Church History* 47 (1978): 363–380.

Todd, Margo, "Humanists, Puritans and the Spiritualized Household," *Church History* 49 (1980): 18–34.

Wilks, Michael, "Misleading Manuscripts: Wyclif and the Non-

Wycliffite Bible," in *The Materials, Sources and Methods of Ecclesiastical History*. Studies of Church History, v.11, ed. Derek Baker (Oxford, 1975): 147–161.

———, "Royal Priesthood: the Origins of Lollardy," in *The Church in a Changing Society: Conflict, Reconciliation or Adjustment* (Uppsala, 1978): 63–70.

Williams, R. L., "Patterns of Reformation in the Theology of William Tyndale," in *Christian Spirituality*, ed. Peter Brooks (London, 1975): 119–139.

Wrightson, Keith and Levine, David, *Poverty and Piety in an English Village. Terling, 1525–1700* (New York, 1979).

Yost, John K., "Protestant Reformers and the Humanist *via media* in the Early English Reformation," *Journal of Medieval and Renaissance Studies* 5 (1975): 187–202.

———, "A Reappraisal of How Protestantism Spread during the Early English Reformation," *Anglican Theological Review* 60 (1978): 437–446.

Catholic Reform

John W. O'Malley

Long either neglected or pursued out of obvious partisanship, the study of Catholicism of the sixteenth and seventeenth centuries is now enjoying a revival. It needs, in fact, not a chapter like this one but a volume of its own to do it justice. The late Hubert Jedin (d. July 16, 1980), whose monumental study of the Council of Trent reached completion in 1975, deserves considerable credit for this increased interest. The high quality and immense quantity of his work on almost all aspects of "the Tridentine era" are only part of his contribution. Just as important are the scholars in Germany and elsewhere whom he trained or inspired over the course of his long career.

Jedin several times indicated that, whereas his own studies dealt primarily with the pre-history and history of the Council, the next stage of research would be studies of the "application" of the Council. For Jedin, the heart of the Tridentine reform was an episcopacy animated by a renewed (or even a new) sense of ministry, as the bishop was transformed from feudatory to pastor.

Scholars, in Germany and Italy especially, have taken up this idea, and we now possess some careful studies about "post-conciliar" bishops and dioceses. These studies sharpen our growing awareness of the critical distinction between what the Council intended and how its decrees were later interpreted and implemented. They have to some extent even displaced Trent itself as the center of interest. Their conclusions already indicate considerable variety among the bishops and show that not all of them were or wanted to be carbon copies of Carlo Borromeo of Milan. Paolo Prodi's study of Gabriele Paleotti, archbishop of Bologna, was one of the earliest and most successful of such works.[1] Prodi's book anticipated the superior

---

[1]Prodi (1959–67). See also, e.g., Cairns (1976). Along with other works, two studies on bishops are reviewed by Venard (1975). Among the more recent studies on Ger-

scholarship now emanating from or influenced by the Centro di documentazione: Istituto per le scienze religiose of Bologna.

Trent assiduously avoided any explicit statement on the critical issue of the pope's place in the Church. Somewhat paradoxically, studies of the episcopacy have in the final analysis demonstrated the importance of the papacy and the Roman Curia in the post-conciliar period. They have indicated how, in conscious or unconscious parallel with secular governments, the Roman bureaucracy continued or intensified a process of administrative centralization. In recent years there have been only a few studies of the post-conciliar Curia, and none of the popes, though there is surely room now for modern biographies of Sixtus V, Paul V, or Urban VIII, to name only a few.[2] Major studies of curial cardinals and officials are also lacking. A full-scale biography of Cardinal Alessandro Farnese, for example, would certainly yield fascinating results. Leonard E. Boyle's *A Survey of the Vatican Archives and of its Medieval Holdings* (Toronto, 1972) is now the standard primer for the most vast and complex depository of sources for such research.

The most important publications of documents relative to the papacy during this period have been the continuation of the *Nuntiaturberichte aus Deutschland*, the *Acta Nuntiaturae Gallicae*, the *Nunziature di Venezia*, and similar series. These documents, ably edited, still await full exploitation by scholars and promise to illuminate more than just political history.[3]

Yet it is politico-ecclesiastical history—or, at least, history "from above"—that scholars concerned with Germany still favor. In general these scholars follow the conventional paths of interest: war, courts, diplomacy, episcopal curias, and the edition of documents, as the continued publication of the *Acta Reformationis Catholicae*, the *Acta Pacis Westphalicae* and other series suggests. Largely under

---

many are Förster (1976), and Becker-Huberti (1978).

I am indebted to Professor Lawrence Duggan of the University of Delaware for allowing me to read his unpublished paper, "New Directions in Scholarship in the Counter Reformation in Germany." An up-to-date listing of sources and studies on the Counter Reformation (as well as Reformation) for all of Europe is to be found in Lutz (1979): 189–225. See also the section entitled "Grundprobleme und Tendenzen der Forschung": 117–88. The *Bibliographie internationale de l'Humanisme et de la Renaissance*, a basic research tool for Catholicism in the early modern period somewhat despite its title, now seems to have its annual publication once again assured.

[2]An interesting work on the reorganization of the Curia after the Council remains unpublished: Tomaro (1973). The studies by Reinhard (1974) and (1975) throw light on some neglected aspects of papal policy.

[3]See Müller (1973), and Jedin (1973).

the inspiration of Ernst Walter Zeeden of the University of Tübingen, scholars have devoted themselves to detecting and describing the actions that produced the two great "confessions" that ushered Germany into the "Confessional Age."

The new bibliography of the writings of the Catholic Controversialists, though not without weaknesses, should facilitate research into the ways Catholic intellectuals responded to the Reformation.[4] Among these intellectuals, Johannes Gropper has emerged as deserving even closer examination, as his theology is seen to approximate the conciliatory positions of Gasparo Contarini and Giovanni Morone.[5] The *Corpus Catholicorum* of the Görres-Gesellschaft continues to provide the most easily available documentary basis for ongoing research in this area.

We still need, however, more studies of the theological and doctrinal shifts that characterized Catholicism in the new era. Catholic historians of the Counter Reformation have often failed to understand that reform of doctrine was Luther's principal concern. Correspondingly, they have thought of Catholic reform in Tridentine terms (Session IV) as "reforming morals" (and institutions) but only "confirming doctrine," though Léopold Willaert tried to address this problem over twenty years ago in his book on post-tridentine theology.[6] For most of the Catholic world Willaert was ahead of his times when he frankly admitted more interest in "ideas and sentiments" than in "events." Since his day, however, the most engaging studies of Catholicism in the early modern era have dealt neither with "event-centered" nor "idea-centered" history. Rather, they have dealt with "religious sentiment," especially in the context of popular piety and pastoral care. Local religious institutions have been explored in the complexity of their social and economic settings.

German historians have shown relatively little interest in this development. Thus, for all his accomplishment, Jedin along with his colleagues and disciples must share leadership in Catholic studies with French scholars influenced by the methods and presuppositions of Lucien Febvre, Gabriel Le Bras, Marc Bloch, Fernand Braudel, Emmanuel LeRoy Ladurie, and others. The focus, therefore, changes abruptly from Germany to France, from the Görres-Gesellschaft to the *Annales* school, and from the Universities of Bonn,

[4]Klaiber (1978). See the review article by Gilmont (1979).

[5]For a general review of scholarship that contains reference to Gropper, see Strnad and Walsh (1978): esp. 284–86.

[6]Willaert (1960). See also now Andrés Martín (1976–).

Münster, and Tübingen to the École Pratique des Hautes Études.[7] Praised by some, damned by others, these French scholars with their sociological and quantifying methods are having a notable impact on Catholic historiography in their own country and elsewhere.[8]

Within France, the seventeenth century has attracted the special attention of scholars interested in Catholicism. The reasons are not difficult to discover. After the Wars of Religion, French culture experienced a new *élan* as it moved towards the Century of Lights. Some recent studies suggest a relationship between the political struggles of the Wars and the renewed religious fervor.[9] More important, the seventeenth century was a century of great French religious figures—Vincent de Paul, Isaac Jogues, Cardinal Bérulle, Jeanne-Françoise de Chantal, Louise de Marillac, Jean-Baptiste de la Salle, and many others. Recent editions of the correspondence and other writings of some of these persons will now facilitate research on them.

If these leading personalities were so outstanding, one is naturally led to ask what "the people" were like and how the Church cared for them. French scholars are currently devoting immense attention to these questions. Pride of place among sources for information about "the people" and the Church's ministry to them are the records of pastoral visitations. The C.N.R.S. has recently begun publication of a *Répertoire des visites pastorales*.[10] This collection is destined to become an extremely important instrument for research into French dioceses. The volumes of the *Histoire des diocèses de France* (Paris, 1968–) and the *Histoire religieuse des provinces de France* (Tours, 1975–) continue to be published and fill a fundamental need. Ernst Walter Zeeden and Hansgeorg Molitor have published a preliminary inventory of printed and unprinted sources for visitations in the Empire.[11]

In Italy the early interest of don Giuseppe De Luca in the "history of piety" had some vague affinities with the French school. De Luca's interest took concrete form in 1951 with the founding of the

[7]There are a number of good accounts of the phenomenon, e.g., Stoianovich (1972), Iggers (1975), Allegra and Torre (1977). See also Burke (1973).

[8]See e.g., Russo (1972), Fenlon (1974), Vauchez (1975).

[9]See e.g., Benedict (1979).

[10]See Venard and Julia (1977).

[11]Zeeden (1977). Noteworthy for its focus on the capitol of Catholicism and its use of the generally neglected archives of the Roman Vicariate is Beggiao (1978).

[12]On De Luca, see e.g., Jedin (1963), and Guarnieri (1972).

Archivio italiano per la storia della pietà.[12] After De Luca's death in
1962, his work was continued and then transformed by his disciple,
Gabriele De Rosa, whose *Vescovi, popolo e magia nel Sud* (Naples,
1971) was one of the first works in Italy to apply the French methods
to "Catholic Reform."[13] The year 1972 was a turning point. In May,
under De Rosa's leadership, the Convegno studi di storia sociale e
religiosa was held at Capaccio-Paestum with some French partici-
pants. That same year, with De Rosa as editor, the *Ricerche di storia
sociale e religiosa* began publication. These initiatives resulted in the
founding at Vicenza in 1975 of the Istituto per le ricerche di storia
sociale e di storia religiosa.[14] Of somewhat similar inspiration ("pas-
sare dalla storia istituzionale a quella della base") is the *Ricerche per
la storia religiosa di Roma* that began publication in 1977. This
series is especially valuable for its regular publication of inventories
of archives.

France has had, however, a generous head-start over Italy. The
results for the Counter Reformation of the new scholarship in
France up to 1971 were surveyed at some length by Jean Delumeau
and are now available in English as *Catholicism between
Luther and Voltaire: A New View of the Counter Reformation* (Philadelphia, 1977). Though already slightly dated (the
Italian edition has a new bibliography) and too narrowly concerned
with France, the book implicitly or explicitly raises most of the major issues facing present or future scholarship in the field. Even more
helpful as a brief guide for research is François Lebrun's listing
(1976) of major sources and studies pertinent for the religious history
of this period in France and the collection (1980) of surveys with annotated bibliographies that he edited.[15] Lebrun's work is complemented by the comprehensive list of "centres de recherches" now
provided in Bernard Plongeron's *Religions et sociétés en occident*
(Paris, 1979).[16]

The very title of Delumeau's book suggests some big issues. Accustomed to view the Counter Reformation as the century that extended
roughly from the Council of Trent to the Peace of Westphalia in
1648, we are now asked to stretch the chronological framework for
at least another century. We are thus made keenly aware that 1648

[13]See Salimbeni (1972), and Lazzarini (1974).
[14]See *Ricerche di storia sociale e religiosa* 7–8 (1975): 489–99.
[15]Lebrun (1976) and (1980).
[16]See also Plongeron and Pannet (1976), and Duboscq, et al. (1979).

was a terminal point determined by German historians interested in German problems and by an older methodology that concentrated on political and military events even when dealing with the Church. In France the year 1648 has little significance for the social structures and the internal religious revival that concern the presently dominant school of historiography. This means that the failures and achievements of the Council of Trent must now be judged in a longer perspective.[17]

The English edition of Delumeau's book adds a subtitle employing the term "Counter Reformation" that the original French edition lacked. This addition can be interpreted as a distortion of the author's intent. Delumeau chose *Catholicisme* as his title and avoided—deliberately, I assume—the conventional labels like "Catholic Restoration," "Catholic Reform," and "Counter Reformation." With Jedin, Delumeau does recognize a legitimate use of "Counter Reformation" to designate the reactionary and retaliatory elements in the religious history of the sixteenth, seventeenth, and even eighteenth centuries (p. xi). But he intends to deal with a broader phenomenon, and indeed to stress "the positive and innovative aspects, the richness and energy, of Tridentine Catholicism."

The fact is that Jedin did not put to rest uneasiness about terminology with the famous essay in 1946 in which he distinguished between Counter Reformation and Catholic Reform.[18] The discussions that preceded and followed that essay have not been mere *lites verborum*, but occasions to search the very meaning of the era and to evaluate it.[19] In 1977 Wolfgang Reinhard again addressed the problem. After a fine analysis based upon a thorough and wide ranging review of scholarship on the period, he opted for the neutral title, "Confessional Age," to replace both Reformation and Counter Reformation.[20] He thus would substitute for a scheme of antithesis a scheme of parallel development, and would view both "confessions" as factors operative in the modernization of European society.

Also in 1977 Gottfried Maron attacked Jedin's understanding of the distinction between Counter Reformation and Catholic Reform as misleading and inadequate to explain what really happened in sixteenth-century Catholicism.[21] According to Maron, Jedin's typi-

---

[17]See Wright (1975b), and Callahan and Higgs (1979).
[18]Jedin (1946).
[19]See, e.g., Venard (1977).
[20]Reinhard (1977).
[21]Maron (1977).

cally Catholic assumption that there was an unbroken continuity between the positive aspects of the Tridentine reform and late-medieval reforms defies the facts. Tridentine Catholicism in all its parts
differed significantly from its antecedents. Maron strongly implies
that the change was not for the better.

Delumeau's most striking thesis is that in the Middle Ages the
"masses" were never Christianized and that their evangelization was
one of the most characteristic achievements of both Reformation
and Counter Reformation. Although the theses of Jedin, Reinhard,
Maron, and Delumeau do not contradict one another on every
point, they are not easily compatible either. This contrast in viewpoints strongly suggests that there is no way of evaluating or adequately conceiving of the "Counter Reformation" unless we know
what the situation was before it got under way and how (or even
whether) it changed it. Though in no way dealing with the
"masses," my own book on preaching at the papal court on the eve
of the Reformation demonstrates, I believe, how a better understanding of *Préréforme* can appreciably influence our evaluation of
Reformation and Counter Reformation.[22] The same would be true
of Adriano Prosperi's book on Giammatteo Giberti and José García
Oro's studies of Ximenes de Cisneros.[23] Similar studies are needed for
almost every aspect of Christian life. The Erasmian reform, treated
elsewhere in this volume, and all other early Humanist reforms must
of course be taken into account.

Of particular interest in this regard is how Catholicism, while
keeping its old organizational structures, actually transformed its effectiveness and modes of operation. Some contemporary research is
now suggesting that the "Counter Reformation" was as interested as
its Protestant equivalents in waging war against "the old religion;" it
was as much characterized by its opposition to "medieval superstition" as by its opposition to Protestantism.[24] A more perplexing but
perhaps related issue, also discussed by Delumeau, is why and how
the evangelized peoples of Europe became "dechristianized" from
the middle of the eighteenth century onwards.

Delumeau's evaluation of the Counter Reformation, "without
however any illusions as to its rigidity" (p. xi), is fairly positive.[25]

[22]O'Malley (1979).
[23]Prosperi (1969), and García Oro (1971). On the general issue, see Duggan (1978).
[24]See, e.g., Wright (1975a).
[25]Delumeau (1977) has recently summarized his evaluation, esp. 85–113.,

Perhaps only in that regard does his book bear much resemblance to H. Outram Evennett's work ostensibly on the same "Counter Reformation."[26] In this they both differ from the more accepted tradition that the era marked a decline—cultural and intellectual at least, but perhaps also economic, social, and political. This evaluation has a long history; partly responsible for its popularity are the German Protestant historians who coined the term and others like John Addington Symonds who sensationalized the supposed repressiveness of the era's institutions. The idea was later taken up by Italian intellectuals like Francesco De Sanctis, Benedetto Croce, and Antonio Gramsci, who applied it broadly to "baroque" Italy. Croce laid the blame for decline principally on the Tridentine Church. The *aggiornamento* of Vatican Council II also helped evoke and confirm an unfavorable assessment of the Tridentine era and the Tridentine Church. Such assessments are repeated by many Italian scholars today, including some like Romeo De Maio who come out of the Catholic tradition.[27] Even in its more secular aspects, scholars in the past tended to "forget" and scorn this period of Italian history rather than study it, as the title of Eric Cochrane's book on Florence indicates.[28]

In an important essay in 1960, H. G. Koenigsberger argued that what happened in Italy during the "era of the baroque" was not decadence but a "shift" of interest.[29] The argument has not convinced everybody, and the thesis was recently challenged in a Canadian journal.[30] Even more recently, Charles B. Schmitt proposed that Italy's loss of leadership in science was due as much to the founding and expansion of theological faculties in the Italian universities after the Council of Trent as it was to more direct ecclesiastical repression.[31]

This discrepancy in evaluation points to some important issues. First, the Counter Reformation evokes from historians different appreciations that depend in part on the national context in which they place it. French historians will be predisposed to view it more favorably since it coincides with the beginning of French cultural and political hegemony. The same is true, with considerable qualification after the sixteenth century, for Spain and its "siglo de oro." It is not true at all for Protestant Germany; it is arguable for Italy.

[26]Evennett (1968).
[27]See, e.g., De Maio (1973). See also Cochrane (1980a).
[28]Cochrane (1973). See also Cochrane (1980b), and, more broadly, Quazza (1971).
[29]Koenigsberger (1960).
[30]Santosuosso (1975).
[31]Schmitt (1979): esp. 388–94.

Secondly, in Italy much more than in France, Catholics have tended to withdraw from the academic and intellectual life of the nation or have allowed themselves to be excluded from its more aggressive aspects. In no other country of Western Europe are the lines between "lay" and clerical cultures so clearly drawn, so well maintained. Today "lay" often means Marxist. It is ironic as well as symptomatic of much deeper problems in contemporary Italian culture that, in a country where Protestantism made hardly any headway and seems, in fact, to have had little appeal, many of the best historians today write not about the central Catholic tradition of their nation but about Italian heretics. Thus in Italy many of those who are equipped with the finest academic training and hold the most prestigious academic posts are inimical to the Counter Reformation on ideological grounds or lack interest in it except in such negative manifestations as the Inquisition or Index.[32]

On one specific problem of Italian history in the Cinquecento, however, a great deal of effort has been expended by both Catholic and lay scholars, by Italians and foreigners. That is the problem of the *spirituali* (or "evangelicals") gathered around Cardinals Contarini and Pole in the 1530's and 1540's.[33] The issue fascinates scholars from different camps because, after several decades of research, it is still not altogether clear where heresy begins or where orthodoxy ends; the case is seen as the first and most dramatic test of whether a moderate or conciliatory middle-of-the-road could be found in the religious crisis; the failure of the *spirituali* and the repression they suffered mark for many historians the real beginning of the Counter Reformation in the negative sense of the term.

Study of the *spirituali* easily suggests, therefore, the Index and Inquisition. These phenomena have long been objects of considerable and partisan interest. Though the records of the Holy Office that survive in Rome continue to be absolutely inaccessible, portions of them have been discovered elsewhere.[34] Moreover, governmental and diocesan records are now available to scholars in various places. From them we have some interesting studies especially for Spain, Venice, and the *Mezzogiorno*.[35] This scholarship shows the Inquisition to have been fairer and more moderate than its critics have

[32]See, e.g., Cochrane (1970–71).
[33]See Gleason (1978). See also Simoncelli (1975) and (1979).
[34]See Tedeschi (1979).
[35]For the Spanish Inquisition in general, with a bibliography of more recent works, see Bennassar (1979). For other areas, see, e.g., Grendler (1977), Borromeo (1977–78), Rotondò (1973), Le Brun (1975).

maintained and also shows a wide variety of working relationships (usually on a cooperative model) between Church and State, between local and Roman authorities.

The studies of the *spirituali* have examined their doctrines and their careers, and thus have demonstrated that the methodologies of the *Annales* school have not altogether prevailed. In fact, an Anglo-American historian has recently argued that the influence of the school is waning; he believes he detects a trend back to narrative and "event-centered" historiography.[36] In Italy, where interest in the French methods has been high during the past decade, admiration has by no means led to the elimination of more traditional subjects and forms of history.[37] The same is true, indeed, even for France. For instance, the teachings on holiness or "spirituality" of the great leaders of Catholicism during the period, an issue to which Evennett called special attention, continues to elicit a large number of studies.[38] Here the *Dictionnaire de spiritualité* (now up to N) is an invaluable resource.

The dissertations on Ignatius Loyola and the early Society of Jesus that the Gregorian University in Rome produces almost every year tend to concentrate on spirituality, or on the Constitutions of the order.[39] Ignatius has not been the subject of a major historical study that has attracted attention outside Jesuit circles, however, for decades. Since the *Monumenta Ignatiana* of the Jesuit Historical Institute in Rome is now completed in a partly revised edition, it will provide a firm basis for new contextualizations of the Jesuit phenomenon. Similar studies are needed for the other new religious orders of the period as well.

The failure of Saint Ignatius to inspire a major study may be due in part—but only in part—to the general competence of Pietro Tacchi-Venturi's two volumes on the early history of the Jesuits in Italy (re-

[36]Stone (1979). But see also Hobsbawm (1980)

[37]Note how little attention Scaduto, e.g., gives works influenced by the French school in his two reviews of scholarship (1976) and (1977). In the latter article he does discuss, however, Rosa (1976). On Rosa's book, see also the opinions in *Critica Storica* 16 (1979): 352–64. See now Stella (1976), and Galasso and Russo (1980-). For a recent study of popular religion in Spain, see Christian (1981).

[38]Despite the recent and lamentable demise of the *Revue de l'histoire de la spiritualité*, there persists in France today a lively interest in the subject; see, e.g., Le Brun (1974). For Italy, see Marcocchi (1979). See also Petrocchi (1978–79). The transformation of sanctity into "heroic" proportions in the Counter Reformation is the subject of a suggestive essay by De Maio (1973): 257–78.

[39]The situation described by Iparraguirre (1972) does not seem to have changed significantly since he wrote.

vised edition in four parts, 1930–51). Mario Scaduto has now published the next two volumes in the series under the title *L'epoca di Giacomo Lainez* (Rome, 1964–74). This study, a worthy successor to Tacchi-Venturi, promises well for the subsequent volumes that Scaduto intends to write.

Francis Xavier, Loyola's closest and most illustrious companion, has received at the hands of the late and long-lived Georg Schurhammer the most painstakingly detailed biography that any Counter-Reformation saint has ever had—and probably ever will have! The fourth, final volume of the English translation of this work has just appeared. Schurhammer's biography is, without apology, a strictly old-fashioned "life and times." Not therefore without its critics, it still stands as a magnificent fund of information about personages and sources that will be of use to historians for years to come.

These works of Tacchi-Venturi, Scaduto, and Schurhammer are also products of the Jesuit Historical Institute that publishes the *Monumenta* and the *Archivum* of the Society of Jesus, just around the corner from the Jesuits' well organized central archives, which are open to scholars. The Institute is now directed by an American historian, Charles E. O'Neill. Other religious orders in Rome maintain similar centers.

The very mention of Xavier's name raises the problem of the foreign missions in sixteenth- and seventeenth-century Catholicism. If the thesis is correct that Catholicism in those centuries was not simply a mixture of some old and some new elements, but a reality so comprehensively different from its medieval antecedent that such distinctions are misleading, then a new consciousness of the worldwide dimensions of its pastoral task certainly contributed to this metamorphosis. Part of the merit of Delumeau's book, despite its preoccupation with France, is the attention it accords the foreign missions, just as part of the weakness of earlier syntheses like Evennett's, Zeeden's, and A. G. Dickens' is their slighting of them.

I have neither the space nor the competence to comment on recent historiography about the Catholic foreign missions. This subject has attracted a great deal of scholarly attention lately, however, and much of the new work seems to be of high quality. The specific issues that have most often been discussed are the "rites controversy" in China and India, the Jesuit reductions in Paraguay, and Las Casas' controversies over slavery.

Awareness that missions were now a major and abiding aspect of the Church's role in the world led to the foundation in 1622 of the Congregatio pro propaganda fide. The 350th anniversary of the Congregation was celebrated in 1972 with a three-volume collection of studies examining different facets of the Congregation's activities over the centuries.[40] The first volume (1622–1700) is pertinent to this survey of research. In spite of the generally high quality of the contributions, the authors are notably reluctant to offer negative criticisms or to raise broader cultural questions—tasks now offered, therefore, to other historians. The archives of the Congregation are open to scholars.

Whether or not England was a "mission" came to be a much agitated question during the period. This issue, with the concommitant postulate that the Catholic "community" in England was discontinuous with its medieval past, has been taken up by John Bossy in his extremely important study, *The English Catholic Community, 1570–1850* (New York, 1976). By placing English Catholicism within the context of English sectarianism and non-conformism, Bossy has restructured the whole approach to it. Just as important from our present perspective, Bossy disregards conventional dates like 1648 and 1688 and, without explicitly arguing to any "Counter-Reformation" character for his chronology, extends his study into the nineteenth century. It comes as no surprise to learn, therefore, that he is influenced by the French schools of "sciences religieuses."

The "mission-consciousness" of Catholics in the sixteenth and seventeenth centuries was not restricted to the newly discovered lands or to territories lost to Protestantism. "Popular missions" to rural populations were just as important and symptomatic of Catholic concerns at the time. Over thirty-five years ago Father Scaduto began to write on the missions of the Italian Jesuits. Of all the subjects explored and exploited by the new French scholarship, few have proved as rewarding as this one, as the pertinent pages of Delumeau indicate.[41]

Because these missions were such well organized pastoral strategies, records survive in archives of the religious orders involved. Corresponding diocesan records are also often available. Since important leaders like Vincent de Paul, Jean Eudes, and Bernadino Realino inspired or took part in these missions, the subject invites study of the interaction between various *élites* and "the people."

---

[40]*Sacrae Congregationis* (1971–76). See also Denzler (1969).
[41]For Italy, see, e.g., Mezzadri (1979), and Faralli (1975).

Further, it yields information that illuminates how "reformed" parishes were meant to function and how they encroached upon other forms of religious organization like the popular confraternity.[42]

In an influential article some years ago, John Bossy argued that the principal characteristic of the Counter Reformation, in so far as it affected the ordinary population, lay in the enforcement of a code of religious observance within a framework of parochial uniformity.[43] For all its success in imposing this stricter discipline on the people, the Counter Reformation thereby fatally weakened the structures of natural kinship in families as well as confraternities. This analysis is, in effect, an indictment.

The part urban lay leaders, cooperating with the hierarchy, played in transforming, even destroying, elements of popular religion in rural areas is now being examined.[44] In fact, it is time to examine critically the tradition that attributes the "Counter Reformation" almost exclusively to the clergy. How, and to what extent, we must now inquire, was the laity involved? If it is true that a new energy vitalized works of mercy in Catholicism and gave them a more effective organization, what part did the laity play in this operation?

With these questions the Church-State issue—reformulated, to be sure—again enters the discussion. It is that issue, broadly conceived, that has engaged much of the Anglo-American scholarship on Venice in recent years.[45] Church-State relationships have a peculiar relevancy for our subject, we must remember, for they largely determined how the decrees of the Council of Trent would be received and made effective.

By again raising the problem of Trent and its implementation, I have brought this review to full circle. Some final observations are in order, however, before concluding. In the course of the review I

---

[42]A related article of considerable importance is Metz (1974–75). A recent article on confraternities that places them in a political context is Harding (1980).

[43]Bossy (1970). See the other articles by the same author (1971), (1973), (1975).

[44]I wish to thank Philip T. Hoffman, California Institute of Technology, for allowing me to read his unpublished paper, "The Church and the Rural Community in the Sixteenth and Seventeenth Centuries."

[45]See, e.g., Grendler (1977) and (1979), Bouwsma (1968), Santosuosso (1973), Wright (1974b). Important, related, but different by its emphasis on social history is Pullan (1971). Also different in orientation would be Olivieri (1972) and (1974). Useful indications for research are provided by Prodi (1973). For the Church-State problem elsewhere, esp. as it engaged some leading personalities of the age, see, e.g., Wright, (1974).

have indicated a number of problems that deserve closer scrutiny by scholars and that can contribute to the debates that are still raging about the era. With deplorable myopia I have hardly mentioned Spain or Latin America, and I have completely ignored Eastern Europe. My excuse is that, for all its fascination, the subject assigned me is vast, sprawling, chronologically ill-defined, and rife with controversial issues. No single problem or set of sources could be pursued in satisfactory detail.

I should, nonetheless, now like to point out four phenomena particularly characteristic of Catholicism during these centuries that deserve considerably more attention than they have as yet received. These phenomena need especially to be located in general cultural and social contexts and then to be assumed into larger syntheses. They are: (1) women, (2) education, (3) preaching, (4) art.

Long before women's studies became fashionable, it was clear that during the early modern period women enjoyed a leadership role in Catholicism that they never enjoyed before or since and that was more prominent, by and large, than that enjoyed by their Protestant sisters. Attention has generally been directed to the founders, reformers, or members of religious orders, especially if they were also authors. Teresa of Avila is the outstanding example, but there is a long list of others like Angela Merici, Maria Maddalena de' Pazzi, Mary Ward, Catherine de Bar, Marie de l'Incarnation, Angélique de Saint-Jean of Port-Royal. The indications that laywomen, particularly among the nobility and upper bourgeoisie, were active in Church reform now needs exploration.[46] Studies along these lines would help clarify the debate about whether Catholicism utilized or neglected the family in its efforts at reform.

In general the laity was interested in establishing schools for its children and seminaries for its clergy; it sometimes happened that these two objectives coincided. Nothing is more typical of Catholicism during this period than its zeal for religious education. In a dramatic shift of *mentalité*, the religious orders began to look upon schools as primary instruments of ministry and pastoral care. True enough, there was a Protestant equivalent of this conviction, but the similarity and differences should make the pursuit of the problem all

[46]See Weaver (1981). Professor Weaver has written an interesting book in which several women are prominent (1978). I wish to thank Kathryn Norberg, University of California, San Diego, for allowing me to read her unpublished paper, "Women, the Family, and the Counter Reformation."

the more rewarding. Though we have collections of studies, editions of documents, and a few important monographs (especially on cate-chisms),[47] there does not yet exist, to my knowledge, an inclusive study of this phenomenon for any country.[48] Moreover, the study of schools leads to a study of patronage, and thus suggests the crudest and most Marxist question of all: who paid for the "Counter Refor-mation"—and why and how?

Trent's words that preaching was the *praecipuum munus* of the bishops did not fall on deaf ears. In the late sixteenth and early seventeenth centuries, a veritable deluge of preaching manuals spilled from the presses in Spain, Italy, France, and Germany. Cor-responding to the manuals were volumes of printed sermons by some of the leading figures of the day. Numerous collections of sermons in manuscript still survive in libraries and archives. This material awaits exploitation by scholars, who should pay as much attention to the form and purpose of the sermons as they do to content, if they wish to do this material justice. It is difficult to imagine material more appropriate for supporting comparisons between high and low culture, between theology and piety, between culture and religion.[49]

Finally, art. Having strolled up and down the streets of a number of "Counter-Reformation" cities and spent an immense amount of time in their museums and churches, I have long been amazed at the ease with which "Counter-Reformation" historians eliminate paint-ing, sculpture, and architecture from their purview. Even Delu-meau, in order to keep his book "an appropriate length" (p. xi), omitted a chapter on art. Yet Victor Tapié has shown how well a study of art monuments can illuminate the "spiritualité collective" of the Counter-Reformation era.[50] The field is admittedly delicate and difficult to study, and requires an uncommon combination of skills. But it should not for that reason be neglected. In the past few

[47]Of particular importance is Bellinger (1970).

[48]I wish to thank Professor Paul F. Grendler, University of Toronto, for allowing me to read his unpublished paper, "The Future of the Counter Reformation in Italy." In that paper Professor Grendler mentions that he is "engaged in a study of Italian prima-ry and secondary education in the Renaissance and Counter Reformation." An impor-tant book on Counter-Reformation education in Italy is Brizzi (1978). For France, see Darricau (1977); for Germany, see, e.g., Seifert (1978).

[49]See O'Malley (1982). There are now two important new books in English on preaching during the Counter-Reformation era: Smith (1978), and Bayley (1980). See also McGinness (1980). For the large context into which much of the preaching of the era must be located, see now Fumaroli (1980).

[50]Tapié (1972) esp. the "Introduction méthodologique": 7–39.

years two important studies of Michelangelo have appeared that try
to relate art to religious sensibilities.[51] A recent book describes the
self-conscious determination during the era to use art for religion,
and again shows that there are ways of investigating the importance
and function of art that go beyond studies of major artists.[52]

I want to thank Professors Paul F. Grendler, University of Toronto, and James M. Weiss, Boston College, for reading this chapter
and offering suggestions for it.

Bibliography

Allegra, Luciano and Torre, Angelo, *La nascita della storia sociale
in Francia* (Turin, 1977).

Andrés Martín, Melchíades, *La teología española en el siglo XVI*
(Madrid, 1976–).

L'art baroque à Lyon: Actes du Colloque (Lyons, 1975).

Batllori, Miguel et al., "La regolata iconografia della Controriforma
nella Roma del Cinquecento," *Ricerche per la storia religiosa
di Roma* 2 (1978): 11–50.

Bayley, Peter, *French Pulpit Oratory 1598–1650* (Cambridge, England, 1980).

Becker-Huberti, Manfred, *Die tridentinische Reform im Bistum
Münster unter Fürstbischof Bernhard von Galen 1650 bis
1678* (Münster/W., 1978).

Beggiao, Diego, *La visita pastorale di Clemente VIII (1592–1600)*
(Rome, 1978).

Bellinger, Gerhard, *Der Catechismus Romanus und die Reformation* (Paderborn, 1970).

Benedict, Philip, "The Catholic Response to Protestantism," *Religion and the People*, ed. James Obelkevich (Chapel Hill,
1979): 168–90.

Bennassar, Bartolomé, *L'Inquisition espagnole (XVe–XVIe siècles)*
(Paris, 1979).

Borromeo, Agostino, "Contributo allo studio dell'Inquisizione e dei
suoi rapporti con il potere episcopale nell'Italia spagnola del
Cinquecento," *Annuario dell'Instituto Storico Italiano per*

---

[51]De Maio (1978), and Steinberg (1980).
[52]Sauzet (1975). See also, e.g., *L'art baroque* (1975), Culley and McNaspy (1971),
Lemmon (1977), Pfeiffer (1976–77), Weil (1974), Pallucchini (1972), Batllori, et al.
(1978).

l'Età Moderna e Contemporanea 29–30 (1977–1978): 219–
76.

Bossy, John, "The Counter-Reformation and the People of Catholic
Europe," *Past and Present* 47 (1970): 51–70.

_____, "The Counter-Reformation and the People of Catholic Ire-
land, 1596–1641," *Historical Studies* 8 (1971): 155–69.

_____, "Blood and Baptism: Kinship, Community and Christiani-
ty in Western Europe from the Fourteenth to the Seventeenth Centuries," *Sanctity and Secularity: The Church and
the World*, ed. Derek Baker (New York, 1973): 129–43.

_____, "The Social History of Confession in the Age of Reforma-
tion," *Transactions of the Royal Historical Society* 5th Ser.
25 (1975): 21–38.

_____, *The English Catholic Community, 1570–1850* (New York,
1979).

Bouwsma, William J., *Venice and the Defense of Republican Liberty* (Berkeley, 1968).

Boyle, Leonard E., *A Survey of the Vatican Archives and of its
Medieval Holdings* (Toronto, 1972).

Brizzi, Gian Paolo, *La formazione della classe dirigente nel Settecento* (Bologna, 1978).

Burke, Peter, ed., *A New Kind of History: From the Writings of
Febvre* (New York, 1973).

Cairns, Christopher, *Domenico Bollani, Bishop of Brescia* (Nieuwkoop, 1976).

Callahan, William J. and Higgs, David, eds., *Church and Society in
Catholic Europe of the Eighteenth Century* (New York,
1979).

Christian, William A. Jr., *Local Religion in Sixteenth-Century
Spain* (Princeton, 1981).

Cochrane, Eric, "New Light on Post-Tridentine Italy: A Note on Recent Counter-Reformation Scholarship," *Catholic Historical
Review* 56 (1970–71): 291–319.

_____, *Florence in the Forgotten Centuries*, 1527–1800 (Chicago,
1973).

_____, "Caesar Baronius and the Counter-Reformation," *Catholic
Historical Review* 66 (1980): 53–58. (a)

_____, "The Transition from Renaissance to Baroque: The Case of
Italian Historiography," *History and Theory* 19 (1980): 21–
30. (b)

Culley, Thomas D. and McNaspy, C. J., "Music and the Early

Jesuits (1540–1565)," *Archivum Historicum Societatis Jesu* 40 (1971): 213–45.

Darricau, Ráymond, "Éducation et pastorale au XVIIe siècle," *Révue d'histoire écclésiastique* 72 (1977): 60–67.

Delumeau, Jean, *Le Christianisme va-t-il mourir?* (Paris, 1977). (b)

———, *Catholicism between Luther and Voltaire: A New View of the Counter Reformation* (Philadelphia, 1977). (a)

De Maio, Romeo, *Riforme e miti nella Chiesa del Cinquecento* (Naples, 1973).

———, *Michelangelo e la Controriforma* (Bari-Rome, 1978).

Denzler, Georg, *Die Propagandakongregation in Rom und die Kirche in Deutschland im ersten Jahrzehnt nach dem Westfälischen Frieden* (Paderborn, 1969).

De Rosa, Gabriele, *Vescovi, popolo e magia nel Sud* (Naples, 1971).

Duboscq, Guy, et al., ed., *La religion populaire* [Actes du colloque international, 1977] (Paris, 1979).

Duggan, Lawrence, "The Unresponsiveness of the Late Medieval Church: A Reconsideration," *Sixteenth Century Journal* 9, 1 (1978): 3–26.

Evennett, H. O., *The Spirit of the Counter Reformation* (Cambridge, England, 1968).

Faralli, Carla, "Le missioni dei Gesuiti in Italia (sec. XVI–XVII): problemi di una ricerca in corso," *Bollettino della Società di Studi Valdesi* 96 (1975): 97–116.

Fenlon, Dermot, *"Encore une Question:* Lucien Febvre, the Reformation and the School of 'Annales,' " *Historical Studies* 9 (1974): 65–81.

Förster, Joachim F., *Kurfürst Ferdinand von Köln* (Münster/W. 1976).

Fumaroli, Marc, *L'Age de c'éloquence* (Geneva, 1980).

Galasso, Giuseppe, and Russo, Carla, eds., *Per la storia sociale e religiosa de Mezzogiorno d'Italia* (Naples, 1980–).

García Oro, José, *Cisneros y la reforma del clero español en tiempo do los Reyes Catolicos* (Madrid, 1971).

Gilmont, Jean-François, "La bibliographie de la controverse catholique au XVIe siècle," *Révue d'histoire écclésiastique* 74 (1979): 362–71.

Gleason, Elisabeth G., "On the Nature of Sixteenth-Century Italian Evangelism: Scholarship, 1955–1978," *Sixteenth Century Journal* 9, 3 (1978): 3–25.

Grendler, Paul F., *The Roman Inquisition and the Venetian Press* (Princeton, 1977).

———, "The *Tre Savii sopra Eresia* 1547–1605: A Prosopographical Study," *Scuola e Vita* 3 (1979): 283–340.

Guarnieri, Romana, "Don Guiseppe De Luca tra cronaca e storia," *Modernismo, fascismo, comunismo: aspetti e figure della cultura e della politica dei cattolici nel '900*, ed. Guiseppe Rossini (Bologna, 1972): 249–362, first edition only.

Harding, Robert R., "The Mobilization of Confraternities against the Reformation in France," *Sixteenth Century Journal* 11, 2 (1980): 85–107. (This entire issue is dedicated to the Counter Reformation).

Hobsbawn, E. J., "The Revival of Narrative: Some Comments," *Past and Present* 86 (1980): 3–8.

Iggers, Georg G., *New Trends in European Historiography* (Middletown, Conn., 1975).

Iparraguirre, Ignacio, "Desmitificación de San Ignacio," *Archivum Historicum Societatis Jesu* 41 (1972): 357–73.

Jedin, Hubert, *Katholische Reformation oder Gegenreformation?* (Lucerne, 1946).

———, *Geschichte des Konzils von Trient*, 4 vols. (Freiburg i/Br., 1949–75). *History of the Council of Trent* (New York, 1957–61).

———, "Don Guiseppe De Luca e la storia della Chiesa," *Rivista di storia della Chiesa in Italia* 17 (1963): 10–14.

———, "Nuntiaturberichte und Durchfürung des Konzils von Trient," *Quellen und Forschungen aus italienischen Archiven und Biblîthiken* 53 (1973): 180–213.

Klaiber, Wilbirgis, ed., *Katholische Kontroverstheologen und Reformer des 16. Jahrhunderts: Ein Werkverzeichnis* (Münster/W., 1978).

Koenigsberger, H. G., "Decadence or Shift? Changes in the Civilization of Italy and Europe in the Sixteenth and Seventeenth Centuries," *Transactions of the Royal Historical Society* 5th Ser 10 (1960): 1–18.

Lazzarini, Antonio, "Studi di storia socio-religiosa," *Quaderni storici* 26 (1974): 568–81.

Lebrun, François, ed., "Directions de recherche," *La religion populaire: Approches historiques*, ed. Bernard Plongeron (Paris, 1976): 109–28.

———, *Histoire des catholiques en France du XVe siècle à nos jours* (Toulouse, 1980).

Le Brun, Jacques, "Bulletin d'histoire de la spiritualité: l'époque moderne," *Révue d'histoire de la spiritualité* 50 (1974): 57–79.

———, "Censure préventive et littérature religieuse en France au début du XVIIIe siècle," *Révue d'histoire de l'Église de France* 61 (1975): 201–25.

Lemmon, Alfred, "Jesuits and Music in Mexico," *Archivum Historicum Societatis Jesu* 46 (1977): 191–98.

Lutz, Heinrich, *Reformation und Gegenreformation* (Munich, 1979), 189–225.

Marcocchi, Massimo, "Per la storia della spiritualità in Italia tra il Cinquecento e il Seicento: Rassegna di studi e prospettive di ricerca," *Problemi di storia della Chiesa nei secoli XV–XVII* (Naples, 1979): 223–65. (The other contributions in this volume are also worth consulting).

Maron, Gottfried, "Das Schicksal der katholischen Reform im 16. Jahrhundert," *Zeitschrift für Kirchengeschichte* 88 (1977): 218–29.

McGinness, Frederick J., "Preaching Ideals and Practice in Counter-Reformation Rome," *Sixteenth Century Journal* 11, 2 (1980): 109–27.

Metz, René, "La paroisse en France à l'époque modern et contemporaine," *Révue d'histoire de l'Église de France* 60 (1974): 269–95; 61 (1975): 5–24.

Mezzadri, Luigi, "Le missioni popolari della Congregazione della Missione nello Stato della Chiesa (1642–1700)," *Rivista di Storia della Chiesa in Italia* 33 (1979): 12–44.

Müller, Gerhard, "Die Bedeutung der Nuntiaturberichte für die Kirchengeschichte," *Quellen und Forschungen aus italienischen Archiven und Bibliotheken* 53 (1973): 168–79.

Olivieri, Achille, "Sensibiltà religiosa urbana e sensibiltà religiosa contadina nel Cinquecento Veneto: suggestioni e problemi," *Critica storica* 9 (1972): 631–50.

———, "Strutture e caratteri della sensibiltà religiosa veneta del Cinquecento: suggestioni e studi," *Critica storica* 11 (1974): 577–93.

O'Malley, John, *Praise and Blame in Renaissance Rome* (Durham, N.C., 1979).

———, "Content and Rhetorical Forms in Sixteenth Century

Treatises on Preaching," *Renaissance Eloquence*, ed. James
J. Murphy (Berkeley, 1982).

Pallucchini, Anna, "Venezia religiosa nella pittura del Cinquecento," *Scuola e Vita* 14 (1972): 159–84.

Petrocchi, Massimo, *Storia della spiritualità italiana*, 3 vols. (Rome, -1978–1979), esp. 2: *Il Cinquecento e il Seicento.*

Pfeiffer, Heinz, "Zum neueren Schriftum über die Kunstätigkeit der Gesellschaft Jesu," *Archivum Historicum Societatis Jesu* 45 (1976): 220–30; 46 (1977): 421–30.

Plongeron, Bernard, *Religions et sociétés en occident* (Paris, 1979).

_____, and Pannet, Robert, eds., *Le christianisme populaire: Les dossiers de l'histoire* (Paris, 1976).

Prodi, Paolo, *Il cardinale Gabriele Paleotti (1522–1597)*, 2 vols. (Rome, 1959–67).

_____, "The Structure and Organization of the Church in Renaissance Venice," *Renaissance Venice*, ed. J. R. Hale (London, 1973): 409–30.

Prosperi, Adriano, *Tra evangelismo e controriforma: G. M. Giberti (1495–1543)* (Rome, 1969).

Pullan, Brian, *Rich and Poor in Renaissance Venice* (Cambridge, Mass., 1971).

Quazza, Guido, *La decadenza italiana nella storia europea* (Turin, 1971).

Reinhard, Wolfgang, *Papstfinanz und Nepotismus unter Paul V. (1605–1621)*, 2 vols. (Stuttgart, 1974).

_____, "Nepotismus: Der Funktionswandel einer papstgeschichtlichen Konstanten," *Zeitschrift für Kirchengeschichte* 86 (1975): 145–85.

_____, "Gegenreformation als Modernisierung? Prolegomena zu einer Theorie des konfessionellen Zeitalters," *Archiv für Reformationsgeschichte* 68 (1977): 226–52.

Rosa, Mario, *Religione e società nel Mezzogiorno tra Cinque e Seicento* (Bari, 1976).

Rotondò, Antonio, "La censura ecclesiastica e la cultura," *Storia d'Italia* [Enaudi] (Turin, 1973): V, 1399–1492.

Russo, Carla, "Studi recenti di storia sociale e religiosa in Francia: problemi e metodi," *Rivista storica italiana* 84 (1972): 625–82.

Sacrae Congregationis de Propaganda Fide Memoria Rerum, 3 vols. (Rome, 1971–76).

Salimbeni, Fulvio, "Vescovi, popolo e magia nel Sud. A proposito di un libro recente," *Nuova rivista storica* 56 (1972): 453–66.

Santosuosso, Antonio, "Religious Orthodoxy, Dissent, and Suppression in Venice in the 1540's," *Church History* 42 (1973): 476–85.

———, "The Italian Crisis at Mid-Sixteenth Century: A Matter of Shift and Decadence," *Canadian Journal of History* 10 (1975): 147–64.

Sauzet, Robert, *Les visites pastorales dans le diocèse de Chartres pendant la première moitié du XVIIe siècle* (Rome, 1975).

Scaduto, Mario, *L'epoca di Giacomo Lainez* (Rome, 1964–74).

———, "Dal Rinascimento alla Controriforma," *Archivum Historicum Societatis Jesu* 45 (1976): 377–93.

———, "Momenti di storia religiosa e di storia culturale italiana tra Cinquecento e Settecento," *Archivum Historicum Societatis Jesu* 46 (1977): 431–56.

Schmitt, Charles B., "Filosofia i scienza nelle università italiane del XVI secolo," *Il Renascimento: Interpretazioni e problemi* (Rome-Bari, 1979): 353–98.

Schurhammer, Georg, *Francis Xavier: His Life, His Times*, trans. Joseph Costelloe, 4 vols. (Rome, 1973–81).

Seifert, Arno, *Weltlicher Staat und Kirchenreform: Die Seminarpolitik Bayerns im 16. Jahrhundert* (Münster/W., 1978).

Simoncelli, Paolo, "Nuove ipotesi e studi sul 'Beneficio di Cristo,' " *Critica storica* 12 (1975): 320–88.

———, *Evangelismo italiano del Cinquecento* (Rome, 1979).

Smith, Hilary Dansey, *Preaching in the Spanish Golden Age* (Oxford, 1978).

Steinberg, Leo, "A Corner of the *Last Judgment*," *Daedalus* 109 (1980): 207–73.

Stella, P., "Devozioni e religiosità popolare in Italia (sec. XVI–XX): interpretazioni recenti," *Rivista Liturgica* 63 (1976): 155–73.

Stoianovich, Troian, *French Historical Method: The Annales Paradigm* (Ithaca, 1972).

Stone, Lawrence, "The Revival of Narrative: Reflections on a New Old History," *Past and Present* 85 (1979): 3–24.

Strnad, Alfred A. and Walsh, Katherine, "Reform und Reformation in neuer Sicht," *Innsbrucker Historische Studien: Sonderdruck* 1 (1978): 253–90.

Tacchi-Venturi, Pietro, *Storia della Compania di Gesù in Italia*, rev. ed., 2 vols. in 4 (Rome, 1930–51).

Tapié, Victor, *Retables baroques de Bretagne et spiritualité du XVIIe siècle* (Paris, 1972).

Tedeschi, John, "Preliminary Observations on Writing a History of the Roman Inquisition," *Continuity and Discontinuity in Church History*, eds. Forrester Church and Timothy George (Leiden, 1979): 232–49.

Tomaro, John, "The Papacy and the Implementation of the Council of Trent, 1564–1588," (Diss., University of North Carolina, 1973).

Vauchez, André, "La spiritualité populaire au moyen âge d'après l'oeuvre d'E. Delaruelle," *Révue d'histoire de la spiritualité* 51 (1975): 281–88.

Venard, Marc, "Autour de la Réforme tridentine en Italie," *Révue d'histoire écclésiastique* 70 (1975): 59–66.

_____, "Réforme, Réformation, Préréforme, Contre-Réforme: Étude de vocabulaire chez les historiens récents de la langue française," *Historiographie de la Réforme*, ed. Philippe Joutard (Paris, 1977): 352–65.

_____, and Julia, Dominique, "Le Répertoire des visites postorales," *Révue d'histoire de l'Église de France* 63 (1977): 213–33.

Weaver, F. Ellen, *The Evolution of the Reform of Port-Royal* (Paris, 1978).

_____, "Women and Religion in Early Modern France: A Bibliographical Essay on the State of the Question," *Catholic Historical Review* 67 (1981): 50–59.

Weil, Mark S., "The Devotion of the Forty Hours and Roman Baroque Illusions," *Journal of the Warburg and Courtauld Institutes* 37 (1974): 218–48.

Willaert, Léopold, *La restauration catholique, 1563–1648* (Paris, 1960).

Wright, A. D., "Federico Borromeo and Baronius," *Center for the Advanced Study of Italian Society*, Occasional Papers No. 6 (Reading, England, 1974): 3–27. (a)

_____, "Why the *Venetian* Interdict?" *English Historical Review* 89 (1974): 534–50. (b)

_____, "The People of Catholic Europe and the People of Anglican England," *The Historical Journal* 18 (1975): 451–66. (a)

_____, "The Significance of the Council of Trent," *The Journal of Ecclesiastical History* 26 (1975): 353–62. (b)

Zeeden, Ernst Walter and Molitor, Hansgeorg, ed., *Die Visitation im Dienst der kirchlichen Reform*, 2nd ed. (Münster/W., 1977).

From 'Popular Religion' to Religious Cultures

Natalie Zemon Davis

Ten years have passed since the publication of Keith Thomas's *Religion and the Decline of Magic* and *Le catholicisme entre Luther et Voltaire* of Jean Delumeau. Both of these important books insisted that religion be given a wide definition, extending beyond formal doctrine to widespread belief and beyond prescribed piety to actual practise. Both looked for boundaries between different systems of dealing with the supernatural: where did magic stop and religion start? where did paganism leave off and Christianity begin? Both described the attack on "superstition" by learned clerics, Protestant and Catholic (though Thomas viewed the Reformed assault as more uncompromising than the Counter-Reformed one), and both saw more effectively regulated, uniform religions emerging from the changes of the sixteenth century. However differently they assessed this outcome, they both agreed that the easy admixture of magic and religion in the medieval church had separated, and that, in Thomas's phrase, "the gulf [had deepened] between the educated classes and the lower strata of the rural population."[1]

From their work and earlier work[2] have been crystallized the problems historians have pursued in the past active decade. What precisely was popular religion? No other sixteenth-century subject has required more self-consciousness from its investigators! Did the task of describing it involve distinguishing the magical and pagan from the religious and the Christian? the "sincere" belief from the one held only out of fear or conformity? Or was it rather a matter of seeing what religion meant to those who said they believed it? What

---

[1]Delumeau (1965, 1971, 1974, 1976, 1978); Thomas (1971), 666.

[2]For bibliography and discussion of earlier work, see Davis (1974), Schmitt (1976), 23–36.

were the various social functions religion played? And were the changes of the late fifteenth to the seventeenth centuries to be interpreted primarily as the successful purging or repression of certain "popular" elements from Protestant and Catholic religions?

As to the definition of "popular religion," scholars agree that it refers to religion as practised and experienced and not merely as defined and prescribed. Beyond this there is so much ambiguity in usage that Carlo Ginzburg and William Christian, Jr. suggest that historians not employ the phrase at all. They may well be right. Against those who claim there exists an age-old, unchanging corpus of popular beliefs, formulas and rituals, they argue that religion must always be studied as the religion of certain groups in a given time and place.[3] But what these groups should be is less clear, and even Ginzburg and Christian differ in their choice. Introducing a collection of essays in *Quaderni Storici*, Ginzburg urges the study of the "religion of the popular classes" or the "subordinate classes" in pre-industrial Europe; a major issue is the range of relationships that can exist between this religion and that of the ruling classes, from convergence to opposition. Christian's study of sixteenth-century Spain focuses on "local religion," a religious style which is shared vertically by peasants, city-dwellers, and kings and which contrasts with universalistic, Erasmian styles brought in by clerical outsiders.[4]

Other interesting publications in recent years move between the same poles of broad and narrow construction. For A. N. Galpern the "people" included anyone who lived in sixteenth-century Champagne, clerics as well as lay people, whose behavior helped one explicate continuity. In Marc Venard's study of religion and the church in sixteenth-century Avignon and its environs, the "popular classes" are more specifically the small merchants, artisans, workers, cultivators, and the poor, whose "modes of religious participation" are contrasted with those of the urban elites and those of the clergy.[5]

These works portray religious cultures—interconnected beliefs and practises—within a framework chosen by the historian as significant. The question to be examined may be the transformation of Catholicism from its medieval to modern forms; Avignon, with its special connections with the papacy and Tridentine reform, is an in-

---

[3]Carlo Ginzburg, (1979), 393–97; Christian (1981), 178–80. See also Vauchez (1976), 429–44; Vovelle (1977), 7–32.

[4]Ginzburg, "Premessa Giustificativa," *Religioni* (1979), 393–97; Christian (1981).

[5]Galpern (1976); Venard (1980) 4, 1755–1799.

teresting case. It may be the implantation of a Protestant society; the Palatinate and adjacent Rhineland (the subject of Bernard Vogler's work), with both Reformed and Lutheran churches, make an interesting case. Or the historian may want to explore the possibilities of religion for creating solidarities and social or personal identities; the villages of New Castile informing Philip II about their shrines and vows, a London turner recording his "Growth" as a Christian, and a Bolognese seamstress telling her spiritual thoughts to her diary provide splendid cases.[6]

What must be established from such cases is not whether they are "popular," but what they represent. As Peter Burke has warned us, the culture of artisans and peasants can vary from milieu to milieu, and when nobles and clerics take part in it, they do so with their own understandings and on their own terms.[7] So Luisa Ciammiti does not claim that her saintly seamstress is typical, but does set her firmly in the world of single women in seventeenth-century Bologna and in a tradition of pious females given scope by their confessors. So Galpern stresses the importance of confraternities throughout Champagne, but notes that the poor did not belong to them. Christian points out that saints act as helpers throughout New Castile, but while villagers drew together around one set of saints, city-dwellers expressed their differences in devotion to separate saints. Both Venard and Vogler discuss distinctive features of their regions in a way that illumines conditions elsewhere. Is the "malleability" and "need to experiment" in Avignonese religious life connected with its open geographical location? Is not the long solicitude of the Palatinate clergy for the daily activities of their flock connected to the existence of the two competing Protestant confessions and political fragmentation there? Does this explain the contrast with the clergy in "the great Lutheran territories, who became functionaries and led a quiet little life"?[8]

The study of religious cultures should, then, be contextual and comparative. It also should be relational. We do not want just to compare peasants with their priests, pastors, landlords, and judges; we want to see them interacting with each other through religion. The priest may be a vigilant agent of the bishop in removing an un-

---

[6]Venard (1980); Vogler (1974, 1976); Christian (1981); Seaver (1980); Ciammitti, (1979), 603–39.

[7]Burke (1978), 23–64.

[8]Ciammitti (1979), 603–39; Galpern (1976), 52–68; Christian (1981), 148–53;

seemly statue from the parish church; he may be the old-time collaborator of the village blacksmith in presenting a blessed and heated key to persons and animals stricken with rabies.[9] Whatever the case, a religious culture should be seen in two-way communication with the structures of authority around it.

The rabies key of Saint Pierre can also open the door to our next concern, the criteria used to understand religious cultures. Though historians have followed Thomas and Delumeau in using the categories "magic," "superstitious," and "pagan" as rightful evidence for sixteenth- and seventeenth-century thought, they are becoming increasingly unwilling to adopt them as terms for interpreting religious practise.[10] New approaches have led to at least three discoveries that we can consider: behavior previously dismissed as irrational or "merely" ritualistic has been found to be significant in defining group identity and social relations; reflection on doctrine has been found among people who, it was thought, had no time even for opinions; and the connection between Catholic and Protestant reform programs and actual experience has been found to be more complex than we knew.

Already in *Religion and the Decline of Magic* Keith Thomas had mentioned that public prayer might have the symbolic function of demonstrating a community's solidarity as well as seeking God's practical help at a time of crisis. Galpern's sensitive examination of the cult of the saints, prayers for the dead, and confraternities went on to show the relation between these activities and a society in which the strong helped the weak in patronage relationships and in which, in the absence of central sovereign authority, people clustered in multiple small groups for mutual support. Galpern insisted, however, that these forms had been relevant to the fourteenth and fifteenth centuries, but were no longer "meaningful" in the sixteenth century—a strained and unconvincing use of the theory of cultural lag. Now William Christian has argued that such devotions can have a continuous role over time not just in reflecting social realities, but in shaping them. Shrines, vows, relics, and the patron saints that went with them in sixteenth-century New Castile created and reinforced corporate responsibility and, by bringing the sacred into di-

---

Venard (1980) 4:1924–31; Vogler (1976), 369–70.
[9]Venard (1977).
[10]See discussion in Davis (1974), Geertz and Thomas (1975).

rect contact with the landscape, strengthened local societies, urban and rural, against outside control. So long as people believed that disasters were mostly the punishments of an angry God and saints for collective sins—and this belief lasted for a long time—so long would they domesticate any reforms toward a universalistic or personal religion into local bargains with heavenly protectors.[11]

In a wide-ranging interpretation of public behavior, religious and secular, in fifteenth-century Florence, Richard Trexler has made the most impressive case for the significance of ritual and suggested how to account for short-term changes: "The purpose of ritual . . . is to achieve goals; it is not obsessive or irrational, but ecologically adaptive." Florentine religion, from processions bearing Our Lady of Impruneta through the streets to the climax of the Mass, helped provide the legitimacy, honor, and trust needed by a commercial republic without a nobility and with a fluid political system based on patronage. Then, when the independence of the republic was threatened from without, religious ritual helped provide identity within by placing innocent boys at the center of a new processional life.[12]

Such approaches have so far been little used in regard to Protestant devotional forms, with their reduction in ritual, but the evidence for such an analysis is being collected. What are the markers for group identity and for social linkage and exclusion when processions and corporate ties around saints and relics have been eliminated? What new powers of social definition are given to words, songs and voices, which play so important a role in the new liturgy? The practise of the Lord's Supper, hitherto studied primarily to assess the success or failure of the Reformation, could be used as an indicator of the community's self-image: the high level of attendance of Protestants in the Languedoc and Geneva; the higher attendance of women than of men in the Palatinate; the non-attendance of people with unresolved quarrels, even when their pastors say they may come; non-attendance of people because they lack decent clothes; disputes about precedence in receiving the sacrament, some wanting social status or political position to count more than ecclesiastical status or sex (that is, nobles and magistrates before Elders; wealthy women with their husbands, not with other women at the back); the reluctance of

---

[11]Thomas (1971), 146–47; Galpern (1976), especially 43–44, 69–71, 94–95; Christian (1981), chs. 5–6.

[12]Trexler (1980), xxiv–xv and throughout.

some believers to drink wine from a goblet touched by so many lips—to give only a few examples.[13]

If we are now more aware of the variation in the symbolic meanings of religious cultures, other studies have revealed the extent to which reflection on doctrine cropped up even in the humblest circles. Already there were the individual "religious skeptics" that Keith Thomas found here and there, such as the Essex husbandman that held "all things cometh by nature;" then there were the villagers of Montaillou, who in the early fourteenth century discussed among themselves at least four different theories about the condition of the soul after death. Now there is Carlo Ginzburg's village miller Menocchio in the hills of Friuli, who for decades had argued with cobblers and priests and anyone who would listen that the world emerged from chaos, that God was everywhere, that Christ was "one of the children of God because we are all God's children," that there was no resurrection of the flesh, that "each person holds his faith to be right, but we do not know which is the right one," that the clergy wanted to be gods on earth, and much more. Whether or not Menocchio's world-view was a blend of an old oral tradition of peasant materialism (as Ginzburg has speculated) with ideas taken from the books he had borrowed, he was responsible for *a ferment of rural discussion* on subjects that went well beyond the everyday needs of crops and families. And it was thirty years before he was denounced to the Inquisition in 1584. Nor are such circles of argument unique. About the same time in a village in Lorraine touched by the Reformation, Noel Journet, former soldier and now local schoolmaster, talks to his cronies about how the Bible is but "fables, dreams, and lies," how Jesus Christ "is a man like others," how magistrates are "tyrants and thieves," how he wants to write a book about a new faith and a God that is not cruel.[14]

In short, recent research has suggested that we widen our sense of the possibilities of religious culture, even in the countryside. More is packed into the meaning of ritual life than we have thought and, even though there may be relatively few Menocchios and Journets, more is going on in local discussions than we have thought. All this is

[13]Garrisson-Estèbe (1980), 241–46; Vogler (1974), 2:713–60; Vogler, "La piété populaire luthérienne dans les pays rhénans au XVIe siècle," Plongeron and Pannet (1976), 138–42. I have tried to give some attention to the interpretation of Calvinist ritual in Davis (1975), ch. 6 and Davis (1981).

[14]Thomas (1971), 166–73; Le Roy Ladurie (1975), chs. 26–27; Davis (1979), 64–71; Ginzburg (1980), 1–17 and throughout; Berriot (1978).

well to bear in mind in considering the origins and impact of Catholic and Protestant reform.

In the interpretation of changing Catholic religious practise, two major approaches emerge. One is represented by the work of Marc Venard on Avignon and its region. Using such indices as wills, Venard finds a supple Catholic practise in the pre-Reformation years, balanced between individual concern for salvation and religious structures which connect with local social institutions, between the cult of the saints and the worship of Christ. He does not think it useful to determine how "pagan" this practise was—there is no single model for a Christian society in his view—and if anything, the "infra-Christian foundation of beliefs and cosmo-biological rites" helped root Catholicism in the region. As with William Christian's "local religion," Avignonese religious culture carried with it a strong sense of the sacred in holy objects, and the support of the popular classes for the extermination of the Waldensians and their subsequent violence against Huguenots was touched off in part by their fear of profanation.

Heresy in the Avignon region is not accounted for, then, by the "religious anguish" found in northern areas of Europe. It comes initially, says Venard, from Waldensian settlements from the Piedmont, which had held tenaciously to their old ways, and then from relatively literate artisans, mostly outside of Avignon, eager for access to the Word and to the liturgy in their own language. The Counter-Reformation finally took hold in the region, aided by the collaboration of the popular classes with their mysticism, violence, processions, confraternities (though not the penitential ones, which were special to the upper classes), and even with their willingness to argue doctrine with Protestants. The Tridentine victory had some irony to it, however, for it weakened those features of Catholic life previously central to popular support, desacralizing it by the exclusive privilege given the Sacred Host above every other form of devotion. Venard makes the interesting suggestion that the predominant role of women in seventeenth-century Avignonese piety (at confession, communion, etc.) reflects their greater tolerance for clericalization. It was their husbands and fathers who lost power when the *curés* took more control over the confraternities and hospitals; now the women could have more scope of their own.[15]

Though arrived at independently, Venard's views have some gen-

[15]Venard (1980), especially 211–82, 367–406, 1755–1839, 1923–57.

eral resemblance to John Bossy's interpretation of Catholic change, first offered in an important essay of 1970 on "The Counter-Reformation and the People of Catholic Europe." Both see a medieval church giving expression to independent social groupings and a Tridentine Church seeking to attain unity through clerically controlled institutions, especially the parish. But whereas the sources for Venard's research have been ecclesiastical and other archives in one locality, Bossy's have been liturgical texts and commentaries on them from different parts of Europe, and his approach to them has been inspired by anthropology. In close examinations of baptism, godparentage, confession, and the Mass, Bossy argued that the medieval church served primarily to make peace between feuding and quarrelling kinship groups, while the Tridentine Church tried to keep peace by ignoring or suppressing particularistic interests. The medieval Mass allowed moments where people could pray for their own kin and friends, living and dead (and possibly even against their enemies), and yet buried enmities in the mutual sacrifice of Christ and in the kiss of peace. The post-Tridentine Mass intensified its sacramental features at the expense of its sacrificial ones, and abandoned the kiss of peace, already weakened by the use of a peace board, which worshippers kissed instead of each other. Unity was even more effectively created in the non-liturgical parish feast of Corpus Christi. The medieval sacrament of confession was made in the open, often involved the reporting of quarrels, and ended in a laying on of priestly hands which reconciled the sinner not only to God but to fellow Christians. The post-Tridentine confession was hidden in a stall where the priest, now more a judge than a peacemaker, could not lay on the hands of social reconciliation, and where the questioning might stress inner states more than outer wrongs. Bossy concludes that the precarious unity created through recognizing and reconciling quarrelling groups had more substance to it than the artificial unity of the Counter-Reformation with its asocial core.[16]

There is much to debate in Bossy's interpretation, and he himself sees parts of it as still exploratory. Can we, for instance, view the Tridentine Church as giving as little leeway to kin groups as he suggests, especially when we look at practise along with prescription?

[16]Bossy (1970, 1973, 1975, 1979, 1981). For the special situation of Catholics in England, Bossy (1976), ch. 6.

Books of hours and rosaries circulate within families as sacred property and do not have a totally individual character; Jesuits teach prayers to be said "in common" for a mother or father "in the assembly of the family" and to be said privately during the *Memento etiam* of the Mass for one's departed "kin, friends, and allies;" families ignore the Tridentine limitation on godparents and, with the connivance of their parish priests, bring in groups of them to the baptismal font; burial practises increasingly stress the family tomb or chapel. Confraternities do not allow themselves to be totally under the thumb of the clergy; laymen of the parish vestry quarrel with their priest; women's gossip (that is, "godsib") networks continue to have authority in the neighborhood.[17] Perhaps Bossy's generalizations will have to be modified somewhat, but nevertheless, he has provided one of the most important and original approaches to religious culture to appear in the last decade.

Studies of Protestant religious culture have been less sweeping in their time frame, but Janine Garrisson-Estèbe, Bernard Vogler, and Gerald Strauss have made interesting statements regarding the impact of the new religions in southern France, the Palatinate, and other parts of Germany in the last half of the sixteenth century. Using records of Reformed synods and consistories and of Lutheran visitations, they find evidence of the persistence of old ways, such as carnival and the fires of Saint John's day, and apathy for the new, such as talking or sleeping during the pastor's sermon. Attendance at catechism, so important in principle for a religion insisting on knowledge of the faith, was sporadic at best—"negligent," "careless" (*fahrlässig, unfleiss*), said the pastors in the Palatinate and elsewhere in Germany—and if the youngsters managed to memorize their catechism, they didn't know what it meant and they forgot it when they grew up. Gerald Strauss concludes from the visitors' reports that "the programmed indoctrination" and "parroting [of the catechism] could not have prompted much religious thinking. . . . A century of Protestantism had brought about little or no change in the common religious conscience and in the ways in which ordinary

---

[17]For example, Emond Auger, *La manière d'ouir la messe avec dévotion et fruict spirituel. Ensemble le manière de bien confesser ses pechez . . . Et quelque prières générales pour toutes sortes de personnes* (Paris, 1571), ff. C iii^r, H i^r–H ii^r. Archives municipales de Lyon, GG3 and GG384 with examples of godparents in the 1570's and 1580's going beyond the Tridentine limitation, already proclaimed in the diocese in 1566. Davis (1978), 99, 107.

men and women conducted their lives. . . . Against this alien code [of the Lutheran clergy], ordinary people maintained a vigorous religious subculture."[18]

There can be little doubt that the religious subculture existed, but it is hard to see from these sources what would be its characteristics, nor is it likely that it would be totally free from Protestant values. Some children mastered their catechism well—throughout the Palatinate, they were reported especially to be girls—and some adults, especially women, could answer for their faith. Mute or mechanical though these people were at their interrogations, they went back to villages and workshops where memorized words were used to tell things in their own way, through stories, the back-and-forth of argument, and exchanged proverbs. Perhaps they had living in their neighborhood not only the cloth merchant who (as Strauss reports) remembered wool prices but not the sermon and the catechism "because he didn't need them so much," but also a Menocchio, like the digger of Germersheim in the Rhineland who denied the resurrection of the dead.[19]

What is clear from the many indices used by Vogler in his regional study is that some features of Protestantism—picked up from sermons sometimes attended and listened to despite the chatter of the young and the snores of the old, the experience of communion taken sometimes, the experience of being summoned before a Reformed consistory or of reporting someone to an elder—influenced the way the popular classes defined their world and the sacred. Christocentric language is used in more than a formulaic way in wills; Psalms and hymns are sung at times of trial; family prayers are said; the consistory is appealed to for the settling of quarrels in Reformed areas. These are not alien matters like the ham hanging from the *conversos'* ceiling. Rather they have been taken over by these communities, at least in part, *on their own terms.* Thus Vogler can talk about a "Protestant style" finally emerging among the masses of people; indeed, it may account for their sharing in the anti-Catholic spirit of the seventeenth-century confessional age. An even better example, provided by Philippe Joutard, is the appearance in Protestant areas of distinctive healing and other folk practises, reproved by

[18]Garrisson-Estèbe (1980), 229–35; [Garrisson-]Estèbe and Vogler (1976), 368–69; Vogler (1974), 771–809; Strauss (1978), chs. 13–14.

[19]Vogler (1974), 787–807, 875; Strauss (1978), 296.

pastors as magical, but nevertheless based on Reformed models and ideas.[20]

Lent does not triumph definitively over Carnival in the sixteenth and seventeenth centuries, but neither are the popular classes unaffected by the historical changes in which they participate. Religious cultures are not merely inherited or imposed; they are also made and remade by the people who live them.

To study these processes further in the age of the Reformation, we can follow the paths opened by these and other valuable publications. What has proved fruitful is the re-examination of the forms of religious life so as to link them in a new way with social and political activity, with feeling and reflection: the rituals that accompany the great stages of life, birth, marriage, and death;[21] the rituals that accompany the different stages of the year in countryside, city, and court;[22] the rituals that can mark an individual life throughout the day or year, including feasting and fasting, and other forms of bodily control; the rituals available for periods of anger, shame, fear, or rejoicing. Pilgrimages, processions, miracles, and shrines can be studied and mapped, vows and ex-votos examined.[23] The social setting for religious behavior can be investigated both in the formal organization of the parish and confraternity and in the informal world of the household and neighborhood circle.[24]

Let me take liturgical and sacramental forms as an example. How can we study them so as to see more clearly what religion means in the sixteenth century and why it changes? First we go well beyond establishing attendance at events of public worship, essential though this is for a start.[25] Following Bossy, we work through the varieties of sixteenth-century liturgical texts and sacramental manuals (many of them available in American and Canadian rare-book collections);

[20]Vogler (1974), 842, 885–89, 928; [Garrisson-]Estèbe and Vogler (1976), 386–87; Garrisson-Estèbe (1980), 277–83, 335–37; Monter (1976), 479; Philippe Joutard, "Protestantisme populaire et univers magique: le cas cévenol," in *Religion populaire* (1977), 145–64. Other useful sources on the implantation of Protestant religious culture are Bertheau (1970), Soman (1980), Kingdon (1972).
[21]Molin and Mutembe (1976); Burguière (1978); Davis (1978); Ariès (1977); Chaunu (1978); Gennep (1960).
[22]Phythian-Adams (1972); Davis (1981).
[23]Henisch (1976); Christian (1972, 1981); Sumption (1975); Turner (1978); Rothkrug (1980); Schmitt (1979); Delumeau (1976), ch. 10 on "Les miracles"; *Ex-voto* (1979).
[24]Gutton (1979), Kingdon (1979), Freeman (1968).
[25]Toussaert (1960), 124–60; Vogler (1974), 650–57.

and then we try to understand them as doctrine, metaphor, and performance.[26] By metaphor I mean all those features of language, ges-
ture, and movement which make statements about human relationships. By performance I mean the actual event, as close as we can
get to it, as experienced by worshippers in a given time and place.

For the reconstruction of the Catholic mass and the Protestant service, the evidence is scattered about in different sources, as we can
see from the French case. It is found in instructions to priest and
pastor:

> Catholic: "The priest kisses the altar and turns toward the
>   people."
> Protestant: "That done, the assembly sings some Psalm."

In the hostile polemical literature:

> Protestant on Catholic: "Messire Jacotin must be very much in
>   love with that table, he kisses it so often; he turns like a
>   Moorish dancer."
> Catholic to Protestant: "The disorder of their Psalm-singing is
>   so great that some are on one verse, some on another . . .
>   Not a zealous sigh during their service, no hand on the
>   breast, perpetually cold as ice."

In advice to worshippers at the back of Books of Hours, and in devotional literature:

> Catholic: "When you see the host elevated say, 'Oh, God eter-
>   nal father, I present this holy sacrifice."
> Protestant: "One must look out that the singing not be light
>   and frivolous, but have weight and majesty."

In educational literature:

> Catholic: "Our mass is so familiar that almost the littlest
>   woman understands what happens next . . . and the least of
>   artisans knows when to say 'Amen'."
> Protestant: "We praise the Lord with a common speech, and
>   almost from the same mouth . . . We pray always from the
>   heart."

In church records which can tell us about seating, whether there are
seats, and about decorum:

> Catholic: "Laughing during mass is a mortal sin." "No one is

---

[26]Turner (1969); Geertz (1973), chs. 4, 15; Dix (1945); Trexler (1980); Davis (1981).

to place any herbs or writings under the altar cloth while mass is being said in hopes of magical work."

Protestant: "There is laughing during the service." "The preacher's sermons are too long, confused, and abusive."

In parodic ceremonies, such as the Feast of Fools, which can tell us about the significance of their object, in diaries and in paintings and woodcuts.[27]

Such evidence must be interpreted without preconceived notions of what constitutes an appropriate demeanor for worship: dogs may be barking and babies crying, yet, whatever the fears of the clergy, people may take away from the experience a concept of the sacred in a characteristic relation to the profane. The question that must be asked is what has to happen to make the liturgical event of the mass appear to be "a lie"[28]—to the celebrants, but here especially to the "popular classes." Is it an enhanced sense of their own religious competence? an intensified resentment at the clergy's economic, political, and emotional power? a rejection of the kind of social hierarchy expressed during the mass? a rejection of sacrifice and patriarchal redistribution as the bases for trust and the flow of goods? Whatever the case, and this list has not exhausted the possibilities, any theory of the popular sources of the Reformation must be able to account for what occurred around the altar and what was created around the pulpit and the communion table.

For confession, the way has been paved by Thomas Tentler's excellent book on the medieval period, Steven Ozment's use of confessors' manuals to illustrate "the burden of late medieval religion," and Bossy's linking of pre-Tridentine confession with the resolution of quarrels and social amity.[29] A fuller view of the performance of confession may help us understand why some sinners ultimately re-

[27]*Missale Romanum, peroptime ordinatum* (Lyon, 1512), f. 108^{r-v}. In the copy in Princeton's Firestone Library there are as well further written instructions in the margin in a sixteenth century hand. [Jean Calvin], *La forme des prières et chantz écclésiastiques* (Geneva, 1542), ff. i 6^r, a 2^r–a 5^r; Pierre Viret, *Les cauteles et canon de la messe* (Lyon, 1563), 91, 113–14; Florimond de Raemond, *L'histoire de la naissance, progrez et decadence de l'hérésie de ce siècle* (Rouen, 1623), 1010–11; *Cy commence une petite instruction et manière de vivre pour une femme seculière* (Paris, n.d. [c. 1520]), f. A viii^v; *Heures a lusaige de lyon nouvellement imprimées et corrigées à Paris l'an mil cinq cens et six* (Paris, n.d. [1506]), ff. 109^r–112^v; Emond Auger, *Continuation de l'institution, Verité et Utilité du Sacrifice de la Messe* (Paris, 1566), 107, 111; Pierre Viret, *Du vray usage de la salutation faict par l'ange a la vierge Marie* ([Geneva], 1556), 59, 73; Jean Benedicti, *La Somme des Pechez* (Paris, 1595), 195–96; Vogler (1974), 659, 667.

[28]On liturgy and lying, see Rappaport (1978).

[29]Tentler (1977); Ozment (1975), 22–27; Bossy (1975).

jected it as a wicked tyranny, while others accepted it or even tried to turn it to their own uses. Drawing from summas, the literature of advice and other primary sources, let us reconstruct Easter confession in a medium-size parish of three hundred families in a French city.[30] There are two vicars ready for "the crowd" (*la foule*). One, following his manual and the recommendations of the last synod, is "gentle, gracious, humble, affable" and allows the sinner to accuse herself in any order she wishes before going on to do the questioning; the other is severe and admonitory, directing the questioning throughout. The people arrive in diverse states. A few have examined their lives already by the ten commandments and the seven deadly sins and may even have brought along notes; most have one or two sins in mind since last Easter or are just in a vague state of apprehension. During the confession, some have trouble understanding the priest's words and he theirs, since they speak a rural dialect or a foreign tongue; others tell of a sinful event as though it were a wondrous or funny story; others, especially the women, conceal things so they will not appear dishonored before the priest; others lay the blame for everything on someone else; some talk about themselves seriously as the center of an important event. Meanwhile, the people in line are pressing forward to overhear what is being confessed ahead and speculating that Pierre is admitting the disobedience to his master he bragged about a month ago at the Three Crowns Inn and that Antoinette is being induced to recount her lascivious behavior with François, currently the subject of gossip on her street.

The experience of confession varies and the Protestant rejection of it may depend less on a view of it as always shameful and frightening than on a broader set of social and psychological circumstances that make the priestly role seem unacceptable in any form. Sinful acts with important public consequences should be treated not in private or as a subject of gossip, but in a public arena, as at a meeting of a Reformed consistory.

A similar approach could be used for the study of private prayer, where the sources are abundant: prescriptive writings of humanists,

---

[30]Benedicti, *Somme*, 215–23 and Book V; Auger, *La manière d'ouir la messe* . . . *Ensemble la manière de bien confesser ses pechez*, ff. D iii^r–F i^r; *Cy commence une petite instruction*, ff. B iv–B ii^v; *Statuta ecclesie Lugduni* (Lyon, n.d. [c. 1488]), ff. b ii^r–b iiii^r; *Statuta synodalia ecclesiae metropolitanae et primatialis Lugdunensis* (Lyon, 1566), 30–36; *Statuts et Ordonnances synodales de l'Eglise metropolitaine de Lyon* (Lyon, 1578), ch. 9.

Protestants, and Catholics; printed and manuscript collections of prayers; prayers penned into the fly-leafs of books; paintings and woodcuts. Here again an effort could be made to understand the prayer as a performance: who is praying, in what setting and when? with what gestures, entreaties, and intentions? Nor need we stop with the numbered Rosary prayers (attacked by Reformers as superstitious and defended by Domincans as "made for everyone, both men and women, lettered and unlettered"), but go on to consider invocations and incantations, even if attacked by both reforms as magical.[31]

Throughout this essay I have been assuming that the most fruitful work on religious cultures would have a comparative perspective, comparing behavior by class, sex, and locality and comparing Protestant and Catholic religious sensibility. I would like to propose that we expand our comparative framework even further to include Jewish religious culture. By this I mean asking the same questions about Jewish communities in Italy and central Europe that we have been asking about "popular religion" in Christian societies, and trying to use the Jewish case to verify our conclusions about the Protestant and Catholic cases. For example, in contrast to what was happening in Christian Europe in the sixteenth and seventeenth centuries, there was a great porousness between rabbinical religion and magic or "superstition." Throughout Jewish society spirits were invoked by calling on their names (mostly angelic, sometimes demonic), amulets were prepared and used, and the rabbis insisted that the amulets worn on the sabbath be approved ones (that is, they had worked for three different persons, were written on kosher parchment, etc.). What was feared was not some pact with Satan, who in any case played little role in Jewish belief, but the idolatry of claiming that the power achieved had come from one's own act rather than God's Name or that of His agents. People were rarely accused of witchcraft, and as for the inevitable Evil Eye, one counteracted it by practical techniques, but did not prosecute those who cast it.

The explanation for this situation is multiple—the widespread interest among learned Jews in mystical Kabbalah, especially after the

[31]White (1951); Tobriner (1975); Snyder (1976); Britnell (1976); Ruth Mortimer, *Harvard College Library . . . French 16th Century Books* (2 vols.; Cambridge, Mass., 1964), nos. 294–313 on Books of Hours. *Alphabet ou Instruction Chrestienne, pour les petis enfans* (Lyon, 1558); Emond Auger, *Formulaire de prières catholiques* (Paris, 1576); Pierre de Bollo, *Le Rosaire de la tressaincte vierge Marie Mere de Dieu* (Lyon, 1604), 21.

expulsion from Spain, the relative decentralization of religious organization (groups of literate males around rabbis), the fluidity of Jewish social structure, the distinctive relation of women to ritual life
and Talmud, the combination of mistrust of each other and utter dependence on each other so characteristic of these precarious Jewish
communities—but it should be evident how our analysis of Christian Europe can benefit from such a comparison.[32]

And perhaps as well we will find similarities in the differences:
the Jewish woman in childbirth reciting Psalm 20, one verse for each
month of pregnancy, and holding her amulet with the three angels
that protect against Lilith; the Catholic woman in childbirth invok-
ing Saint Margaret and placing an amulet with prayers to her on her
stomach; the Protestant woman in her good-luck childbirth girdle,
calling to the Lord while her midwife recites charms over her.[33]
Each can teach us what is particular to a religious culture and what
is common to the people of sixteenth-century Europe.

Bibliography

Abrahams, Israel, *Jewish Life in the Middle Ages*, ed. Cecil Roth
    (London, 1932).

Ariès, Philippe, *L'homme devant la mort* (Paris, 1977).

Aymard, A., "Contribution à l'étude du folklore de la Haute Au-
    vergne. Le sachet accoucheur et ses mystères," *Annales du
    Midi* 38 (1926): 237–347.

Barriot, François, "Hétérodoxie religieuse et utopie politique dans
    les 'erreurs estranges' de Noël Journet (1582)," *Bulletin de la
    société de l'histoire du protestantisme français* 124 (1978):
    236–48.

Bertheau, Solange, "Le consistoire dans les Eglises Réformées du
    Moyen-Poitou au XVIIe siècle," *Bulletin de la sociètè de l'his-*

---

[32]Trachtenberg (1977); Abrahams (1932); Pollack (1971); *Magic and Superstition*
(1975); Scholem (1965); Patai (1967); Simonsohn (1977), chs. 6–7. For a general introduction to the large body of literature on Jewish society and culture in the early
modern period, see Jacob Katz, *Tradition and Crisis. Jewish Society at the End of the
Middle Ages* (New York, 1971) and H.H. Ben-Sasson, ed., *A History of the Jewish People* (Cambridge, Mass., 1976).

[33]Trachtenberg (1977), 139, 105–106, 169, 202; *Magic and Superstition* (1975), nos.
164–76. *La vie de madame saincte Marguerite vierge et martyre avec son oraison*
(n.p., n.d. [c. 1515]), ff. A vi^v–A viii^r; Aymard (1926); Thomas (1971), 188.

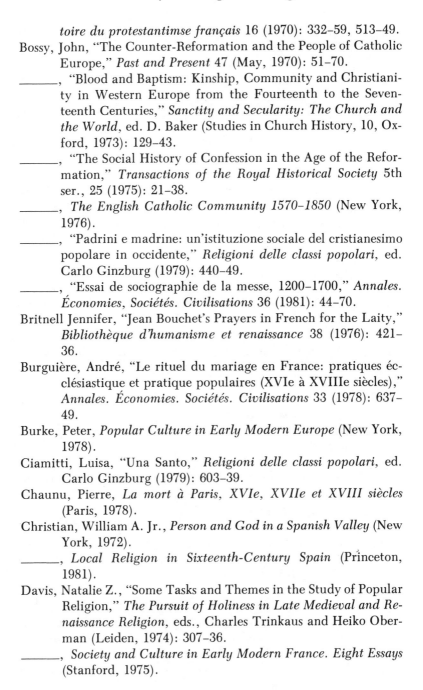

toire du protestantimse français 16 (1970): 332–59, 513–49.

Bossy, John, "The Counter-Reformation and the People of Catholic Europe," *Past and Present* 47 (May, 1970): 51–70.

———, "Blood and Baptism: Kinship, Community and Christianity in Western Europe from the Fourteenth to the Seventeenth Centuries," *Sanctity and Secularity: The Church and the World*, ed. D. Baker (Studies in Church History, 10, Oxford, 1973): 129–43.

———, "The Social History of Confession in the Age of the Reformation," *Transactions of the Royal Historical Society* 5th ser., 25 (1975): 21–38.

———, *The English Catholic Community 1570–1850* (New York, 1976).

———, "Padrini e madrine: un'istituzione sociale del cristianesimo popolare in occidente," *Religioni delle classi popolari*, ed. Carlo Ginzburg (1979): 440–49.

———, "Essai de sociographie de la messe, 1200–1700," *Annales. Économies, Sociétés. Civilisations* 36 (1981): 44–70.

Britnell Jennifer, "Jean Bouchet's Prayers in French for the Laity," *Bibliothèque d'humanisme et renaissance* 38 (1976): 421–36.

Burguière, André, "Le rituel du mariage en France: pratiques écclésiastique et pratique populaires (XVIe à XVIIIe siècles)," *Annales. Économies. Sociétés. Civilisations* 33 (1978): 637–49.

Burke, Peter, *Popular Culture in Early Modern Europe* (New York, 1978).

Ciamitti, Luisa, "Una Santo," *Religioni delle classi popolari*, ed. Carlo Ginzburg (1979): 603–39.

Chaunu, Pierre, *La mort à Paris, XVIe, XVIIe et XVIII siècles* (Paris, 1978).

Christian, William A. Jr., *Person and God in a Spanish Valley* (New York, 1972).

———, *Local Religion in Sixteenth-Century Spain* (Princeton, 1981).

Davis, Natalie Z., "Some Tasks and Themes in the Study of Popular Religion," *The Pursuit of Holiness in Late Medieval and Renaissance Religion*, eds., Charles Trinkaus and Heiko Oberman (Leiden, 1974): 307–36.

———, *Society and Culture in Early Modern France. Eight Essays* (Stanford, 1975).

————, "Ghosts, Kin and Progeny: Some Features of Family Life in Early Modern France," *The Family*, eds. A. S. Rossi, J. Kagan and T. K. Hareven (New York, 1978): 87–114.

————, "Les conteurs de Montaillou," *Annales. Économies. Sociétés. Civilisations.* 34 (1979): 61–73.

————, "The Sacred and the Body Social in Sixteenth-Century Lyon," *Past and Present* 90 (Febr., 1981): 40–70.

Delumeau, Jean, *Naissance et affirmation de la Réforme* (Paris, 1965).

————, *Le catholicisme entre Luther et Voltaire* (Paris, 1971).

————, "Les réformateurs et la superstition," *Actes du Colloque L'Admiral de Coligny et son temps* (Paris, 1974): 451–87.

————, *La mort des pays de Cocagne. Comportements collectifs de la Renaissance a l'âge classique* (Publications de la Sorbonne, "Etudes," 12; Paris, 1976).

————, *La peur en Occident, XVIe–XVIIIe siècles* (Paris, 1978).

Dix, Dom Gregory, *The Shape of the Liturgy* (London, 1945).

Ex-Voto du terroir marseillais, Exhibition at the Archives communales de Marseille, October 1978–January 1979 (Marseille, 1979).

Freeman, Susan Tax, "Religious Aspects of the Social Organization of a Castilian Village," *American Anthropologist* 70 (1968): 38–49.

Galpern, A. N., *The Religion of the People in Sixteenth-Century Champagne* (Cambridge, 1976).

Garrisson-Estebe, Janine, *Protestants du midi*, 1559–1598 (Toulouse, 1980).

————, and Vogler, Bernhard, "La génèse d'une société protestante: Étude comparée de quelques registres consistoriaux languedociens et palatins vers 1600," *Annales. Économies. Sociétés. Civilisations* 31 (1976): 362–78.

Geertz, Clifford, *The Interpretation of Cultures* (New York, 1973).

Geertz, Hildred and Thomas, Keith, "An Anthropology of Religion and Magic, Two Views," *Journal of Interdisciplinary History* 6 (1975): 71–109.

Gennep, Arnold van, *The Rites of Passage*, tr. M. B. Vizedom and G. L. Caffee (Chicago, 1960).

Ginzburg, Carlo, *Religioni della classi popolari*, ed. Carlo Ginzburg, Special number of *Quaderni Storici* 41 (May-August, 1979).

————, *The Cheese and the Worms. The Cosmos of a Sixteenth-*

Century Miller, tr. John and Anne Tedeschi (Baltimore, 1980).

Gutton, Jean-Pierre, *La sociabilité villageoise dans l'ancienne France* (Paris, 1979).

Henisch, Bridget Ann, *Feast and Fast. Food in Medieval Society* (University Park, Pa., 1976).

Kingdon, Robert, "The Control of Morals in Calvin's Geneva," *The Social History of the Reformation* ed. Lawrence P. Buck and Jonathan W. Zophy (Columbus, 1972): 3–16.

_____, "Protestant Parishes in the Old World and the New: The Cases of Geneva and Boston," *Church History* 48 (1979): 290–304.

Le Roy Ladurie, Emmanuel, *Montaillou, village occitan de 1294 à 1324* (Paris, 1975).

Magic and Superstition in the Jewish Religion. An Exhibition organized by the Maurice Spertus Museum of Judaica (Chicago, 1975).

Molin, Jean-Baptiste and Mutembe, Protais, *Le rituel du mariage en France du XIIe au XVIe siècle* (Theologie historique, 26; Paris, 1976).

Monter, E. W., "The Consistory of Geneva, 1559–1569," *Bibliothèque d'humanisme et renaissance* 38 (1976): 468–84.

Muchembled, Robert, *Culture populaire et culture des élites* (Paris, 1978).

Ozment, Steven E., *The Reformation in the Cities. The Appeal of Protestantism to Sixteenth Century Germany and Switzerland* (New Haven, 1975).

Patai, Raphael, *The Hebrew Goddess* (New York, 1967).

Phythian-Adams, Charles, "Ceremony and the Citizen: The communal year at Coventry, 1450–1550," *Crisis and Order in English Towns, 1500–1700* eds. Peter Clark and Paul Slack (Toronto, 1972): 57–85.

Plongeron, Bernard, ed., *La religion populaire dans l'occident chrétien. Approches historiques* (Paris, 1976).

_____, and Pannet, Robert, eds., *Le christianisme populaire. Les dossiers de l'histoire* (Paris, 1976).

Pollack, Herman, *Jewish Folkways in Germanic Lands (1648–1806). Studies in Aspects of Daily Life* (Cambridge, Mass., 1971).

Rappaport, Roy, *Ecology, Meaning and Religion* (Richmond, Ca., 1978).

Religion populaire (Dauphiné, Savoie Provence, Cévennes, Valais, Vallée d'Aoste, Piémont), special number of *Le monde alpin et rhodanien. Revue régionale d'ethnologie* 5 (1977).

La religion populaire en Languedoc du XIIIe siècle à la moitié du XIVe siècle (Cahiers de Fanjeaux, II, Toulouse, 1976).

Rothkrug, Lionel, *Religious Practices and Collective Perceptions: Hidden Homologies in the Renaissance and Reformation*, special number of *Historical Reflections/Réflexions historiques* 7 (Spring, 1980).

Sauzet, Robert, *Les visites pastorales dans le diocèse de Chartres pendant la première moitié du 17e siècle* (Paris, 1975).

Schmitt, Jean-Claude, " 'Religion populaire' et culture folklorique," *Annales. Economies. Sociétés. Civilisations* 31 (1976): 941–53.

———, *Le saint lévrier. Guinefort, guérisseur d'enfants depuis le XIIIe siècle* (Paris, 1979).

Scholem, Gershom, G., *Major Trends in Jewish Mysticism* (New York, 1965).

Seaver, Paul, "The Puritan Work Ethic Revisited," *Journal of British Studies* 19 (1980): 35–53.

Simonsohn, S., *History of the Jews in the Duchy of Mantua* (Publications of the Diaspora Research Institute, 17; Jerusalem, 1977).

Snyder, Lee Daniel, "Erasmus on Prayer: A Renaissance Reinterpretation," *Renaissance and Reformation/Renaissance et Réforme* n.s. 12 (1976): 21–27.

Soman, Alfred and Labrousse, Elisabeth, "Le registre consistorial de Coutras, 1582–1584," *Bulletin de la société de l'histoire du protestantisme français* 126 (1980): 195–228.

Soulet, Jean-François, *Tradition et réformes religieuses dans les Pyrénées centrales au XVIIe siècle* (Pau, 1974).

Strauss, Gerald, *Luther's House of Learning. Indoctrination of the Young in the German Reformation* (Baltimore, 1978).

Sumption, Jonathan, *Pilgrimage. An Image of Medieval Religion* (Totowa, N.J., 1975).

Tentler, Thomas N., *Sin and Confession on the Eve of the Reformation* (Princeton, 1977).

Thomas, Keith, *Religion and the Decline of Magic* (London, 1971).

Tobriner, Alice, "Vives' Prayers in English Reformation Worship," *Catholic Historical Review* 61 (1975): 505–15.

Toussaert, Jacques, *Le sentiment religieux en Flandre à la fin du moyen age* (Paris, 1960).

Trachtenberg, Joshua, *Jewish Magic and Superstition. A Study in Folk Religion* (New York, 1977).

Trexler, Richard C., *Public Life in Renaissance Florence* (New York, 1980).

Turner, Victor W., *The Ritual Process. Structure and Anti-Structure* (Chicago, 1969).

_____, and Turner, Edith, *Image and Pilgrimage in Christian Culture. Anthropological Perspectives* (New York, 1978).

Vauchez, André, "Conclusion," *La Religion populaire en Languedoc du XIIIe siècle à la moitié du XIVe siècle* (1976): 429–444.

Venard, Marc, "La clef de Saint Pierre de Faucon. Une nouvelle vision de croyances populaires à l'aube du XVIIe siècle," *Actes du 99e congrès national des sociétés savantes, Besançon, 1974* (Paris, 1977): 1:197–208.

_____, *L'église d'Avignon au XVIe siècle* (4 vols.; Lille, 1980).

Vogler, Bernard, *Vie religieuse en pays rhénan dans la seconde moitié du XVIe siècle* (1556–1619) (3 vols.; Lille 1974).

_____, *Le clergé protestant rhenan au siècle de la Réforme* (1555–1619) (Paris, 1976).

Vovelle, Michel, "Conclusions" *Religion populaire (Dauphiné, Savoie, Provence, Cévennes, Valais, Vallée d'Aoste Piémont)* (1977): 7–32.

White, Helen C., *The Tudor Books of Private Devotion* (Madison, 1951).

Society and the Sexes

Joyce Irwin

Debate over the proper role of women in relation to men is not an innovation of the twentieth or even the nineteenth century. The "woman question" was a lively issue among the many others of the sixteenth century. The debate itself, waged in the context of humanism, drew attention to women of the ancient world. Thus the historical interest in "society and the sexes" extends back for centuries but has been provided renewed vigor and new directions by the feminist movement of the last fifteen years. To some extent the renewed vigor has resulted in a rediscovery of materials known to previous generations but neglected for several decades. In the biographical studies of women, for instance, recent research is in some respects scarcely an advance upon nineteenth-century research. Certainly the view that women have been neglected by historical research itself neglects the extensive efforts of nineteenth-century writers. In some cases, the twentieth-century contribution is simply the availability in English language of information previously available in German or French. In other cases, however, the methods and perspectives of twentieth-century historians have opened new paths of research. Social historians and feminists have not been satisfied to study individual women or the views of men concerning women, but have attempted to investigate the role and status of women as a class. Because of the relative newness of the method and the vastness of the topic, results in this area are still sketchy. Meanwhile, such areas as the medical history of women have advanced little in the past century.

The present essay focuses primarily on recent research published in English language, most of which is commonly available in American libraries. The recent publication of *The Women of England From Anglo-Saxon Times to the Present,* edited by Barbara Kanner, allows me to restrict my comments to continental Europe. Rosemary Masek's survey of English materials in that book is far more extensive than is possible here. Exclusion of England also helps rectify the imbalance created when British queens and Puritan theologians dominate the attention of American scholars of womanhood.

General Studies

The demand for textbooks in women's studies has given rise to several good chapters on women in the Renaissance and Reformation in books devoted to the larger study of women in European history or in church history. In most general approaches the same themes recur: Renaissance humanism made possible a much higher level of education among women of the upper classes; the Reformation gave married life new respectability, but at the same time closed one vocational avenue for women—that of the cloister. Other questions arouse more controversy. Did the Protestant reforms improve upon previous views of women? Did Protestant women have greater opportunities for religious leadership than lay Catholic women? Did educated women of the aristocracy achieve a greater degree of independence and power than previously? The evaluation of the best researched essays is generally mixed, if not predominantly negative. After looking beyond the superficial evidence, most writers tend to agree with Vern Bullough: "The more things change, the more they remain the same."[1]

Joan Kelly-Gadol, for instance, finds that the political transformation from feudalism to the modern state deprived noblewomen of the positions of power which had made courtly love possible.[2] Baldassare Castiglione, far from increasing women's dignity by arguing for married love rather than adulterous courtly love, "established . . . a fateful bond between love and marriage" which made women dependent on men both in the family and in public life.[3]

By contrast, Sherrin M. Wyntjes, in the same volume, emphasizes the merits of Christian humanism for female aristocrats and the benefits of the Reformation for middle-class women. The spiritual equality taught by humanists and reformers gave women "the right to criticize the church just as men did."[4] The elevation of marriage to a "cooperative relationship of mutual responsibility"[5] allowed ministers' wives important roles in furthering the Reformation. Women of various social positions took advantage of this "period of

[1]Bullough (1974), 195.
[2]Kelly-Gadol (1977), 160.
[3]Kelly-Gadol (1977), 155.
[4]Wyntjes (1977), 171.
[5]Wyntjes (1977), 173.

upheaval"[6] to engage in social, political, and religious activities previously unexplored. Only as the century came to an end did a conservative reaction bring an increasingly rigid definition of the proper role of women.

More qualified in its assertions, yet in basic agreement with Wyntjes, is the essay of Jane Dempsey Douglass. At much greater length than Wyntjes, Douglass discusses the new theology of marriage, comparing the views of Luther and Calvin. She also points to the effects of the Reformation on marriage law, public education and church life, and to the activity of women both as supporters and as opponents of the Reformation. Lest their independent role be overstated, however, Douglass notes that "the only 'women's liberation' of interest to the sixteenth-century Reformation was the elimination of the monastic view of women, sex, and marriage which had flourished both in the monastery and among the laymen."[7]

As if to counteract the emphasis on Protestantism's elimination of the monastic way, Rosemary Ruether and Eleanor McLaughlin included in their recent book of essays a chapter of women's religious communities of the sixteenth century. Ruth P. Liebowitz points out the variety and vitality of religious women during the Counter Reformation. Without questioning the theological basis for religious orders, "women who sought an active apostolate were highly innovative in terms of defining new spiritual vocations and institutional structures appropriate to express them."[8] Angela Merici, Mary Ward, and Louise de Marillac founded orders dedicated to action— education, nursing, charity—rather than contemplation. Yet they met with considerable resistance from the church hierarchy and eventual restrictions on their independence. The story as a whole, then, is "a very mixed epic."[9] These women of the sixteenth century failed to achieve all they attempted, yet they "helped to lay the groundwork for a more modern view of women as a whole."[10]

Not only did the Protestants make religious vocations impossible for women of their circles, but they also, according to Eleanor L. McLaughlin, limited the feminine in theology. Whereas in the Middle Ages there are occasional uses of feminine imagery to refer to God (specifically by Anselm of Canterbury and Julian of Norwich),

[6]Wyntjes (1977), 186.
[7]Douglass (1974), 313–4.
[8]Liebowitz (1979), 133.
[9]Liebowitz (1979), 146.
[10]Liebowitz (1979), 147.

the Reformers, with their "rationalistic and spiritualizing tendency,"[11] denied the feminine aspects of religious experience. The emphasis on transcendence rather than immanence, spirit rather than flesh, resulted in a dichotomizing theology which left its followers lacking the wholeness symbolized by the naming of God as Mother and Sister as well as Brother, King, and Lover.[12]

Biography

The traditional and still valuable mode of studying women of the Reformation has been biography. There are numerous lives of queens, and learned ladies have been studied with considerable frequency. The Renaissance itself produced a number of "lives of famous women," beginning with Boccaccio.[13] Humanists were, of course, primarily interested in ancient women, but by the seventeenth century some such works became good sources of information on contemporary women.[14]

In the nineteenth century, women of the sixteenth century began to receive extensive biographical treatment, sometimes in general histories of women, sometimes in histories of Reformation women. Particularly strong in the study of French women is Louis Marie Prudhomme's *Biographie universelle et historique des femmes célèbres*. Ernestine Dietsch Diethoff's *Edle Frauen der Reformation und der Zeit der Glaubenskämpfe* includes Protestants, princesses, and poets, all with the purpose of demonstrating why women should keep to their housewifely roles. Lives of six still virtually unknown women of the Low Countries are discussed by Elisabeth Johanna Hasebroek in *De vrouwen der hervorming*. In English James Anderson has published two volumes of *Ladies of the Reformation*, the first including women of England, Scotland, and the Netherlands, the second women of Germany, Switzerland, France, Italy, and Spain.

A similar format, but with different national groupings, has been followed more recently by Roland Bainton.[15] In three volumes Bain-

[11]McLaughlin (1976), 51.

[12]McLaughlin (1976), 52.

[13]Giovanni Boccaccio, *Concerning Famous Women*, trans. Guido A. Guarino (New Brunswick, New Jersey: Rutgers University Press, 1963). For a list of other such works, see Bond (1904), 80–82.

[14]See, for instance, Joh. van Beverwyck, *Van de Uitnementheyt des Vrouwelichen Geslachts* (1643).

[15]Bainton (1971, 1973, 1977).

ton treats us to readable, reliable, and well-documented sketches of women from virtually all European countries. Equally, if not more, ambitious is the chronologically comprehensive history of Elise Boulding. In spite of the fact that Boulding is not a specialist in any historical epoch, her treatment of the Renaissance and Reformation provides a useful overview.

Other recent efforts have been more modest, though no less valuable as well-painted pieces of the larger picture. Charmarie Jenkins Blaisdell has studied the role of Renée de France as an influential noblewoman in the midst of the religious and political struggle between Reform and Counter-Reform. The stories of women who were less disposed to dissimulate for political reasons are told in the martyrologies, which have also been the focus of recent research.[16]

Two recent books of essays have focussed on another category: learned woman. J. R. Brink believes it possible to speak of a "tradition of learned women before 1800," though admittedly the connections become clearer in the seventeenth century than earlier. In fact, Christine de Pisan, subject of an essay by Leslie Altman, "regarded herself as an isolated phenomenon."[17] C. J. Blaisdell's essay on Marguerite de Navarre and her circle illuminates the connections between learned noblewomen in France.[18] A possible family tradition is suggested in the case of Caterina Corner (Cornaro), an ancestor of Elena Lucretia Cornaro Piscopia, who received a degree from the University of Padua in 1678. The latter woman is the subject of an essay in another recently published collection on learned women. Patricia H. Labalme, editor of *Beyond Their Sex: Learned Women of the European Past*, examines Piscopia against the backdrop of other women in early modern Venice. An essay by Paul Oskar Kristeller in the same volume looks at women in Italy at an earlier point in the Renaissance, while Natalie Z. Davis chooses several female writers from 1400 to 1820 in order to point out the relationship between gender and historical writing. Overall, this collection is less uniform in approach than the first, but it has the merit of rooting the topic more deeply in its historical context.

By comparison with the efforts of the nineteenth century, the products of the twentieth century seem rather meager, though they may be more sophisticated—or at least "up-to-date"—in their

---

[16]See Abbott (1980) and Olson (1980).
[17]Brink (1980), 3.
[18]Brink (1980), 36–53.

methods and presuppositions. Future scholarship might well make more use of our predecessors' results, however, both as sources of information on lesser-known women and as interesting historical documents in their own right.

The "Woman Question"

Historians of literature have long been attuned to the "querelle des femmes" to a degree unknown among historians in general. The latter might well mention a few names such as Baldassare Castiglione, Marguerite of Navarre, and John Knox as bringing the question of woman's nature to public attention. Yet such isolated references hardly take on the character of a serious debate. Literature scholars, on the other hand, are often content to limit their attention to literary depictions of the sexes. Moreover, such scholars are usually interested in the literature of only one country. Hence, an important contribution to scholarship would be a comprehensive discussion of sixteenth-century writers' views on the roles of the sexes, drawn from literature, politics, philosophy, theology, and science. Although this would require broad vision and varied skills, much of the groundwork has been laid.

Early in this century, Marie Alphonse René de Maulde la Clavière gave us a lengthy "study of feminism," portraying the liberated vision of the women of the Renaissance, particularly in France. These women dreamed of a new, more powerful role in society, but, as the author sees it, they failed utterly.

> A dream indeed—all these schemes of happiness which had flashed across the gloomy background of realities like dissolving views on the wall of a lecture-room: the blue sea, the blazing sun, appearing but for a moment, left the blackness deeper still.[19]

A conservative social mood—best observed in Puritanism—pushed women back into their subordinate status.

Less interested in accusation than in description, Ruth Kelso (1956) gathered from the "literature of gentility" an ideal picture of Renaissance woman. From a bibliography of eight hundred ninety-one items, Kelso produced a composite portrait of the model noblewoman in each of the facets of her life: "training," "studies," "vocation," "love and beauty," and "the lady at court." As such the work

---

[19]Maulde la Clavière (1905), 475.

is extraordinarily valuable, but it does not eliminate the need for analysis of these same sources in their historical context.

As an effort in this direction, the recent book of Ian Maclean, *The Renaissance Notion of Woman*, is both exciting and disappointing. While offering chapters entitled "Theology, mystical and occult writings," "Medicine, anatomy, physiology," "Ethics, politics, social writings," and "Law," Maclean completes his text in only ninety-two pages. His footnotes, which take up another eighteen pages, are an extremely valuable source of references to both primary and secondary sources. Yet the text itself jumps too quickly across time and intellectual space to offer the reader a meaningful view of the whole. Asserting that Aristotelian scholasticism united theologians (Catholic and Protestant), lawyers, and physicians, Maclean sees a correlation between the decline of Aristotelianism as a scholarly method and the decline of the Aristotelian view of women. Both trends were in progress toward the end of the sixteenth century; the half century between 1580 and 1630 saw a lively debate and an impressive scholarly output which pointed to a "shift in scholarly attitudes to the female sex."[20]

While Maclean's book suffers from too broad a view in that he makes Aristotelianism the only category of discrimination, Manfred P. Fleischer loses the larger picture in his analysis of the *Disputatio nova contra mulieres* (1595), one of the significant works also discussed by Maclean. Fleischer refuses to take seriously the anti-Socinian polemics of this work, attributed to Valens Acidalius, even though Socinianism can be recognized as a matter of great concern to Saxon theologians. As a result Fleischer treats the entire debate too literally, although he may be excused by virtue of the fact that so many writers of the seventeenth century made the same mistake.

While Fleischer provides a commentary on one episode in the ongoing discussion of woman's nature and Maclean offers a framework for the entire discussion, the need remains for a study combining the virtues of both—a detailed analysis of specific texts within a broad interdisciplinary perspective. Such a study should make use of Maclean's other book, which pursues the topic in seventeenth-century French literature.[21] Also significant, though one-sided, is Rogers' (1966) study of misogyny in literature. More specific contributions are those of McKendrick (1974), Ornstein (1941), Seidel (1979),

[20]Maclean (1980), 89.
[21]Maclean (1977).

Johnson (1973), and Cherry (1973). Wright (1955) and Utley (1970) provide general introductions to the debate on women, at least as it was known in England.

Theology and Religious Life

The attitudes of the major reformers toward women have been well researched, particularly as these impinge on their doctrines of marriage. Numerous excerpts from Luther's writings have been included in anthologies of women's history.[22] Bainton's sketch of Katherine von Bora gives a folksy view of life with her famous husband.[23] An earlier work of the same author concisely summarizes Reformation theologies of sex, love, and marriage.[24] Steven Ozment pursues one aspect of the topic by focussing on the reformers' opposition to vows of celibacy,[25] while Jane Dempsey Douglass depicts the many facets of the new theology of marriage as they affect women. Luther's affection for Katherine, his harsh criticism of the disparagers of women, his defense of the sanctity of marriage and parenthood can easily shape a picture of Luther as one who worked to raise the status of women. Yet his earthy personality and his emphasis on marriage as a remedy for sin can also provide the evidence for labelling him a male chauvinist.[26] Resolution of this conflict is not to be expected from future research but from a realistic approach to a man who was more willing than most to reveal his humanness.

By contrast, Stauffer's (1971) treatment of John Calvin's relationship with family and friends is disappointingly thin. We have little occasion to be troubled by off-the-record comments by John Calvin. Nevertheless, the same problem of ambiguity arises here as well. On the basis of Calvin's scripture commentaries, John H. Bratt finds "a qualified but definite subordination of woman and a qualified but definite supremacy of man."[27] Whether one should stress the "quali-

----

[22]Clark and Richardson (1977); O'Faolain and Martines (1973).

[23]Bainton (1971).

[24]Bainton (1957). The bibliography in this work gives several references to German research on this topic.

[25]Ozment (1980), 381–396.

[26]Notorious in some feminist circles is the comment attributed to Luther, "Men have broad shoulders and narrow hips, and accordingly they possess intelligence. Women have narrow shoulders and broad hips; women ought to stay at home, . . . for they have broad hips and a wide fundament to sit upon, keep house, and bear and raise children." (*Table Talk*, no. 55).

[27]Bratt (1976), 1.

fied" or the "definite" depends to a great extent on seeing Calvin in the context of his age, as Charmarie Blaisdell points out.[28]

Before an evaluation of the attitudes of the major reformers can be made, much more research needs to be completed. Not only the precursors of Puritan spokesmen on marriage and family such as Bullinger and Bucer need further study, but also those theologians whose influence was confined to the Continent. Comparisons with radical reformers on the one hand and with Roman Catholics on the other would help to rectify the imbalance of attention to the two major reformers. A recent attempt to portray the variety of attitudes toward women within the Radical Reformation is my sourcebook, *Womanhood in Radical Protestantism, 1525–1675.* In contrast to some general assertions about Anabaptist women, I find little evidence that women's status in sixteenth-century sects was more free and equal than in established churches. Not included in this compilation were Polish Antitrinitarians, who have been said to have encouraged women's leadership. Such evidence as one finds in George Williams' *The Polish Brethren*[29] is inconclusive, however. A high priority for future research should be a compilation of sources from the Catholic Reformation that would include theological analyses of womanhood as well as biographical information about the lives of individual women. Also important would be a study of Reformed and Lutheran theologians of the late sixteenth and early seventeenth centuries, particularly as this period saw a lively interest in the woman question and produced a large number of notable women.

Social history

The field of social history can also provide a context for studies of Luther and Calvin. To judge whether a particular reformer is "progressive" or "reactionary" depends not only on a comparison with the thought of his contemporaries, but also on a knowledge of actual circumstances.

A study of marriage customs across Europe, for instance, reveals that the institution was in a state of flux quite apart from the reformers' proposed changes. Edward Benson asserts that many writers were out of touch with their own situation: "Rules for marriage choice were changing, and with them the rules for married life, but

---

[28]Blaisdell (1976), 20.
[29]George Huntston Williams, ed. and trans., *The Polish Brethren*, 2 vols., Harvard Theological Studies, no. 30 (Missoula, Mont., 1980).

many contemporaries, Marguerite [of Navarre] among them, understood neither the depth or the speed of the change."[30]

Christiane Klapisch-Zuber (1979) has recently studied the increasing role of the church in wedding rites in Tuscany from the fourteenth to the sixteenth century. Through the iconographic representation of the "Marriage of the Virgin," focussing on the wedding ring, Klapisch-Zuber sees folk rituals being absorbed by the power of the Church, which then abhorred and eliminated them in the sixteenth century. The church's appropriation and standardization of the marriage ceremony in France during the sixteenth and seventeenth centuries is discussed by André Burguière (1978), who also notes the correlation between this process and increased emphasis on paternal preeminence within the family. Both authors tend to view the changes as an effort on the part of the Church to gain power.

John K. Yost examines attitudes toward marriage as a mode of life and evaluates the changes in a much more positive light than Burguière. Rather than a takeover of folk practice by the Church, Yost sees, at least among civic and Christian humanists, a closing of the gap between spiritual and worldly values: "What was taking place amounted to a reintegration of life style and value system."[31]

Other studies of marital relations in the sixteenth century are more limited in scope, reflecting the archival research of local or regional historians. E William Monter (1979) observes that in late sixteenth-century Geneva a new marriage pattern evolves as women begin to marry closer to age 24 than to 20. Marriage court records are providing informaton on husband-wife relations in Württemberg and Constance for researchers Virginia E. DeMarce (1980) and Thomas Safley (1980). While a vast amount of such evidence may be available, it remains to be seen whether the significance of the results is proportionate to the effort involved in gathering the information.

Lest it be thought that women were to be found only in the home, some researchers are intent on demonstrating women's work in various trades. Because economic history is itself a relatively recent enterprise, there are far fewer contemporary reflections on the sixteenth-century occupational status of women than on their marital role. Hence, extensive archival research is a prerequisite to any comprehensive evaluation of the economic function of women in the ear-

[30]Benson (1979), 275.
[31]Yost (1977), 151.

ly modern period. Important steps are being taken in this direction by Natalie Z. Davis in the study of Lyons and by Merry Wiesner Wood in the study of Nuremberg.[32]

Women of a higher social class have been the subject of attention by Nancy L. Roelker, who found the number of aristocratic female leaders among the Huguenots remarkable. The combination of a weakened French crown and humanistic education provided the background from which noblewomen—particularly widows—found opportunities for independence and influence within Calvinism.[33] A complementary article by Gordon Griffiths (1979) examines the piety of Louise of Savoy and her role in the reform of the Catholic Church.

Looking at city women, on the other hand, Natalie Davis finds a more complex picture in which women in both Catholic and Reformed circles became active in various ways as religious change made new roles possible. Each church had its own strengths as far as women were concerned. "Both forms of religious life have contributed to the transformation of society."[34] At the same time, "neither, of course, eliminated the subject status of women."[35]

Davis' balanced portrait of French city women in the era of religious change is likely to be confirmed in its main points by evidence yet to be brought to light from other geographical areas. Not only will it be important to have more studies of Protestant women in particular locations, such as that of Miriam Chrisman (1972) on Strasbourg women, but it will also be valuable to learn of those women who remained Catholic, whether by choice or by circumstance.

Science and Medicine

One area in which little recent research is available is the history of science and medicine as it relates to women. Undoubtedly this reflects the fact that the history of science has never received much attention from church historians or even secular historians. An imaginative recent book touching on the sixteenth century is Carolyn Merchant's *The Death of Nature*, where the repression of women and the exploitation of nature are linked to the rise of the scientific method and technology. The book, while well researched, does not

[32]Davis (1979); Wood (1981).
[33]Roelker (1971/72; 1972).
[34]Davis (1975), 94.
[35]Davis (1975), 93.

introduce unfamiliar primary sources but integrates a vast amount of secondary material into a broad interpretive framework. The relevant chapter of Maclean's *The Renaissance Notion of Woman* offers more ideas for further primary research.

My much narrower essay, discussing the relationship between embryological theory and Christological theology among Calvinists and certain Anabaptists, reveals some implications for beliefs concerning the nature of women.[36] A related note shows the conflicting use of a specific biblical verse as confirmation of both Galenic and Aristotelian embryological thought.[37]

Future research on related topics might well make use of the extensive bibliography on medicine and sexuality by Hugo Hayn (1886). He includes not only physiological topics such as fertility, pregnancy, and birth, but also folkloric topics such as personal hygiene and sexual morality.

Suggestions for the Future

In this essay I have emphasized recent research in the area of "society and the sexes," while at the same time reminding the reader that our present feminist wave has had precursors who also created an impressive scholarship. Many writers of both the present and the earlier feminist phases have been motivated by a desire to make a polemical point. The divisive nature of theological conflict has been compounded by the emotional issues of sexuality. The result has been that some paint a rosy picture of the Reformation's bringing about a better life for women, while others bemoan the reformers' elevation of married life. As long as the task has been to argue one side or the other, women's history in its present phase has merely been recovering the ground lost since the last phase.

With the coming of the second decade of the women's movement, it is possible to move beyond polemics to an acceptance of the variety and complexity of the evidence involved. Such recognition frees researchers from treading the same old paths again in hopes of coming to a final verdict. Just as sixteenth-century historians in general have moved beyond debating the merits of the Reformation in favor of examining its component parts, so historians of women should concentrate on analysis rather than evaluation.

For this purpose it is important to be as broadly informed about

[36]Irwin (1978a).
[37]Irwin (1978b).

the various aspects of the century as possible. Interdisciplinary studies—though demanding—are essential to a fuller understanding of the ways in which men and women related to each other. At the same time there is room for careful specialized studies as building blocks for a larger structure. Two large microfilm collections on women's history—*The Gerritsen Collection of Women's History*[38] and *History of Women*[39]—have made research on European women possible on a wider scale. It is to be hoped that scholars will identify hitherto neglected facets of the topic through these collections.

My own intuition is that the richest field of unexplored material lies in that chronological space pointed out by Ian Maclean. Because histories of the Reformation so often end with the Council of Trent, the decades between 1580 and 1630 are generally not "claimed" by Reformation researchers. In the case of "Society and the Sexes," if not also in other areas, it could be argued that the crucial chapter is missing when the story ends with an earlier date. Perhaps the developments of that period will ultimately have to be credited to the account of the seventeenth century, but Reformation historians would do well to look into their own claims in the area.

Bibliography

Abbott, Leona Stucky, "Women in the Anabaptist Martyrologies," paper delivered at Sixteenth Century Studies Conference, St. Louis, October 24, 1980.

Anderson, James, *Ladies of the Reformation* (London, 1855; 1857).

Bainton, Roland Herbert, *What Christianity Says About Sex, Love and Marriage* (New York, 1957).

_____, *Women of the Reformation in Germany and Italy* (Minneapolis, 1971).

_____, *Women of the Reformation in France and England* (Minneapolis, 1973).

_____, *Women of the Reformation from Spain to Scandinavia* (Minneapolis, 1977).

---

[38] *The Gerritsen Collection of Women's History*, from the Kenneth Spencer Research Library at the University of Kansas. Available through Microfilming Corporation of America, Glen Rock, New Jersey.

[39] *History of Women. A comprehensive collection based on the holdings of nine major libraries.* Available through Research Publications, Inc., Woodbridge, Connecticut.

Bell, Susan, *Women: from the Greeks to the French Revolution* (Belmont, California, 1973).

Benson, Edward, "Marriage Ancestral and Conjugal in the 'Heptaméron'," *Journal of Medieval and Renaissance Studies* 9 (1979): 261–275.

Biéler, André, *L'homme et la femme dans la morale calviniste* (Geneva, 1963).

Blaisdell, Charmarie Jenkins, "Renée de France between Reform and Counter-Reform," *Archiv für Reformationsgeschichte* 63 (1972): 196–225.

———, "Response to 'The Role and Status of Women in the Writings of John Calvin'," in *Renaissance, Reformation, Resurgence*, ed. Peter de Klerk (Grand Rapids, 1976).

Bomli, P. W., *La femme dans l'Espagne du siècle d'or* (The Hague, 1950).

Bond, R. Warwick, ed., *The nobility of women, by William Bercher, 1559* (London, 1904).

Boulding, Elise, *The Underside of History: A View of Women Through Time* (Boulder, 1976).

Bratt, John H. "The Role and Status of Women in the Writings of John Calvin," *Renaissance, Reformation, Resurgence*, ed. Peter de Klerk (Grand Rapids, 1976).

Brink, J. R., ed., *Female Scholars: A Tradition of Learned Women Before 1800* (Montreal, 1980).

Bullough, Vern L., *The Subordinate Sex* (Baltimore, 1974).

Burguière, André, "Le rituel du mariage en France: pratiques ecclésiastiques et pratiques populaires (XVIe–XVIIIe siècle)," *Annales. Économies, Sociétés–Civilisations* 33 (1978): 637–649.

Cherry, Caroline Lockett, *The Most Unvaluedst Purchase: Women in the Plays of Thomas Middleton* (Salzburg, 1973).

Chrisman, Miriam, "Women and the Reformation in Strasbourg 1490–1530," *Archiv für Reformationsgeschichte* 63 (1972): 143–167.

Clark, Elizabeth and Richardson, Herbert, *Women and Religion: A Feminist Sourcebook of Christian Thought* (New York, 1977).

Davis, Natalie Zemon. *Society and Culture in Early Modern France* (Stanford, 1975).

———, "Women in the *Arts Mechaniques* in Sixteenth Century

Lyons," *Mèlanges en hommage de Richard Gascon*, ed. Jean-Pierre Gutton (Lyon, 1979).

DeMarce, Virginia Easley, "Comparative Use of the Wurttemberg Marriage Court by Men and Women in the Sixteenth Century," paper delivered at Sixteenth Century Studies Conference, St. Louis, October 25, 1980.

Diethoff, Ernestine Dietsch, *Edle Frauen der Reformation und der Zeit der Glaubenskämpfe* (Leipzig, 1875).

Douglass, Jane Dempsey, "Women and the Continental Reformation," *Religion and Sexism*, ed. Rosemary Radford Ruether (New York, 1974).

Fleischer, Manfred P., " 'Are Women Human?'—The Debate of 1595 Between Valens Acidalius and Simon Gediccus,"*Sixteenth Century Journal* 12, 2 (1981), 107–122.

Griffiths, Gordon, "Louise of Savoy and Reform of the Church," *Sixteenth Century Journal* X/3 (1979), 29–36.

Hasebroek, Elisabeth Johanna, *De vrouwen der hervorming*, 2 vols (Amsterdam, 1859).

Hayn, Hugo, *Bibliotheca Germanorum gynaecologica et cosmetica*, 2nd ed. (Leipzig, 1886).

Irwin, Joyce L., "Embryology and the Incarnation: A Sixteenth-Century Debate," *Sixteenth Century Journal* IX/3 (1978): 93–104. (a)

———, "Hebrews 11:11 as Embryological Proof-Text," *Harvard Theological Review* 71/3–4 (1978): 312–316. (b)

———, ed., *Womanhood in Radical Protestantism* (New York, 1979).

Johnson, Marilyn L., *Images of Women in the Works of Thomas Heywood* (Salzburg, 1973).

Kanner, Barbara, ed., *The Women of England: From Anglo-Saxon Times to the Present* (Hamden, Connecticut, 1979).

Kelly-Gadol, Joan, "Did Women Have a Renaissance?" *Becoming Visible: Women in European History*, eds. Renate Bridenthal and Claudia Koonz (Boston, 1977).

Kelso, Ruth, *Doctrine for the Lady of the Renaissance* (Urbana, 1956).

Klapisch-Zuber, Christiane, "Zacharie où le père évincé. Les rites nuptiaux toscans entre Giotto et le concile de Trente," *Annales. Economies-Sociétés-civilisations* 34 (1979): 1216–1243.

Labalme, Patricia H., ed., *Beyond Their Sex: Learned Women of the European Past* (New York, 1980).

Liebowitz, Ruth P., "Virgins in the Service of Christ: The Dispute over an Active Apostolate for Women During the Counter-Reformation," *Women of Spirit*, eds. Rosemary Ruether and Eleanor McLaughlin (New York, 1979).

McKendrick, Melveena, *Woman and Society in the Spanish Drama of the Golden Age* (London, 1974).

McLaughlin, Eleanor L., "Male and Female in Christian Tradition: Was There a Reformation in the Sixteenth Century?" *Male and Female: Christian Approaches to Sexuality*, eds. Ruth Tiffany Barnhouse and Urban T. Holmes, III (New York, 1976).

Maclean, Ian, *Woman Triumphant: Feminism in French Literature, 1610–1652* (Oxford, 1977).

———, *The Renaissance Notion of Woman: A Study in the Fortunes of Scholasticism and Medical Science in European Intellectual Life* (Cambridge, 1980).

Maulde la Clavière, R. de, *The Women of the Renaissance: A Study of Feminism*, trans. George Herbert Ely (London, 1905).

Merchant, Carolyn, *The Death of Nature: Women, Ecology, and the Scientific Revolution* (New York, 1980).

Molin, J. B., and Mutembé, P., *Le rituel du mariage en France du XIIe au XVIe siècle* (Paris, 1974).

Monter, E. William, "Historical Demography and Religious History in Sixteenth Century Geneva," *Journal of Interdisciplinary History* 9 (1979): 399–427.

O'Faolain, Julia and Martines, Lauro, *Not in God's Image* (New York, 1973).

Olson, Jeannine Fahl, "Crespin's Female Martyrs," paper delivered at Sixteenth Century Studies Conference, St. Louis, October 24, 1980.

Ornstein, Jacob, "La misoginía y el profeminismo en la literatura castellana," *Revista de Filología Hispánica* 3 (1941): 219–32.

Ozment, Steven, *The Age of Reform, 1250–1550* (New Haven, 1980).

Prudhomme, Louis Marie, *Biographie universelle et historique des femmes célèbres*, 4 vols. (Paris, 1830).

Roelker, Nancy Lyman, "The Appeal of Calvinism to French Noblewomen in the Sixteenth Century," *The Journal of Interdisciplinary History* 2 (1971/72): 391–418.

_____, "The Role of Noblewomen in the French Reformation," *Archiv für Reformationsgeschichte* 63 (1972): 168–195.

Rogers, Katharine M., *The Troublesome Helpmate: A History of Misogyny in Literature* (Seattle, 1966).

Sachs, Hannelore, *The Renaissance Woman* (New York, 1971).

Safley, Thomas, "Marital Litigation in the Diocese of Constance," paper presented at the Sixteenth Century Studies Conference, St. Louis, October 25, 1980.

Seidel, Michael A., *Satiric Inheritance: Rabelais to Sterne* (Princeton, 1979).

Stauffer, Richard, *The Humanness of John Calvin*, trans. George Shriver (Nashville, 1971).

Utley, Francis Lee, *The Crooked Rib: An Analytical Index to the Argument about Women in English and Scots Literature to the End of the Year 1568* (Columbus, Ohio, 1944; reprint: New York, 1970).

Wheaton, Robert, and Hareven, Tamara K., *Family and Sexuality in French History* (Philadelphia, 1980).

Wood, Merry Wiesner, "Paltry Peddlers or Essential Merchants? Women in the Distributive Trades in Early Modern Nuremberg," *Sixteenth Century Journal* 12, 2 (1981): 3–14.

Wright, Louis B., *Middle-Class Culture in Elizabethan England* (Chapel Hill, 1935).

Wyntjes, Sherrin, "Women in the Reformation Era," *Becoming Visible: Women in European History*, eds. Renate Bridenthal and Claudia Koonz (Boston, 1977).

Yost, John K., "Changing Attitudes Towards Married Life in Civic and Christian Humanism," *Occasional Papers of the American Society for Reformation Research* 1 (1977): 151–166.

The Confessional Age: The Late Reformation in Germany

James M. Kittelson

Germany in the second half of the sixteenth century is a land of golden opportunity for students of the Reformation. Put simply, by comparison with the many excellent and highly sophisticated works that treat the 1520's and 1530's in general and the leading figures of these decades in particular, the years after the Peace of Augsburg are a virtual wasteland. With but a few exceptions,[1] not even the tidal wave of research that followed the publication of Bernd Moeller's seminal essay on the urban Reformation[2] could breach the breakwater of mid-century. Scholars have instead been consumed with starting and restarting the German Reformation without investigating its conclusions. In so doing, they have, will-nilly, fostered the impression that the fires of reform died out sometime shortly after Luther's death, banked by the bickering of his epigoni and crushed under foot by the territorial princes.

Yet, much is at stake in the Late Reformation. At the very least no evaluation of the Reformation as a whole is possible without a clear understanding of what enduring changes may have flowed from the inchoate reform movement of the early years. This lack is doubly deplorable because it has reinforced the trend in recent historiography to question the traditional place of both the Renaissance and the Reformation in the development of modern civilization.[3] To scholars in the late 20th century for whom formal religion holds much diminished importance, the mere establishment of new confessions and new churches is not a matter of great significance by comparison with the great themes of state building, social and economic

---

[1]Greyerz (1980); Rublack (1978); Weyrauch (1978); Abray (1978); Kittelson (1977).
[2]Moeller (1972), 41–115.
[3]Noted in Bouwsma (1979) and Spitz (1979).

change, or religious belief and behavior at the popular level. Nonetheless, due in part to their traditionally idealist bent towards *Geistesgeschichte*, Reformation historians have left virtually untouched the problem of the Reformation's enduring consequences in terms of its continuing political significance, its institutions, or even its day-to-day beliefs and practices. Consequently, it is presently not possible to render anything like a full assessment of the abiding effects of the German Reformation. In the context of such plain ignorance, it should come as no surprise that non-specialists tend to regard the Reformation as an event in church history but not as a distinct period in the history of Europe as a whole.

Yet, on the face of it even in Germany the Reformation clearly did not stop unfolding with the Peace of Augsburg. By the end of the sixteenth century Protestant Germany featured newly-established churches that adhered to lengthy and detailed confessions whose truth as a guide for belief and behavior was continually pressed upon entire populations through church visitations, schools, welfare systems, and marriage and morals courts, all of which scarcely existed during the first half of the century. It is also certain that formal religion continued to play a powerful role in Imperial politics, if only because the Augsburg Confession was formally inserted into the German constitution by the Peace of Augsburg that ended the Schmalkald Wars. Additionally, it is only in the late Reformation that Luther's evangelical religion was taught in universities as well as in catechisms, thereby evolving into one of the three main-line "isms" of Latin Christianity alongside Roman Catholicism and Calvinism. There is therefore no justification for ignoring the Late Reformation even though it featured no commanding theologian of the stature of Luther, Calvin, or Zwingli.

Even given this state of the art, certain tentative hypotheses regarding the period may be put forth, largely as a result of recent work or work in progress. These focus upon the development of Lutheranism into a coherent orthodoxy, the final establishment of Protestant churches and other attendant institutions in cities and territories, and the effects of the new religion at the popular level. Nonetheless, even in these three areas the basic research remains far from complete.

Certainly for filial reasons, the best studied area, at least in terms of volume and access to the fundamental information, remains the development of the Lutheran tradition from Luther's death in 1546 to the Formula and Book of Concord in 1577 and 1580.[4] The most notable feature of this scholarship is that, contrary to the history of Calvinism, the question of whether the Formula and those theologians who contributed to it were true to Luther has not been much at issue. Exceptions to this rule center on the suggestion that some Lutherans, notably Melanchthon and Brenz, were willing to go farther than Luther in discussing predestination, and nearly universal agreement that Luther's doctrine of the two kingdoms was virtually ignored by his followers.[5] Scholars commonly account for the willingness of Lutherans to accord such high authority within the church to the prince by referring to their training in the humanist tradition and to the political realities they confronted when constructing churches within territorial principalities.[6]

Nonetheless, on the basic theological issues of justification, authority, the sacraments, and the church there is little suggestion that the Formulators deviated from Luther or even developed his basic theological insights, whether within or without directions Luther himself had already indicated. The Formula, while perhaps viewed as rather more normative in certain Lutheran circles in the United States than on the Continent or elsewhere,[7] is a decidedly unsystematic document, though it has not been treated as such. Indeed, consensus has it that one of the hallmarks of late sixteenth-century Lutheranism, as demonstrated by the resolution of the controversies that sprang up following Luther's death, was to be intentionally unsystematic and to refuse to speculate beyond the Scriptures and beyond Luther himself about issues that subsequently agitated, for example, those in the Reformed tradition.[8]

If only as an aside, it must be added that recent literature on the development of Lutheranism to the Formula of Concord has a second salient characteristic. Straightforward historical accounts, e.g., of the Formula's *Entstehungsgeschichte*, have by and large given way to treatments that serve the dogmatic purposes of contemporary Lutheran theologians, at least if publications from the recent anni-

---

[4]There is no standard, published bibliography. For a beginning guide, see Spitz (1977).

[5]Elert (1962), 126ff and Estes (1968), 5–25. The most noteworthy general critique is Heppe (1859), 273ff.

[6]E.g., Pauck (1961), 101–143 and Estes (1968).

[7]The discussion by Cochrane in Spitz (1977), 63f. and the literature cited there.

[8]This judgment does not apply to the "orthodox" theologians of the seventeenth century. See Haikola (1958), 9–12, 106–107 and Preus in Spitz and Lohff (1977), 86–101.

versary observations of the Formula and the Augsburg Confession are any guide. It is most interesting that, although the standard accounts of Lutheranism in the second half of the sixteenth-century are hopelessly dated and inaccessible to most scholars, virtually no attempt to supplement, much less to replace, them is even in progress. Rather, most recent essays on the subject have treated the Formula's applicability to current theological and ecclesiastical problems, and frequently in the most explicit manner possible.[9]

The combination of what may be called a principally dogmatic interest in late sixteenth-century Lutheranism with historical research that is limited for the most part to the early years of the Reformation has left a number of critical questions unanswered. They may be gathered together by means of a comparison of the development of Lutheranism and Calvinism as distinct confessions. Was there something in the "structure of Lutheranism," as Elert would have it (at least in translation), that prevented its development into *and* wide agreement with a highly systematic set of theological propositons that was so characteristic of the Reformed tradition by the end of the sixteenth-century? In this regard it should be noted that the major controversies that followed Luther's death, whether Majoristic, Flaccian, or Christological, grew from the efforts of a theologian or a group of theologians to spell out Lutheran teaching on issues that had not been discussed earlier. These efforts might be regarded as having had a systematizing thrust, and they were rejected in the Formula. Additionally, Lutheranism lacked the ministrations of Italian Thomists such as Jerome Zanchi or Peter Martyr Vermigli. Yet, as the most casual reading of the Formula or the works of its progenitors will reveal, the Lutherans of the late sixteenth-century were fully versed in dialectic and fully capable of splitting hairs with the most acute Calvinist, even though they steadfastly refused to go beyond resolving the precise issues that lay before them.

Surely one resolution of this problem lies in that most neglected of all areas of research, the history of Lutheran universities in the late sixteenth and early seventeenth centuries.[10] Unfortunately, scholars have so far evinced scant interest in how the Lutheran version of Latin Christianity was conveyed to what amounted to two genera-

---

[9]The view in *ibid.*, 1, 5, where six of the twelve essays are termed "historical" but deal exclusively with the Formula's reception. In Lohff and Spitz (1977), nine of the twelve essays are exclusively dogmatic. Continental observations have commonly had a rather different focus, e.g., *Zeitschrift für Bayerische Kirchengeschichte* (1980), Schöne (1978), Brecht and Schwartz (1980).

[10]Beginnings include Paulsen (1919).

tions of Lutheran pastors, whose acquiescence, at the very least, made possible the Formula's wide acceptance. In this regard there is evidence from Strasbourg in the person of Johann Marbach, the President of this city's Company of Pastors for almost thirty years, that the doctrine of the *ubiquitas Christi* and the Formula's understanding of election or predestination may have been current among Lutheran churchmen as early as 1547.[11] Additionally, Marbach undoubtedly learned these ideas as a student at Wittenberg, where Luther himself chaired his doctoral disputation. Certain troubling questions follow. How did Marbach (and others?) learn these doctrines? Who taught them? How, in detail, were they taught? All of this may ignore the dramatic events that led to the Formula, but these questions and similar ones are vital to any understanding of the development of Lutheranism. Put simply, in spite of all that has been done, the development of Lutheranism as a distinct confessional tradition is still a very poorly understood subject, at least in purely historical terms.

The increasing interest of secular historians in the actual establishment of Protestant churches in Germany and their functioning is another likely factor in the relative lack of research on the purely historical development of Lutheranism as a distinct confession. Volker Press's monumental work on the Palatinate will stand as a model for all future studies in this area. Through a careful examination of the archival sources Press discovered that it was not Calvinism as such that led to the highly-structured and highly-centralized Palatine administrative system if only because the first church order was composed by Marbach and endured relatively unchanged. Rather, both politicians and clergy perceived a need for such structures in a time of great religious controversy.[12] Bernard Vogler's detailed, if diffuse, treatment of the development of the Protestant clergy in the Rhenish territories tends to buttress Press's conclusions, albeit from a different perspective. In sum, even as the administrative structures of the churches became ever more detailed and routinized, the clergy developed into a professional class with a common education and standardized requirements for entry and promotion that tended to ignore birth. Naturally, they also shared a single confessional stance.[13] The picture emerges, then, not of a Reformation that lost momentum sometime after Luther's death, but of religious changes

---

[11]Kittelson (1977)and the ms. Mc 181 (Universitätsbibliothek Tübingen).
[12]Press (1970).
[13]Vogler (1976).

that were consolidated and firmly implanted at least among Germany's intellectual and political elites.

No other area of Germany has been studied with such detail in this regard as the Palatinate. Yet, on the face of it, the remainder of Protestant, and Catholic, Germany would appear to feature this same process of consolidation along the twin paths of confession-building and church-building. Strasbourg, for example, as late as 1598 finally adopted a new church order by which the city officially subscribed to the Formula of Concord and became decisively Lutheran. Colmar's reform was complete only by the late sixteenth century, while it was not until the same period that the episcopal cities of Würzburg, Bamberg, Trier, Mainz, Salzburg, Passau, Freising, and Eichstätt were forcibly returned to being securely Catholic.[14] Perhaps, therefore, it is time to discard the picture of a Lutheranism that turned moribund after 1546. To be sure, Luther's heirs were unable to gain many new territories after mid-century, but they appear to have consolidated the gains of the 1520's and 1530's by creating—where allowable by Imperial law—churches that endured and that subscribed to a common confession. Consequently, Lutheranism, both as a confession and as a group of institutions, is a creation as much of the late Reformation as of the years before Luther's death.

All of the above is by now rather widely accepted, if poorly understood in detail and therefore subject to wide-ranging revision. But what of the impact of changes at the level of formal confessions and administrative structures upon the religious beliefs and behavior of the ordinary German Lutheran? Here the field of Reformation history has recently received a fundamental challenge by one of the most startling books of the last decade. Briefly, on the basis of his reading of visitation reports for all of Protestant Germany, Gerald Strauss concludes that "the burden of proof ought now at last to be placed where it belongs: upon those who claim, or imply, or tacitly assume, that the Reformation in Germany aroused a wide-spread, meaningful, and lasting response to its message." To the extent that they relied on catechisms, sermons, and exhortations, Protestant clergymen failed to change the religion of ordinary Germans and, therefore, the Reformation itself was a failure.[15]

These findings have been challenged through a case study at the

---

[14]Adam (1922); Greyerz (1980); Rublack (1978).
[15]Strauss (1978), 303, 307–308.

evidentiary level.[16] Nonetheless, they remain very important both because they are based upon massive research into the primary sources and because they tend to reinforce the current trend to question the Reformation's traditional place in the development of modern civilization. It is possible, of course, for defenders of the older and still dominant interpretation to argue that, in principle, it is not necessary to demonstrate enduring changes at the popular level in order to establish that the Reformation was a distinct period in European history and therefore merits study in its own right.[17] The difficulty is that such an approach is likely to leave unbelievers unconvinced. Those who are persuaded that "real" history is "social" history and that the only noteworthy changes are those that occurred across the broadest possible spectra of society tend to ignore such things as confession-building and church-building as merely the work of elites, notwithstanding the fact that the Protestant clergy in Germany became first a professional and only then a social class in the process. It is therefore not too much to suggest that the future of Reformation history may hinge on the results of further research into the late Reformation in general and its broad effects in particular.[18]

At present, because so little work has been done or is even being considered, this future is very cloudy. What follows, then, are suggestions for further work that should be regarded as something of a research design to determine what, if any, lasting changes flowed from the Reformation. Additionally, these questions are those that appear, at present, to be fundamental to such an undertaking, and will in all likelihood change as research continues.

As indicated earlier, the development of Lutheranism into a reasonably coherant confession, i.e. the Formula of Concord, still stands in need of research on two grounds. First, scholars need to investigate the sources of the disagreements that plagued Luther's heirs after his death. It is understandable, but nonetheless striking, that the outpouring of publications around the anniversaries of the Augsburg Confession and the Formula and Book of Concord has virtually ignored those who gave rise to the controversies that made it necessary to establish concord. Perhaps it was too much to expect that the trouble-makers—Osiander, Melanchthon, Flaccius, Major,

---

[16]Kittelson (1982).

[17]Bouwsma (1979) takes this position explicitly and Spitz (1979) does so implicitly.

[18]For more detail, see Kittelson (1982).

Amsdorf—should be invited to a feast that celebrated peace. None-theless, the failure to study these figures in detail[19] and to under-stand the controversies in their terms leads implicitly to one of two conclusions: either the central figures were in fact vain speculators and troublemakers or they were weak people who reacted foolishly to external circumstances such as the Interim or the development of Calvinism. On the face of it, neither of these conclusions is terribly satisfactory, if only because they assume the existence of a continu-ous and truly Lutheran tradition that would not have been apparent to many late-sixteenth-century observers.

These conclusions are also unsatisfactory because they ignore ele-ments within Lutheranism during Luther's own life-time that may well have contributed to the controversies that sprang up after his death. One of these may have been the very methods that were used to teach Luther's theology to his followers. At the very least, the re-introduction of Aristotle into the curriculum at Wittenberg and Melanchthon's use of *loci communes* to convey the evangelical reli-gion, with Luther's approval, were devices to allow Lutherans to confront new theological issues as they arose. Melanchthon's much maligned *Augustana Variata* of 1540 that caused so much difficulty after 1555 is in fact one instance of such an attempt to make received truths speak to new circumstances.[20] If so, then the decision at Naumberg in 1561 to allow the *Variata* as an explanation of the *In-variata* appears not only as a political concession to the Elector Pala-tine but also to be consistent with the intentions of the *Variata*. In sum, just as in the developments from Calvin to Calvinism, the very methods the Lutheran theologians used may have had affects upon their conclusions. But only the most careful study of the antagonists, without preconception regarding who was right either by the stan-dard of the Formula or of Luther himself, will shed much further light on the "structure" of Lutheranism in the sixteenth century.

At the same time the elements for unity need further study. In ad-dition to knowing what Lutheran clergymen were taught during their university studies during the decades after 1540, it is also vital-ly important to understand how they were socialized, to use the cur-

---

[19]The great exception is the work of Kolb, noted in the bibliography.

[20]Müller (1980), 164ff. Elert (1962), 90, remarks "It was the great accomplishment of the first two generations of Lutheran dogmaticians and theologians, of Melanchthon above all, that . . . they understood how to make Luther's doctrine of justification the central point and reference point of all theology." Others, e.g. Bouman (1977), 87ff., and those he cites, have not been so positive.

rent term, during their early years in the pastorate. In this regard, one of the principal features of every evangelical church order was the establishment of some formal assembly of pastors that met regularly to discuss the business of the local parishes. In the countryside these meetings commonly occurred around the annual visitation, while in the larger towns they took place monthly, bi-weekly, or even weekly. Moreover, individual churches developed local confessions that probably served as standards for admittance and undoubtedly developed from wide-ranging discussions among the local corps of pastors. The point is quite simple: in these discussions and meetings, as well as in the universities or the publications of the controversialists, a general Lutheran consensus was already being built in the 1550's and 1560's. Unfortunately, almost nothing is known about even the content of these local confessions, one of which, that of Saxony, played a vital role in the textual history of the Formula.[21]

Finally, what part did the politicians play in generating and enforcing concord? There can be no doubt that princes and city governments looked with extreme displeasure upon religious controversy, especially within their own jurisdictions, as Johann Sturm's fate in Strasbourg in 1581 and the fate of theologians in Heidelberg and Jena somewhat earlier well illustrate. In addition, Duke Christoph of Württemberg and his relationship to Jacob Andreae[22] in the work of concord suggest that princes gave warm support to every effort to put an end to all the bickering and name-calling. But for what reasons? Surely they could simply have expelled from their territories whoever was in the minority in any religious dispute and so be done with it. But this they most emphatically did not do, at least not immediately. Rather, they seem to have given the theologians opportunities to dispute in what might be taken as an effort to reach the truth of the matter. As much appears to have been especially the case when the parties claimed to be true to Luther and the Augsburg Confession.[23] Is it possible, then, that the political security of evangelical towns and principalities was thought to be so closely tied to adherence to the Augustana that the politicians felt themselves severely limited in the range of political decisions they could make on confessional matters? The answer to this question requires a careful

[21]Müller (1980), 164ff; Kittelson (1977); Bizer (1952); Hauschild in Lohff and Spitz (1977); Pfeiffer (1980), 2–19.

[22]Schindling (1977); Kolb (1977), 9ff.

[23]E.g. in Strasbourg, see Kittelson (1977).

reconstruction of diplomatic relations among the Estates of the Empire and between them and the Emperor himself. The sheer frequency of Imperial Diets in the second half of the century suggests that this was a particularly active period in Imperial politics, and it goes almost without saying that formal religion was one of the issues. Here may lie at least a partial explanation for the high level of political participation in the creation of Lutheranism.

The second major area of concern must be the process of church building that was occuring during this same period. This subject has received so little study that it is not even possible to determine whether there emerged by the end of the century a typical pattern for the organization of Lutheran churches. Certainly the central notion that polity was a matter of adiaphoron to Lutherans is reflected in the fact that there were no major controversies over the issue such as plagued the Reformed. Yet, a comparison of the church orders would reveal whether there nonetheless existed a widespread consensus about how the church should be administered and who should do the administering. It is also apparent that some elements in these orders (the nature of Christian liberty in the Brandenburg-Nuremberg order and the degree of consanguinity allowable for marriage in Strasbourg) were inserted at the behest of the secular authorities. At an absolute minimum, then, these church orders, frequently the largest single piece of legislation within a city or principality, contain the agreed-upon reforms of the Reformation at the most practical level imaginable. They consist, so to speak, of the combined agenda of church and civil authorities for the reordering of Christendom in accord with true doctrine.[24] Only by knowing in some detail what this agenda was will it be possible to determine whether, for example, Lutheranism was indeed socially and politically passive in comparison with the Reformed tradition.

Albeit poorly developed for the latter half of the century, the above have nonetheless been traditional subjects of research for Reformation scholars and can be readily pursued with traditional methods. The functioning and effects of the new institutions are another matter. Partially because scholars have so concentrated upon the early decades and have therefore not confronted these issues, the fundamental questions and methods for investigating them have simply not been developed. And yet, here more than anywhere else lies the answer to the basic question, "Did the Reformation in Ger-

[24]Kittelson (1976) and the literature cited there.

many have any abiding consequences for more than Germany's political and intellectual elites?"

At first glance the day-to-day functioning of the new institutions of the Reformation and the detailed institutional history their study entails might seem in principle to have little to do with the average German Protestant. Yet, it is vital to determine how the new churches, schools, public welfare systems, and civil marriage and morals courts worked in order to ascertain which institutions affected the lives of the common people most directly. Then, as now, the formal legislation did not tell the whole story. One illustration is the commonplace that by the end of the sixteenth century Lutheran churches had become virtually an arm of the civil government, and that therefore the doctrine and practice actually preached was what the civil authorities found congenial. As much would indeed seem to be the case from a casual reading of the church orders and of the views of the churchmen and politicians who enacted them. Yet, recent work strongly suggests that Lutheran churches retained an unexpected independence of judgment even in moments of controversy.[25] Consequently, at least in the realm of religion, the church, i.e. the clergy, itself continued to be a dominant and quasi-independent force in the lives of average citizens. Indeed, given that schools commonly had religious as well as educational purposes and that pastors commonly served on marriage and morals courts, it is likely that religious convictions continued to be a socially creative, as well as a politically disruptive, force well into the late sixteenth century and beyond. Just how and to what extent cannot be known without studying the actual functioning of the new institutions.

Finally, and above all, it remains to be determined whether the Reformation engendered any noteworthy changes in religious belief and behavior at the popular level. With the publication of Strauss's book and a rejoinder to it, this area of study has become fraught with difficulty.[26] On the surface, the existence of relatively plentiful source materials in the form of instructions to visitors and their detailed accounts of religious life in the towns and villages of Germany would seem to render a final determination of this issue rather easy. One ought to be able simply to read the reports and present the results. The problem is that Strauss has done so in general for all Germany (including Strasbourg) and concluded that the Reformation

---

[25]See n. 21 above.
[26]For the following Strauss (1978), 285–288 and Kittelson (1982).

failed, while the present author has done so in detail for Strasbourg alone and concluded that the reformers there succeeded.

Further research is certainly needed. But it is likely that without some agreed-upon methods results in the future will be just as contradictory as present findings. In a sense, the difficulties lie with the documents themselves. What is to be made, for example, of the common declaration in the visitation reports that "there is nothing in particular about which to complain?" Was this the result of a "soft questionnaire" and lax procedures or is it to be regarded as having followed from a careful judgment that the religious situation was more or less as the visitors would have had it? To put the matter differently, are people who were discovered and named by the visitors and who would be regarded today as certifiably insane to be taken as evidence of a continuing folk religious tradition? Because a few people engaged in exorcism and the casting of sign, is it to be concluded that this was a wide-spread practice that most people hid from the inspectors?[27] In sum, *what* in this massive amount of material and *which* of its students are to be believed?

Certain considerations are obvious. First, in every case careful attention must be paid to the exact intentions and objectives of late-sixteenth-century churchmen. To be sure, they wished to reform the morals of every unregenerate philanderer and drunk in Germany just as they wished to guarantee the sure arrival of every German into the Kingdom of God. But their objectives in the visitations were more modest; they tried to find and discipline the immoral and to make certain that first the children and then the populace as a whole knew the basic articles of the Christian faith. Additionally, they probably counted success or failure on the basis of objectives in this latter order of magnitude. It is therefore simply unrealistic to pluck the lofty desires from the reformers' published works, compare them to the results of the visitations, and then conclude that the reformers failed. Even Luther confessed that he hadn't enough Christians in all Saxony to form a single congregation of believers.

Secondly, not only the results of the visitations but also the actual functioning of the institutions of reform must be placed in their precise local circumstances before arriving at any global conclusions regarding the impact of the Reformation at the most basic levels of society. In the sixteenth century it did not take a general conflagra-

---

[27]The tendency of Strauss (1978), 302ff. and Davis in Trinkaus and Oberman (1974), 307–336. For the counter approach, see Midelfort (1972), (1981).

tion to disrupt the work of the church; local political unrest could do perfectly well. Nor did it require a general famine to disrupt a local social welfare system or a general plague to empty a local school system.[28] Without taking local circumstances into account, no balanced judgment regarding the enduring consequences of the Reformation is possible.

Finally, as a consequence of both the above, sampling techniques either in the gathering or the presentation of the evidence simply will not do the job. Churches and schools that were functioning perfectly well one year could perfectly well fall into ruins but a few years later due to local wars, plague, or crop failure. Consequently the religious beliefs and behavior of the masses need to be treated on a year-to-year and parish-to-parish basis. Here, then, chronology becomes of the utmost importance.

Yet, even these three considerations scarcely solve the problem of selection from the masses of detail contained in these instructions and reports. It may in fact be that here, as elsewhere,[29] some form of team research could help resolve this most vexing issue. With such an approach it might even be possible to generate some statistical means of actually counting instances of deviation in belief and behavior as a portion of total population and thereby overcome the wildly varying degree of specificity in the reports. At the very least such an approach would provide a continuing check on the findings of one scholar by another and therefore lend credance to the results of the whole.

As the foregoing indicates, the greatest single obstacle to a general assessment of the Reformation's enduring consequences lies in the state of research. This lack is itself a stumbling-block to further work because the scholar has so few reliable guideposts for his or her own work. Withal, however, perhaps the greatest problem lies in the nature of the sources themselves. With but a few exceptions, noted below, the marvelous critical editions of source materials available for the earlier period do not exist for the second half of the century. The work that will be done will therefore be primarily archival with all the critical, paleographical, linguistic, and logistical problems that follow. Perhaps because the Center for Reformation Research

---

[28]For example, the judgment of Winckelmann (1922) that the post-Bucer years were disastrous for Strasbourg's welfare system ignores the fact that resources were insufficient to meet the rapid inflation of the time.

[29]The cooperative projects of the various divisions of the Sonderforschungsberiech Spätmittelalter und Reformation in Tübingen come to mind.

has so well collected and catalogued microfilm copies of the theologians' writings[30] and the Sonderforschungsbereich Spätmittelalter und Reformation in Tübingen is performing a similar work for the *Flugschriften*, these will be the first areas researched. But it would be a pity if the work stopped there, because the questions of church-building, of the functioning of the new institutions of the Reformation, and of its abiding effects would be left untouched in large measure. As noted at the outset, Germany in the second half of the sixteenth century is a land of golden opportunity for students of the Reformation.

Bibliography

1. Source Collections

Bauer, Hans, ed., *Rothenburger Gymnasial-Matrikel 1559 bis 1671* (Würzburg, 1973).

Bekenntnisschriften der evangelisch- lutherischen Kirche (Göttingen, 1952).

Bernhardt, Walter, *Die Zentralbehörden des Herzogtums Württemberg und ihre Beamten 1520–1629* 2 vols. (Stuttgart, 1973).

Bizer, Ernst, ed., *Confessio Virtembergica. Das württembergische Bekenntnis von 1551* (Stuttgart, 1952).

Brecht, Martin, et al., eds., *Johannes Brenz. Werke*, 3 vols. (Tübingen, 1970–).

Center for Reformation Research, *Sixteenth Century Bibliography*, 19 vols., (St. Louis, 1975–).

Eger, Wolfgang, *Verzeichnis der protestantischen Kirchenbücher der Pfalz* (Koblenz, 1975).

Ernst, V., ed., *Briefwechsel des Herzogs Christoph von Wirtemberg* (Stuttgart, 1899).

Lutz, Heinrich, and Kohler, Alfred, eds., *Das Reichstagsprotokoll des kaiserlichen Kommissars Felix Hornung vom Augsburger Reichstag 1555* (Wien, 1971).

Pollet, J. V., ed., *Julius Pflug. Correspondence*, 4 vols. (Leiden, 1969–).

Reu, Johann, ed., *Quellen zur Geschichte des Katechismus-Unterrichts* (Gütersloh, 1911).

---

[30]Center for Reformation Research (1975–).

Richter, Aemelius Ludwig, ed., *Die evangelische Kirchenordnungen des sechszehnten Jahrhunderts* 2 vols. (Weimar, 1846).

Sehling, Emil, et al., eds., *Die evangelische Kirchenordnungen des XVI. Jahrhunderts* 14 vols. (Leipzig and Tübingen, 1902–).

Themel, Karl, ed., "Dokumente von der Entstehung der Konkordienformel," *Archiv für Reformationsgeschichte,* 64 (1973): 301–305.

Vornbaum, Reinhold, ed., *Die evangelische Schulordnungen des XVI Jahrhunderts* (Gütersloh, 1860).

2. Literature

Abray, Lorna Jane, "The Long Reformation: Magistrates, Clergy, and Laity in Strasbourg, 1520–1598" (Unpublished Ph.D. diss: Yale, 1978).

Adam, Gottfried, *Der Streit um die Prädestination im ausgehenden 16. Jahrhundert* (Neukirchen-Vluyn, 1970).

Adam, Johann, *Evangelische Kirchengeschichte der Stadt Strassburg bis zur französischen Revolution* (Strassburg, 1922).

Allbeck, Willard Dow, *Studies in the Lutheran Confessions* (Philadelphia, 1952).

Barton, Peter F., *Um Luthers Erbe. Studien und Texte zur Spätreformation: Tilemann Heshusius (1527–1559).* (Witten, 1972).

Benecke, G., *Society and Politics in Germany 1500–1750* (London, 1974).

Benrath, Gustav Adolf, "Die kurpfälzischen Kirchenvisitationen im 16. Jahrhundert," *Blätter für Pfälzische Kirchengeschichte,* 42 (1975): 17–24.

Binder, Ludwig, "Die Augsburgische Konfession in der siebenbürgischen evangelischen Dirche," *Zeitschrift für bayrische Kirchengeschichte* 49 (1980): 54–85.

Bizer, Ernst, *Studien zur Geschichte des Abendmahlsstreits im 16. Jahrhundert* (Darmstadt, 1962).

Bouman, Herbert J.A., "Retrospect and Prospect: Some Unscientific Reflections on the Four Hundredth Anniversary of the Formula of Concord," *Sixteenth-Century Journal,* 8 (1977): 85–104.

Bizer, Ernst, *Studien zur Geschichte des Abendmahlsstreits im 16. Jahrhundert* (Darmstadt, 1962).

Bouwsma, William J., "The Renaissance and the Drama of Western Civilization," *American Historical Review,* 84 (1979): 1–16.

Brecht, Martin, *Kirchenordnung und Kirchenzucht in Württemberg vom 16. bis 18. Jahrhundert* (Stuttgart, 1967).

_____, and Schwarz, Reinhard, eds., *Bekenntnis und Einheit der Kirche. Studien zum Konkordienbuch* (Stuttgart, 1980).

Calinich, Robert, *Der Naumburger Fürstentag 1561* (Gotha, 1870).

Davis, Natalie in Charles Trinkaus and Heiko Oberman, eds., *The Pursuit of Holiness in Late Medieval and Renaissance Religion* (Leiden, 1974): 307–336.

Ebel, Jobst, "Jakob Andreae (1528–1590) also Verfasser der Konkordienformel," *Zeitschrift für Kirchengeschichte*, 89 (1978): 28–119.

_____, "Die Herkunft des Konzeptes der Konkordienformel," *Zeitschrift für Kirchengeschichte*, 91 (1980): 237–282.

Elert, Werner, *The Structure of Lutheranism*, trans. W. A. Hansen (St. Louis, 1962).

Engel, Peter, *Die eine Wahrheit in der gespaltenen Christenheit. Untersuchung zur Theologie Georg Calixts* (Göttingen, 1976).

Estes, James, "Church Order and the Christian Magistrate according to Johann Brenz," *Archive for Reformation History*, 59 (1968): 5–25.

_____, "The Two Kingdoms and the State Church according to Johannes Brenz and an Anonymous Colleague," *Archive for Reformation History*, 61 (1970): 35–50.

_____, "Johannes Brenz and the Problem of Ecclesiastical Discipline," *Church History*, 41 (1972): 464–479.

_____, "Johannes Brenz and the Institutionalization of the Reformation in Württemberg," *Central European History*, 6 (1973): 44–59.

Fleischer, Manfred, "The Institutionalization of Humanism in Protestant Silesia," *Archive for Reformation History*, 66 (1975): 256–274.

Forde, Gerhard O., *The Law-Gospel Debate. An Interpretation of its Historical Development* (Minneapolis, 1969).

Franz, Gunther, *Die Kirchenleitung in Hohenlohe in den Jahrzehnten nach der Reformation* (Stuttgart, 1971).

_____, "Reformation und landesherrliches Kirchenregiment in Hohenlohe," *Württembergisch Franken*, 58 (1974): 120–152.

Fritz, F., *Ulmische Kirchengeschichte vom Interim bis zum dreissigjährigen Krieg* (Stuttgart, 1934).

Gensischen, Hans-Werner, *We Condemn. How Luther and 16th-century Lutheranism Condemned False Doctrine*, trans. Herbert J. A. Bouman (St. Louis, 1967).

Greyerz, Kaspar von, *The Late City Reformation in Germany. The Case of Colmar, 1522–1568* (Wiesbaden, 1980).

Haikola, Lauri, *Gesetz und Evangelium bei M. Flaccius* (Lund, 1952).

———, *Studien zu Luther und zum Luthertum* (Uppsala, 1958).

Hareide, Bjarne, *Die Konfirmation in der Reformationszeit. Eine Untersuchung der Lutherischen Konfirmation in Deutschland 1520–1585* (Göttingen, 1971).

Hartman, J., and Jäger, K., *Johann Brenz*, 2 vols. (Hamburg, 1840–42).

Haug, Otto, "Die evangelische Pfarrerschaft der Reichsstadt Schwäbisch Hall in Stadt und Land," *Württembergisch Franken*, 58 (1974): 359–373.

Heppe, Heinrich, *Geschichte des deutschen Protestantismus in den Jahren 1555–1581*, 3 vols. (Marburg, 1852–59).

Hermelink, Heinrich, *Geschichte der evangelischen Kirche in Württemberg von der Reformation bis zur Gegenwart* (Stuttgart and Tübingen, 1949).

Hinkel, Helmut "Ein Konfessionsstreit in Dieburg in den Jahren 1582–1584," *Archiv für mittelrheinische Kirchengeschichte*, 26 (1974): 97–106.

Hollweg, Walter, *Der Augsburger Reichstag von 1566 und seine Bedeutung für die Entstehung der reformierten Kirche und ihres Bekenntnisses* (Neukirchen, 1964).

Jungkuntz, Theodore R., *Formulators of the Formula of Concord: Four Architects of Lutheran Unity* (St. Louis, 1977).

Kittelson, James M., "Humanism and the Reformation in Germany," *Central European History*, 9 (1976): 303–322.

———, "Marbach vs. Zanchi: The Resolution of Controversy in Late Reformation Strasbourg," *The Sixteenth-Century Journal*, 7 (1977): 31–44.

———, "Successes and Failures in the German Reformation: The Report from Strasbourg," *Archive for Reformation History*, 73 (1982).

Klug, Eugene F., *From Luther to Chemnitz on Scripture and the Word* (Grand Rapids, Mich., 1971).

Koch, Ernst, "Striving for the Union of the Lutheran Churches: The Church-Historical Background of the Work Done on the Formula of Concord at Magdeburg," *Sixteenth Century Journal*, 8 (1977): 105–121.

Kolb, Robert, "Georg Major as Controversialist: Polemics in the Late Reformation," *Church History*, 45 (1976): 455–468.

———, "Dynamics of Party Conflict in the Saxon Late Reformation: Gnesio Luthersns vs. Philippists," *Journal of Modern History*, 49 (1977): D1289–1305.

———, *Nikolaus von Amsdorf (1483–1565): Popular Polemics in the Preservation of Luther's Legacy* (Nieuwkoop, 1978).

———, "Augsburg 1530: German Lutheran Interpretations of the Diet of Augsburg to 1577," *Sixteenth Century Journal*, 11 (1980): 47–61. (a)

———, "Good Works are Detrimental to Salvation: Amsdorf's Use of Luther's Words in Controversy," *Renaissance and Reformation/Renaissance et Réforme*, 4 (1980): 136–151. (b)

Leder, Klaus, *Kirche und Jugend in Nürnberg und seinem Landgebiet 1400 bis 1800* (Neustadt/Aisch, 1973).

Lempp, Wilhelm, *Der Württembergische Synodus, 1553–1924* (Stuttgart, 1929).

Lieske, Reinhard, *Protestantische Frömmigkeit im Spiegel der kirchlichen Kunst des Herzogtums Württemberg* (München, 1973).

Lohff, Wenzel, "Legitimate Limits of Doctrinal Pluralism According to the Formula of Concord," *Sixteenth Century Journal*, 8 (1977): 23–38.

———, and Spitz, Lewis W., eds., *Widerspruch, Dialog und Einigung. Studien zur Konkordienformel der Lutherischen Reformation* (Stuttgart, 1977).

Mager, Inge, "Lutherische Theologie und aristotelische Philosophie an der Universität Helmstedt im 16. Jahrhundert," *Jahrbuch der Gesellschaft für niedersächsische Kirchengeschichte*, 73 (1975): 83–98.

Meinhold, Peter, ed., *Kirche und Bekenntnis* (Wiesbaden, 1980).

Midelfort, H. C. Erik, *Witch Hunting in Southwest Germany 1562–1648. The Social and Intellectual Foundations* (Stanford, 1972).

———, "Madness and the Problems of Psychological History in the Sixteenth Century," *Sixteenth Century Journal*, 12 (1981): 5–12.

Moeller, Bernd, *Imperial Cities and the Reformation: Three Essays*, trans. H. C. Erik Midelfort and Mark U. Edwards (Philadelphia, 1972): 41–115.

Müller, Gerhard, "Alliance and Confession: The Theological-Historical Development and Ecclesiastical-Political Significance of Reformation Confessions," *Sixteenth Century Journal*, 8 (1977): 124–140.

_____, "Das Konkordienbuch von 1580," *Zeitschrift für Bayerische Kirchengeschichte*, 49 (1980): 161–178.

Müller-Volbehr, Jörg, *Die geistlichen Gerichte in den Braunschweig-Wolfenbüttelschen Landen* (Göttingen, 1973).

Nebe, Otto H., *Reine Lehre. Zur Theologie des Niklas von Amsdorff* (Göttingen, 1935).

Neumeyer, Heinz, *Kirchengeschichte von Danzig und Westpreussen in evangelischer Sicht* (Rautenberg, 1971).

Olson, Oliver K., "Theology of Revolution: Magdeburg, 1550–1551," *Sixteenth Century Journal*, 3 (1972): 56–79.

Pauck, Wilhelm, *The Heritage of the Reformation* (New York, 1961).

Paulsen, Friedrich, *Geschichte des gelehrten Unterrichts auf der deutschen Schulen und Universitäten* (Leipzig, 1919).

Pfeiffer, Gerhard, "Nürnberg und das Augsburger Bekenntnis, 1530–1561," *Zeitschrift für bayerische Kirchengeschichte*, 49 (1980): 2–19.

Planck, Gottlieb Jakob, *Geschichte der Entstehung, der Veränderung und der Bildung unsers protestantischen Lehrbegriffs vom Anfang der Reformation bis zu der Einführung der Konkordienformel*, 5 vols. (Leipzig, 1788–1800).

Press, Volker, *Calvinismus und Territorialstaat. Regierung und Zentralbehörden der Kurpfalz, 1559–1619* (Stuttgart, 1970).

Reller, Horst, "Die Auswirkungen der Universität Helmstedt auf Pfarrer und Gemeinden in Niedersachsen," *Jahrbuch der Gesellschaft für niedersächsische Kirchengeschichte*, 74 (1975): 35–52.

Röhrich, Timotheus-Wilhelm, *Geschichte der Reformation im Elsass und besonders in Strassburg* 3 vols. (Strassburg, 1830–1832).

Roth, Friedrich, *Augsburgs Reformationsgeschichte*, 4 vols. (Munich, 1901–1911).

Rublack, Hans-Christoph, *Gescheiterte Reformation. Frühreformatorische und protestantische Bewegungen in süd- und westdeutschen Residenzen* (Stuttgart, 1978).

Salig, Christian August, *Vollständige Historie der Augsburgischen Confession*, 3 vols. (Halle, 1730–1735).

Schindling, Anton, *Humanistische Hochschule und freie Reichsstadt. Gymnasium und Akademie in Strassburg, 1538–1621.* (Wiesbaden, 1977).

Schöne, Jobst, ed., *Bekenntnis zur Wahrheit. Aufsätze über die Konkordienformel* (Erlangen, 1978).

Schornbaum, Karl, "Zum Tag vom Naumburg," *Archiv für Reformationsgeschichte*, 8 (1911): 181–214.

———, "Markgraf Georg Friedrich von Brandenburg und die Einigungsbestrebungen der protestantischen Stände," *Archiv für Reformationsgeschichte*," 17 (1921): 161–193.

Schulze, Albert, *Bekenntnisbildung und Politik Lindaus im Zeitalter der Reformation* (Nürnberg, 1971).

Schütz, Werner, "Jakob Andreae als Prediger," *Zeitschrift für Kirchengeschichte*, 87 (1976): 221–243.

Seeling, Werner, *Johannes Willing (1525–1572), ein Schicksal zwischen Luthertum und Calvinismus. Versuch einer Biographie* (Zweibrücken, 1972).

Simon, Matthias, *Evangelische Kirchengeschichte Bayerns* (Nürnberg, 1952).

Spitz, Lewis W., "The Course of German Humanism," in *Itinerarium Italicum. The Profile of the Italian Renaissance in the Mirror of its European Transformations*, ed. by Heiko A. Oberman with Thomas A. Brady, Jr. (Leiden, 1975).

———, "The Formula of Concord, Then and Now," *Sixteenth Century Journal*, 8 (1977): 9–21.

———, "Periodization in History: Renaissance and Reformation," in *The Future of History* ed. by Charles Delzell (Nashville, 1979).

———, and Lohff, Wenzel, eds., *Discord, Dialogue and Concord. Studies in the Lutheran Reformation's Formula of Concord* (Philadelphia, 1977).

Strauss, Gerald, *Luther's House of Learning. Indoctrination of the Young in the German Reformation* (Baltimore, 1978).

Vogler, Bernard, *Le Clergé Protestant Rhènan au Siécle de la Réforme (1555–1619)* (Paris, 1976).

Voit, Hartmur, *Nikolaus Gallus* (Neustadt/Aisch, 1977).

Walter, Jörg, *Rat und Bürgerhauptleute in Braunschweig 1576–1604. Die Geschichte der Brabantschen Wirren* (Braunschweig, 1971).

Wartenburg, Gunther, "Die Confessio Augustana in der albertinischen Politik unter Herzog Heinrich von Sachsen," *Zeitschrift für bayerische Kirchengeschichte* 49 (1980): 44–53.

Weyrauch, Erdmann, *Konfessionelle Krise und soziale Stabilität. Das Interim in Strassburg (1548–1562)* (Stuttgart, 1978).

Winckelmann, Otto, *Das Fürsorgewesen der Stadt Strassburg vor und nach der Reformation bis zum Ausgang des sechszehnten Jahrhunderts* (Leipzig, 1922).

Wolf, Gustav, *Zur Geschichte der deutschen Protestanten, 1555–1559* (Berlin, 1888).

Zeeden, Ernst Walter, and Molitor, Hans-Georg, eds., *Die Visitation im Dienst der kirchlichen Reform* (Münster, 1967).

Index of Names